New Documentary

Praise for the first edition of *New Documentary: A Critical Introduction*:
'It's refreshing to find a book that cuts through the tired old debates that have surrounded documentary film and television. It heralds a welcome new approach', *Sight and Sound*

'This book is going to be essential reading for any media teacher with a serious interest in documentary and is highly recommended for centres selecting "Documentary" as one of the two "Textual Topics" on AQA's Media spec', *In The Picture*

New Documentary provides a contemporary look at documentary and fresh and challenging ways of theorising the non-fiction film. As engaging as the original, this second edition features thorough updates to the existing chapters, as well as a brand new chapter on contemporary cinema release documentaries.

This new edition includes:

- Contemporary films such as *Capturing the Friedmans*, *Être et avoir*, *Farenheit 9/11*, *The Fog of War* and *Touching the Void* as well as more canonical texts such as *Hoop Dreams* and *Shoah*.
- Additional interviews with influential practitioners, such as director Michael Apted and producer Stephen Lambert.
- A comprehensively revised discussion of modern observational documentary, including docusoaps, reality television and formatted documentaries.
- The work of documentary filmmakers such as Nicholas Barker, Errol Morris, Nick Broomfield, Molly Dineen and Michael Moore and the work of Avant-Garde filmmakers such as Chris Marker and Patrick Keiller.
- Gender identity, queer theory, performance, race and spectatorship.

Bruzzi shows how theories of documentary filmmaking can be applied to contemporary texts and genres, and discusses the relationship between recent, innovative examples of the genre and the more established canon of documentary.

Stella Bruzzi is Professor of Film and Television Studies at the University of Warwick. Her previous publications include the co-edited collection *Fashion Cultures: Theories, Explorations and Analysis* (2000, with Pamela Church Gibson) and *Undressing Cinema: Clothing and Identity in the Movies* (1997). Her most recent publication is *Bringing Up Daddy: Fatherhood and Masculinity in Post-War Hollywood* (2005).

New Documentary
Second edition

Stella Bruzzi

Routledge
Taylor & Francis Group

LONDON AND NEW YORK

First edition published 2000
by Routledge

This edition published 2006
by Routledge
2 Park Square, Milton Park, Abingdon, Oxon OX14 4RN

Simultaneously published in the USA and Canada
by Routledge
270 Madison Ave, New York, NY 10016

*Routledge is an imprint of the Taylor & Francis Group, an informa
business*

Typeset in Galliard by
Keyword Group Ltd
Printed and bound in Great Britain by
Antony Rowe Ltd, Chippenham, Wiltshire

British Library Cataloguing in Publication Data
A catalogue record for this book is available from the British Library

Library of Congress Cataloging-in-Publication Data

Bruzzi, Stella, 1962–
    New documentary: a critical introduction / Stella Bruzzi. – 2nd ed.
        p. cm.
    Includes bibliographical references and index.
    ISBN 0-415-38525-3 (hardback : alk. paper) –
    ISBN 0-415-38524-5 (pbk. : alk. paper) 1.
Documentary films – History and criticism.   1.   Title.
    PN1995.9.D6B78 2006   2006006456
    070.1'8dc22

ISBN10: 0-415-38525-3 (hbk)
ISBN10: 0-415-38524-5 (pbk)

ISBN13: 9-78-0-415-38525-1 (hbk)
ISBN13: 9-78-0-415-38524-4 (pbk)

Contents

Figures

Acknowledgements

Once again I would like to extend warmest thanks to my editor Rebecca Barden, in the first instance for proposing this second edition and then for her assistance with preliminaries such as the outline. I am also immensely grateful to Rebecca's replacement Natalie Foster and to her editorial assistant Aileen Storry. For the first edition of *New Documentary* several filmmakers were kind enough to allow me to interview them about their work and I would like to thank them again for their time: Nick Barker, Chris Terrill, Nick Shearman, Rachel Bell and Mark Fielder. For the second edition I interviewed Nick Shearman again and also Michael Apted and Stephen Lambert, whose contributions have proved invaluable. I would also like to mention for their enthusiasm and insightfulness all the students at Royal Holloway, University of London who took my documentary courses over the 13 years I taught there – and of course my Media Arts colleagues, who made my time there so enjoyable and stimulating. This book would never have been written without the love of my family, especially my husband Mick whose interest, encouragement and support sustained me throughout. The first edition was dedicated to my son Frank, who was born as I was still writing. As I embarked upon this revised edition whilst on maternity leave to look after his sister Phyllis, it seems only right that I should dedicate this new edition to both of them.

Introduction

There have been several key developments in documentary film and television production since the first edition of this book appeared in 2000. In terms of generic renewal, the important evolutions that have taken place in recent years have been the renewed popularity of documentaries in the cinema (in the wake of Michael Moore's *Bowling for Columbine*) and the advent of reality television and its close relative the formatted documentary. What both of these indicate is that documentary has become a global commodity in a way it simply was not a mere six years ago. These recent interventions also serve to consolidate and reinforce the central tenet of the first edition of *New Documentary*, namely that documentaries are performative acts, inherently fluid and unstable and informed by issues of performance and performativity. The latter have become increasingly forefronted as defining concerns of documentary, from the continued rise of docuauteurs such as Michael Moore, to the centrality of performance to reality television and finally to the increased presence of reconstruction in historical documentary where the use of drama has become almost a prerequisite.

Because documentary output has evolved so dramatically over the past few years it did not seem sufficient, when approaching this second edition, to merely tack on a new chapter. All existing chapters have been reviewed and updated, and some have been more radically overhauled. Major changes have been made to the discussion of 'docusoaps', for example, with which the old chapter on British observational documentary television concluded. Although some docusoaps have survived, the sub-genre – which had been such a major component of popular television, particularly in Britain – died around the millennium, almost as abruptly as it had risen. In the wake of the phenomenal global success of Endemol's *Big Brother* has come 'reality television', which in turn has spawned formatted documentaries such as *Wife Swap* and *Faking It*. Under the revised title of 'New Observational Documentary', Chapter 4 now gives far more prominence to the rise of 'factual entertainment' since docusoaps by focusing on reality television and formats. Although for slightly different reasons, Chapter 3 on documentary journeys has been similarly overhauled to take into consideration a wider range of documentaries and now includes discussions of *Sherman's March, Hotel Terminus, Seven Up* and *Hoop Dreams*. It is hoped that this chapter now offers a more comprehensive analysis of why the journey has been such an enduring nonfictional narrative structure. Chapter 5's discussion of documentary images of the president now includes more recent examples, such as Michael Moore's critique of George W. Bush in *Fahrenheit 9/11* and finally Chapter 7 is an entirely new chapter in which I offer an analysis of four of the most significant and popular cinema-release documentaries since 2000: *Être et avoir*, *The Fog of War*, *Capturing the Friedmans* and *Touching the Void*.

New Documentary was and is primarily a work of theory. In the first edition I remarked that 'theoretical writing on documentary has, by and large, not kept pace with developments in critical and cultural theory', a claim that is still valid but should perhaps be modified in the light of some recent publications, such as Michael Renov's *The Subject of Documentary* in which Renov reassesses and develops previous arguments about and definitions of documentary, particularly in relation to fiction film and subjectivity. Although my book's thesis is historically broad, *New Documentary* is not intended as a general introduction to nonfiction film and television. Because of this continued emphasis on a thesis (the belief, as laid out at greater length later in this Introduction, that documentary should be viewed as a performative act) to have singled out a particular *historical* moment might seem odd. However, this concluding chapter, through its analysis of four notable documentaries, also offers *historical* proof of the pervasive influence now of performative ideas, an influence amply supported by the domination on the small screen of reality television and its subsidiaries. The emphasis of *New Documentary* remains the British, American and European (primarily French) documentary traditions, within both cinema and television. To expand the book's terrain further than I already have would have made the project unwieldy and probably incoherent. A stated aim of the first edition was to tackle more contemporary documentaries that are, by and large, available for study and viewing. I have stuck by this when revising my original book, as I have stuck by my other intention of offering an alternative way to understand documentary in relation to the performative. The problematisations of the 'real' that have taken place both within theory and within practice since the publication of Judith Butler's *Gender Trouble* in 1990 seem so fundamental that it now would be blinkered to offer a view of documentary that did not encompass them. To pursue the same metaphor a little, applying notions of performativity to documentary has been, to me, akin to finding a new pair of spectacles through which to look at nonfiction film and television. As I did in the first edition of *New Documentary*, I will now divide this Introduction into a section on 'Theory' and an explanation of 'Organisation and structure'.

Theory

As my underpinning rationale is the importance of performativity in relation to documentary, the first issue relating to how documentary has hitherto been theorised needs to be addressed. There has been a consistent necessity amongst those who have written about documentary to make sense of an otherwise unmanageable number of texts, movements and historical moments through the construction (or imposition) of a family tree that seeks to explain the evolution of documentary along linear, progressive lines. The most influential and widely used writer on documentary has been Bill Nichols, whose numerous books on the subject have no doubt shaped most courses on documentary in universities since the 1980s. Nichols has offered the most influential documentary genealogy; there are others, such as Paul Rotha's early 'evolution of documentary' outlined in *Documentary Film* in 1936 or Erik Barnouw's genealogy of sorts in *Documentary: A History of the Non-fiction Film* (1993), but Nichols' 'family tree' is the one that has stuck, although hybrid, eclectic modern films have begun to undermine his efforts to compartmentalise documentaries. Nichols has, to date, identified five modes: the Expository, the Observational, the Interactive, the Reflexive and the Performative. He is keener on some modes than on others (the Interactive and the Reflexive, particularly) but his categories are often – and increasingly – defined negatively, that is in terms of what they do *not* as opposed to *do* represent.

After the publication of the first edition of *New Documentary* it was clear that some people saw this critique of Bill Nichols' schema as unfairly aggressive and, paradoxically, defensive (a term used as I recall in a review of my book by Jane Roscoe); what I perhaps did not make clear was that I made particular use of Nichols' genealogical paradigm because it has become so important and influential. On some undergraduate courses Nichols' modes are attributed as if they are not one way of looking at documentary history and production, but *the* way. Nichols himself has indicated he believes this to be the case when he writes, for example, by way of an introduction to the performative mode in the mid-1990s (the 'new mode in town'): 'Things change. The four modes of documentary production that presented themselves as an exhaustive survey of the field no longer suffice' (Nichols 1994: 93). Since when could Nichols' four earlier modes (at this time: the Expository, the Observational, the Interactive and the Reflexive) offer 'an exhaustive survey' of documentary? Like any other map for understanding documentary, Nichols' 'family tree' is necessarily circumscribed by his own preferences and areas of knowledge; of much more enduring interest than these reductive categories is Nichols' detailed engagement with individual documentary texts. As Michael Renov remarks in *The Subject of Documentary*, Nichols' *Representing Reality* was a 'groundbreaking study' (Renov 2004: 22) – but not for its pedalling of a Darwinian model of documentary history. Maybe as a result of this omniscience, the definitions Nichols offered in the mid-1990s of his 'modes' were excessively crude (it seems to me, for instance, that when Nichols comes to adding the performative mode in *Blurred Boundaries* in the mid-1990s, he feels compelled to perpetuate the family tree rather than admit that, because of increased documentary heterogeneity and complexity, the compartmentalisation of documentary has become too reductive). The table that sets out the modes in this book is breathtakingly simplistic, and exemplifies the fundamental problem with the 'family tree' which is that it imposes a false chronology onto what is essentially a theoretical paradigm, so the Expository documentary is attributed to the 1930s, the Observational Documentary to the

1960s, and so on through to the Performative documentary, attributed to the 1980s–90s (Nichols 1994: 95). The years between the Second World War and the advent of observational cinema in the 1960s must have been, if one follows this model, numbingly dull. The chronology offered here is hugely problematic. It is, for example, simply not tenable to maintain that voice-over (the *sine qua non* of the Expository mode) is any less popular a device in non-fiction film now than it was; narration is everywhere, likewise observation – frequently in the same documentary.

A problem with the Nichols 'family tree' is that, in order to sustain itself, wildly heterogeneous documentaries are forced to co-exist, very uncomfortably at times, within one mode – a dilemma that is examined more specifically in Chapter 2 of this book. Since *Blurred Boundaries* Nichols has himself engaged with such issues. In *Introduction to Documentary* he suggests a slightly different configuration of documentary groups, now arguing for six modes starting with the Poetic (a new category in which he places films that emphasise 'visual associations, tonal and rhythmic qualities, descriptive passages' [Nichols 2001: 33]), which is followed by the more familiar Expository, Observational, Participatory (the renamed 'Interactive mode'), Reflexive and Performative. It is entirely legitimate to suggest that there are different types of documentaries that display or prioritise different formal characteristics; what is less tenable, however, is Nichols' previous contention that such categories follow on from each other, a problem that Nichols himself addresses to an extent in *Introduction to Documentary* when he writes: 'These six modes establish a loose framework of affiliation within which individuals may work; they set up conventions that a given film may adopt; and they provide specific expectations viewers anticipate having fulfilled' (Nichols 2001: 99).

If, however, it is the case as Nichols had in fact identified earlier that 'None of these modes expel previous modes; instead they overlap and interact. The terms are partly heuristic and actual films usually mix different modes although one mode will normally be dominant' (Nichols 1994: 95), then have such genealogical tables become redundant? The result – whether conscious or not – of having imposed this 'family tree' on documentary history is the creation of a central canon of films that is exclusive and conservative. With this in mind, I have attempted here to present a not overly prescriptive underpinning theorisation of documentaries that helps to suggest links between diverse kinds of documentary filmmaking, from independent art house films to the most popular forms of televisual factual entertainment.

An insistent implication of Nichols' 'family tree' is not merely that documentary has pursued a developmental progression towards greater introspection and subjectivity, but that its evolution has been determined by the supposedly generic quest of documentary filmmakers for better and more authentic ways to represent reality, with the implied suggestion that, somewhere in a utopian future, documentary will prove able to collapse altogether the difference between reality and representation. Documentary and fiction are forever the polarities that are invoked in this debate and Nichols' 1990s genealogy bizarrely begins with

'Hollywood fiction' whose deficiency is the 'absence of "reality"' (Nichols 1994: 95).[1] The inverted commas around 'reality' are significant here, as if the real can never be authentically represented and that any film, whether documentary or fiction, attempting to capture it will inevitably fail. Michael Renov (1986: 71–2) likewise asserts

> it is important to recall that the documentary is the cinematic idiom that most actively promotes the illusion of immediacy insofar as it forswears 'realism' in favour of a direct, ontological claim to the 'real'. Every documentary issues a 'truth claim' of a sort, positing a relationship to history which exceeds the analogical status of its fictional counterpart.

It is certainly unlikely that either Nichols or Renov have ever been so naïve as to be unwilling or unable to ascribe to the relationship between reality and representation a fruitful dialectical relationship; however, when working with much writing on documentary of the past 20 years it sometimes seems necessary to remind theorists that such a dialectic need not be instinctively treated with distrust. And sometimes it becomes necessary to remind ourselves that reality does exist and that it can be represented without such a representation either invalidating or having to be synonymous with the reality that preceded it.

Repeatedly invoked by documentary theory is the idealised notion, on the one hand, of the pure documentary in which the relationship between the image and the real is straightforward and, on the other, the very impossibility of this aspiration. In this vein Brian Winston somewhat hysterically suggests that, in the future, documentary will simply be mounting a panicked rear-guard action against marauding fakery:

> It seems to be likely that the implications of this technology [for digital image manipulation] will be decades working themselves through the culture. However, it is also clear that these technological developments, whatever else they portend, will have a profound and perhaps fatal impact on the documentary film. It is not hard to imagine that every documentarist will shortly (that is, in the next fifty years) have to hand, in the form of a desktop personal video-image-manipulating computer, the wherewithal for complete fakery. What can or will be left of the relationship between image and reality?
>
> (Winston 1995: 6)

Winston here is obviously writing before docusoaps, before reality television and before the penetration into documentary production of a more relaxed as well as knowing acceptance of performative fluidity. Since Winston wrote this, it has become even clearer that the authenticity of documentary is *not* thrown into doubt because a couple of charlatans exhibit the 'wherewithal' to create fake documentaries. To paraphrase *This is Spinal Tap*, the most adored *faux* documentary of all time: it's a fine line between the real and the fake, and what is of far more interest to documentarists at the moment it seems to me is the complexity and productiveness of the relationship between the two. Reality television has rendered the binary opposition identified by Winston simplistic, although some distrust is still evident in more recent writing as when Renov remarks whilst talking about popular nonfiction forms on American television, such as *Cops* and *America's Most Wanted*:

> the growth of hybrid media forms that, while trafficking in the 'real', occasionally even miming the tropes of a documentary style, cannot be said to adhere in any meaningful way to the standards of a documentary praxis (as to ethics, rhetoric, or pedagogy) developed over the past seventy years.
>
> (Renov 2004: 21–2)

Too often in the past documentary was seen to have failed (or be in imminent danger of failing) because it could not be decontaminated of its representational quality, as Erik Barnouw (1993: 287) suggested when declaring

> To be sure, some documentarists claim to be objective – a term that seems to renounce an interpretative role. The claim may be strategic, but it is surely meaningless. The documentarist, like any communicator in any medium, makes endless choices. He (sic) selects topics, people, vistas, angles, lens, juxtapositions, sounds, words. Each selection is an expression of his point of view, whether he is aware of it or not, whether he acknowledges it or not.

Barnouw's claim is simple but erroneous: that the minute an individual becomes involved in the representation of reality, the integrity of that reality is irretrievably lost. What is, time and time again, entered into is the perennial Bazin vs Baudrillard tussle, both of whom – from polar perspectives – argue for the erosion of any differentiation between the image and reality, Bazin because he believed reality could be recorded, Baudrillard because he believes reality is just another image. Because the ideal of the pure documentary uncontaminated by the subjective vagaries of representation is forever upheld, all non-fiction film is thus deemed to be unable to live up to its intention, so documentary becomes what you do when you have failed.

The intention of *New Documentary* is to question such theoretical assumptions from a variety of perspectives, both theoretical and historical. As indicated above, the book is an indirect response to the impact of Judith Butler's writing on critical theory. The underpinning idea of *New Documentary* is that the pact between documentary, reality and the documentary spectator is far more straightforward than many theorists have made out: that a documentary will never be reality nor will it erase or invalidate that reality by being representational. Furthermore, the spectator is not in need of signposts and inverted commas to understand that a documentary is a negotiation between reality on the one hand and image, interpretation and bias on the other. Documentary is predicated upon a dialectical relationship between aspiration and potential, that the text itself reveals the tensions between the documentary pursuit of the most authentic mode of factual representation and the impossibility of this aim. This is not a new phenomenon – the fissures are there in Huston's war documentaries, for instance, or the 'collage junk' films of Emile de Antonio – it just has not been talked about much within the parameters of documentary theory, a body of work that has assumed and prioritised (although not exclusively) the documentarist's putative desire to attain the 'grail' of perfect authenticity.

Another influence as I conceived of this book was the writing on documentary of Noël Carroll, who argues combatively and wittily with how film studies has theorised the nonfictional image. At the start of 'Nonfiction film and postmodernist skepticism' Carroll identifies, as I have above, the central dilemma of theory to be the belief that documentary is 'necessarily biased' because 'motion picture technology is inherently and necessarily selective', and that any claims it might have to objectivity are thus 'foreclosed a priori' (Carroll 1996b: 283). As Carroll goes on to make clear:

> This argument contains two notions worth scotching: first, that there is something about nonfiction film, due to its inherent nature, that renders it, in contradistinction to other things (such as sociological treatises), uniquely incapable of objectivity; and second, that selectivity guarantees bias.
>
> (p. 283)

It became important to me to marry in some way Carroll's philosophical precision and skepticism with notions of performativity and the belief that a documentary's meaning, its identity is not fixed but fluid and stems from a productive, dialectical relationship between the text, the reality it represents and the spectator. In addition to Carroll, the writing of Dai Vaughan has been significant in this, particularly his belief – cited at other times in *New Documentary* – that 'What makes a "documentary" is the way we look at it' (Vaughan 1999: 84). Vaughan then argues that 'To see a film as documentary is to see its meaning as pertinent to the events and objects which passed before the camera: to see it, in a word, as signifying what it appears to record' (pp. 84–5). Although Vaughan acknowledges the 'theoretical difficulties' of this definition, he is eager 'to avoid the labyrinth of rules and exceptions, and exceptions to the exceptions, which awaits anyone who tries to identify documentary by generic or stylistic criteria' (p. 85). What both Carroll and Vaughan accept – and this has the potential to be hugely liberating – is that filmmakers and spectators alike comprehend the inherent difficulties with representation in the nonfiction film but that this understanding does not invalidate either the documentary film or the documentary pursuit; that a documentary itself is the crucial point at which the factual event, the difficulties of representation and the act of watching a documentary are confronted – if not resolved.

The dominant theoretical preoccupations directly criticised by Carroll and indirectly cited by Vaughan are relatively recent interventions. Many antecedents of the modern documentary were not so haunted by issues of bias, performance and authorial inflection – Esfir Shub did not consider the fact/fiction divide between her portrayal and Eisenstein's of Russia's recent political history to be particularly significant, identifying the fictionalised *Battleship Potemkin* as the catalyst to her search for newsreel material with which to compile another film to 'show the revolutionary past' (Jay Leyda, quoted in Macdonald and Cousins 1996: 58). In this frame of mind, the repeated use of Eisenstein's dramatisation of the storming of the Winter Palace in *October* as a piece of newsreel is not so anomalous. The suspicion with which Robert Flaherty's reconstructions in *Nanook of the North* or *Man of Aran* is now frequently treated stems not from an understanding of why he reconstituted an Arran family or recorded their dialogue in a studio (technical limitations, a desire to make a record of a lost way of life, and so on) or of how such films may have been understood for what they were by contemporary audiences. Likewise, John Grierson's early definition of documentary in light of Flaherty's work as 'the creative treatment of actuality' (Rotha 1952: 70) has been viewed as contradictory. As Winston (1995: 11) suggests: 'The supposition that any "actuality" is left after "creative treatment" can now be seen as being at best naïve and at worst a mark of duplicity'.

And yet, as Winston later points out, Grierson himself differentiated between documentary and other, lesser, forms of non-fiction film, and openly acknowledged the 'contradictions' in his definition by stressing repeatedly that the element which documentaries possessed but which other forms of non-fiction film lacked was 'dramatisation' (Winston 1995: 103). Grierson, the Soviets, Paul Rotha and other early practitioners and theorists were far more relaxed about documentary as a category than we as theorists have become, and it is intriguing how, as particularly the additions to this revised edition demonstrate, documentary has in various ways returned to its more relaxed roots with dramatisation, performance and other forms of fictionalisation and narrativisation becoming once more predominant.

Worries over authenticity and the evolution of documentary are frequently linked to the increasing sophistication of audio-visual technology. Whereas technical limitations certainly influenced the kinds of documentaries that were feasible in the 1930s when Grierson was first writing, this is no longer the case, so the return we are currently witnessing to a more fluid definition of documentary must have another root. The role of American *cinéma vérité* has proved the crucial historical factor in limiting documentary's potential and frame of reference, and it is significant that, although many theorists suspect and criticise direct cinema, most of them dedicate a large amount of time to examining it. Richard Leacock and his fellows believed that the advancements in film equipment would enable documentary to achieve authenticity and to collapse the distance between reality and representation, because the camera would become 'just a window someone peeps through' (Donn Pennebaker quoted in Winston 1993: 43). As Errol Morris has bluntly put it:

> I believe that *cinéma vérité* set back documentary filmmaking twenty or thirty years. It sees documentary as a sub-species of journalism. ... There's

no reason why documentaries can't be as personal as fiction filmmaking and bear the imprint of those who made them. Truth isn't guaranteed by style or expression. It isn't guaranteed by anything.

(Quoted in Arthur 1993: 127)

As Morris's timescale suggests, it has taken time for documentary filmmaking to rid itself of the burden of expectation imposed by direct cinema; furthermore, virtually the entire post-*vérité* history of non-fiction film can be seen as a reaction against its ethos of transparency and unbiased observation. Ironically, the aesthetics of observational/*vérité* cinema have become the *sine qua non* of *faux* documentaries, the way to signal, therefore, the fakery of the documentary pastiche in series such as *Tanner '88, The Office* or *The Thick of It* and films such as *This is Spinal Tap, Man Bites Dog* and *A Mighty Wind.* It is no longer technical limitations that should be blamed for documentary's 'contradictions' but rather the expectations loaded onto it by its theorisation. It can legitimately be argued that filmmakers themselves (and their audiences) have, much more readily than most theorists, accepted documentary's inability to give an undistorted, purely reflective picture of reality. Several different sorts of non-fiction film have now emerged that propose a complex documentary truth arising from an insurmountable compromise between subject and recording, suggesting in turn that it is this very juncture between reality and filmmaker that is at the heart of any documentary.

Documentary practice and theory have always had a problem with aesthetics – or to be more precise with aestheticisation; as John Corner observes, 'The extent to which a concern with formal attractiveness "displaces" the referential such as to make the subject itself secondary to its formal appropriation has been a frequent topic of dispute' (Corner 1996: 123). What has occurred in the past few years especially (in what Corner – when writing about reality television – has referred to as a 'postdocumentary' age [Corner 2002: 257]) is that the aesthetics of documentary – the acknowledged imposition of narrative structure, for example, or stylisation – have now become overt as opposed to clandestine components. The discussion in Chapter 1 of Abraham Zapruder's 8-mm recording of the assassination of President Kennedy posits that there is an inverse relationship between style and authenticity: the less polished the film the more credible it will be found. The latter chapters of this book confront the problems of aestheticisation and accept authorship and stylisation as intrinsic to documentary. Likewise, the role performance plays in documentary has become, in several instances, not the death of documentary but rather a crucial way of establishing its credibility, as the dialogue on the subject of control between Molly Dineen and Geri Halliwell in *Geri* illustrates. The later films of Nick Broomfield take this notion of constructed truth a stage further as they build themselves around the encounters between subjects and Broomfield's on-screen alter ego – encounters that, in turn, form the basis for a reflexive dialogue with the spectator on the nature of documentary authenticity. Likewise, the stylistic excesses of Errol Morris's documentary features, the visual tricks used in other recent films such as *The Kid Stays in the Picture* or *Tarnation* or the way in which *Être et avoir* has had to be reassessed in the light of the legal battles that have followed its release and concomitant success have necessarily served to indicate the continued reflexivity of much documentary practice. What has emerged in recent documentary practice is a new definition of authenticity, one that eschews the traditional adherence to observation or to a Bazinian notion of the transparency of film and replaces this with a multi-layered, performative exchange between subjects, filmmakers/apparatus and spectators.

When arguing against Bill Nichols' presupposition that objectivity in the documentary is impossible, Noël Carroll points out that, because documentaries do not, on the whole, reveal the process of their construction, it does not follow that they automatically deny the existence of these processes (Carroll 1996b: 293). To conclude, Erik Barnouw's assumption is that the intervention of the camera necessarily distorts and alters human behaviour, *ergo* that the resulting piece of film cannot be objective or truthful so that film is deemed to have failed. Why failure? It is perhaps more generous and worthwhile to simply accept that a documentary can never be the real world, that the camera can never capture life as it would have unravelled had it not interfered, and the results of this collision between apparatus and subject are what constitutes a documentary – not the utopian vision of what might have transpired if only the camera had not been there. If one is always going to regret the need for cameras and crews and bemoan the inauthenticity of what they bring back from a situation, then why write about or make documentaries? Instead, documentaries are performative acts whose truth comes into being only at the moment of filming – a moment that, in turn, signals the death of the documentary pursuit as identified by critics such as Erik Barnouw. The paradox that now dominates – as documentaries seem more spontaneous and authentic because they show the documentary process and the moment of encounter with their subjects – is that they also flaunt their lack of concern with conforming to the style of objectivity.

Organisation and structure

Although the above introduction to documentary theory has touched on some of the ways in which this book has structured its arguments, I will conclude by outlining briefly its organisation of material. Part I comprises two chapters: the first deals with the issues of film as record or archive, the second with documentary's use of narration. These discussions are intended to function as a polemical introduction to the problems posed by seeing documentary as an eternal conflict between objectivity and subjectivity, positing that accidental film, such as Abraham Zapruder's home movie footage of Kennedy's assassination, exemplifies non-fictional film at its most objective, whilst the use of narration – an overt intrusion of the filmmaker's bias and didactic point of view – exemplifies documentary at its most subjective. As both discussions conclude, such categorical definitions are crude and invalid, Chapter 1 by focusing on the dialectical re-use of archive material in documentaries such as *The Fall of the Romanovs, Millhouse:*

A White Comedy and *The Atomic Café,* and Chapter 2 by pointing out the very different relationships established between the voice-over and the image in films such as *The Times of Harvey Milk, Hôtel des invalides* and *Sunless.* Chapters 3 and 4 follow on from an introduction that looks in more depth at the problems posed to an understanding of documentary practice by direct cinema – or more precisely the way in which the exponents of direct cinema defined their achievements. Chapter 3 takes as its starting point the importance to observational documentary of the moment of encounter, discussing a series of examples that I have bracketed loosely together as 'journey documentaries': *Seven Up* and *Hoop Dreams* as illustrative of documentaries made over a long time period, *Shoah* and *Hotel Terminus* as examples of investigative documentaries about the Holocaust and *London* and *Sherman's March,* which are constructed around a series of chance meetings that then dictate the courses their narratives take. The subsequent discussion in Chapter 4 of factual entertainment on television, concluding with an analysis of the impact of reality television, looks at the role of performance in observational situations. Part III then tackles the question of performance in documentary, from, broadly speaking, the perspectives of the subject-performer and the director-performer. Chapter 5 examines the ways in which the American presidential image has evolved from the era of Kennedy in the early 1960s to George W. Bush since 2000. The starting point for this discussion is the representation of Kennedy in the direct cinema documentaries *Primary* and *Crisis,* progressing to the disillusionment with the presidential image that follows Nixon's use of the television broadcast as a platform for lying, then including a discussion of Clinton era documentaries such as *The War Room* and *Feed* alongside the various feature films about American presidents released in the 1990s and concluding with an examination of Michael Moore's vilification of George W. Bush in *Fahrenheit 9/11.* Chapter 6 looks at documentaries that are themselves performative, adopting as its point of departure the use of the term by J.L. Austin and Judith Butler (thereby understanding the term 'performative' in a very different way to Bill Nichols in *Blurred Boundaries*). The films of Nicholas Barker, Errol Morris, Molly Dineen and Nick Broomfield are examined as exemplary of the thesis that underpins this whole book: that documentaries are inevitably the result of the intrusion of the filmmaker onto the situation being filmed, that they are performative because they acknowledge the construction and artificiality of even the non-fiction film and propose, as the underpinning truth, the truth that emerges through the encounter between filmmakers, subjects and spectators. Chapter 7 is new to this edition and uses a discussion of four important documentaries of the new millennium (*Être et avoir, The Fog of War, Capturing the Friedmans* and *Touching the Void*) as illustrative of the renewed success of documentaries in the cinemas and, concomitantly, as a means of demonstrating how this moment of popularity for the feature documentary suggests a healthy synergy between history and theory: that the understanding of documentaries as performative acts has become increasingly prevalent in and relevant to practice.

Part I

Ground rules

To initiate an analysis of documentary as a perpetual negotiation between the real event and its representation (that is, to propose that the two remain distinct but interactive) this opening section will juxtapose the notion of film as record with the use of voice-over. This is not an arbitrary selection, but a decision to establish this book's underlying thesis that documentary does not perceive its ultimate aim to be the authentic representation of the real through an examination of (a) the component of documentary that uniquely exemplifies the ideal of a non-fictional image's 'purity' (film as record), and (b) the component that most overtly illustrates the intrusion of bias, subjectivity and conscious structuring of those 'pure' events (narration). In 1971 the German documentary dramatist Peter Weiss offered a definition of documentary theatre that is pertinent to this argument. In 'The Materials and the Models', Weiss argues that, whilst documentary theatre 'refrains from all invention; it takes authentic material and puts it on the stage, unaltered in content, edited in form' (Weiss P. 1971: 41), it also 'presents facts for examination' and 'takes sides' (p. 42). Weiss manifestly does not automatically perceive the imposition of a structure (whether through editing or other means) to mean the loss of objectivity, instead he advocates documentary theatre rooted in dialectical analysis, the principal components of which are the raw material and the theatrical model. His intention in a play such as *The Investigation* – as he intimates later in 'The Materials and the Models' – is to extract from the material 'universal truths', to supply 'an historical context' and to draw attention to 'other possible consequences' (p. 43) of the events encompassed by the play. The raw material is incapable of drawing out or articulating the truths, motives or underlying causes it both contains and implies, so it falls to the writer to extract this general framework. Weiss's notes towards a definition of documentary theatre suggest that documentary is born of a negotiation between two potentially conflicting factors: the real and its representation; but rather than perceive this to be a problem that must be surmounted – as it is perceived in much documentary film theory – Weiss accepts this propensity towards a dialectical understanding of the factual world to be an asset and a virtue.

The intention here is to examine documentary film along the lines that Weiss uses to examine documentary theatre. Although theoretical orthodoxy stipulates that the ultimate aim of documentary is to find the perfect way of representing the real so that the distinction between the two becomes invisible, this is not what one finds within the history of documentary filmmaking. Part of the intention behind these opening paragraphs is thereby to reconsider the documentary 'canon' as it has been laid out by reinstating some of the influential figures who have not conformed to the history imposed by much documentary theory, and who have adopted an attitude to their filmmaking comparable to that of Weiss towards the creation of documentary theatre. Both the discussion of film as record and the discussion of voice-over conclude by suggesting that the dialectical relationship between the event and its representation is the backbone of documentary filmmaking.

1 The event

Archive and newsreel

Documentary is persistently treated as a representational mode of filmmaking, although at its core is the notion of film as record. In its examination of documentary's purported struggle for objectivity, this opening chapter will be concerned with the relationship between film as record and as representation, centred on the idea – or ideal – of an original unadulterated truth; although many of the films to be cited also contain a voice-over, this analysis will focus on the use of newsreel and other raw or accidental footage and archive. The material to be considered will be the Zapruder footage of the assassination of President Kennedy, the compilation films of Emile de Antonio and *The Atomic Café*.

The crux of the problem when considering the potential differences between film as record and as representation, is the relationship between the human and the mechanical eye. Dziga Vertov posited a relationship between the eye and the kino-eye (the latter he referred to as the 'factory of facts' [Michelson 1984: 59]), espousing the idea that cinema's primary function was to show what the human eye could see but not record:

> In fact, the film is only the sum of the facts recorded on film, or, if you like, not merely the sum, but the product, a 'higher mathematics' of facts. Each item of each factor is a separate little document, the documents have been joined with one another so that, on the one hand, the film would consist only of those linkages between signifying pieces that coincide with the visual linkages and so that, on the other hand, these linkages would not require intertitles; the final sum of all these linkages represents, therefore, an organic whole.
>
> (Michelson 1984: 84)

For a compiler of images and a recorder of life, such as Vertov, the recording procedure is always subservient to the facts being committed to film; the mechanical eye is simply capable of showing and clarifying for its audience that which initially stands before the naked eye. The act of filming concretises rather than distorts and is in itself a way of comprehending the world. Later the French documentarist and theorist Jean-Louis Comolli returns to the relationship between the human eye and its mechanical counterpart, but reaches very different con-clusions, believing that, through the advent of photography

> the human eye loses its immemorial privilege; the mechanical eye of the pho-tographic machine now sees *in its place,* and in certain aspects with more sureness. The photograph stands as at once the triumph and the grave of the eye.
>
> (Comolli 1980: 122–3)

Comolli, from a perspective that acknowledges the ambivalence of the mechan-ical eye, argues that Bazin, for one, is naïve to think that, because the camera records a real event, 'it provides us with an objective and impartial image of that reality' as 'The *represented* is seen via a *representation* which, necessarily, trans-forms it' (p. 135).

The underpinning issue is whether or not the intervention of the filmmaker and, therefore, the human eye renders irretrievable the original meaning of the events being recorded. Linda Williams, like many other recent writers on docu-mentary, detects a loss of faith 'in the ability of the camera to reflect objective truths of some fundamental social referent', a loss which she goes on to say 'seems to point, nihilistically ... to the brute and cynical disregard of ultimate truths' (Williams 1993: 10). Later Williams comments that 'It has become an axiom of the new documentary that films cannot reveal the truth of events, but only the ideologies and consciousness that construct competing truths – the fic-tional master narratives by which we make sense of events' (p. 13), so doubting entirely that the image-document itself can mean anything without accompany-ing narrativisation and contextualisation. The problem with Williams' analysis is that it expediently singles out examples (such as *The Thin Blue Line* and *Shoah*) rooted in memory and eye-witness testimony, films that intentionally lack or exclude images of the events under scrutiny, thus making a plausible case for a 'final truth' (p. 15) to be dislodged in favour of a series of subjective truths.

Whilst not advocating the collapse of reality and representation, what this chapter will attempt is an analysis of film as record from an alternative perspec-tive, namely that documentary has always implicitly acknowledged that the 'doc-ument' at its heart is open to reassessment, reappropriation and even manipulation without these processes necessarily obscuring or rendering irre-trievable the document's original meaning, context or content. This relationship between form, the spectator and the document is crucial. Dai Vaughan argues that:

> The photograph – once we are sure that it *is* a photograph – cannot lie. But it can be falsely labelled ... If we accept that documentary is best defined as a way of perceiving images, we cannot evade the implication that it is blind to the falsity of labels. Documentary will be consequent upon what it appears to show, rather than upon what it necessarily does show; and the relationship between the two is a matter for the filmmakers' ethics,

inaccessible to the viewer. Yet the assumptions which the viewer makes
about this relationship, on the basis of signals intended or unintended, will
inform his perception of the film. To make a documentary is therefore to
persuade the viewer that what appears to be *is*.

(Vaughan 1999: 59)

The document (here Vaughan's document is a photograph) is not empty of
meaning, although it can be devoid of interpretation; and interpretation, within
a documentary, is the filmmaker's most significant explanatory tool and one
which, according to Vaughan, is used to inform the way in which a document is
in turn interpreted or understood by the viewer.

The fundamental issue of documentary film is the way in which we are invited
to access the 'document' or 'record' through representation or interpretation, to
the extent that a piece of archive material becomes a mutable rather than a fixed
point of reference. Talking about a television documentary that allegedly used
footage of one event to represent another event for which no cine footage exists,
Vaughan asks 'How ought we to designate such a sequence?' (Vaughan 1999:
85). Vaughan argues that if the footage's 'true provenance' is not given (footage
allegedly of the Warsaw ghetto uprising of April 1943 was actually of the rising of
August–October 1944) then 'we must surely say that its use was documentary but
mendacious'. If, conversely, its provenance had been acknowledged then,
Vaughan concludes, 'I would defend it as a legitimate fictive usage' (p. 85), for as
he had argued earlier: 'What makes a film "documentary" is the way we look at it
… To see a film as documentary is to see its meaning as pertinent to the events
and objects which passed before the camera: to see it, in a word, as signifying what
it appears to record' (pp. 84–5). A filmmaker such as Emile de Antonio does not
disregard the documentary source of his films, nor are his films mere formalist
exercises that tread the post-modern path of disputing the distinction between the
historical/factual and the 'fake' or fictive. The provenance of his archive is not in
doubt, even if he invites his viewers to look at the archive in a particular, guided
way. Rather his films and those, such as *Atomic Café*, which have been overtly
influenced by his 'collage junk' method, play on the complexity of the relationship between historical referent and interpretation; they enact a fundamental
doubt concerning the purity of their original source material and its ability to
reveal a truth that is valid, lasting and cogent. De Antonio's films do not simply
deny or suppress the existence of an independent truth contained within the raw
footage they re-edit and comment upon, and it is perhaps this sort of equivocation that problematises the perception of archive's role in documentary.

Film as accidental record: 'the Zapruder film'

To test some of the assumptions about film as record and its transmutation into
archive it seems appropriate to turn to the most notorious piece of accidental
footage: Abraham Zapruder's 22 seconds of 8-mm film showing the assassination of President Kennedy, 22 November 1963, in Dallas, Texas. Several factors

make 'the Zapruder film', as it is commonly known, an interesting example. The film is the work of a very amateur cameraman, a classic piece of home movie footage that Zapruder simply intended as a family record of the President's visit. The discrepancy between quality and magnitude of content and the Zapruder film's accidental nature make it particularly compelling. The home movie fragment almost did not happen as Abraham Zapruder, a local women's clothing manufacturer, had left his Bell and Howell camera at home on the morning of 22 November because of the rain, but had been persuaded by his secretary to go back and fetch it; it also almost looked quite different, as Zapruder found his position on the concrete block just in front of the 'Grassy Knoll'[1] at the last minute. Additionally, as illustrated in the film itself, it is evident that this position gave Zapruder a view of the motorcade that was partially obscured by a large road sign, tantalisingly blotting out certain details of the assassination. In keeping with this accidental quality is Zapruder's own tentativeness when discussing the film before the Warren Commission, commenting humbly, 'I knew I had something, I figured it might be of some help – I didn't know what' (quoted in Wasson 1995: 7). Similarly important is Zapruder's lack of expertise as a camera operator. The silent film jolts in response to the shots and Zapruder finds it difficult to keep Kennedy centre frame: at the crucial moment when the fatal head shot hits him, the President has been allowed to almost slide out of view, leaving the most famous frames of amateur film dominated, almost engulfed, by the lush green grass on the other side of Elm Street. 'Zapruder' became shorthand in American film schools in the years following the assassination for a piece of film of extremely low technical quality whose content was nevertheless of the utmost significance.[2] For Bazin, the apotheosis of the photograph is the similarly artless family snapshot whose documentary equivalent would be the home movie. So it was that students and others sought to emulate the style of the Zapruder footage; as Patricia Zimmerman comments with reference to home movies, 'the American avant-garde has appropriated home-movie style as a formal manifestation of a spontaneous, untampered form of filmmaking' (Zimmerman 1995: 146). The home movie is, virtually by definition, the documentation of the trivial, the personal and the inconsequential, events of interest only to the family group involved. What makes Zapruder's home movie exceptional is that it happens to capture an event that is not private and trivial but public and of huge importance. Footage that by accident rather than design captures material this monumental transgresses the boundaries between the official and unofficial uses of broadcast film, offering an alternative point of view, a perspective that is partly predicated upon the absenting of the film *auteur*, the conscious creator of the images. Zapruder's accidental home movie, like George Holliday's similarly spontaneous video recording of the beating of Rodney King by members of the LAPD in March 1991, became the official text of the events it recorded.

Why is this combination of the accidental, the amateur and the historically significant event so engaging? If one were to devise a method for classifying archive material in accordance with its purity or level of distortion, the Zapruder film would be at the top of the scale. Paul Arthur comments on the 'mutual agreement' between film theorists such as Siegfried Kracauer and Bela Balazs that 'newsreels and documentary reportage in general are "innocent" or "artless" due to their lack of aesthetic reconstruction' (Arthur 1997:2); he goes on to quote Kracauer when positing that 'it is precisely the snap-shot quality of the pictures that makes them appear as authentic documents' (p. 3), concluding that 'the absence of "beauty" yields a greater quotient of "truth"' (p. 3), thereby establishing an inverse ratio between documentary purity and aesthetic value. The Zapruder film, by these criteria, is exemplary in its rawness, innocence and credibility as a piece of non-fiction evidence or documentation. Zapruder, unlike those who copied him, is not consciously manipulating his amateur status, and it is this naïveté that audiences still find compelling, as exemplified by the preponderance of 'the accidental video witnessing of spectacular events' (Ouellette 1995: 41) that dominates the American series *I Witness Video*. Andrew Britton mentions, as if it is a foregone conclusion, that 'there can be no such thing as a representation of the world which does not embody a set of values', so ensuring that the documentary's 'greatest strength is its availability for the purpose of analysis and ideological critique' (Britton 1992: 28). There is no space in this claim for non-fiction images such as the Zapruder film, accidental footage that is not filmed with a conscious or unconscious set of determining values – 'value', in Britton's estimation, being automatically attached to the author/filmmaker as opposed to a film's content. Yet historical documentaries are made up of such non-critical fragments as the Zapruder footage. Within such a context, the film's 'value' is presumed to be that, because of the singular lack of premeditation, intention and authorship, it is able, unproblematically to yield the truth contained within its blurry, hurried images; but therein lies its problem and the factual film's burden of proof.

The Zapruder footage very quickly became an object of fetishistic fascination. As film that shows the moment of Kennedy's death, its 'imagery operating as the equivalent of the snuff film', the Zapruder frames bear uneasy comparison with the pornographic ideal of 'going all the way' to the moment of death (Simon 1996: 67). However, the fact that for 12 years the images were only known as single frames published in the Warren Commission Report[3] into the assassination or *Life* magazine, which secured the rights to the Zapruder film on the night of the assassination for $150,000, inevitably rendered them mysterious. By 1975, when the film was first broadcast, the rights had been returned to the Zapruder family, although the original footage now belongs to the US government, which paid the heirs of Abraham Zapruder £10million to keep it in the national archives (a deal that was agreed on the day John Kennedy Jr died in a plane crash). In the immediate aftermath of the assassination, the Zapruder film was thus not available as film, although the surrounding events were: the arrival of the motorcade at Parkland Memorial Hospital, Jackie Kennedy accompanying her husband's coffin on Air Force One's flight back to Washington, the funeral, the arrest and subsequent murder live on television of Lee Harvey Oswald. The absence of the key assassination images was exacerbated by the presence of these surrounding pieces of tape and film and by the knowledge that the Zapruder film was all the time being examined, re-examined and reenacted by the Warren Commission. Such absence or lack was especially marked when considering the fatal shot to Kennedy's head, as these frames (Nos. 313–15) were deemed too traumatic to show (*Life* omitting them from early publications of the film), or, as occurred in the published Warren Commission Report, were distorted, as two frames (314 and 315) were 'accidentally' reversed, which gave the impression that Kennedy's head was thrust forward by the impact of the bullet, thus supporting their lone gunman theory. When these frames did become readily accessible, the 'involuntary spasm' shown as the bullet hits Kennedy itself 'became the site of an investigatory fetish' (Simon 1996: 68), the Zapruder film's most over-scrutinised images.

Although the Warren Commission said that 'Of all the witnesses to the tragedy, the only unimpeachable one is the *camera* of Abraham Zapruder' (my italics; *Life* Magazine, 25 November 1966, quoted in Simon 1996: 41), its status as evidence is ambiguous: it can show that President Kennedy was assassinated but is unable to show how or by whom, because Zapruder's camera (and it is revealing that the apparatus is singled out for unimpeachability and not the man) is effectively facing the wrong way – at the President and not at who shot him. Other photographic material, taken from the opposite side of Elm Street, which could potentially reveal more about the positions of the assassins – such as Orvill Nix's film and Mary Moorman's photograph – has been allegedly subjected to greater Security Services intervention and violation,[4] although the Warren Commission did omit Zapruder frames 208–11 from its final report, despite the assertion that the first bullet struck Kennedy at frame 210 (Simon 1996: 40).

If documentary putatively aspires to discover the least distortive means of representing reality, then is not footage such as the Zapruder film exemplary of its aim? It is devoid of imposed narrative, authorial intervention, editing and discernible bias and yet its contents are of such momentous significance that it remains arguably the most important piece of raw footage ever shot. The Zapruder film as a piece of historical evidence has severe limitations. Despite its value as explicit raw footage, the truth that its frames can reveal is restricted to verisimilitude of image to subject; the non-fictional image's mimetic power cannot stretch to offering a context or an explanation for the crude events on the screen, thus proposing two levels of truth: the factual images we see and the truth to be extrapolated from them. Or is that 'truths'? One of the consistently complicating aspects of the Zapruder film is that it has been both 'unimpeachable' and 'constantly open to multiple interpretations' (Simon 1996: 43), an open series of images that can be used to 'prove' a multitude of conflicting or divergent theories about the assassination. This is the footage's burden of proof: that, as an authentic record, it functions as incontrovertible 'evidence', whilst as a text incapable of revealing conclusively who killed President Kennedy it functions as an inconclusive representation. What the Zapruder film demonstrates, is an irresistible desire (on the part of theorists and probably practitioners as well) for manipulation, narrativisation or conscious intervention, despite the avowed detestation of such intrusions upon the factual image. The Zapruder footage has, for example, led Heidi Wasson to speculate wildly that the footage 'becomes the threshold to an imaginary and real space where seemingly contradictory rituals are re-enacted' (Wasson 1995: 10). Exemplifying this duality, the Zapruder footage's continuous paradox is that it promises to reveal what will always remain beyond it: the motivation and the cause of the actions it depicts. This has, in turn, led consistently to two impulses, the first being to focus obsessively on the source material itself, to analyse, re-analyse, enhance, digitally re-master Zapruder's original in the vain hope that these images will finally reveal the truth of who killed Kennedy, the second being to use the same sequence of images as the basis for an interpretation of the assassination that invariably requires and incorporates additional, substantiating material, usually drawing from an ever-dwindling number of eyewitnesses and an ever-increasing pool of conspiracy theorists. Although Zapruder's footage is an archetypal example of accidental, reactive and objective film, it has rarely been permitted to exist as such because, as Bill Nichols comments, 'To re-present the event is clearly *not* to explain it' (Nichols 1994: 121).

It is this central inadequacy that has led to a peculiar canonisation of certain emotionally charged pieces of film and video, images that could be termed 'iconic'. Recently the transmutation occurred with the endlessly repeated and equally endlessly inconclusive shots of the mutilated car in which Princess Diana and others were killed in a Paris underpass on 31 August 1997. Although these images could really only tell us that Diana, Dodi Fayed and Henri Paul had died, they were, alongside the hastily edited compilation documentaries that started running on the afternoon of the crash, played again and again as if, miraculously, they would suddenly prove less inconclusive, or indeed that looking at them hard enough would enable us to reverse the events they confirmed. The endlessly repeated images of the second plane plunging into the Twin Towers on 9/11 (2001) has been used as a similarly collective site of national and global trauma, and it is significant that – no doubt because viewers' responses to such images have become so preconditioned – Michael Moore in *Fahrenheit 9/11* chose to represent the terrorist attacks on the World Trade Centre through an audio track of those moments laid onto black leader, only cutting later to footage of distraught New Yorkers trying to comprehend what is going on. Moore has omitted the iconic archival moments of 9/11. The iconic status afforded the 9/11, Diana and Zapruder footage, is the result of other factors; imbuing the images with significance beyond their importance as mere film or video, they function as the point where diverse and often conflicting mythologising tendencies, emotions and fantasies collide. A comparably hyperbolic and intense language was adopted to describe the deaths of JFK and Diana – 'the day the dream died', 'the end of Camelot' – and the mass outpouring of grief that followed them more than adequately repressed the shortcomings and failings of the individuals struck down. The images of the attacks on New York came to represent the wounding of an entire nation if not the western world. The Zapruder film has become the dominant assassination text, onto which is poured all the subsidiary grief, anger, belief in conspiracy and corruption surrounding the unresolved events it depicts. The text is simple, its meaning is not; as Roland Barthes observes, 'Myth is not defined by the object of its message, but by the way in which it utters this message: there are formal limits to myth, there are no "substantial" ones' (Barthes 1957: 117).

With each repeated viewing of the Zapruder film, do we still simply see it for what it is, see the death? This question might seem needlessly obfuscating, but at issue is how we look at any image that is so familiar that we already know it intimately before we begin the process of re-viewing. Iconic documentary material such as this is, in part, forever severed from its historical and narrative contextualisation. The killing of President Kennedy is perpetually reworked in the present; each theory about who killed Kennedy and why urges us to impose a closure on these malleable images, adopting the language of certainty ('who killed Kennedy will be shown here for the first time'[5]) whilst knowing presumably that they will be superseded in due course by a new theory, a new set of certainties. The Zapruder film remains the core text of the Kennedy assassination, 'invisibly back-projected on all the other film evidence' (Simon 1996: 47), and our obsession with it is in no small part due to our ambivalent desire to have it both reveal and keep hidden the truth behind the 'world's greatest murder mystery'.[6] Its iconic and fetishistic status is due to its familiarity and its instability as evidence; Zapruder captures a public death and presents us with a personal viewing experience (a home movie) – as Errol Morris comments, 'we're there ... it's happening before our eyes'.[7] If a piece of archive footage becomes so familiar that a mere allusion to one detail or one frame triggers off a recollection of the whole, then the experience of watching that film is not simply that of observing the representation of an actual event. The Zapruder film has significance beyond the sum of its parts; despite its subject matter, it begins to function like a melodrama, to comfort the viewer almost with its known-ness, its familiarity. Knowing the end ironically frees us to speculate upon alternatives ('what if ?', 'if only'), to reconstruct the sequence just as we see it relentlessly repeating the very events we are trying to suppress. This is particularly the case when it comes to the frames immediately prior to the shot hitting Kennedy's head; the pause (even at real speed) between gun shots always seems implausibly long, Kennedy is slumping into his wife's arms and Zapruder has almost lost him from view when suddenly the right side of his head explodes. In that hiatus between points of intense violence, the impulse is to re-imagine history.

The Zapruder film shows us everything and it shows us nothing; it is explicit but cannot conclusively confirm or deny any version of the assassination. Perhaps, cynically, one could proffer this as the reason for its enduring mystique, that because it will never solve the murder mystery it is a perfect fantasy text. Too often the indissoluble ambivalence of the Zapruder film is forgotten in favour of an 'anything goes' approach to it as a historical document that has no meaning until it has been interpreted or given a story, an attitude that Wasson succumbs to when treating the footage as just another cultural artefact, suggesting that the 'film *qua*, film quickly dissolves, becoming intimately linked to the cultural phenomena which infuse it' (Wasson 1995: 10). This conclusion resembles the inflexible formalism of Hayden White (1987: 76) as he says that 'any historical object can sustain a number of equally plausible descriptions or narratives'. The essential ambiguity surrounding Zapruder's images hinges on the awareness that their narrativisability does not engulf or entirely obscure their veracity. Nichols is thereby wrong to believe that inconclusive pieces of film record such as Zapruder's leave the event 'up for grabs' (Nichols 1994: 121–2); what is 'up for grabs' is the interpretation of that event. If the footage's realness is merely to be fused with its imaginative potential, then why is the actual Zapruder film so different from and more affecting than its imitators, all of which effectively represent the same event? There have been countless reconstructions of the home movie fragment, from a dream sequence in John Waters' *Eat Your Makeup* (1966) in which Divine parodies Jackie Kennedy reliving the day of the assassination, to the countless more earnest versions made for quasi-factual biopics, to the documentary restagings of the events undertaken (from the Warren Commission onwards) to attempt to establish the facts. One anomaly is that the closer or more faithful the imitation is to the Zapruder original, the more it emphasises its difference from it. An interesting example of a Zapruder re-enactment is the accurate reconstruction undertaken for *The Trial of Lee Harvey Oswald* (David Greene, 1976), a film made before copies of the Zapruder were widely available. The Zapruder simulation is repeatedly used during the hypothetical trial of the film's title, and those in the courtroom are shocked by what they see. But whilst Oliver Stone's *JFK,* in a comparable courtroom situation, uses the real Zapruder footage digitally enhanced, enlarged and slowed down (thus compelling the cinema spectator to identify directly with the diegetic audience's horror), the reconstruction for *The Trial of Lee Harvey Oswald* differs from its prototype in one crucial respect: it omits the blood and gore of the fatal shot to Kennedy's head. This is citation, not replication – a mythologised rendering of the original, brutal snuff movie.

   The ultimate, uncomfortable paradox of the Zapruder film as raw evidence is that the more it is exposed to scrutiny, with frames singled out and details digitally enhanced, the more unstable and inconclusive the images become. The industry of what Don Delillo has termed 'blur analysis'[8] has always flourished, but the results are confusing and frequently fanciful, despite Simon's assertion that

> The film must be slowed down to be legible; its twenty-two seconds go by too fast for its vital content to be adequately studied. As a result, it speaks its own impossibility as film. ... Its status as evidence relies simultaneously on duration and its arrest, film and still frame.
>
> (Simon 1996: 48)

Run at proper speed, the Zapruder footage is brief and incomplete; the action starts and stops convulsively, in mid-action. This indeterminacy is the overriding characteristic of accidental footage, its jolting, fragmentary quality not only producing an unfinished narrative, but also preventing a conscious viewpoint from being imposed on the images by either the person filming or the audience. The speed with which the assassination occurs is thereby a crucial factor, as Noël Carroll (1996a: 228), intimates: 'Unexpected events can intrude into the viewfinder – e.g., Lee Harvey Oswald's assassination – before there is time for a personal viewpoint to crystallize'.

The paradox remains, however, that it is only when viewed at proper speed that the true impact of Kennedy's death becomes apparent. In his analysis of the trial of the LAPD officers accused of beating Rodney King in March 1991, Bill Nichols suggests that, far from being an elucidating technique, the slowing down of the original George Holliday video tape could be used to distort the facts, as the LAPD defence team demonstrated with their assiduous dissection of the same footage that the prosecution alleged proved their case for police brutality to corroborate their case for acquittal. The defence argument

> appeared to fly in the face of common sense. But it took the *form* of a positivist, scientific interpretation. It did what any good examination of evidence should do: it scrutinised it with care and drew from it (apparent) substantiation for an interpretation that best accounted for what really happened.
>
> (Nichols 1994: 30)

Similar distortions have occurred around the Kennedy assassination. Two examples are the magnifications of a piece of film and a portion of a photograph – Robert Hughes's film showing the Texas School Book Depository and Mary Moorman's photograph showing the Grassy Knoll. Both have been digitally enhanced to the point of allegedly revealing shady figures at a window or crouched behind a picket fence. The evidence, in the enhanced versions, might be convincing, but played at real speed or unmagnified these two records of the assassination day appear inconclusive, the results of a desperate desire to find something plausibly human amidst the play on light and shade. One person's figure is another person's shadow.

The Zapruder film (and Holliday's video of Rodney King) make us perhaps question 'the truth-bearing capacities of film' (Simon 1996: 48). This returns us to the notion that Abraham Zapruder's camera, though able to produce an unfailingly authentic record of the Kennedy assassination, is pointing the wrong way, that the film may just be one of many texts that can be used to explain the assassination, not the only one. Still one of the most compelling investigative films made about the assassination and its aftermath is Emile de Antonio's *Rush to Judgement* (1966) on which he collaborated with lawyer Mark Lane. Lane had written a book of the same name, published on 15 August 1966, that took issue with key areas of the Warren Commission Report, made public on 27 September 1964. Neither the book nor the film attempts to solve the 'murder mystery' of the assassination, but merely to insinuate that the Warren Commission's conclusions are unconvincing and that there are grounds for arguing that there had been a conspiracy to kill Kennedy; hence the adoption in both of an examination/cross-examination structure. As Lane stipulates in the documentary's first piece to camera, the film will be making 'the case for the defence'. More tantalising than the inconclusiveness of the Zapruder footage is the lack of testimony from Lee Oswald, Oswald having been shot in the basement of the Dallas police headquarters by Jack Ruby on 24 November as he was being escorted to the County Jail. *Rush to Judgement* is the first of several television and film attempts to give Oswald's defence a 'voice'.[9] The majority of the film's interviewees support the theory that Kennedy was shot at least once from the front as seems logical from the movement backwards of the President's head in the Zapruder footage; it is ironic and apposite, therefore, that the majority of de Antonio's witnesses are facing the Grassy Knoll, and so literally looking the other way from Zapruder. With the absence of any archive material of the assassination itself, *Rush to Judgement* is reliant on memory presented, within its prosecutional framework, as testimony. The difference between the Zapruder film and *Rush to Judgement* is the difference between the event and memory, between a filmed representation of a specific truth and the articulation of a set of related, contingent versions. In a film such as *Rush to Judgement* the human eye replaces the mechanical eye as the instrument of accurate or convincing memory; as the photographic evidence yields fewer rather than more certainties, the eye-witnesses interviewed by de Antonio and others usurp its position. The obvious problem with the growing dependency (from the 1960s onwards) on interviews as evidence not (supposedly) overly manipulated by the *auteur*-director, is that what can too easily be revealed is a series of truths (or what individuals take to be truths) not a single, underpinning truth. Just as the Zapruder film remains an inconclusive text, so *Rush to Judgement* ensures that the assassination inquiries are not closed by the appearance of one hastily compiled report, having one interviewee, Penn Jones, state directly to camera at the end of the film:

> I would love to see a computer, faced with the problem of probabilities of the assassination taking place the way it did, with all these strange incidents which took place before and are continuing to take place after the assassination.[10] I think all of us who love our country should be alerted that something is wrong in the land.

The fundamental discrepancy between 'raw' archive material as exemplified by the Zapruder film and a memory/interview-based documentary such as *Rush to Judgement* highlights the source for the growing disillusionment with the notion of image as document. If pieces of unpremeditated archive as ostensibly uncontaminated and artless as Zapruder's or Holliday's home movies can produce contradictory but credible interpretations, then the idea of the 'pure' documentary which theorists have tacitly invoked is itself vulnerable. In *Il Giorno della Civetta* the Sicilian writer Leonardo Sciascia adopts the artichoke as a metaphor for describing the authorities' pursuit of the Mafia: that no matter how many leaves the police or the judiciary tear away, they never reach its heart, or if they do, its heart proves to be a strangely inconclusive place. Likewise the hounding of the 'pure' documentary; for is it not the case (as with gruesome reality television or the stop-frame 'blur analysis' to which the Zapruder and Holliday films have both been subjected) that the closer one gets to the document itself, the more aware one becomes of the artifice and the impossibility of a satisfactory relationship between the image and the real? Not that reality television (by which I mean its first incarnation: programmes based on unedited video material frequently of crimes and cop chases [see Dovey 2000]) should be doubted and immediately classified as manipulative fiction, but even the least adulterated image can only reveal so much. The very 'unimpeachability' or stability of the original documents that form the basis for archival non-fiction films is brought into question; the document – though showing a concluded, historical event – is not fixed, but is infinitely accessible through interpretation and recontextualisation, and thus becomes a mutable, not a constant, point of reference. A necessary dialectic is involved between the factual source and its representation that acknowledges the limitations as well as the credibility of the document itself. The Zapruder film is factually accurate, it is not a fake, but it cannot reveal the motive or cause for the actions it shows. The document, though real, is incomplete.

The compilation film and Emile de Antonio

As a consequence of this, archive material has rarely been used unadulterated and unexplained within the context of documentary film, rather it has primarily been deployed in one of two ways: illustratively, as part of a historical exposition to complement other elements such as interviews and voice-over; or critically, as part of a more politicised historical argument or debate. The former usage, as exemplified by series such as *The World at War, The Vietnam War, The Nazis: A Warning From History, The People's Century* or *Auschwitz: The Nazis and the Final Solution* is straightforward in that it is not asking the spectator to question the archival documents but simply to absorb them as a component of a larger narrative. Within this category of archive-reliant documentary, the origin of the footage is rarely an issue, as the material is used to illustrate general or specific events and is usually explained by a voice-over and interviewees. The alternative political approach to found footage – for which the derivation of such archive is a significant issue and which frequently uses such material dialectically or against the grain – has a long-standing history and is more complex. The 'compilation film' (a documentary constructed almost exclusively out of retrieved archive) was pioneered by Soviet filmmakers Esther Shub and Dziga Vertov in the 1920s, both of whom worked within a revolutionary tradition which believed in political, instructive and inspirational cinema. The importance of Shub particularly was that she applied to non-fiction film (although the Soviets endlessly debated the validity of the fiction/non-fiction divide – see Tretyakov *et al.* 1927) the 'montage of attractions' most readily associated with Sergei Eisenstein, who Shub had worked with. Jay Leyda comments of Shub's films that they

> brought back to life footage that had hitherto been regarded as having, at the most, only the nature of historical fragments. By the juxtaposition of

these 'bits of reality', she was able to achieve effects of irony, absurdity, pathos and grandeur that few of the bits had intrinsically.

(Leyda 1983: 224)

Two stages of 'compilation' are indicated here, one which involves collation and discovery and another which requires assimilation and analysis. Shub's method was to both focus on the original footage and recontextualise it. Exemplary of Shub's way of working is the film she made to commemorate the February 1917 overthrow of the imperial family, *The Fall of the Romanovs* (1927) – a revolutionary, pro-Bolshevik film that was, nevertheless, largely dependent on antipathetic, pro-Tsarist material. It thereby exhibits the dependency upon dialectical collision between the inherent perspective of the original archive and its radical re-use that remains a characteristic of the compilation documentary. In the summer of 1926, Shub travelled to Leningrad where she found that much of the relevant pre-Revolutionary newsreel footage had been damaged or had disappeared, although she did come across the private home movies of Nicholas II and some 60,000 metres of film, of which she chose 5,200 metres to take back to Moscow (Leyda 1996: 58–9). Of her structuring of this found footage, Shub says:

In the montage I tried to avoid looking at the newsreel material for its own sake, and to maintain the principle of its documentary quality. All was subordinated to the theme. This gave me the possibility, in spite of the known limitations of the photographed events and facts, to link the meanings of the material so that it evoked the pre-Revolutionary period and the February days.

(Leyda 1996: 59)

The significant observation here is the idea that a clear distinction exists between 'newsreel' and 'documentary', and, following on from this, that whilst the newsreel is limited to showing events, it is the function of a documentary to provide structure and meaning. A documentary, a structured and motivated non-fiction film, does not aspire to convey in as pure a way as possible the real material at its core because this is what newsreel or other comparable forms of amateur, accidental and non-narrative film do.

Shub's compilation film technique conforms to the tradition of dialectical, political filmmaking, to the idea expressed by Eisenstein that 'the expressive effect of cinema is the result of juxtapositions' (Eisenstein 1926: 147). The events retraced in *The Fall of the Romanovs* do not just 'speak for themselves', and Shub's intention is to use archive material severed from its original context to offer a reinterpretation of events and to effect 'the politicised activation of "suppressed" ideas or the inversion of conventional meanings' (Arthur 1997: 2). In *The Fall of the Romanovs*, Shub both straightforwardly tells the story of the events leading up to the revolution and passes commentary on why it occurred. Juxtapositions are frequently set up via the film's brief intertitles. Near the beginning, one such intertitle draws attention to the vast expanses of land owned and overseen by a wealthy few, followed by a piece of film illustrating this claim that concludes with an exterior shot of what we subsequently learn is the sumptuous residence of the governor of Kaluga. Following the exterior shot, there is an intertitle 'And next to them – this', followed by images of tiny peasant mud huts. The implications of social injustice are quite obvious, but, like Eisenstein, what Shub then does, once the initial juxtaposition has been established, is to intercut a variety of images that further illustrate this social difference without feeling the need to explicate them. Shub's method is not to disappear the archive's origins and potential original meaning as Arthur implies (it remains significant that the images of the governor of Kaluga descending the steps of his vast residence with his wife on his arm is home movie footage – personal material that, of itself, signals immense privilege) but rather to preserve that meaning whilst simultaneously imposing a fresh interpretative framework. Hayden White dwells on the idea that it is narrative that gives the real historical event cogency, arguing that it is only through the presence of a story that the inherent meaning of events can be revealed or understood and that 'To be historical, an event must be more than a singular occurrence, a unique happening. It receives its definition from its contribution to the development of a plot' (White H. 1987: 51). Conversely, Shub and others who followed her do not condemn the unnarrativised event as indecipherable until it has been positioned within a developmental structure, rather they posit that there is a fruitful dialogue to be had between original newsreel, home movie footage and the like and the critical eye of the filmmaker (and the implied new audience). A documentary, as Tretyakov and others intimate, will never be merely the Zapruder film or the Kaluga governor's home movie, it will always be, to some degree, the creative treatment of actuality.

The most important compilation documentary filmmaker has been the American Emile de Antonio, who made a series of documentaries, from *Point of Order* (1963) to *Mr Hoover and I* (1989), which scrutinised and assessed recent American history. His films are notably Soviet in their intent: formally radical and rooted to the idea that meaning is constructed through editing, they mirror de Antonio's Marxist intentions and his distrust of more conventional documentary modes such as observational cinema and the use of didactic narration; they use archive material provocatively and dialectically and compel audiences to think, to question and to seek change.[11] De Antonio is a strong advocate of bias and of the foregrounding of opinion, thereby undermining the notion that documentary is principally concerned with transparency and non-intervention. It is therefore ironic that the question of authorship has frequently plagued compilation filmmakers: Shub found that critics considered *The Fall of the Romanovs* not to be her film and de Antonio had *Point of Order* (a re-editing of the televised 1954 McCarthy vs Army hearings) excluded from the 1963 New York film festival on the grounds that 'it was television and not film' (Weiner 1971: 10).[12] De Antonio's work offers the most comprehensive articulation of the ideas first expressed by Shub about the polemical potential of archive film. One interviewer terms de Antonio's method 'radical scavenging' (Weiner 1971): revisiting existing footage to construct out of it an alternative and maybe even directly oppositional narrative from that which it inherently possesses.

Just as Shub and those who follow her create a dialectical relationship between original film and its recontextualisation, so they do not believe that the marked clarity of their own political position will stand in the way of audiences formulating their own opinions. In one interview, whilst attacking American *cinéma vérité* ('Only people without feelings or convictions could even think of making *cinéma vérité*'), de Antonio states: 'I happen to have strong feelings and some dreams and my prejudice is under and in everything I do' (Rosenthal 1978: 7). This 'prejudice' informs de Antonio's treatment of his audience; his films are difficult, they 'make demands on the audience' (Weiner 1971: 13), thus immediately recalling Eisenstein's view, with reference to *Strike,* that film should plough the audience's psyche. Like Eisenstein's, de Antonio's films are furtively didactic. Despite his films' democratic intention (not wanting to teach but to reveal) de Antonio wants his audience to arrive at the same conclusion as himself, a method he calls 'democratic didacticism' (Waugh 1985: 244). This term neatly embodies de Antonio's particular brand of archive documentary that instructs without divesting the spectator or the re-edited archive of independence of thought. De Antonio's films aim to convince the audience of the arguments put forward, they are passionate as well as intellectual and articulate, constructed around 'a kind of collage junk idea I got from my painter friends' of working with 'dead footage' (Rosenthal 1978: 4).[13] 'Collage junk' is central to de Antonio's notion of 'democratic didacticism' as it is through the juxtaposition of 'people, voices, images and ideas' that he is able to develop a 'didactic line' that nevertheless eschews overtly didactic mechanisms such as voice-over (Weiner 1971: 6). De Antonio refutes entirely the purely illustrative function of archive material, instead the original pieces of film become mutable, active ingredients. Imperative to de Antonio's idea of 'democratic didacticism', though, is that the innate meaning of this original footage, however it is reconstituted, is never entirely obscured. One vivid, consistent facet of de Antonio's work is that his collage method does not attack hate figures such as Richard Nixon, Joseph McCarthy or Colonel Patton directly, but rather gives them enough rope by which to hang themselves – turning often favourable original footage in on itself.

To witness McCarthy's demise on live television is far more effective (both live in 1954 and in 1963, the date of *Point of Order's* release) than being told, with hindsight, that the American political establishment finally realised that the junior senator was a bigoted, drunken liar. De Antonio is fond of recounting how, despite years of trying, McCarthy's counsel, Roy Cohn, was unable to nail de Antonio for manipulation of the facts: 'There is no finer flattery nor more delicious treachery than verbatim quotation' (Tuchman 1990: 66). Several of the sequences in *Point of Order* belie this innocence, the most ostentatious example being the end of the film. In this sequence de Antonio imposes a narrative structure (in as much the same way as Peter Weiss does in his documentary play *The Investigation*) that shows McCarthy continuing a bumbling, verbose diatribe against Senator Symington, while those present pack their bags and clear the chamber, concluding with a final shot – a photograph – of the empty committee chamber. De Antonio constructs this sequence using a collage of disparate, not necessarily sequential images, using such non-synchronous material to suggest that the establishment, who previously had sustained him, finally turns its back on McCarthy. The duality of *Point of Order* is that de Antonio constructs its narrative and meaning out of footage over which, in the first instance, he had no authorial control, hence Cohn's distrust of de Antonio as well as his inability to find libellous bias in the film. De Antonio succinctly identifies the mechanism whereby this duality is possible when commenting, 'Honesty and objectivity are not the same thing. Nor are they even closely related' (Weiss 1974: 35). *Point of Order* is 'honest' in that all the images it collates are irrefutably real, and yet it is not 'objective' because those same images have been resituated to suit and argue de Antonio's perspective of the events they show. What a film like *Point of Order* elucidates very clearly is the problem of equating the image ostensibly without bias with the truth (and the cameras deployed for the McCarthy vs Army hearings are as non-interventionist as possible, simply focusing on who is speaking). His 'collage junk' films are an astute, ironic dismantling of this assumption.

De Antonio's work clearly illustrates not only that original footage is open to interpretation and manipulation, but that general theses can be extrapolated from specific historical images and that the historical event does not only reside in the past but is inevitably connected to the present. De Antonio's Marxism thus underpins all his documentaries. Walter Benjamin in 'Theses on the Philosophy of History' suggests that historical materialists should disassociate themselves from the victors of history and the maintaining of the status quo and instead 'brush history against the grain' (Benjamin 1955: 259). De Antonio adopts a similar stance, as his films seek to draw out the subsidiary, buried, unofficial text of American history. In certain instances the link between past and present is explicitly made, as in *In the Year of the Pig* (1969) in which de Antonio, in a documentary which spans the years between French colonial rule of Vietnam and the Tet Offensive of 1968, examines the (then) contemporary war in direct relation to the history of imperialist intervention in Indochina. De Antonio's intention is to offer the 'intellectual and historical overview' (Rosenthal 1978: 9) lacking, he argued, from the blanket but unanalytical newsreel coverage of the war. Whereas so many subsequent films about Vietnam (*Dear America,* for instance) marginalize the problem of American intervention in Vietnam by stressing the personal effect of the war on the GIs, *In the Year of the Pig* dwells almost exclusively upon historical contextualisation. The photomontage sequence which opens the film, contrasts (with black leader in between) the image of a Civil War soldier who died at Gettysburg with a photograph of a GI in Vietnam with 'Make war not love' daubed on his helmet. This counterpointing highlights the imminent loss of life awaiting the troops in Vietnam; it also represents the immorality, as de Antonio sees it, of the American position, that 'our cause in Vietnam was not the one that boy had died for in 1863' (Crowdus and Georgakas 1988: 168), hence the reprise of the Gettysburg image – in negative and accompanied by a scratchy version of *The Battle Hymn of the Republic* – at the end of the film. Both *In the Year of the Pig's* cumulative structure and its use of individual images serve the desire to endlessly contextualise and reassess the present. A universal truth that

Figure 1.1   In the Year of the Pig
Source: Courtesy of BFI Stills, Posters and Designs

emerges through the film via the many images of cultivation and farming, Ho Chi Minh walking through the jungle and GIs lying dead amidst the undergrowth is that any attempt to defeat the North Vietnamese will always be futile, for not only have they suffered and recovered from a cycle of attacks and invasions throughout history, but their endurance is symptomatic of their lifestyle, their affinity with the land and the American inability to conquer it. Vietnam in this context represents stability. Complementing this overall argument are the potent specific images, such as the sequence showing French colonisers in white hats and suits being pulled in rickshaws by some Vietnamese, getting out at a café where a Moroccan in a fez brusquely dismisses the Vietnamese when they hold out their hands for payment. For de Antonio this 1930s scene 'encapsulates the whole French colonial empire' (Crowdus and Georgakas 1988: 167), and is 'the equivalent of a couple of chapters of dense writing about the meaning of colonialism' (Crowdus and Georgakas 1988: 167). This may be an overestimation of its capacity (much of the scene's impact stems from its contextualisation within a confrontational and polemical film), but the sequence nevertheless reflects upon itself as a historical document and upon its contemporary relevance to the much later American aggression.

The most enduring aspect of de Antonio's work is its use of collage techniques to offer an ironic and humorous critique of American history – a quality directly echoed by *The Atomic Café*, to be discussed at the end of this chapter. *Millhouse: A White Comedy* (1971), notable as a pre-Watergate anti-Nixon film, is, as the title suggests, a documentary comedy. Like most of de Antonio's films, how *Millhouse* came to be made is just as important as what it says or how it says it. The film was the major reason for de Antonio's presence (on whom the FBI had already amassed a substantial file) on Nixon's 'enemies' list, something of which he was inordinately proud, claiming that the ten White House files on him were, above the film awards he had won, his 'ultimate prize' (Rosenthal 1978: 8). Whilst he was cutting *Painters Painting*, de Antonio received an anonymous telephone call from someone saying he had stolen all the Nixon footage from one of the television networks and that he was willing to give de Antonio the material for nothing if he would make a film out of it. De Antonio agreed, and 200 cans of films were dropped off

Figure 1.2   Millhouse: A White Comedy
Source: Courtesy of BFI Stills, Posters and Designs

one night at the building where he was editing. In order to preserve the anonymity of his source and to ensure that the FBI could not trace the material, de Antonio had all the film's edge numbers erased. This is characteristic de Antonio 'derring-do'. Because of the sensitivity of their subject matter, most of his films attracted secret service or police attention (which never ultimately prevented their release): whilst setting up *Rush to Judgement* witnesses were intercepted and scared off before de Antonio could interview them; the film, tapes and negatives of his interview with the Weathermen (the basis for *Underground*) were subpoenaed by the FBI – an action which prompted many from Hollywood to rally to his support; he was arrested, along with the Ploughshares 8, for demonstrating outside a nuclear plant during the production of *In the King of Prussia*. The documentaries are an audacious fusion of intention, content and form; they are both personal and universal. *Millhouse,* on a basic level, is an expression of de Antonio's own personal hatred for Nixon's 'essential creepiness' (Weiner 1971: 4–5) which he always thought would be Nixon's final undoing.[14] In addition, the film is a complex attack on the political system that sustained Nixon and permitted him to repeatedly resuscitate his career despite his endless shady dealings. The comic and political elements are necessarily intertwined, as Nixon afforded so many opportunities for satire; *Millhouse*'s 'Six Crises' structure, for instance, ironically mimics Nixon's pre-presidential memoirs, *Six Crises*. From the early years spent hounding Alger Hiss in 1948 (and the absurd discovery of some incriminating film in a pumpkin in Whittaker Chambers' garden)[15] or smearing his opponent Helen Gahagan Douglas's name during their 1950 senatorial contest, Nixon's 'creepiness' and comic potential serially endangered his progression as a politician.

An essential component of the dialectics that inform *Millhouse* is the tussle at its heart between its comic and its serious political tendencies. Nixon (as opposed to his manipulation by de Antonio) is frequently the direct source of the film's comedy. *Millhouse* consistently focuses upon and derives humour from Nixon's painstaking and painful reconstructions of his own media persona, particularly at moments of crisis. As de Antonio comments:

> What Nixon has been able to do in his political life is totally transform his exterior, his external personality. ... Nixon is packaging himself, and that is the importance of the Checkers speech. The Nixon of Checkers is a different creature than the Nixon of Cambodia 1970, or the Nixon of the 1968 campaign, or the Nixon who went to China.
>
> (Weiss M. 1974: 32)

The power of *Millhouse* is that it makes a logical link between Nixon's perpetual reinvention of himself (his courting of the media and his superficiality) and the appropriateness of the 'collage junk' method that fabricates meaning from juxtaposing an eclectic group of images. De Antonio observed that Nixon was paradoxically obsessed with the media and overly preoccupied with 'shielding himself from the American people' (Weiss M. 1974: 32), of hiding his innate untrustworthiness behind a faltering masquerade of Horatio Alger little-man-made-good sincerity. Satirical compilation films are inherently dependent upon the surface value of archive, and the opening sequence of *Millhouse* establishes the tone for much of the ensuing attack on Nixon's superficiality and the values it represents, as Nixon's wax effigy in Madame Tussaud's is assembled to the announcement 'The President of the United States' and the bombastic strains of *Hail to the Chief. Millhouse* dismantles Nixon's self-created image, piecing together an excruciating caricature of the 'poor, wretched, clumsy mixed-up man' as de Antonio calls him (Crowdus and Georgakas 1988: 174). De Antonio's Nixon resembles a puppet, a dummy that has learnt a series of mannerisms. There are, for example, the two rapid montages of Nixon executing his most memorable gesture of raising both hands above his head in a V and the overlapping of Nixon's 1968 'I see a day' convention speech with Martin Luther King's earlier 'I have a dream' (from which, *Millhouse* insinuates, it was plagiarised). Nixon's performances masked a vacuum at their core – a point underlined in an interview specially shot for *Millhouse* with a high school companion who, despite being his friend, 'can't think of an anecdote' to tell about Nixon.

The comic moments of *Millhouse* often centre upon Nixon's perception and performance of himself. An exemplary sequence would be the one centring on Nixon's arrival at the White House after his victory in 1968. The sequence is as follows:

> Part of a specially shot interview with an aide explaining how Nixon described himself as 'an intellectual' and 'called himself at one point the egghead of the Republican party'. Cut to:

> Archive of an early presidential press conference at which Nixon, flanked by his family, itemises his hobbies as reading and history, stressing that he does not read Westerns or watch much television, in the process making a dig at his predecessor Lyndon Johnson by quipping, 'we've removed some of the television sets', an aside that is greeted with laughter. Cut to:

> A continuation of the first interview in which the aide, barely able to suppress a smirk, recounts how Nixon told him he would rather be teaching 'in a school like Oxford' and writing books. Cut to:

> Lengthy sequence showing an evening of White House entertainment comprising an instrumental, expressive dance version of *Satisfaction,* a song to Nixon ('Mr Nixon is the only one'), a homophobic joke by Bob Hope (who is also the MC), Nixon thanking Hope by quoting James Thurber who 'once wrote that the oldest and most precious national asset of this century is humour' and wishing him well for the show's overseas tour (presumably of Vietnam).

In this sequence, the comedy results from de Antonio's juxtaposition of collated material to ridicule Nixon's pompous opinion of his own intellectuality. The attacks on him are direct (as in the interview) and indirect (as in the juxtaposition of Nixon's self-aggrandisement with some particularly tawdry White House entertainment); Nixon also shows himself up by quoting James Thurber during a sequence putatively illustrative of his intellectuality. The power of a sequence such as this resides in its effortless ability to make us laugh at Nixon and signalling a very clear point of view without resorting to direct authorial intervention or overtly didactic means. The analytical montage in this sequence also serves to demonstrate de Antonio's (and our) intellectual superiority to Nixon, a patronising tone that characterises many comic compilation films.

This analytical, intellectual approach to historical documentary filmmaking is manifested not merely in the way Nixon the individual is reassessed, but in how the system he epitomises is also scrutinised. As de Antonio comments, 'This film [*Millhouse*] attacks the System, the credibility of the System, by focusing on the obvious and perfect symbol for that system' (Weiner 1971: 4). Repeatedly, what de Antonio attempts in his documentaries is not the articulation of a solution to a problem but the exposure of what is wrong, the infinitely corruptible and corrupting political and ideological system that dominated America during the period he was making films (1963–89). In this, the films remain both democratic and radical. Through charting Nixon's shady history and through the comic analysis of Nixon's chaotic relationship with his image, the successful 1968 presidential candidate comes to be depicted as a puppet, a figurehead of a machine.[16] The serious political intent of *Millhouse* is most clearly manifested in sequences that focus upon Nixon's role as leader; this is when de Antonio vents his political hatred, as exemplified by the documentary's sequence concerning Vietnam and the escalation of the conflict under the Nixon administration. The sequence, near the end (like Eisenstein, de Antonio increases the complexity and aggression of his montage sequences progressively through his films), begins with a résumé of the history of American interference in Vietnam, subsequently arriving at the present. The contemporary section of the sequence is as follows:

A speech by Nixon in which he comments, 'In the previous administration we Americanised the war in Vietnam. In this administration we are Vietnamising the search for peace'. Cut to:

A map of Indochina being gradually shaded black – North and South Vietnam followed by Cambodia and then Laos, over which a woman's voice quotes Mao Tse Tung: 'The people may be likened unto water and the guerrilla band unto fish'. Cut to:

Graphic stating the South Vietnamese casualties of war to date (1,000,000) and the number of refugees (6,000,000). As this graphic fades, the woman's voice quotes from the *New York Times:* 'In this year, 1971, more civilians are being wounded in the three countries of Indochina and more made refugees than at any time in history', a statement that continues over the same Nixon speech as before, this time mute.

Nixon's speech continues, this time with synch sound, as he pledges that his aim is for South Vietnamese forces to 'assume full responsibility for South Vietnam', a comment overlaid onto footage of South Vietnamese soldiers marching. Cut to:

The filled in map of Indochina accompanied by the woman's voice-over: 'Two and a half Hiroshimas a week'. Cut to:

Another Nixon speech in which he promises that the US stand to gain nothing from the Vietnam war except 'the possibility that the people of South Vietnam will be able to choose their own way in the world'. Superimposed onto Nixon as he speaks is a long list of American companies who are profiting from the war. Cut to:

A protest march.

The target here is Nixon's mendacity concerning the escalation of the war in Indochina under his administration, each image and piece of sound (and it is interesting that the narrated quotations function as components of the collage) being used to embellish this point. The sequence is raw and intense, reaching a crescendo with the significantly uncredited piece of voice-over making the elliptical comment 'two and a half Hiroshimas a week' and the scrolling list of American companies sustaining the war. Illustrative of the dangerous as opposed to comic potential of Nixon's untruthfulness, this sequence also emphasises his part in history and his political role; the moment at which Nixon is mute as the voice-over recounts the South Vietnamese casualties of the conflict so far being a reminder of both his untrustworthiness and his impotence.

As exemplified by *Millhouse: A White Comedy*, de Antonio's style combines comedy with acute and angry political commentary. His documentaries are overtly confrontational, radical in both form and content. De Antonio's preoccupation was American post-war political history; he distrusted politicians and sought an intellectual mode of filmmaking capable of magnifying their flaws and exposing both the shortcomings of the electoral system and the inadequacy (as de Antonio saw it) of conventional documentary forms to radically reassess notions of factual representation and analysis. His ethos of 'collage junk' has been copied and reworked many times, and has become an instrumental component of documentaries of historical analysis. From it can be taken several things, most importantly the twin notions that all documentaries, because the product of individuals, will always display bias and be in some manner didactic, and that there is no such thing as incontrovertible truth, as each document or factual image, when made to conflict with another, finds its meaning irretrievably modified. Contextualisation, not merely the image itself, can create meaning; history, which de Antonio refers to as being the theme of all his films (Crowdus and Georgakas 1988), is perpetually modified by its re-enactment in the present.

Modern examples: Historical television documentaries; *The Atomic Café*

De Antonio saw himself as a pioneer of a 'new' documentary form that prioritised the compilation and juxtaposition of interviews and archive. The 1960s was very much the era of the observational documentary (and drama documentary) focusing upon the present, on actions that were unfolding contemporaneously with the filmmaking process. By the 1970s, more emphasis was placed upon contextualisation and history, and with this arrived an increased dependency on compilation and interviews. The two traditions of archive documentaries have persisted: the historical television series or strand that uses archive material illustratively and films such as *The Atomic Café* (which thanks de Antonio in the end credits), which adopt the polemical, confrontational style of de Antonio.

The conventional television use of archive is largely non-dialectical, the purpose of its retrieved archive being to demonstrate what has already been or is in the process of being signalled by other information sources such as the voice-over or the words of interviewees. Arguably it is thus the more didactic, formal aspect of a series such as *Cold War* (Jeremy Isaacs, 1998), namely its voice-over, that defines its identity. Within this hierarchy, words guide the audience's responses to the archival image, whether this is Kenneth Branagh's voice-over or the words of eye-witnesses and the testimonies of experts. During Episode 2 ('Iron Curtain, 1945–1947') there is a short sequence that exemplifies both uses of the voice to determine and define our interpretation of found footage. Telling the story of the immediate aftermath of World War Two at the time of the British, American and Soviet control of Germany, a terse piece of narration ('Berlin – the final battlefield') prefaces familiar aerial shots of a devastated German capital (endless rubble, buildings reduced to shells), followed by a more personalised account of the period by a German female interviewee recounting being raped by a Russian soldier which, in turn, is intercut with footage of women hanging their heads or looking pleadingly at the camera. Within this short *Cold War* sequence there are two distinct uses of archive. The Berlin footage (which one could term 'iconic' in that it has become so much part of the way in which we collectively recall the end of the war) is inserted to substantiate the information, already elliptically given in the voice-over, that the city, in 1945, had been the site of the Nazis' final resistance and capitulation against the Allied forces. In this the visual material performs a corroborative, illustrative function within what is effectively a documentary lecture on the beginnings of the Cold War; the images are contextualised and explained even as they appear, and their viewing, whilst enhancing our assimilation of the events under discussion, does not promote debate or argument. The audience is not invited to speculate upon the origins of the material or any possible discrepancy between original and current meaning; this use of archive is not combative or political, and the edits between images and voice offer a cumulative as opposed to a dialectical understanding of the event they represent.

The second use of archive exemplified by the above sequence (in a similarly non-interventionist vein) is the insertion of general or non-specific images to accompany the distressing recollection by the woman interviewee of her first experience of rape. Although, once more, the archive is used illustratively, the relationship between word and image differs from that of the preceding example in that there is only an inferred or contrived correlation between the two. We have no means of knowing what the actual motivation for the women's despair in these images is, they are only given a specific connotation (that women were regularly raped by the occupying Russian soldiers in Berlin) by being juxtaposed with the interviewee's personal account. It is often the case that there is no footage available to illustrate a verbal description of a past event, so a filmmaker must resort to generic images that offer an approximate representation. This use of generic archive provokes a common slippage in historical documentaries, namely that the non-specific image ('desperate women' in Berlin circa 1945) has imposed upon it a new, precise and, by definition, transient signification that may or may not correlate with its original meaning. The 'generic' use of archive is an economic measure used in *Cold War* and other similar documentaries to convey to the audience the memories invoked by eye-witness or expert accounts; the raped woman herself is not represented by the images, but her trauma and its potential emotive effect on us is. An audience understands this convention which, in turn, suggests that the same archival images could be recycled again and used as the 'figurative' representation of an entirely different story or situation. Paul Arthur sheds doubt upon the entire enterprise of using archive footage within a documentary context, when commenting that the dissonance between personal recollection and images

> raises the spectre of ... partiality. Documentarists who would never dream of restaging an event with actors do not hesitate in creating collages that amount to metaphoric fabrications of reality. The guarantees of authenticity ostensibly secured by archival footage are largely a myth.
>
> (Arthur 1997: 6)

As de Antonio's films showed, it is possible for re-used footage to retain vestiges of its original meaning, however reconfigured, a potential that Arthur's blanket condemnation excludes, although it remains legitimate to argue that the use of generic footage in *Cold War* is manipulated into illustrating a memory which is imposed rather than innate, and so retains a mythic quality.

The People's Century (BBC/WGBH, 1997) was an example of a series that used archival images differently, despite its stylistic similarities with other big historical series, adhering to one important device: the direct linking of interviewees and archive, so the eye-witness testimonies are specifically and graphically correlated to the images used as illustration. When the subject is the student anti-war demonstrations at the end of the 1960s, it would not, one assumes, have been difficult to find images of Jeff Jones of the Weathermen to accompany his interview for the series. Others interviewed for the same episode, however, were not known figures but had coincidentally been captured on film and subsequently tracked down by the filmmakers. Within the framework of *The People's Century*, the original footage is not treated as neutral or as generically figurative, instead it becomes concretely illustrative of what is being said around it. *The People's Century* constructs a bridge between personal history, oral history and the official history of the historical image, a link that is, in the use of generic archive, almost assumed not to exist. As is the case with the Berliners in the images used to accompany the woman's account of her rape, the figures in the original archive are depersonalised, extricated from their original circumstances, and find themselves condemned to perpetual anonymity and worse, in a sense, to have never existed. Most significant in *The People's Century*, therefore, is the reinstatement of these 'anonymous' individuals captured on camera into the official recorded history of this century; the ultimate verification of the notion that archive functions as the substantiation of memory.

A series such as *The People's Century* retains the idea that historical footage possesses an inherent meaning, although this signification is not positioned within a dialectical framework as it might be in 'collage junk' documentaries. The continuation of de Antonio's style of politicised compilation film is better exemplified by a film such as *The Atomic Café* (Kevin Rafferty, Jayne Loader, Pierce Rafferty, 1982), a satirical indictment of American Cold War propaganda in the 1950s that owes much to the comic montage conventions of a film such as *Millhouse*. *The Atomic Café* is predicated upon a simple central thesis: that the

Figure 1.3   The Atomic Café
Source: Courtesy of BFI Stills, Posters and Designs

government's and the establishment's deliberately misleading and scare-monger-
ing representation of the threat of nuclear war in the 1950s is ripe for ironic
reassessment, and as such the film offers a distillation of de Antonio's 'collage
junk' method. It is a film that had a huge impact at the time of its release, is still
(with its release on video and the appearance of Loader's accompanying CD-
ROM *Public Shelter*) widely viewed, and has exerted considerable influence on
how 1950s Cold War America is represented. *The Atomic Café*, like de Antonio's
documentaries, is exhaustive; it took five years to compile and edit, and makes
substantial use of forgotten film from obscure 1950s government film catalogues. It uses official material to subversive ends, consistently imposing on the
archive an opinion and meaning that is completely at odds with its original intention. Out of propaganda, *The Atomic Café* constructs ironic counter-propaganda; out of compiled images from various sources it constructs a
straightforward dialectic between the past and the present. *The Atomic Café*
operates a similar duality to that found in the majority of politically motivated
compilation films, that the archive documents are respected on their own terms
as 'evidence' at the same time as they are being reviewed and contradicted by
their recontextualisation. As a result, the original material, despite the montage
editing techniques deployed, is what remains memorable about the film; it is significant, for example, that many of the reviews from the time of the film's release
focus on the 1950s propaganda rather than the film's formal qualities.

Broadly speaking, there are two types of sequence in *The Atomic Café*: those
that leave the original archive relatively unadulterated and those that more
overtly play around with different pieces of footage to create, through contrapuntal editing, a distinct narrative structure and ideological point. One section
of *The Atomic Café* that is frequently remarked upon intercuts the cartoon 'Burt
the Turtle' with the informational film 'Duck and Cover' in which children and
families are instructed to follow the turtle's example and cover themselves with
whatever is to hand if the bomb strikes. The immediate response to this sequence
is to laugh, primarily at the comic ineptitude and naïveté of the notion that cow-
ering under a picnic blanket or tucking oneself under a school desk is adequate
protection against an atomic blast, but also at the government's belief that anyone would find this propaganda credible. There are several official films throughout *The Atomic Café* that provoke much the same response: the cartoon film
about a doctor and his patient suffering from 'nuclearosis'; the nuclear family
(sic) at the end who, after surviving a bomb in their shelter, re-emerge with
father saying stoically that they have not suffered that badly and now have 'nothing to do except await orders and relax'. In these instances it might be overly
simplistic to state that 'the documents speak for themselves' (Titus 1983: 6), for
the pleasure derived from merely observing the archive that Pierce Rafferty has
found is necessarily modified or compromised by what it is immediately or generally juxtaposed against. The 'Duck and Cover' sequence, for example, runs into
a more formally radical and manipulative sequence. First, there is part of a televised (and one presumes rigged) question-and-answer session about the nuclear
threat between members of the public and 'experts'. A woman asks how far from

the centre of the blast would one have to be to survive, to which the reply given is 12 miles. This is juxtaposed with another contemporary 'expert' (presumably not a government stooge) describing how it would be futile (a word he repeats) to think of survival even in a bomb shelter within a 2,000 square mile radius of the blast, which in turn is juxtaposed with the 'nuclearosis' cartoon making assurances about the effectiveness of small shelters within the home. After a piece of similar archive showing homes being built with shelters and proudly display-ing a 'we are prepared' sticker, there appears another sceptical academic remark-ing that shelters, far from acting as a deterrent, will ironically prompt the USA and the USSR to contemplate the possibility of nuclear conflict all the more readily. Within these five minutes, reconstituted footage is used in both ways hitherto mentioned: it is left relatively unadulterated and is overtly manipulated to construct an argument. What is strikingly presented in the latter part of the sequence (in the clear knowledge that 'Duck and Cover' and the laughter it pro-voked will impinge on this) is the idea that archive can be recontextualised to produce a counter-argument, or in this instance a piece of counter-propaganda. Within this there is a dominant text suggesting that the government fabricated an unrealistic image of nuclear war and the possibilities of survival alongside a subtext revealing that this was done not naïvely but in full possession of the avail-able scientific facts about nuclear blasts and fall-out (it is hugely important in this respect that the realistic opinions are put forward by academics of the time not by individuals speaking with hindsight).

A sequence that has prompted some questioning of documentary method has been *The Atomic Café*'s opening, which concerns the first hostile nuclear strikes against Japan. After opening with footage of the first ('Trinity') atom bomb test in the New Mexico desert, *The Atomic Café* begins its examination of Hiroshima. The sequence starts with an interview with Paul Tibbets (cap-tain of the Enola Gay, the American plane carrying the atomic bomb) and a fighter plane taking off, intercut with Japanese civilians walking through city streets and a single, sharply dressed Japanese man filmed from a low angle as he looks up at a brilliant blue sky. Subsequently, the film returns to Tibbets' voice over-laid onto footage of a bomber plane (not identified as the Enola Gay) manoeuvring itself out of the line of the atomic blast; Tibbets is explain-ing his decision to leave the area as quickly as possible when he realised the extent of the damage, a level of destruction represented by some intensely familiar footage of a city flattened except for a few isolated shells of buildings. After the subsequent American nuclear attack on Nagasaki, film of burnt and maimed survivors being subjected to physical examinations follows on from a perhaps unintentionally critical Tibbets stating that the US forces sought 'vir-gin targets' which had not suffered previous bomb damage in order to carry out 'classroom experiments' on the effects of radiation – an interview that cul-minates in the pilot's throwaway speculation that the guilt engendered by these atomic attacks was possibly the catalyst for the US government's subse-quent decision to say as little as possible about the reality of nuclear war. Paul Arthur is one of those to have taken issue with the opening of *The Atomic*

Café, seemingly particularly preoccupied with the use of the isolated, 'generic' Japanese man in the Hiroshima section:

> In context, the montage sequence makes a discursive leap that frays our intuitions of documentary protocol, adopting a narrative editing trope that both heightens dramatic anticipation and elicits pathos for a specific individual. Since we may reasonably doubt that this man was an actual victim of the bombing, his function within the sequence is confusing. The fact that he does not belong to the scene portrayed becomes important, and misleading, in ways that related substitutions do not.
>
> (Arthur 1997: 5)

Arthur's contention appears to be that the conventions of generic archive somehow are not appropriate to individuals for whom we may feel pathos. It is dubious that an audience for *The Atomic Café* would be troubled by the likelihood that the Japanese man was not a victim of the Hiroshima bomb; instead, this sequence would probably be viewed as symbolic as opposed to accurately representative, but Arthur's problems with the sequence are interesting because of what they suggest about the political manipulation of images. Arthur would presumably feel happier with a comparable sequence in Barbara Margolis' *Are We Winning, Mommy?: America and the Cold War* (1986), another epic documentary about America in the nuclear age in which the start of the Cold War is far less elliptically portrayed. *Are We Winning, Mommy?* views the bombing of Hiroshima as a direct result of President Truman's growing conviction, after the Potsdam conference, that Stalin, like Hitler, was bent on world domination. The Trinity test and the subsequent attacks on Japan are thereby placed within a clear political framework, whilst *The Atomic Café* eschews such linearity of argument and, like de Antonio, seeks to be democratic and not overly guiding. *Are We Winning, Mommy?* offers an often brilliant historical overview of the Cold War (and likewise took five years to make), whereas *The Atomic Café* is an agitational film, a piece of counter-propaganda that does more than observe the post-war nuclear escalation. *Are We Winning, Mommy?* elects to make its position explicit, whilst *The Atomic Café* works through insinuation.

To return to the opening of *Atomic Café*. The unsuspecting, smart Japanese man is an Everyman figure, a representative character who not only functions as a cog within the Hiroshima narrative – a personalised reaction to the imminent arrival of the Enola Gay – but as a more abstract presence within the subliminal subtext underpinning the whole film: that what was being practised in the 1950s was an elaborate form of disavowal whereby the American government knew but denied and actively suppressed the true horrors of nuclear arms under a ludicrously inane arsenal of propaganda films. The inevitable destruction of any individual caught by a nuclear blast is the knowledge that informs the rather beautiful shots of the lone Japanese man (brought back for *The Atomic Café*'s final vitriolic montage as he is juxtaposed with a reprise of 'Duck and Cover'); Americans – like him – would stand no chance if directly hit, and it is one of the documentary's poignancies that the largely American audience is compelled to identify with someone who is effectively 'the enemy'. Within a collage film such as *The Atomic Café* some of the archival documentation has a dual contextualisation, being given an immediate meaning and one that pertains to the overall perspective of the film. If the documentary is to work as an agitational text (as one that provokes its audience into awareness and action as well as increasing its historical knowledge) it has to be able to use or manipulate its original documents into a polemical thesis. This would be impossible if, as Arthur would have it, every piece of archive was forced to perform a denotative function. The implied target of *The Atomic Café* is the actively repressive American governments and authorities of the 1950s; like de Antonio before them, Rafferty, Loader and Rafferty are attacking the system that, in this case, fabricated the Cold War, forcing a parallel with the similarly nuclear-obsessed Reagan governments of the 1980s. Like the wiser contemporary audiences of *The Atomic Café*, it is also suggested that the original viewers of the 1950s propaganda were not so gullible that they believed Burt the Turtle; they too denied what they had known since the end of the war: the blanket destruction of Hiroshima and Nagasaki. It is imperative to consider the opening Japan sequence, complete with all its strongly manipulative editing, as the basis for the remainder of the film, as the mini text that informs the whole. With disavowal, acknowledgement precedes repression. In *The Atomic Café* the documentation (made accessible to Americans at the time) of the destruction of Hiroshima and Nagasaki precedes the propaganda for the building of bomb shelters (later renamed fall-out shelters when the position that one could survive the bomb itself became untenable) and other measures to ensure survival. Just as it is unlikely that Americans truly believed that consuming tranquillisers and tinned food in a subterranean bunker would save them, so we, the current audience, have the Japan footage as the images which shape our responses to the silliness that ensues. *The Atomic Café* is more than a clever piece of counter-propaganda that reverses the original meaning of the archive it uses, it confronts its audience with the complex series of manoeuvres that sustained the Cold War and its accompanying propaganda.

Conclusion

The place of archive in documentary has altered somewhat since the first edition of *New Documentary*. The most significant shift has been the rise of dramatic reconstruction as a supplement to or even replacement for archival material. As Paul Arthur notes (in an article about the return of the essay nonfiction film), 'documentary's first principles have gotten a solid thrashing of late as nonfiction filmmakers … revive the forbidden practice of dramatic reenactment' (2003a: 58). The use of drama within the framework of nonfiction does not necessarily alter how we might or might not classify a film as a documentary, for as Dai Vaughan has argued (in an essay quoted earlier) 'What makes a film "documentary" is the way we look at it' (Vaughan 1999: 84). What dramatisation does do is change the way in which we are being invited to respond emotionally and intellectually to the images in question. The blending of documentary footage and dramatic reconstruction within the framework of a documentary, impacts differently upon our viewing experience than a similar blurring of the boundaries might in a piece of fiction. In *JFK* Oliver Stone mixes the Zapruder footage with reconstruction – or 'his own simulated *vérité*' as Linda Williams classifies it, from which he constructed 'a grandiose paranoid countermyth of a vast conspiracy' (Williams 1993: 11). As Williams sees it, Stone is driven by a belief that 'it is possible to intervene in the process by which truth is constructed' (p. 11) and to use reconstruction as a means of challenging the official line on the assassination of John Kennedy. *JFK*, however, is a cinematic version of television's 'docudrama', a genre that is based on fact but which identifies itself (via the use of actors and the presence of a script) as a fictionalised version of these facts. The use of reconstruction within a documentary should be perceived differently. The current vogue is for reconstruction to be used often alongside more traditional documentary methods, such as archive and interviews, and despite Janice Hadlow (then Channel 4 Commissioning Editor for History, currently Head of BBC Four) warning on *Happy Birthday BBC2* (2003) that filmmakers venture into reconstruction at their peril, documentaries have become obsessed with it. A significant reason for the rise in clearly signposted reconstruction was the inevitable fallout from the admitted restaging of scenes for docusoaps such as *Driving School*. The BBC's response to admissions on the part of the programme makers that certain sequences were restaged or faked was to issue uncompromising new guidelines about 'Staging and re-staging in factual programmes' (quoted on page 131 of this book), which, among other things, stipulated that an action should only be re-staged if 'clearly signalled' to the audience. One way in which restaging can be 'clearly signalled' is through the use of reconstruction – using actors to impersonate documentary subjects. If there is any doubt about a scene's authenticity then (on British television at least) the word 'reconstruction' often appears in the corner of the screen. Increasingly, this signage is no longer needed as dramatisations become increasingly differentiated from 'real' archive or specially shot documentary sequences. Frequently the inauthenticity as it were of the reconstructed scenes is emphasised, as indeed it was in a film such as Errol Morris's *The Thin Blue Line*, in which the reconstructions of the night of the murder under examination are linked through editing to specific eye-witness accounts and are heavily stylised (a slow motion shot of a cup of coffee flying through the air; an extreme close up of a car indicator light accompanied by Philip Glass's portentous score) so as to ensure that their reconstructedness is never in doubt.

Recent use of reconstruction is idiosyncratic and has established certain generic oddities and tendencies. For example, it is rare for the actors in reconstructed scenes shot for documentaries to speak lines audibly or, on English speaking television, to speak them in English (in Laurence Rees's *Auschwitz: The Nazis and the Final Solution* [BBC, 2005] one convention is exemplified as the German officers in the reconstructions speak in German; in Kevin Macdonald's cinema documentary *Touching the Void* the other convention is illustrated by the actors portraying Joe Simpson and Simon Yates who are seen talking, but not so we can decipher what they're saying). Reconstruction is therefore purely illustrative of words and archive used elsewhere in a documentary; it is padding. Then there is what could be termed the '*Walking With Dinosaurs* syndrome' when a so-called documentary (re)constructs plausible but hypothetical historical scenes, a convention invented by the BBC's hugely successful dinosaur series in which Kenneth Branagh's voiceover talked about families of smaller dinosaurs being threatened by a hungry, larger carnivorous one. Reconstruction here comprises the invention of characters that could have existed but of whom there is no record. This extreme form of reconstruction is now to be found quite regularly amongst usually primetime, bigger budget documentaries such as Channel Four's *Ancient Egyptians* (2003), which again offers a fanciful dramatised history of the period, replete with fictionalised conversations and invented personal feuds and families or BBC1's *Oliver Cromwell: Warts and All* (2003) transmitted the same month in which dramatisations of Cromwell's life (Cromwell is played by Jim Carter) exist alongside traditional narration (read by Christopher Eccleston) and interviews with historians.

Reconstruction can perform a liberating function, particularly to a historical subject for which no archive is readily available; however, there have been too many examples recently of gratuitous reconstruction. *The Miner's Strike* (BBC2, 2004), which interviewed some extremely articulate ex-miners, still felt the need to reconstruct the events these talking heads had so vividly just recounted, even though the interviews could be – and were – juxtaposed with powerful existing archive of, for example, the clash between miners and police at Orgreave colliery. Similarly, *The Four Minute Mile* (BBC2, 2004) deemed it necessary to re-enact the closing moments of the 1954 race despite the existence – and the producers' use of – famous and iconic authentic archive of Bannister's record-breaking run. Bar a handful of close-ups, these reconstructions added very little to the story. This arguably confusing convention of placing reconstruction (often of the half-hearted, semi-audible variety) alongside authentic archive rarely offers new insights or creates a dialectical counterpoint to the more traditional archive and interview material; more commonly it is little more than a florid way of reiterating the same ideas in fancy dress. One recent documentary to use reconstruction as part of a collage that included real archive and interviews was BBC2's *Dunkirk* (2004), a stylistically ambitious three-part series based on eyewitness accounts that interwove black and white archive with reconstructed colour footage, all filmed in a highly contemporary style (restless camera, crisp editing and CGI). Put alongside each other in much the same way as Oliver Stone had done in *JFK*, the archive sequences become energetic, dramatic renditions of the British salvage operation. *Dunkirk* was watchable and well received; however, one cannot help but have the sneaking suspicion that the reconstructions were there as a means to show off – and to show that television can go some way to replicate the awesome special effects of Steven Spielberg's *Saving Private Ryan*. That reconstruction has become such an indispensable element of so much television documentary is exemplified by the formal change in Laurence Rees's work from *The*

Nazis: A Warning from History (1997) to *Auschwitz: The Nazis and the Final Solution* (2005). It seemed inconceivable at the time of *The Nazis* that Rees would resort (or stoop?) to reconstruction. In a traditional manner that earlier series juxtaposed only authentic archive and interviews, while the latter inserted several dramatised reconstructions of, for example, the Nazis discussing the building and running of their most notorious death camp. In another complication, while the words of interviewees were, if they did not speak English, simultaneously translated, the German spoken in the reconstructions remained audible and the scenes subtitled. What are the conventions here? It is as if, having 'dumbed down' the series by inserting dramatised sequences, Rees then decided to intellectualise it again by making these reconstructions more of an effort to watch than the more generically straightforward interviews. In a sense, reconstruction has come full circle as now it is used interchangeably with archive in many instances – much as it was in the 1920s in the USSR. What is missing, however, is the political intent behind the reconstructions. Now they are used to heighten and render more accessible the latent drama of the documentary situation.

This chapter has taken issue with the central tenet of much theoretical writing on documentary, namely that a successful documentary is contingent upon representing the truth at its core as objectively as possible. Documentary film is traditionally perceived to be the hybrid offspring of a perennial struggle between the forces of objectivity (represented by the 'documents' or facts that underpin it) and the forces of subjectivity (that is the translation of those facts into representational form). The discussion of the Zapruder film of Kennedy's assassination posited the impossibility that a single piece of film, even one as accidental and unpremeditated as it is, can be a full and intelligible record of an event without being in some way contextualised or set alongside other sources of information. The realisation, however, that the authentic document might be deficient or lacking should not precipitate a representational crisis as it too often does. As the compilation films discussed for the remainder of this chapter exemplify, documentaries are predicated upon a negotiation between the polarities of objectivity and subjectivity, offering a dialectical analysis of events and images that accepts that no non-fictional record can contain the whole truth whilst also accepting that to re-use or recontextualise such material is not to irrevocably suppress or distort the innate value and meaning it possesses. These 'collage junk' films are ostensibly democratic in that they do not overtly intervene upon original film material. In the next chapter voice-over narration is examined as arguably the most blatant example of intervention on the part of the documentary filmmaker. As de Antonio sees it, narration is a fascist act that proclaims a film's didacticism.

2 Narration

The film and its voice

How and why did documentary narration acquire its miserable reputation, whilst still remaining one of the most commonly used devices in non-fiction film-making? Voice-over, in both documentaries and fiction films, is an extra-diegetic soundtrack that has been added to a film. On the whole such a voice-over gives insights and information not immediately available from within the diegesis, but whereas in a fiction film the voice-off is traditionally that of a character in the narrative, in a documentary the voice-over is more usually that of a disembodied and omniscient narrator. The negative portrayal of voice-over is largely the result of the development of a theoretical orthodoxy that condemns it for being inevitably and inherently didactic. Within this book's critique of the manner in which documentary's history has been depicted as an endless pursuit of the most effective way of representing the 'purity' of the real, this analysis of voice-over will question its condemnation as the imposed destroyer of the 'pure' film image, questioning along the way the oversimplified perception of voice-overs as all in some manner pertaining to the most basic 'voice of God' model. We have been 'taught' to believe in the image of reality and similarly 'taught' how to interpret the narrational voice as distortive and superimposed onto it. The endpoint of this discussion will be the various ways in which the classic voice-over has been modified and its rules transgressed through the insertion of ironic detachment between image and sound, the reflexive treatment of the narration tradition and the subversion of the archetypal solid male narrator in a documentary such as *Sunless*. The diversity of the form strongly suggests that an overarching definition of voice-over documentaries is distortive in itself.

The 'problem' at the heart of discussions of narration is the question of how one views the relationship between sound and image. In 1930 filmmaker and theorist Paul Rotha argued that sound films were 'harmful and detrimental to the culture of the public' (Rotha 1930: 408). Rotha, long before Christian Metz, automatically classified film as a purely visual medium to which sound could do irreparable damage, stating that, 'Immediately a voice begins to speak in a cinema, the sound apparatus takes precedence over the camera, thereby doing violence to natural instincts' (Rotha 1930: 406). The 'one legitimate use for the dialogue film' according to Rotha was the topical newsreel, for here the appeal was not aesthetic or 'dramatic' but factual. Underpinning Rotha's objections is a belief in the purity of film predicated upon its visual impact alone, arguing that a silent film has a more lasting effect on its audience than a sound film and displaying an undeniable romanticism when positing that 'No power of speech is comparable with the descriptive value of photographs' (Rotha 1930: 405). Unlike the Soviets who, at the end of the 1920s, supported sound if deployed as another tool with which to 'strengthen and broaden the montage methods of influencing the audience', but warned against the 'commercial exploitation' of synchronised sound which would instead 'destroy the culture of montage, because every mere *addition* of sound to montage fragments increases their inertia' (Eisenstein *et al.* 1928: 234), Rotha is troubled by the idea that sound will contaminate the image. So it is with documentary: whereas what could be termed the alternative narration tradition, like the Soviets, advocates a 'contrapuntal use of sound vis-à-vis the visual fragment of montage' (Eisenstein *et al.* 1928: 234), most of the time voice-over is perceived as a threat, as didactic and anti-democratic.

Voice-over is the unnecessary evil of documentary, the resort of the 'unimaginative and incompetent' (Kozloff 1988: 21). Direct Cinema pioneer Robert Drew, in an article combatively entitled 'Narration can be a killer', contends that only documentaries that eschew narration as a structuring device can 'work, or are beginning to work, or could work, on filmic-dramatic principles', that only films that tell a story directly (without voice-over) can 'soar' into a utopian realm 'Beyond reason. Beyond explanation. Beyond words'. As Drew dogmatically concludes, 'words supplied from outside cannot make a film soar', so 'narration is what you do when you fail' (Drew 1983: 271–3). Drew's objections to narration are echoed by the majority of theoretical writing about documentary, which, along with certain practitioners, has cemented the view expressed above by promoting the idea that the term 'voice-over', when applied to documentaries, signifies only the didactic single, white, male tones of *The March of Time* and its sorry derivatives. Most to blame for this negative perception of voice-over documentaries has been Bill Nichols' definition of the 'expository mode' as didactic, the oldest and most primitive form of nonfiction film. As I have argued at greater length in my Introduction, the fundamental problem with Nichols' 'family tree' of documentary modes is that it elides differences between films that are similar in one formal respect whilst simultaneously imposing a false chronology onto documentary history. Nichols maintains that the expository style was 'the *first* thoroughly worked out mode of documentary' (my italics; Nichols 1983: 48), but it serves Nichols' and not documentary history's ends to maintain that this is so. The non-fiction films of the silent era (or as Nichols no doubt perceives it: the era of documentary chaos) are too numerous to list here, but the work of Dziga Vertov, for one, was neither didactic and voice-over led nor undertheorised.

The coherent history of documentary film is thus deemed to have begun around the time of the Second World War. The most oft-cited example of the narration-led documentary form is Louis de Rochemont's *The March of Time*, a monthly film magazine that ran from 1935–51 and used archive and dramatisation in the reconstruction of what it deemed to be significant current events. In the episode recounting the Battle of Britain, for example, this pivotal confrontation is re-enacted using a handful of bomber planes, newsreel footage and reconstructions. Above all *The March of Time* offered a synthesis, a viewer's digest of a cycle of events that had already reached a conclusion, and within this strict, instructional framework its booming, relentless voice-over ('Time marches on!') inevitably took on the role of teacher. This sort of commentary was dubbed the 'voice of God', with all the insinuations of patriarchy, dominance, omniscience that term harbours. The standard assumption as far as documentary theory is concerned is that whereas synch sound 'helps anchor the meaning of the images' (Nichols 1981: 200) thereby preserving their dominance, narration is an intrusion which interferes with this automatic prioritisation of the image whilst concomitantly immobilising and distancing the spectator through its dictatorial methods. Documentary's 'tacit proposal' to its audience is, as Nichols sees it, 'the invocation of, and promise to gratify, a desire to know' (Nichols 1981:205), a function exemplified by the use of direct address, readily characterised as instructive and 'overwhelmingly didactic' in its domination of the visuals (Nichols 1983:48) and of audience response. The omniscient narrator offers the dominant – if not the only – perspective on the footage on the screen. Nichols is worth quoting at length on what he terms

> 'The expository mode' as inherent within much of his seminal writing on the subject are the dangerous assumptions and slippages that colour much theorisation of documentary's deployment of commentary: The expository text addresses the viewer directly, with titles or voices that advance an argument about the historical world. ... The expository mode emphasises the impression of objectivity, and of well-established judgement. This mode supports the impulse towards generalisation handsomely since the voice-over commentary can readily extrapolate from the particular instance offered on the image track. ... Exposition can accommodate elements of interviews but these tend to be subordinated to an argument offered by the film itself, via an unseen 'voice of God' or an on-camera voice of authority who speaks on behalf of the text. ... Finally, the viewer will typically expect the expository text to take shape around the solution to a problem or puzzle: presenting the news of the day, exploring the working of the atom or the universe, addressing the consequences of nuclear waste or acid rain, tracing the history of an event or the biography of a person.
>
> (Nichols 1991: 34–8)

As identified in this passage, the primary features of narration-led documentaries are: that, by blending omniscience and intimacy, they address the spectator directly; they set out an argument (thus implying forethought, knowledge, the ability to assimilate); they possess a dominant and constant perspective on the events they represent to which all elements within the film conform; they offer a solution and thereby a closure to the stories they tell. It is hardly surprising, therefore, that Nichols, in the earlier *Ideology and the Image* had made a direct comparison between the Expository documentary form and 'classical narrative cinema' (Nichols 1981: 97). Carl Plantinga is one of the many subsequent critics to have accepted the chronology supplied by Nichols, thus conflating the direct address form's simplicity with being 'naïve and politically retrograde' (Plantinga 1997: 101). Although Plantinga – unlike Nichols – subsequently identifies variants within the expository mode, differentiating between formal, open and poetic exposition, he is ultimately only providing subdivisions within Nichols' monolithic category, as, predictably, the 'formal' submode is the most rigid whilst the other two are more experimental and by implication 'better' and more advanced (pp. 106–18). Any attempt at rigid classification seems bound to dismiss or find fault with voice-over documentaries more readily than with any other mode. To such an extent has the conventional trajectory dominated, that the differences between narration-led documentaries are simply elided, and even a film as unconventional as Buñuel's *Land Without Bread* is assumed to conform to the traditional 'narration is bad' model. Not only does Nichols arbitrarily decide that voice-over is the dominant feature of otherwise vastly divergent films, but he creates a definition of expository documentary that fits only a portion of the films that might reasonably be assumed to conform to that category. *The March of Time* or *The Times of Harvey Milk* might explain, solve and close a sequence of events, but the same cannot be said of Franju's *Hôtel des invalides,* Chris Marker's *Sunless* or even more straightforward films such as Joris Ivens' *The Spanish Earth* and John Huston's *The Battle of San Pietro*. In bracketing together *Night Mail* and *The Battle of San Pietro* as prime examples of films utilising a 'voice of God' commentary (Nichols 1991: 34), despite Auden's scripted narration for the former being conspicuously poetic and Huston's voice-over in the latter being equally conspicuously ironic, Bill Nichols is only classifying (or condemning) the documentaries through their appropriation of one distinctive formal device. However varied the use of narration has been both before and after *The March of Time,* the overriding view is that the documentary voice-over is the filmmakers' ultimate tool for telling people what to think. This gross oversimplification covers a multitude of differences, from the most common use of commentary as an economic device able to efficiently relay information that might otherwise not be available or might take too long to tell in images, to its deployment as an ironic and polemical tool.

Conventional 'voice of God' narration: *The World at War, The Times of Harvey Milk*

Two examples of conventional 'voice of God' documentaries are *The World at War,* Thames Television's 24-part series about World War Two, and *The Times of Harvey Milk* (1984), Robert Epstein's emotive, Oscar-winning film about the gay San Francisco supervisor who was shot dead on 27 November 1978 by fellow Supervisor Dan White. Big, historical series such as *The World at War* or, more recently, *The Nazis: A Warning from History* (1997) and *Cold War* (1998) are, by nature, instructive, in that they have taken an event or a series of events from history which they subsequently 'tell' the television audience about. This approach to documentary is compatible with – and in some manner is an extension of – John Reith's conception of public service broadcasting in the UK. Reith's dictum that factual broadcasting in this country should both educate and entertain came from an elitist conception of the role of the media, that the BBC had a sense of moral obligation to its audience to impart worthwhile information. This is the 'filmmakers as teachers and audience as willing pupils' model of documentary, very much dependent on the understanding that the former have dedicated a substantial amount of time and resources to acquiring the requisite knowledge (historical information, interviewees, archive, etc.) to assume their academic superiority over the latter. There are various common factors that link historical series such as those cited above: the use of actors' voices for the narration, the deceptively simple compilation of archive to illustrate specific points (often belying the assiduous research that has gone into the selection),[1] the interviewing of 'experts' and eye-witnesses. One of the most famous recent voice-overs is Laurence Olivier's for *The World at War*. Olivier, unlike the younger and less well known Samuel West, for instance, who narrated *The Nazis* and later Laurence Rees's follow-up series *Auschwitz: The Nazis and the Final Solution*, has the particular seniority that results from having been England's most universally acclaimed and respected classical actor.[2] This 'star' persona is exploited by Jeremy Isaacs' series, especially when it comes to Episode 20: 'Genocide', the programme which tackles the Final Solution. This episode opens with Olivier (for the only time in the series) delivering a scripted, formal piece to camera, in which he warns 'you will find it [the ensuing programme] grim viewing, but watch if you can. This happened in our time, but must not happen again', and in which he also asserts that the following film 'shows *how* it was done and *why* it was done'. There are several underlying issues that colour this opening address, the first being the suggestion that Olivier, however sincere, is 'acting', performing pre-scripted lines. Here he has broken one of the 'rules' of documentary voice-over which is to remain separate and disembodied from the images commented upon.[3] The issue of subjectivity is also present in the ideological implications of Olivier's words: that the events about to be shown form part of a closed historical sequence by which the audience will be moved and which, if they look and listen attentively, they will be able to prevent from recurring. What 'Genocide' implicitly offers, therefore, is the surety that it can contain and explicate the 'truth', and this it does by adopting a classic and simple cause–effect linear structure guided by Olivier's voice-over.[4]

The methods deployed for telling the story of the Final Solution are exemplified by the opening sequences. The first images of 'Genocide' (immediately following Olivier's piece to camera and prior to the title sequence) are two tracking shots following the railway lines either side of the Auschwitz gates. The immediate point of spectator-identification is thereby with the victims of the Nazi extermination programme, and what the film subsequently seeks is an explanation for this final journey. The film adopts two structuring strategies or routes of inquiry, the first is to have the narration 'interpret' the events depicted, the second is to chart a linear historical trajectory through these events, from the late 1920s to the final liberation of the camps. The former is an example of the most common deployment of voice-over as a means of making sense of a montage of images that otherwise would not be explicable; the latter is a frequently adopted measure for telling such a monumental story. The voice-over in *The World at War* makes sense of, and creates links between, the images it is covering. An early example in 'Genocide' is the archival sequence that begins with footage of Himmler attending skiing championships and a Nazi youth camp, followed by neo-Darwinian Nazi propaganda films showing animals demonstrating the 'survival of the fittest' laws of nature, and concluding with images of race and plough horses, medical examinations of 'perfect' humans and a variety of group sporting activities. Without Olivier's narration outlining and offering an opinion on Nazi racial philosophy which sought a 'race of supermen' and 'pedigree humans', these images could arguably be open to interpretation, or at least the logic binding them together might be obscured. The pivotal narrative figure for the episode is Heinrich Himmler, appointed by Hitler as Reichsführer of the SS, whom the voice-over describes at the outset as the one who 'refines the philosophy of Nazism'. The selection of Himmler is not arbitrary but expedient and to a degree reductive, as what happens through this episode of *The World at War* is that all the historical events represented in terms of narrative unity refer back, however tangentially, to this one individual. The conventional cause–effect structure pursued by 'Genocide' is in danger of permitting the inference that, had Himmler not existed, the Final Solution would not have happened, or more generally of conforming to what Marxist historian E.H. Carr derogatorily labels the 'bad King John theory of history', whereby history is interpreted as 'the biography of great men' and their evil counterparts, and that 'what matters in history is the character and behaviour of individuals' (Carr 1961:45). The voice-over in *The World at War* steers the telling and thereby the comprehension of its subjects and abides by a determinist view of history whereby 'everything that happens has a cause or causes, and could not have happened differently unless something in the cause or causes had also been different' (Carr 1961:93). *The World at War* as a series does not follow a strictly chronological structure, although each episode is set out in a linear fashion. In 'Genocide' this means that the interviews with SS officers, camp survivors, Anthony Eden and all the other figures are in some way related to Himmler and the blame attached to him as the key architect of the Final Solution at the outset of the film. A residual effect of this is to stop the audience from probing deeper into less straightforward issues such as Nazi ideology and the practicalities of the mass exterminations. The programme likewise shies away from taking issue with its subjects as it maintains its supposedly objective stance. Eden, for example, is not made to confront the inadequacy of being more concerned with the reception in the House of Commons to his 1943 statement regarding the treatment of the European Jews than with the issue of why, despite this information, the Allies did so little to intervene. The version of the Holocaust offered in 'Genocide' is simplified but not distorted.

As Jeffrey Youdelman remarks at the outset of 'Narration, Invention, and History', the common (but he argues misguided) reaction to documentary narration is that the use of a voice-over necessarily suppresses the voices of the documentary subjects themselves, that narration-led films are directly opposed to films which, using 'oral history interview techniques', capture 'for the first time the voice of the people who have shared in the making of working-class history and culture' (Youdelman 1982: 454). Youdelman ends his article by not reviling but praising those filmmakers who advocate the use of 'commentary, intervention, and invention', and who believe in 'taking responsibility for the statement the film was making' (Youdelman 1982: 458). Youdelman here envisages the dialectical co-existence of an authorial 'voice' and factual representation.

The 'voice' of a documentary such as *The Times of Harvey Milk* is easily discernible: supportive of Milk, his politics and his sexuality; saddened by his death; angered by the law's treatment of his murderer. As with the choice of Olivier for *The World at War,* the decision to use Harvey Fierstein as the narrator for *The Times of Harvey Milk* is indicative of the film's stance towards its subject. Fierstein, a well-known gay writer and actor, has an immensely distinctive voice (gravel mixed with treacle) that immediately makes the film into a statement about gay politics. The question of bias, however, is astutely handled by the film; although its narration is still highly selective and is unashamedly biased towards Milk, Epstein is careful to ensure that Harvey Milk is not simply a significant gay figure but more of a democratic Pied Piper with a more universal charisma.

The film starts with a news flash announcing the deaths of Harvey Milk, the first 'out' gay man to be voted into public office in California, and Mayor George Moscone; the narration is soon brought in (over news stills) telling us that Milk 'had already come to represent something far greater than his office'. This observation is subsequently underlined as the film soundtrack cuts to the voice of Milk himself (thinking he could be the target of assassins) taping his will and commenting that he saw himself as 'part of a movement'. Harvey Milk is portrayed as a figure who represents, in the true Lukácsian sense, social forces and attitudes far greater than himself, his is an individual destiny that gives '*direct* expression to general destinies' (Lukács 1937: 152), and this idealisation of him would seem to stem directly from the coercive voice-over. This could undoubtedly also be said of *The World at War*'s treatment of Himmler, that he too was a representative figure who could function as an assimilation of Nazi ideology and action towards the Jews. But whereas *The World at War* maintains a superficial impartiality towards its material, *The Times of Harvey Milk* deftly insinuates that the film's central ethos is not grafted on but innate, that the visuals corroborate the narration but are not subservient to it. There are, for example, moments when the interviewees (all friends and supporters of Milk) substantiate the notion of him as an idealised representative figure: Sally Gearheart, an academic, saying, about her attitude the night of Harvey's murder, 'don't you realise the course of history has been changed', or Tony Anniano, a gay schoolteacher, commenting about the violence that followed White's conviction for manslaughter that 'you can replace a glass door ... but you can't replace Harvey' or Tory Hartmann confirming the idea of Milk as a symbolic figure when she recounts how 'it took his death' to make people see how important it was to 'come out'. The role allotted Fierstein's narration is confirmatory as opposed to purely instructional, so the 'voice' of *The Times of Harvey Milk* ostensibly comes from the active collusion between filmmakers, form, subjects and archive.

The Times of Harvey Milk is using the conventionalised voice-over-led documentary structure not to pseudo-objective ends, but as a tool in a subjective enterprise – the film's 'voice'. The image of Harvey Milk proffered by the documentary is wholly complimentary (there is one mention of Milk's short temper but little else that is negative), but the information is imparted so as to seem that this is the only accurate portrayal. *The Times of Harvey Milk* maintains its right to be selective and to emphasise what it chooses, and, as Bill Nichols posits, 'our attention is not on how the filmmaker uses witnesses to make the point but on the effectiveness of the argument itself' (Nichols 1991: 37). At times it does this in a flagrantly manipulative manner; this is not a clinical analysis of a series of events but an emotional eulogy, and as such it wants to bring its audience round, to make us feel as well as think the same way it does. To achieve this, Epstein deploys a variety of narrative devices, one of which is to construct a conflict around which the rest of the action revolves between Milk and White. As the film's central axis, this confrontation is personal, political and ideological. That Milk and White were such starkly different people, antagonists on the San Francisco board and representatives of vastly different values and beliefs, goes towards setting up the final confrontation: White's murder of Milk. Several strands running through the film can be traced back to this symbolic duel and the collisions that result from it. *Harvey Milk* is clearly an 'authored' film, and yet it also abides by the formal unity associated with expository documentaries; not only is it driven by a strong narration, but its narrative is structured around a series of collisions that emanate from the central Milk vs. White opposition that heighten, explicate and crystallise the debates enacted therein such as gays and lesbians vs. evangelical bigots, minority communities vs the white, middle-class, heterosexual majority.[5] It does not, however, put Dan White's case, which is more complex and troubled than the film makes it appear.[6]

About 50 minutes into the subsequently chronological documentary, the opening sequence is repeated (from a slightly different camera angle), thus signalling that the dominant narrative (Milk's significant if brief political career) is reaching its conclusion. The film's first 'ending' is thus the spontaneous candlelight march that occurred on the night of Milk's death. The manner in which the film builds up to this tragic, celebratory climax is deeply reminiscent of the funeral sequence that crowns Douglas Sirk's *Imitation of Life:* it is simply willing one to cry, and in so doing uses every technique of manipulation at its disposal. After the Feinstein news flash, the film cuts to a protracted sequence of interviews with the same friends and colleagues that have proffered choric opinions of Milk throughout, each talking about their immediate responses to hearing the news that morning and what they did afterwards. This section concludes with Billy Kraus waiting to join the march towards City Hall, and wondering why there were so few people there ('is this all that anybody cared?'). Having reached this moment of extreme pathos and Billy Kraus reporting how he was assured that the march had not reached him yet, there is then a cut to footage of the actual march: a wide street filled, as far as the eye can see, with people holding candles (this is not unlike the similarly delayed revelation of quite how many people are in attendance at the funeral in *Imitation of Life*). After the intensity of the build up to the march, these archive images work as an emotional release, a cinematic outpouring of grief, replete with Mark Isham's correspondingly poignant trumpet music. The cathartic spell this sequence casts is really only broken when Tory Hartmann says over the continuing footage of the march, 'Harvey would have loved this' – a brief respite before she too (in front of the camera) succumbs to tears. This false ending culminates in the respective funerals of Milk and Moscone, the former taking precedence over the latter. In many ways, *Harvey Milk* is a consummate melodrama and this build up to a moment of crisis,triumph or extreme emotion is a formal technique repeated several times.

It may come as a shock to some viewers that the funeral march is not the end of the film. After a fade to black the final section commences, dedicated to the trial and sentencing of Dan White and the street violence that greeted the verdict. There is something anticlimactic, un-Aristotelian about this transition, abruptly reminding those watching that this is more documentary than melodrama. Again, however, the underlying aim of this final stage appears to be to link the history of Milk's fatal conflict with White to wider issues, in particular justice and retribution. Clearly everyone involved in the film, both in front of and behind the camera, considered White's sentence lenient (there is even a strong hint of disappointment on television news reporter Jeannine Yeoman's face as she says 'I thought he might get the chair'). What the film achieves is a mimicking in those watching of the paradoxical emotions felt by the liberals in the film: that whilst they might be politically opposed to capital punishment and violence, they emotionally could not come to terms with the injustice, as they perceived it, of White's conviction for voluntary manslaughter.[7] Just as Epstein's film manifests both stylistically and formally its solidarity with Milk, so it also barely masks his and his fellows' antipathy towards White. For one, there are no specially shot interviews of Dan White's friends and family, so the film continues to make use of interviews with the same collection of Milk's friends. This has the effect of imposing an emotional continuum on the film that compels the audience to react to the last section through the feelings engendered by what has preceded it. We are automatically distanced from Dan White: we see him, his wife and friends only in news archive; even his tearful confession (played on tape to the courtroom) is not given to us 'unadulterated' but comes after a pre-emptive piece of voice-over has warned that the prosecution's gamble of using this to prove White's guilt backfired, as jurors found themselves feeling sorry for him. As an explanation of the violence that followed the verdict, there is a montage of interviews voicing cynical speculations on the reasons for White's 'light' sentence: that had he killed only the heterosexual Moscone, or had he been black, then White would have been convicted of murder. Ultimately, there is a strong sense (as the surety and calm of Milk's ethos is restored by the pre-credits sequence) that all violence and ugliness in *The Times of Harvey Milk* stems directly from White.

The World at War and *The Times of Harvey Milk* offer two examples of traditional voice-over as an explanatory and persuasive tool. They use expository narration, however, in different ways; whereas *The World at War* maintains a semblance of instructional objectivity, the degree of bias in *Harvey Milk* is evident throughout. The tonal differences between the two make definitions of the expository mode difficult. In their persuasiveness, both films could be termed 'propaganda', in that they set out to win the audience round to the validity of their points of view. The 'problem' with this is that documentary theory has been too eager to collapse the notions of 'persuasion' and 'falsification'; a slippage which stems from an adherence to the belief that to display bias is tantamount to creating a fiction out of facts, as the outspoken opinions of Robert Drew attest. As Noël Carroll argues, 'A film may be successfully persuasive without bending the facts' (Carroll 1996a: 235); a documentary may present the filmmakers' point of view through such overt means as a biased voice-over without forfeiting the claim to be a documentary. The extent to which material has been assimilated, concentrated and selected in traditional expository documentaries makes theorists uneasy, as does the domination of commentary and of a single perspective. This is not, however, to say that *The World at War* or *Harvey Milk* are pedalling 'lies'. Even when Carr is attacking an individualist, determinist approach to history, he is not maintaining that history does not include individuals, merely that they 'act in context, and under the impulse of a past society' (Carr 1961: 35). *The World at War* has, out of necessity, been selective in its use of material. Carroll again argues against assuming that selectivity and bias are interchangeable, commenting that whilst selectivity may 'make bias possible' or may even 'in some contexts invite bias ... it does not *guarantee* bias' (Carroll 1996b: 284). The questionable belief behind the theorisation of the narration-led documentary is that the voice-over automatically becomes the dominant and therefore subjectifying force behind every film in which it is substantially used, that its didacticism stems from its inevitable pre-eminence in the hierarchy of documentary devices. Instead, it should be acknowledged that a strong voice-over rarely renders the truth contained within the image invisible, that in effect these narration-led documentaries are films – even the least radical amongst them – that suggest that documentaries, far from being able to represent the truth in an unadulterated way, can only do so through interpretation, which in the case of narration is of the most overt and blatant kind.

This interpretative function is not, however, necessarily at the expense of independent thought; it is not invariably the case that to 'tell' rather than to 'show' the facts is to immobilise the audience, to render them incapable of seeing the material before them in any way which might contradict the perspective of the film. The truth, therefore, does not only become apparent when the overt intervention of the filmmaker is minimised. This is why another common ellipsis in documentary theory – that form and ideology are corollaries – is likewise questionable. The inflexibility detected in the 'expository mode' has itself been a consistent characteristic of the theoretical writing that discusses it. Orthodox attitudes towards narration-led documentaries are thereby generally dependent upon the shaky assumption that films that share a formal device (the voice-over) also share an attitude and an ideological aim, that narration is a form of 'preaching' and the voice-over a device 'authoritarian by nature, elitist and paternalistic' (Youdelman 1982: 464). In 'Cinema/Ideology/Criticism', Comolli and Narboni recognise a category of political filmmaking into which both *The World at War* and *The Times of Harvey Milk* would fit: Category (d), which comprises

> those films ... which have an explicitly political content ... but which do not effectively criticise the ideological system in which they are embedded because they unquestioningly adopt its language and its imagery.
>
> (Comolli and Narboni 1969: 26–7)

Whilst this *Cahiers du cinéma* editorial is willing to positively acknowledge the ambivalence of, for example, the films of Costa-Gavras, when a comparable duality between content and form is approached within a documentary context, formal conservatism is presumed to override any other political or ideological position. Narration is assumed to be undemocratic and inherently distortive. There is therefore the suspicion that a voice-over has the capacity to violate the 'truth' revealed in the image. Pascal Bonitzer (1976: 326) asserts that a film's commentary 'should not do violence to the image', and yet the traditional opinion of voice-over is predicated upon the belief that it cannot but help violate, distort or compromise the image. The voice-over thereby prevents the event being represented from 'speaking', as if a film can possess only one point of view which will inevitably be that of the voice-over if there is one of any substance. If synch sound and the reproduction of the voice was 'the "truth" which was lacking in the silent film' (Jean-Louis Comolli in Silverman 1988: 44), then why has the voice-over been so vilified? The traditional explanation lies in the disembodiment of the classic documentary narrator. Bonitzer (1976: 322) emphasises the voice-over's Otherness when he refers to it as:

> ... that voice of knowledge *par excellence* in all films, since it resounds from offscreen, in other words from the field of the Other. In this system the concern is to reduce, insofar as possible, not the informative capacity of commentary but its assertive character and, if one likes, its *authoritative* character – that arbitration and arbitrariness of the voice-off which, to the extent that it cannot be localised, can be criticised by nothing and no one.

Important here is not merely the identification of the voice-over's Otherness, but that such a voice achieves a certain authority through being both an arbitrator and arbitrary; capable of being both reasonable and logical as well as irrationally selective. That this dubious power is so often invested in a white, male, middle-class and anonymous voice necessarily cements the voice-over form as repressive and anti-radical. Kaja Silverman posits that, in Hollywood films, 'male subjectivity is most fully realised (or perhaps it would be more accurate to say most fully "idealised") when it is least visible' (Silverman 1988: 164). A case can be found for arguing something comparable in relation to the non-fiction film: that the 'voice of God' is a composite of various different manifestations of universality and power that include masculinity and anonymity. However, the reductivism that has plagued discussions of documentary's implementation of voice-over lies in the persistent refusal to either acknowledge any differences between *actual* voices or to distinguish between very different uses of the voice within the documentary context. The use of a female voice-over offers the most overt challenge to the narrowness of such criticism, but one can also point to the deliberately ironic and distanced narration in films such as *Land Without Bread, The Battle of San Pietro* and *Hôtel des invalides.*

Ironic narration: *Hôtel des invalides; The Battle of San Pietro*[8]

In 1966 Scholes and Kellogg stated that 'a narrator who is not in some way suspect, who is not in some way open to ironic scrutiny, is what the modern temper finds least bearable' (quoted in Kozloff 1988: 102). This use of 'ironic scrutiny' has been evident in the use of commentary in documentaries since well before the 1960s (see the use of intertitles in Shub's *Fall of the Romanov Dynasty*), but forms part of an alternative tradition (of which Buñuel, Huston and Franju are notable exponents) whose idiosyncrasies have too frequently been subsumed with uncritical alacrity into the mainstream. As there is an alternative practical tradition, so there is an alternative (if stunted) critical tradition which prioritises the potential rather than the deficiencies of the expository mode. Alberto Cavalcanti is one such dissenting voice who, in the 1930s, writes of how he regrets the relegation of the voice-over to the 'comparatively minor role of providing continuity and "story" in travelogues, newsreels and documentary' since the advent of 'talkies' (Cavalcanti 1939: 29). What interests Cavalcanti are just the ironic possibilities of narration that modern critical orthodoxy have marginalised; that, for instance, the 'effect ... which no audience can resist' of Joris Ivens' *The Spanish Earth* 'arises from the contrast between the cool, tragic dignity of Hemingway's prose on the one hand, and the terrors of the images on the other' (p. 29). To Cavalcanti, a film's 'poetic effect' results from the juxtaposition of 'rational', interpretative narration and emotive images; that 'while the picture is the medium of statement, the sound is the medium of suggestion' (pp. 37–8).

Although one might not necessarily want to categorise all such films as 'poetic', what Cavalcanti highlights is the challenging, radical effect of electing not to correlate image and sound. Similarly Bonitzer debates the use or otherwise of the 'free confrontation' between different narrative elements in documentary when challenging the 'seductiveness' of the dictum *'let the event speak'*, commenting that, 'This is an interesting formula not only because in it can be read the elision of (the author's) point of view toward the event in question, but also because it displaces this "question of point of view" – which is so important for "politics" – to a problem of *speech*' (Bonitzer 1976: 320). The corollary of this, Bonitzer finds, is that the 'eye is carried by the voice' but a voice which remains '*without subject*' (p. 320). The analyses of Cavalcanti and Bonitzer offer pertinent insights into the paradox of the narration-led documentary form: that although the voice is considered 'dominant' over the images and thus to serve a didactic function, it may be powerless in comparison with that image. Films such as *Hôtel des invalides* and *The Battle of San Pietro* break the documentary's version of the cinematic illusion on which this contradiction is formulated, namely the creation of a 'classic' style that elides differences or tensions.

The traditional voice-over form emphasises the unity, and imaginary cohesion of its various elements; so the dominance of the narration covertly serves to emphasise the incontrovertibility of the images by refusing to dispute and doubt what they depict. Narration could thereby be viewed as a mechanism deployed to mask the realisation that this mode of representation, and indeed its inherent belief in a consistent and unproblematic truth, are perpetually on the verge of collapse, that commentary, far from being a sign of omniscience and control, is the hysterical barrier erected against the spectre of ambivalence and uncertainty. Indeed, many of the unconventional voice-overs signal their doubt that such a neat collusion between voice and image can ever be sustained, that even narration is not invariably allied to determinism, but has the potential to be a destabilising component of a dialectical structure that intentionally brings cracks and inconsistencies to the surface. In certain documentary films – when voice-over becomes a truly subversive tool, and one not bound by the conservatism of the expository form – the narration becomes a component capable of engendering such a dialectical distance, one that both draws the audience into sympathising for the image and sets them critically back from it.

In *Hôtel des invalides,* a documentary about Paris's military museum and allegedly Franju's personal favourite among his short films (Durgnat 1967: 47), the distance between official subject and critical tone is both consistent and pronounced. Unlike a more explicitly political voice-over film such as Ivens' *The Spanish Earth* in which Hemingway's committed voice-over directly interprets the images (as when he says over shots of soldiers going to battle: 'This is the true face of men going into action. It is a little different from any other face you'll ever see') *Hôtel des invalides* is dialectical in that its narration does not provide explicit commentary and criticism, but rather creates the space in which such interpretations can occur. This is not to say that Franju's pacifism is hard to detect, but merely that it is only insinuated and never laid bare, notably through the increasingly absurd and strained relationship between the patter emitted by the guide escorting us and visitors around the armoury museum and the images and juxtapositions that comprise the tour (the 'misguided tour' as Durgnat defines it (p. 47)). Noël Burch's contention that *Hôtel des invalides* is so ambiguous that 'it can be read either as an attack on war, or (on a level that is perhaps less sophisticated but still perfectly cogent and perfectly 'natural' to a good many people) as a flag-waving patriotic film' (Burch 1969: 159) is both ingenuous and naïve. Yes, the film was commissioned by the French Ministry of the Army, but they were not entirely satisfied with the result, and their discontent no doubt resulted from detecting the thinly veiled tensions between thesis and antithesis. There is, for example, the sequence which cuts from a low angle shot of Napoleon over which the voice-over comments 'legend has its heroes' to the image of a wheelchair-bound veteran being wheeled to the foot of the statue by a nurse, to which the narrator adds 'war has its victims'. As Franju cuts between the petrified monument and the still living soldier, it remains unclear whether the soldier is looking at Napoleon, or indeed whether he can see or understand the objects his eyes happen to have alighted upon; as a result of this uncertainty, the issue of difference and tension between myth and the present is left for the spectator to ponder. The point of synthesis is the moment of viewing.[9] The constant, nagging demotion of the trappings and icons of past glory is a characteristic of *Hôtel des invalides*, but its 'openness' as a text stems from the lack of Hemingway-esque directional commentary. Take the juxtaposition between yet another shot of Napoleon (to which the guide simply adds, 'the Emperor') and his stuffed horse and dog, two of the more bizarre objects by which the museum remembers him; or the narrator introducing 'The bronzed head of General Mangin's statue' as the camera rather sumptuously pans around the head to reveal that half of it has been blown away. In both these examples what is signalled is the discrepancy between the brutality of war and the safety of its remembering, the one necessarily impinging on the other, so the mummification of experience witnessed in the army museum itself becomes an act of violence. Like the iconic wheelchair, the bland voice-over and the smiling, oblivious couple whose guided tour we are ostensibly following, trundle blithely on, so the swelling anger is ours and not the text's. *Hôtel des invalides* reaches no conclusion as such, although it suggests plenty. As the war orphans march crocodile fashion out of the gates and a flock of birds swings through the air (a reprise of an earlier sequence) the film appears to have made little definite progress. The 'progress', however, has been made by those making sense of the film's elisions and complex juxtapositions – primarily between voice and image, in which the confrontation between official thesis and subversive antithesis is encapsulated.

There are similar moments of disjuncture in John Huston's *The Battle of San Pietro*, the second film in Huston's wartime documentary trilogy – although built into this documentary's use of irony and detachment is a more involved debate around the limitations of narration itself. *The Battle of San Pietro* and *Hôtel des invalides* elicited similarly negative responses from the bodies that funded them, and Huston's US Army superiors excised certain material when shown the completed version in 1944. *The Battle of San Pietro* is usually noted for being a 'classic direct-address documentary' (the narration is by Huston himself) as well as for its use of ironic commentary (Nichols 1981: 185ff). The film's use of irony links it to the tradition of intellectual, anti-establishment documentaries exemplified by *Land Without Bread* and, of course, *Hôtel des invalides*. Huston, for example, contradicts General Mark Clark's opening piece to camera declaring the cost of the hostilities in the Italian campaign not to have been 'excessive' by cutting from Clark to images of dead soldiers being stretchered onto a truck. Huston's voice-over (which he reputedly worked on 'in his tent at night while enemy shells continued to explode nearby' [Hammen 1996: 147]) is inconsistent; the laboured irony of the film's early sequences, for instance, gives way to a purely descriptive narration during the battle scenes, which took place between 8 and 15 December 1943. Some of the censorship problems Huston encountered were indirectly related to these tonal shifts. US Army records reveal several memos calling for the removal of footage showing identifiable dead American soldiers being hauled onto a truck, overlaid with excerpts from interviews they recorded whilst still alive.[10] There is a powerful sense of immediacy to much of *The Battle of San Pietro*, and as Hammen speculates, 'How Huston was able to function as an artist in the situation is difficult to fathom. He reportedly moved continuously in the face of enemy small arms and mortar fire from one cameraman to the next, explaining to each exactly what he wanted from their footage' (Hammen 1996: 147).[11]

The army requested further cuts to be made to the final, post-liberation reel, a section of *San Pietro* that raises further questions about the limitations and use of documentary narration. The reasons for the Chiefs' dissatisfaction with this final section seems to have been that it is tedious and detracts from the ostensible purpose of the film, one memo from Charles Stodter, Assistant Chief, Army Pictorial Service, remarking that 'the ending is somewhat long, particularly the sequence showing the children', and another from Curtis Mitchell, Chief, Pictorial Branch, suggesting that the same images be cut as they have 'little to do with the American soldier and [convey] little information about him to the public' (Culbert 1990). To return to the distinction between the overt, official subject of *The Battle of San Pietro* – namely, the American 1943–1944 Italian campaign and the more universal, emotional subtext of human loss – this is the film's primary dialectic and, to borrow Eisenstein's terminology, the former is the documentary's 'tonal' register (its definite rhythms and movements) whilst the latter is its 'overtonal' or subliminal undercurrents. Huston, having interwoven with clarity and precision image, commentary, irony and passion, dispenses with such rationality when it comes to the conclusion of *San Pietro*, a sequence that is almost abstract in its dependency on raw emotion and an absence of intellectual and historical interpretation. It is as if all the astute counterpointing that precedes the entry into the devastated town was surface, the recognisable ploys of propaganda which fail wholeheartedly to prepare us for Huston's elegiac finale, arguably the heart of the film in which the dialogue between text and spectator is reduced (or rather refined) to the transference of unmediated feeling. This scene, in which the inhabitants of San Pietro re-emerge from their hiding places in the mountains, stands apart from the rest of the film by its lack of narration except of the most minimal, functional kind.[12] The passage where this lack is most pronounced follows the information about there still being German booby traps in the town and the explosion of a building. A body is spied in the rubble; a man, beside himself with grief, is comforted by friends;

a piece of choral music is laid over the images; the man hugs the dead, dust-covered body of what is probably his wife; he turns to look at the camera with an expression of pleading and anger; after which there is a sharp edit (as if the camera cannot bear this burden and has to look away) to two mothers sitting together, both simultaneously breastfeeding and crying. In the man's desperate gaze out to the spectator there is at once contained the desolation of what is captured in the image, the impotency of being the one doing the watching, and the intention in Huston to convey both this fractured relationship and his underpinning theme that the defining truth of war is loss. The man's gaze functions as metaphoric shorthand for the complexity of emotions and intellectual responses encompassed by this untraditional and thereby 'inadequate' propaganda film. Huston, by the end, conveys rather than explains the battle for San Pietro and what it meant to witness it. It is apposite, therefore, that the film brings us back from such an acute moment of despair through images rather than narration. Again this entails looking out to camera, but this time it is the laughing, inquisitive, trusting and self-conscious children whose gazes we meet. These ironically recall General Clark's awkwardness at the beginning of the film – his reluctance at first to address the camera as if avoiding it.

The loss of voice at the end of *San Pietro* is, paradoxically, as eloquent as the previous scenes packed with loquacious commentary. In Alain Resnais' *Nuit et brouillard* there is a sequence detailing the uses to which the Nazis put the remains (the hair, bones, fat) of the millions they exterminated. At one point Cayrol's otherwise calm and poetic narration falters: 'With the bones ... they made fertiliser, or tried to. With the bodies ... but words fail', the ensuing shots being of a bucket piled high with severed heads intercut with the headless bodies they once belonged to packed into boxes like sardines. The commentary then resumes: 'With the bodies, they tried to make soap', describing the horrors of the image they accompany. *Nuit et brouillard* here reflexively signposts the inadequacy of words, whilst ironically emphasising the descriptive powers of the film's otherwise lyrical commentary, the necessity of words to the power of the overall film.[13] Conversely, Huston's unremarked descent into silence in *The Battle of San Pietro* creates a tension between images and words as it conveys the actual insufficiency of words to offer comfort or make images manageable. Voice-over is no longer a controlling mechanism.

The classical fictional model of the voice-over is as the revelation of a person's inner thoughts or the use of the internal monologue to 'turn the body "inside out"' (Silverman 1988: 53). As Silverman (p. 53) continues:

> The voice in question functions almost like a searchlight suddenly turned upon the character's thoughts; it makes audible what is ostensibly inaudible, transforming the private into the public.

In direct contrast to this, the words delivered by a documentary voice-over are, traditionally, public or collective utterances, and, to return to Cavalcanti's distinction between the 'rationality' of sound and voice as opposed to the 'emotional stimulus' provided by images (Cavalcanti 1939: 30), the words introduce, interpret or explain images that might otherwise, in a multitude of ways, remain incoherent. The ostensible purpose of the 'voice of God' model is to absent personality and any notion of the internal monologue, to generalise, to offer an omniscient and detached judgement, to guide the spectator through events whilst remaining aloof from them. As Mary Ann Doane (1980: 43) elaborates, 'it is precisely because the voice [in a documentary] is not localisable, because it cannot be yoked to a body, that it is capable of interpreting the image, producing the truth'. What consequently occurs when a documentary narration falters, stops or acknowledges its inadequacy, as occurs in both *Nuit et brouillard* and *The Battle of San Pietro*, is that the personal, subjective potential of that voice-over is unexpectedly permitted to surface, a rupturing of convention that forces a reassessment of the text/narration relationship and how that relationship impinges on the effect a film has on the spectator. Addressing the issue of words' insufficiency and by literally ceasing to speak, as Huston does in *The Battle of San Pietro*, paradoxically brings to the documentary voice-over the intimacy associated with its fictional counterpart; the diminution of the voice, the acknowledgement of its failure, is in this instance the powerful expression of the 'inner voice', the subjective presence within the documentary. With *The Battle of San Pietro* the tacit documentary 'pact' that the voice-over will remain objective, 'rigorously extradiegetic' and '[assume] autonomy as a discourse' (Guynn 1990: 157) inevitably disintegrates. Guynn later posits that the spectator of a documentary cannot 'identify with the voice of the commentary as he does with the camera, because the voice addresses him [sic]' (p. 159). Not only is the contention that we cannot identify with a voice that addresses us hugely problematic, but the relationship between a documentary's voice-over and its audience can be far more complex than Guynn believes. By the very revelation of tensions and cracks on the surface of the non-fictional (and in this case propagandists) film, *San Pietro* constructs a richly ambiguous relationship between narration and audience which can encompass both the moments of intimacy and emotional revelation (when the words 'fail') and the more conventional public and direct mode of address (when the words can respond to the images). The unease with which Huston adopts the traditional expository form also creates an openness that allows for a far more active, interventionist spectatorship.

In *The Battle of San Pietro* and *Hôtel des invalides*, the documentary's inherent instability (the act of faithful documentation) is signalled through the tension between official and unofficial message or intention and the emphasised inability of the voice-overs to convey the essence of what is being represented. What is in need of being dismantled, is the conventionalised understanding of what a commentary's role is within the documentary, and to achieve this the actual voice – its audibility, its tone and gender, its effect – must likewise be re-examined. Increased personalisation is the most consistently used means of altering the role of a documentary's narrator; Hemingway's informal, conversational tone in *The Spanish Earth*, by breaking down the rigid formality of the traditional

narration (telling us, for example: 'I can't read German either') makes us seriously question the 'voice of God' mode and thus the validity of the critical orthodoxy upon which traditional analyses of narration are predicated. Alternative
means of address have included the use of silence (*San Pietro, Nuit et brouillard*),
the use of openly political narration (*Land Without Bread, The Spanish Earth,
The Last Bolshevik*), the use of multiple voices (*Dear America*) and the use of
women's voice (*Sunless, Are We Winning, Mommy?, Handsworth Songs*). The last
of these options is the most recognisably confrontational, as it challenges, from
several angles, the conceptualisation of the documentary voice-over as a repressive ideological, patriarchal tool.

The woman's voice: *Sunless*

In 'The Photographic Message' Barthes, when discussing the relationship of text
to photographic image, argues that 'the closer the text is to the image, the less
it seems to connote it' (Barthes 1977: 26), that an image's connotative function
('the imposition of second meaning on the photographic message proper' (p.
20)), is reduced by the literalness of any accompanying text. There is a parallel
to be drawn here with the use of voice-over in documentaries. The traditional
expository mode of direct address relies on proximity between text and image:
the words explicate the visuals, telling the spectator how he or she should interpret them; the potential for secondary, connotative meaning is limited. A crucial
component of such an 'unproblematic' narration has traditionally been held to
be the masculinity of the 'voice of God', the traditional tones of authority and
universality. In less recent documentaries, the mere presence of a female voice-
over would tamper with this unity, as deviance from the single, male voice could
be argued to subvert that surety, engender doubt and divest the disembodied
male voice of its 'discursive power' (Silverman 1988: 164). As French feminist
Annie Leclerc observes:

> Man has always decided what can be talked about, and what cannot ... How
> can female thought of any substance come into being if we are constrained
> to think along lines laid down by man ... As yet, I am only really able to
> think one thing: that female thought can exist, must exist so as to put an
> end at last, not to male thought itself, but to its ridiculous – or tragic –
> soliloquy.
>
> (quoted in Moi 1987: 78–9)

Leclerc's suggestion is that the very presence of a female voice in a traditionally
male environment is a means of creating a critical distance, of making one think
about the use and adequacy of 'man-made' words.[14] Although the use of
women's voices in non-fiction filmmaking has greatly increased over the past
decade, the manner in which the expository mode has been theorised has not
taken such historical changes into account. There are two ways in which, in the
UK for example, the woman's voice has started to be heard: as a detached,

omniscient narrator in the 'voice of God' mould and as the voice of the woman filmmaker from behind the camera. Differences are emerging between the two categories in terms of actual quality of voice. The female narrator is more often than not authoritative, relatively deep voiced; popular actresses and personalities used in the UK include Jancis Robinson, Zoë Wanamaker, Lindsay Duncan and Juliet Stevenson. This differs greatly from earlier notable uses of female narration in documentaries such as *Are We Winning, Mommy?* or *Handsworth Songs* in which the women's voices heard in voiceover are less definite, more idiosyncratic, personal and probing.

Both these documentaries are indicative of documentary's realisation in the 1970s and 1980s that a woman's voice embodied protest because women had traditionally been sidelined by history and documentary alike, a stance exemplified by the opening piece of narration in *Handsworth Songs* (John Akomfrah/Black Audio Film Collective, 1986). Following a mute montage of shots establishing the visual backdrop for this documentary about the Birmingham race riots of 1985, the first bit of narration is laid over archive material of the then Home Secretary Douglas Hurd talking to residents of Handsworth in the aftermath of the violence:

> It's the eleventh day of September 1985 and the Home Secretary is standing in a Handsworth street, with confused eyes. The masses saw him struggle for composure and they heard him mutter to journalists: 'These are senseless occasions, completely without reason'. Somebody said behind him, 'The higher the monkey climb, the more he will expose'.

The first thing one notices about this voice-over – bar the fact that it is a woman who is speaking it – is that the narrator is making no attempt to disguise the fact that she is reading; there is a formality to the intonation and modulation as well as to the writing (the rather old-fashioned rendering of the date, for example) that is immediately at odds with the chaotic, hand-held images. The contrapuntal use of the female voice continues as its distanciation from the visual text serves to mimic and convey the alienation of Douglas Hurd from the residents of Handsworth. As with the similar use of reported speech in Patrick Keiller's *London*, the intention here is to undermine the Conservative government as quoting Hurd's comment about the motivelessness of the riots is used to suggest his lack of understanding and to accentuate how out of touch he and his government are with their disaffected people. The political statements being made via the voice-over of *Handsworth Songs* are intensified by the use of a female narrator to voice them.

This more personal, individual woman's voice is now frequently to be found in documentaries in which a female director can be heard from behind the camera, narrating and asking questions. It is intriguing that filmmakers such as Molly Dineen, Jane Treays or Lucy Blakstad, who all interject their own voices into their films, have very similar voices and styles of delivery: wispy, middle-class and rather self-consciously unauthoritative. Whereas women narrators in mainstream film and television conform more readily to the masculine voice-over model, the director–narrators fall more into the category of woman's voice as other.

The equation that seems perpetually to have been made is between the woman's voice as physical utterance and the 'voice' as the metaphoric accessing of women's inner selves, their thoughts and identities. This attitude assumes that gender is an issue, principally because the gender of the 'universal' male voice is hardly remarked upon, whereas the specificity of the female voice too frequently is. The extreme examples of feminists conflating the 'voice' (in both its actual and metaphoric guises) with sex and gender are to be found in the writings of Luce Irigaray and Hélène Cixous, who, responding to patriarchy's over-reliance on seeing and looking, link a woman's 'voice' directly with her body and thoughts, so the adoption of a feminine voice necessarily offers the potential for anti-patriarchal radicalism. Echoing this idea that to 'let women speak' is a polit-ical act, both Doane and Silverman in their respective discussions of the female voice in (largely fictional) cinema, identify as the reason for the critical impor-tance granted women's voices film's ready correlation (supported by the twinned mechanisms of fetishism and voyeurism) between the visual domain and the fem-inine. As Silverman comments, Freudian psychoanalysis (to which most analyses of cinema as vision-centred are indebted) stipulates that 'vision provides the agency whereby the female subject is established as being different and inferior' (Silverman 1988: 17), so an active voice can be mobilised to counter the passive position thereby allocated to women. The female voice-over offers another instance of drawing attention to the frailty of the documentary endeavour to rep-resent reality in the most seamless way possible. It is not the voice of universal-ity but of specificity, and signals the impossibility and the lack that the single male voice-over frequently masks. The 'lack' at the heart of documentary filmmaking and, more importantly, how it has been interpreted, is its inability to accomplish its purported aim to give as authentic a representation of reality as possible. The traditional voice-over can be construed as one of the symbolic substitutes for this loss of control and omniscience. A female commentary is thus an overt tool for exposing the untenability of documentary's belief in its capacity for imparting 'generalised truths' faithfully and unproblematically. This breaking down of tra-dition and expectation is particularly pronounced in documentaries such as *Sunless* that use the gender of the woman's voice-over in a significant way, a politicisation of the voice that is not evident in the use of women as narrators of conventional expository documentaries.

The relationship between image and female commentary in Chris Marker's *Sunless* is complex: the voice-over is spoken by a woman (in the English-language version, Alexandra Stewart), who in turn states that she is relaying not her own thoughts and observations but those contained within a series of letters from the fictional Sandor Krasna, the contents of which find parallels in the film images themselves. The boundaries between these various personae are far from rigid and thus the central relationship between image and words, traditionally so log-ical, becomes, in *Sunless*, fluid and mutable. The illogicality of this relationship, rather than functioning as a release from conventional constraints, has continued to trouble critics who, in turn, have constructed various means of imposing order on the film's central dynamic. Terrence Rafferty, for example, suggests that,

> The far-flung documentary images of *Sunless* are assembled as an *autobiography* – the film has no subject except the consciousness, the memory of the man who shot it – yet Marker attributes this consciousness to the invented 'Sandor Krasna', removes it from himself to a yet more spectral entity.
>
> (My italics; Rafferty 1984: 286)

Jan-Christopher Horak and Edward Branigan likewise conflate Marker and the female commentary, Horak saying about the films up to and including *Sunless:*

> While rejecting the ever-present but invisible commentators of traditional documentary films, Marker's films are inscribed by the presence of their invisible narrators. However, it is not the 'voice of God' of classical newsreels and documentaries that is heard, *but rather the personal and highly recognisable voice of the author, Chris Marker,* who speaks to his audience directly from offscreen.
>
> (My italics; Horak 1997: 50)

Branigan collapses the differences between 'voices' still further when referring throughout his discussion of *Sunless* to the spoken words of the 'cameraman' [sic], for example:

> During the prologue, the cameraman states that one-day he will juxtapose the image of the three children with black leader at the beginning of a film. ... I would like to suggest that the film *Sunless* is a cautionary tale. The cameraman is aware that in remembering images he has filmed, he may be too late in recognising their significance and emotional value.
>
> (Branigan 1992: 212, 215)

All of these (male) critics prove themselves overly eager to rid *Sunless* of its complexity, favouring the reimposition of the hierarchical structure dominating the majority of voice-over documentaries predicated upon the assumption that the (usually male) commentary is the automatic corollary of the 'author' behind it, and that the images are purely illustrative of that amalgamated point of view. *Sunless* is thus perceived to be 'autobiographical', to contain the 'highly recognisable' voice of Chris Marker, and its narration is interpreted as nothing more than the collected statements of the 'cameraman', although the film itself consistently problematises such notions of centralisation. Branigan's conclusions are particularly crude (and offensive if one considers that a female narrator becomes a camera*man*). In needing to create a locus for the film's meaning, he fabricates a composite persona of the 'cameraman', who, apart from indicating once again that the image is to be prioritised over the words (a dubious contention when considering *Sunless*), even fails to take into account the roles Marker acknowledges for himself when, in the final credits, he claims responsibility for 'conception and editing'.[15] Clearly all these discussions of *Sunless* come from an unerringly *auteur*-ist position, the reductivism of which fails to recognise the effects – on the spectator as well as the text – of the film's deliberate dissipation of point of view.

By means of comparison, one could cite the very different use Marker makes of voice-over and letters in *The Last Bolshevik*. In this later (1993) documentary about the forgotten Russian filmmaker Alexander Medvedkin, who died on the eve of Perestroika in 1989, the narrator (in the English version, Michael Pennington) straightforwardly operates as the verbalisation of Marker's thoughts, the film taking the form of six letters from him to Medvedkin. In the pre-title sequence an exchange between Medvedkin and Marker is documented, the former berating the latter for never writing even a few lines, and the latter replying (via the narrator) 'Dear Alexander Ivanovich, now I will write to you ...'. The voice-over in this instance is readily identified as the 'I' of the film and as the mouthpiece for Chris Marker; conversely, the narration of *Sunless* functions to create rather than collapse critical distance, the essential schism between the gender of the actual voice and that of either the fictional writer of letters (Krasna) or the director (Marker) being a differentiation that is emphasised throughout the film. What characterises the female voice-over is the inconsistency of its reported relationship with Krasna. At times it indicates a disturbing lack of independent thought, as if content to be simply a vehicle for translating pearls of wisdom from the venerable traveller; a feeling that is most pronounced when sentences are prefaced by one of the catalogue of servile utterances such as 'he wrote me ...', 'he told me ...', 'he described to me ...', which lend the female voice-over a Desdemona-esque passivity as the receptacle for the Great Man's tales.[16] There are other moments, however, when the narrator comments upon what she is told, and there are quite protracted passages between the observations initiated by an explicit directive from Krasna during which it becomes unclear whether she is voicing independent thoughts perhaps triggered off by her dialogue with Krasna or whether she is merely continuing with the reading and relaying of the letters.

There is one particularly multi-layered series of sequences which exemplifies the confusions and contortions, beginning with the revisiting of the locations for *Vertigo*. The reverential *Vertigo* sequence ('in San Francisco I made a pilgrimage to a film I've seen 19 times') is the closest *Sunless* gets to being openly personal and autobiographical: an imaginary dialogue between a film-maker and one of his favourite films which in turn leads to the reflexive consideration of 'his' own (as it turns out imaginary) film. With childish obsessiveness, *Sunless* relives *Vertigo,* visiting the San Francisco flower shop where 'James Stewart spies on Kim Novak – he the hunter, she the prey?', following the same city streets down which Scottie trailed Madeleine, 'he' (Krasna?) had followed all the film's trails even to the cemetery at the Mission and the art gallery in which Madeleine contemplates Carlotta Valdes' portrait with its spiralled hair – 'the spiral of time'. This is not just a replica journey but a new, interpretative one, responding to, analysing, reworking Hitchcock's film, perhaps as we are being asked to do whilst watching *Sunless*. As the *Vertigo* sequence draws to a close by referring back to *Sunless* and the shot of the children in Iceland with which Marker's film had opened, the relationship of Marker to the film he has ostensibly created is once more complicated, as the voice-over refers to that first image as the 'first stone of an imaginary film' which 'he' will 'never make' but which nevertheless bears the name 'Sunless'. Thus *Sunless*, the visual and aural material its audience is engaged in watching, is cast into the realm of the imaginary, coming to comprise little more than a tendentious collection of memories and travel footage held loosely together by a voice-over whose origins and authenticity remain obscured to the end.

This obscurity spills over into how the film approaches the issues of representation and recollection, the main underlying questions raised by the image and the voice-over. Throughout *Sunless* there is a running analysis of the interconnection between film and memory, two things which the normative documentary model might prise apart but which here are perceived as equivalents. Memory is personal history, subjective recollection prone to the distortions of 'Chinese whispers', whilst documentary film is conventionally the representation and objective collation of a collective past, a generalised history that can legitimately assume its place within a factual context. *Sunless* works against such a simplistic dichotomy, proposing as analogous the acts of remembering and filming in a sequence where the erosion of the divisions between image, voice-over and letters are particularly pronounced:

> I remember that month of January in Tokyo – or rather I remember the images I filmed in that month of January in Tokyo. They have substituted themselves for my memory – they *are* my memory. I wonder how people remember things who don't film, don't photograph, don't tape? How has mankind managed to remember? I know – the Bible. The new bible will be an eternal magnetic tape of a time that will have to reread itself constantly just to know it existed.

Unlike the classic expository documentary, this rumination does not suggest a finite or definite correspondence between image and narration; whilst the voice-over discusses means of remembering, of how memories are constructed, the images show people praying at temples in Japan for the beginning of the Year of the Dog. In the place of an analysis of these images is an analysis of the event–film relationship that necessarily preoccupies much theorisation of documentary: does memory exist independently of being filmed, or is memory constructed through being recorded? The act of remembering thus becomes synonymous with the act of recording, and although the means by which this is achieved may have changed (hence the cursory reference to the Bible), the equivocal outcome remains consistent. To return to the initial issue of how the voice-over in *Sunless* functions: as some writers seek to clarify the identity of the narrator and her place within the Krasna/Marker/voice-over triangle, so they likewise wish to replace the intellectual elasticity exemplified by the above passage of commentary with a controllable and contained series of gestures and ideas. Edward Branigan begins, rather implausibly, by suggesting that *Sunless* be categorised as a travelogue (which is to impose one kind of 'order' on it), before going onto suggest that the film is 'an instance of postmodernism rather than travelogue', and so constructing another 'logic' by which it can become manageable (Branigan 1992: 207–8). Whilst this search for coherence is understandable, it seems more appropriate with a film such as *Sunless* to take it on its own terms, to accept that there are three sources for the narration, and that the relationship between them remains oblique. This discordance is more interesting than striving to 'discover' in the film a unity of purpose; take the mention of Sei Shonagon's lists. In *The Pillow Book* Sei Shonagon, as the narrator of *Sunless* states, notes down things that, in her everyday life, attract, displease and fascinate her, in no particular order and with no particular end in sight. One of the categories cited by the *Sunless* narrator is that of 'Things which quicken the heart', which in *The Pillow Book* are as follows:

> Sparrows feeding their young. To pass a place where babies are playing. To sleep in a room where some fine incense has been burnt. To notice that one's elegant Chinese mirror has become a little cloudy. To see a gentleman stop his carriage before one's gate and instruct his attendants to announce his arrival. To wash one's hair, make one's toilet, and put on scented robes; even if not a soul sees one, these preparations still produce an inner pleasure.
>
> It is night and one is expecting a visitor. Suddenly one is startled by the sound of rain-drops, which the wind blows against the shutters.
>
> (Sei Shonagon 1971: 51)

This list of 'Things that quicken the heart' is personal, idiosyncratic and, one suspects, ephemeral in that, on another day, Sei Shonagon might have compiled a totally different list. This is not a definitive list of 'things that quicken the heart' nor one that will necessarily be recognisable to those who read it; instead, what the list makes one do is to think, however fleetingly, of what would be in one's own list of 'things that quicken the heart'. *Sunless* works in a not dissimilar way on its audience: it offers up images that fluctuate between the domains of the personal or the mundane (the essence as well of *The Pillow Book*) and the historical or generally recognisable (the essence of the classic documentary), which are in turn juxtaposed against a transgressive and ambiguous voice-over that only sporadically coincides with them. The film's dominant thesis becomes: beyond the moment, beyond the collision of image and sound in front of one at any one time, there is no grander meaning, tomorrow's list of 'things that quicken the heart' is not constrained by today's, one image or piece of voiceover is not conditioned by that which preceded it.

Whereas traditional voice-over documentaries are about closure, *Sunless* remains intentionally open, and within this openness the female narration (in its distance from both Marker and Krasna) provides a space for the interpretations of the 'data' or 'files' to take place, files which are usually linked by a random association rather than causality. Likewise the narrator/Marker/Krasna triangle. It is not sufficient to identify the female voice as being Marker's or the 'cameraman's' (Rafferty, draws a parallel between 'the unseen protagonist of *Sunless* [and] the man with the movie camera' (Rafferty 1984: 286)), for this fails to assist the act of watching *Sunless* or aid us in our understanding of its lack of narrative or closure and its emphasis on the mundane, the inconsequential and the ephemeral. Instead, the film is inviting us to enjoy its randomness, and in this it is playing with the notion of what constitutes a documentary. As Marker (1984: 197) has noted, 'the word "documentary" leaves a trail of sanctimonious boredom behind it. But the idea of making files ... suits me well'. It is pertinent that Marker usually works within more conventional forms of documentary, and that all his films (whether the more overtly political ones or the more personal and subjective ones)[17] then go on to participate in a dialogue about the nature of filmmaking rather than blithely accept the harsh parameters and make do. *Sunless* can only be made to conform to the traditional expository model it nominally belongs to if, as has been attempted, one unproblematically correlates the voice-over with Marker; then, quite conventionally, the images and the narration in the film would explicate and consolidate each other. By not definitively establishing mutuality, however, Marker refuses to clarify or classify the film, as the voice-over (if it is not Marker's 'voice') is a fictional construct within a documentary framework.

Conclusion

Sunless raises several problems and questions about narration in documentary and the way it has been interpreted. It is not possible to say about Marker's film that, 'The authoring presence of the filmmaker is represented by the commentary and sometimes the (usually unseen) voice of authority will be that of the filmmaker him- or herself' (Nichols 1991: 37). Even in *The Battle of San Pietro* (which Nichols cites as an example of the actual voice of the narrator being that of the filmmaker and thus a direct verbalisation of Huston's point of view) is not so easily compartmentalised, as the narrator's words do not consistently coincide with what one infers to be Huston's opinions and feelings. The voice-over in *The Battle of San Pietro* literally disintegrates, disappears at times and signals more clearly the collapse of this presumed symbiosis between voice and argument. The false opposition set up by most theoretical discussions is between the 'raw' visual material (which, if it could be left unadulterated, would provide us with a 'truer' representation of the events being recorded) and the forces of subjectivity such as the voice-over that endlessly thwart its objective nobility. Thus, narration (endlessly subsumed into the far more specific category of the 'voice of God') has come to signify documentaries at their most distortive and fictionalising because of the connotations of individualism, instruction and so on that the actual presence of a *voice* conjures up. Many voice-over documentaries, however, do not conform to the 'voice of God' model, and yet their diversity has been underplayed. Films such as *The Battle of San Pietro* or *Sunless* engender in their audiences doubt about the hierarchical binary oppositions that dominate thinking about documentary: that to show is more real than to tell, that the image contains a truth that a narration actively interferes with, that any subjective presence destroys the possibility of objectivity completely. By the time we get to *Sunless* and its multiple confusions of 'voices' the standard theories become untenable. Brian Winston notes that breaking norms can in itself be 'positioned as a deliberate blow against hegemonic practice. For instance, it can be argued that *A propos de Nice* and *Land Without Bread* depart from the norms exactly to critique them' (Winston 1995: 86); one could extend this and suggest that not only are such films critiquing the norms but they are permitting a concomitant diversity of reaction and thought from their audiences. For the films that adopt the non-'voice of God' narration model, the actual documentary comes out of an acknowledgement, refinement and rejection of how commentary and its supposedly inherent didacticism is conventionally perceived. In addition to this, narration becomes a dialectical tool; even when it is most conventionally used as in *The World at War* or *The Times of Harvey Milk,* the limitations of the voice-over do not preclude the possibility of an alternative interpretation being left open and accessible to the audience. Once again, therefore, documentary becomes a negotiation between the film and its subject, of which the narration is a constituent part. Voice-over does not signal the obliteration of the 'purity' of the factual image, although it may offer an alternative and even contradictory view of it.

Part II

The legacy of direct cinema

In the Introduction to this book, American documentary filmmaker Errol Morris was quoted as saying that '*cinéma vérité* set back documentary filmmaking twenty or thirty years' (quoted in Arthur 1993: 127). Morris is here referring to direct cinema, popularly but erroneously known by its French name. Direct cinema is often viewed as the single most significant intervention into documentary filmmaking history, so what is wrong with it? Morris takes issue with various direct cinema beliefs: that American *cinéma vérité* filmmakers (such as Richard Leacock and Donn Pennebaker) approached documentary filmmaking as a means of recording events; that they attempted to deny and absent their own personal perspective; that, through their observational methods, these filmmakers could get to the truth in a way that other forms of documentary filmmaking could not. Similarly, Emile de Antonio, whose polemical, personal films also directly challenged direct cinema's belief in observation, commented

> *Cinéma vérité* is first of all a lie, and secondly a childish assumption about the nature of film. *Cinéma vérité* is a joke. Only people without feelings or convictions could even think of making *cinéma vérité*. I happen to have strong feelings and some dreams and my prejudice is under and in everything I do.
>
> (Rosenthal 1978: 7)

What is wrong with direct cinema is essentially what its exponents said about what the films did, not necessarily what the films themselves achieved. De Antonio's prime target here is the belief of American *cinéma vérité* that any film could or should be objective. Because Robert Drew and those who followed him were fond of recounting what their films were about and how they should be interpreted, theorists and practitioners alike have tackled direct cinema in accordance with how it has defined itself. This has remained the crucial problem and the reason for the observational form – ostensibly so liberating – setting back documentary for twenty or thirty years.

The observational mode, despite the vigorous arguments mounted against it, remains extremely influential, for it freed both the style and content of documentary. The films of Drew, Leacock, Pennebaker, the Maysles brothers and Wiseman focused on the individual, the everyday, the contemporary; they attempted to keep authorial intervention to a minimum by adopting a more casual, observational style that had as its premise the desire to follow action rather than dictate it, to see and record what happened to evolve in front of the cameras. Of course, these aims, as Morris and de Antonio point out, were unrealistic, but nevertheless, an understanding of direct cinema is seminal to any study of documentary. This section of *New Documentary* will not rehash the same old discussions of the 1960s pioneers but will instead look at the important influence that American observational documentary has had on more modern work; in this Introduction I will tackle specifically the issue of why direct cinema's legacy has proved so problematic to the evolution of documentary practice and theory alike. Most practitioners recognise, by now, that documentary film can never offer a representation of real events indistinguishable from the events themselves, although theory has not yet come to terms with the value of such a realisation.

The resigned and stale understanding of documentary film and its history stems largely from two factors (and consequently from their intersection). The theoretical problem – discussed earlier – is that documentary history has too easily been circumscribed and confined by the imposition of a 'family tree' structure, an understanding of its evolution that assumes that one style of filmmaking begets and is rendered obsolete by the mode that replaces it. The practical problem posed by documentary – which will be examined here – relates directly to the practice and critical evaluation of direct cinema. Direct cinema is a 'problem' because its exponents believed (although not all – and one of the failings of documentary theory has been to sideline the dissenting or questioning voices of Fred Wiseman, for example, or at times David and Albert Maysles) that, with the advent of portable equipment and with the movement's more informal style, they could indeed show things as they are and thus collapse, better than any other form of documentary, the boundary between subject and representation. This is the established and conventionalised mission of observational documentary: to offer a real possibility of showing events and people in as unadulterated a state as possible. It seems inconceivable that a current documentary filmmaker would utter naïvely, as Richard Leacock did about his relationship with John Kennedy during the making of *Primary,* that the then presidential candidate forgot at times that he was even being filmed. Cameras were not that small and Kennedy was an astute politician. The direct cinema 'problem' is that most of its great American exponents stood by the authenticity of their filming methods and the end results they achieved, and by and large the copious theoretical discussions of these films have sought merely to dismantle, dismiss and reject this truth claim by scavenging for sequences, edits and shots that contradict the direct cinema mantra. *Vérité* is a sticking place because it successfully 'proves' two mutually exclusive things: that documentary's driving ambition is to find a way of reproducing reality without bias or manipulation, and that such a pursuit towards unadulterated actuality is futile.

Practitioners and theorists alike have assumed that direct cinema's ethos is objectivity, and that, in turn, 'objectivity' and 'observation' are synonymous.

This elision has proved highly detrimental to the conventionalised perception of direct cinema. Bill Nichols comments of observational documentary that it 'appears to leave the driving to us' (Nichols 1983: 52), that the filmmakers' paramount desire is to absent themselves (and, by this, Nichols and they mean their subjective influence) from the filmmaking process and the resulting films, so that 'in pure *cinéma vérité* films, the style seeks to become "transparent" in the same mode as the classical Hollywood style' (Nichols 1983: 49). For Nichols and others the observational style is problematic because it implies the filmmakers' loss of voice, thereby insinuating that 'pure' observation comes at the expense of commitment, interventionism and authorship. This is an inadequate conflation, and to question Nichols' strident pronouncements one can pluck any number of examples from the observational 'canon'. To suggest that the voice of Drew Associates is absent from *Crisis* is to downplay the socio-political potential of the observational style, which in this instance clearly suggests a preference for Robert Kennedy over George Wallace.[1] It is the critical possibilities of the observational mode that have been historically downplayed, but which have been taken up in the modern era.

The disparity between the observational ideal and much observational directing practice hinges on the troublesome notion of 'purity', evoked by Nichols and others in relation to observational documentary. Brian Winston, when talking about Roger Graef's work in the 1970s, says that he 'uses the *purest* of direct cinema modes. However complex the topic, he eschews interviews and narration. In the hands of his long-time collaborator and cinematographer Charles Stewart, the style of these films is *minimally interventionist*' (Winston 1995: 208; my italics). What is clearly being held up for approval here is the grail of pure documentation, a piece of 'pure' observation being thought of as necessarily superior to and 'better' at doing what it has set out to do (that is, represent a series of non-fictional events) than its more mendacious cousins deploying such 'false' mechanisms as voice-over, interview and the actual presence of the filmmaker. Not only are observation and objectivity being wrongly conflated, but also assumptions are being made about style and the use of technology. The technological innovations that paved the way for direct cinema in America and *cinéma vérité* in France in the early 1960s – lightweight cameras, portable sound equipment, stock that could be used in lower light conditions – led to a less formal, more responsive style of filmmaking and a concomitant adherence to an ideological belief in the possibility of accurate representation. One critic who immediately subsumes all these different elements into one is Stephen Mamber when arguing

> At its very simplest, *cinéma-vérité* can be described as a method of filming employing hand-held camera and live, synchronous sound. This is a base description, however, for *cinéma-vérité* should imply a way of looking at the world as much as a means of recording. ... The essential element of *cinéma-vérité* ... is the use of real people in undirected situations.
>
> (Mamber 1972a: 79)

Technology, style and attitude become one.

In examining the zealous pronouncements of the 1960s observational film-makers themselves, it becomes instantly apparent how this misjudgement occurred, for it was they who cemented the view that the belief in purity and objectivity was sustainable. There is a certain evangelical quality about many of the comments, such as Al Maysles' statement 'I regard our films as the purest form of cinema' or his brother David's belief that 'we don't impose anything on the people we film. We are the servants of our subjects rather than the other way round' (Kolker 1971: 185). Absent entirely from this description of their methods is any fundamental acknowledgement of the filmmaking process itself being the intervention that invariably makes all the difference, and this is how American *cinéma vérité* has been accepted and defined: as naïve, simplistic and misguidedly idealistic. But as a result of such fervent utterances – to which one could add many others such as Robert Drew's assertion that 'the film maker's personality is in no way directly involved in directing the action' (quoted in Winston 1993: 43) – this perception of direct cinema has stuck.

Why this poses such a problem is that 'purity' in this context is unobtainable, there are always too many other issues spoiling the communion between subject and viewer across a transparent screen, and so the majority of the criticism levelled at *vérité* in America has focused on moments which show the films to have failed in their messianic endeavour. The films are easy targets in this respect, precisely because of the impossibility of their designated aims. Having eschewed the ostensibly authoritarian devices of previous documentary modes (narration, archive, thesis-led structures) observational documentary rather rashly proclaimed itself not to need any methods beyond observation (a definitively passive activity), and this included authorial intervention. By a process of osmosis, it seemed, the subject matter was to be conveyed to the audience. As Noël Carroll (1996a: 225) suggests, no sooner had 'the cinema of truth' arrived as an idea, 'than critics and viewers turned the polemics of direct cinema against direct cinema': Carroll perhaps fails to go far enough with this assertion, because it is the very quality of the *vérité* statement of intent, its alleged purity, that provokes critics and viewers to turn against it. As Carroll continues, 'Direct cinema opened a can of worms and then got eaten by them' (p. 225).

Comparing the statements by the Maysles brothers and one of their films (*Salesman*, 1969) illustrates the discrepancy between execution and ideal. The film is guilty of several violations of direct cinema's code: it uses non-diegetic music on two occasions; it edits (for effect) sequences out of chronological order; it is highly selective in what and who it chooses to focus upon. These are all elements that, to some degree, are the impositions of the filmmakers; they are tools of interpretation. Such manifestations of a subjective presence are only problematic because of the way in which direct cinema defined its own aims, to many other documentary filmmakers the cutting together, for example, of two sequences temporally separate but thematically related (as occurs in the juxtaposition of Paul, the focal salesman, travelling by train and the bible selling convention he participates in) would not be an issue. The Maysles in interview have felt compelled to dismiss or qualify this sequence as uncharacteristic, as 'dictated' by content. As a technique, such parallel editing makes them both 'a little nervous' (Levin 1971: 278); later in this interview they stipulate that the purpose of observational film editing was merely to compress material, not to manipulate it. There are other instances of 'impurity' in *Salesman:* the superimposition of the Beatles' *Yesterday* over the conclusion of another unsuccessful selling attempt by Paul; the ironic use of the similarly extra-diegetic *If I Was a Rich Man* overlaid onto a sequence of Paul driving from one failed sale to another. Perhaps the Maysles' justification for these impositions would be that both tracks initially had a diegetic source – a gramophone in the first instance, a car radio in the second. One of the more troubling examples of manipulation in *Salesman,* because it suggests more than a deployment of supportive narrative methods, is the very end of the film. The Maysles brothers have referred to their decision to prolong the final shot of Paul looking, apparently despairingly, out of a hotel window, calling this, rather coyly, a 'fictionalisation' (Levin 1971: 276), but they have not explained the whole manner in which this final sequence is edited. One of the things the sequence strongly evokes is the growing alienation of Paul, a markedly less successful bible salesman than his colleagues, culminating in the final shot. *Salesman* concludes with an end of the day discussion between the salesmen the film has been following, cutting between what seem to be two sides of the same room. What the viewer does not expect, however, is that the sequence comprises material from two different sources: a hotel room from much earlier in the film (offcuts from sequences already seen) and a hotel room from later on, after the salesmen have reached Florida. This falsification potentially alters the sequence's whole meaning. Because of where it is presumed to come in the overall sequence of events, Paul's vacant gaze out of the window conveys resignation, defeat, despair and the imminent loss of his job. When, however, it is realised that this shot comes from earlier in the film – from before Paul's plight was fully realised – it begins to take on alternative and less bleak meanings: Paul might just have been getting hungry waiting for the other three to get ready. The Maysles brothers have simply applied the most basic of Lev Kuleshov's discoveries: that what matters above all else is that a sequence of shots *appears* to be logical, not necessarily that it *is;* the issue is whether or not this is appropriate to a piece of direct cinema, to which the answer has to be no.

No, that is, until one comes across statements by direct cinema filmmakers that contradict (or at least admit the shortcomings of) the ideal of the pure image. In another interview from the one quoted above, Albert Maysles says something quite different about the nature of the truth observational documentary can discover:

> We can see two types of truth here. One is the raw material, which is the footage, the kind of truth that you get in literature in the diary form – it's immediate, no one has tampered with it. Then there's the other kind of truth that comes in extracting and juxtaposing the raw material into a more

meaningful and coherent storytelling form, which finally can be said to be more than just raw data.

(Levin 1971: 277)

Here, Albert Maysles is admitting the difference between rushes and a film when he draws a distinction between the truth of the 'raw data' and that of the finished, edited product. In creating the final sequence of *Salesman* out of disparate images and unchronological bits of film, the Maysles brothers are thus constructing the underlying truth of the film: that Paul is not just the narrative core of the film, but its emotional core as well; a tragic, failed figure with whom the filmmakers and the audience alike sympathise and empathise. The end of *Salesman* is a subjective manipulation of events to suggest a character and story that the Maysles brothers, presumably, felt was implicit in the material they had acquired. This, however, is a far cry from the professed ideals of direct cinema, and highlights the issues underlying the 'problem' of purist observational film. With virtually every step, *Salesman* (like many of its contemporaries) denies the validity of the notion of filming 'undirected situations'; besides the anomalies cited above, there are other instances which suggest that sequences were more than likely set up (shots of subjects just happening to enter hotel rooms whilst the camera's running; one bible selling sequence in which a neighbour enters and fails to look in any way surprised at the presence of the Maysles brothers at their friends' dining table).

The key issue is that observational cinema has been mis-defined, and has misdefined itself. Any documentary, including observational ones, testifies to the absence rather than the presence of purity at its heart. Having presented itself as the mode most capable of collapsing the difference between image and reality, of best representing an unadulterated truth, direct cinema suffers particularly harshly from such a realisation. If one strips the films of the theoretical baggage they come burdened down by, they offer less stifling, more exciting possibilities. *Salesman* and *Meet Marlon Brando*, or the political films *Primary* and *Crisis* (discussed in Chapter 5), show the notion of documentary purity to be deeply flawed, but this is not what makes them significant and interesting. Rather, it is the suggestion that the dynamism of the documentary text is predicated upon and created by the central dialectical relationship between content or unadulterated truth and representation, not destroyed by it.

The core of direct cinema films is the encounter before the camera, the moment when the filmmaking process disrupts and intrudes upon the reality of the world it is documenting. This neither invalidates it as a means of recording and conveying that reality, nor does it mean that documentary is simply an elaborate fiction. In the case of Paul Brennan, *Salesman* suggests that his portrayal is founded on the truth that he was a struggling bible salesman before the filming began. He is also created afresh during filming with the Maysles brothers; particularly in sequences in which he is flagrantly playing to the camera (singing in the car and talking directly to camera, delivering a monologue in his wavering Irish brogue), Paul is quintessentially offering a performance of himself in a comparable manner to Brando in *Meet Marlon Brando*. The final composite 'Paul', whom the film evokes and the audience identifies with, amalgamates both these facets: the shown and the implied. In both the contemporary forms of observational documentary to be discussed here, the same juxtaposition is paramount.

Docusoaps and other recent evolutions in televisual observational documentary indicate that the puritanism of early direct cinema has been replaced by more realistic expectations that permit the correlation within one film of observational practice and more obtrusive filmic elements. Likewise, the journey film is entirely the result of capturing an encounter – capturing, therefore, the collision between the off-screen, establishing truth that was there before the cameras turned up, and the truth that emerges from the dialogue that intrusion elicits. In journey documentaries (the subject of Chapter 3) the search for a subject is prioritised over any straightforward conclusion, and the films concomitantly emphasise that a documentary and its thesis can only evolve at the point of filmmaking and that the encounter is the most tenable reality a film offers. This premise, ironically, has its origins in American *cinéma vérité*, in statements such as Albert Maysles' 'I've always been interested to see what happens when two strangers meet' (Levin 1971: 282). The difference between Albert Maysles' perception of the accidental encounter and that enacted in more recent documentaries is that the significance for Maysles lies in the new-found ability to observe the meeting between strangers in as discreet a way as possible; to filmmakers such as Apted, Lanzmann and McElwee the accidental encounter directly involves them and is much more overtly reminiscent of the interactive strain of *cinéma, vérité* found in the films of Jean Rouch. The origins of journey films, docusoaps and reality television, however, lie in the work of early observational documentary: the overriding interest in people as subjects over theses; the prioritisation of the mundane occurrence over the monumental event; a predilection for following subjects and actions as opposed to leading and constructing them.

Much of the remainder of this book will, from a variety of angles, examine the legacy of direct cinema and the manner in which subsequent filmmakers have largely ignored the pronouncements of the observational filmmakers themselves in favour of engaging with and developing the techniques they pioneered. The chapters immediately following this Introduction will focus on two documentary forms (the journey documentary and modern observational television, culminating in reality television and the closely related formatted documentaries) that inherently display the impossibility of collapsing the boundary between the event and its representation. Both sub-genres or modes emphasise the moment of encounter between filmmakers and subjects around which a documentary is constructed and which no documentary can totally mask, whether this is Jane McDonald in *The Cruise* beckoning Chris Terrill and his camera or Claude Lanzmann pressing a Holocaust survivor to speak about the past. Both forms thereby realise and illustrate the deficiencies of how direct cinema defined itself, questioning the foundations of observational cinema whilst still indicating and incorporating its practical strengths – namely, that, unlike more historical or thesis-driven forms of documentary, it can capture unpremeditated, surprising and potentially destabilising moments on camera. Unlike their direct cinema prede-cessors, however, the filmmakers and factual genres to be discussed in the follow-ing chapters understand these accidental moments as having been made by, rather than being independent from the filmmakers' intrusion into the subjects' world; that the important truth any documentary captures is the performance in front of the camera.

3   Documentary journeys

The influence of direct cinema has been widespread. The next chapter will discuss the problems of this legacy largely with reference to popular television documentary, whereas the journey documentaries to be examined here (primarily from cinema but also from television), signal the influence of direct cinema upon more intellectual documentary filmmaking. Of particular narrative significance to the documentaries I have bracketed together here as 'journey films' is the notion of a journey based on encounters – most frequently between filmmaker and subjects, but also between different subjects and also (more obliquely) between the spectator and film. The encounter (and more particularly the chance encounter) was central to the *cinéma verité* and direct cinema traditions, and continues to be a significant factor of many observational documentaries. The majority of the journeys around which the following documentaries are structured are unplanned, and the notion of taking a chance, of seeing where an unpremeditated journey will lead is central to all. What these otherwise eclectic documentaries also have in common is reflexivity: they all adopt, to differing extents, the journey as a means of probing the nature of documentary, the documentary subject and nonfictional representation, an engagement with the essence of representation that direct cinema in particular lacked.

Journey films are structured around encounters and meetings that are often accidental or unplanned; a corollary of this is that a preoccupation with an end point rarely predominates. These characteristics recall direct cinema's interest in the moment when people meet and change; they also very clearly recall direct cinema's French counterpart, *cinéma vérité,* exemplified by Jean Rouch and Edgar Morin's *Chronique d'un été* (*Chronicle of a Summer*) which opens with the filmmakers (who, like several later observational filmmakers, trained as anthropologists)[1] discussing embarking upon a film study of happiness, followed by two women collaborators going out onto the streets of Paris to collate material for the film, Nagra and microphone in hand. The essential difference between this *cinéma vérité* approach and that of Robert Drew and his followers is the ostentatious forefronting of the filmmaking process; the crew of *Chronique d'un été* do not hide behind the supposed transparency of film, they do not remain anonymous *auteurs*. Many journey documentaries borrow from both observational traditions: the close attention to detail and personality of direct cinema and the focus upon the moment of encounter with the filmmaker of *cinéma vérité*. The narrative device of the journey is variously interpreted here as: the journey of making a film or series of films over a number of years (*Seven Up* and its sequels and *Hoop Dreams*), an examination of historical events that takes the form of an actual journey undertaken by the filmmaker (*Hotel Terminus, Shoah*) and a physical journey across terrain (as in *Sherman's March* and Patrick Keiller's *London*).

Direct cinema was founded upon an uncomfortable paradox, that whilst the films were putatively concerned with the unpredictable action not dictated by the filmmakers, they also desired and sought ways of imposing closure on their ostensibly undetermined action. Nichols and others have thereby drawn parallels between direct cinema documentaries and the classical Hollywood style, intimating that both modes of filmmaking emphasise transparency (the disguise of the cinematic apparatus); it could be added that both modes also demonstrate a desire for certainty or the desire for narrative closure. Robert Drew's quest for subjects with an in-built 'crisis structure' (a series of events that are predestined to follow a logical, closed path) or the imposition of a clear ending onto *Salesman,* for example, are illustrative of direct cinema's tendency to give coherence and logic to the potentially incoherent and illogical material observational films could easily unearth. The journey documentaries examined here challenge these notions of certainty, predictability and transparency by enacting the very uncertainty that dictates documentary production because, by taking the form of actual journeys, the films demonstrate how the foundation for any documentary is chance or the notion of not knowing what, during the course of making a film, the filmmakers are going to discover.

The term 'journey', applied to documentary, is either a very concrete term or a deeply nebulous one. In the chapter in *Claiming the Real* entitled 'Chronologic' Brian Winston argues that 'journey films solved actuality's big narrative problem – closure. How should films finish? Obviously, a journey film ends with the end of the journey' (Winston 1995: 104). Winston links journeys exclusively to time, observing that the journey through time has commonly been used as a means of creating logic ('chrono-logic') out of potentially shambolic or unrelated events; thus he categorises city films such as *Berlin: Symphony of a City* and *Man with a Movie Camera,* as journeys because they construct a narrative around the passage of time, usually the passing of a single day. This 'became documentary's preferred way of capturing the urban experience' (Winston 1995: 104), a means of making potentially incoherent images and events cohere within the panoply of the 'city film'. Winston then similarly ascribes 'chrono-logic' to non-city documentaries such as Jennings' *Listen to Britain* whose 'strongly inscribed diurnal pattern' Winston posits compensates for the film's otherwise weak narrative (Winston 1995: 105). There are various types of documentaries that do, though, feature literal journeys, the most obvious example being the travelogue, the documentary equivalent of the road movie. Contemporary television still possesses an interest in the documentary as exploration: great train journeys, travel shows, individuals – usually a celebrity – going in search of a place or a person or even an idea, following a trail or arriving at a special destination. Series such as Michael Palin's *Around the World in 80 Days* or his homage to Hemingway are simply structured around a journey focusing on Palin's actual travels in pursuit of a particular experience and a specified knowledge. Winston's point is essentially that documentary journeys are about passing through and ordering time, that journeys give coherence to an otherwise fragmentary series of events and images. Journeys, therefore, impose logic. The travel film, however, contradicts this: it is more of an actual journey, a journey through time and space, but it is also fundamentally not structured around an argument or indeed around a desire to impose narrative cohesion; it is simply a chronicle of events linked by location, personality or theme.

The quest, whether or not it is related to an actual journey, is a pervasive documentary impulse; the dilemma, though, has been how to give structure to that dangerously unstructured instinct. The twin impulse, amongst theorists in particular, has been to push random events into a narrative, a structure, a logical form. What is intriguing about films otherwise as different as *Shoah* and *London* is that, like the sequential but not necessarily developmental travelogue, they share a distrust of predetermined logic: they pursue narratives that are only superficially closed by their concluding images and words and are more preoccupied with charting moments of encounter and examining the act of journeying than of reaching a fixed destination. Winston, however, focuses on the enthusiasm for completeness and linearity – as if the very act of embarking upon a journey is determined by its end – and quotes Roland Barthes on 'Completeness'. Barthes, under the subheading 'To depart/to travel/to stay', states that completeness is the 'basic requirement of the readerly', later adding that a narrative without its requisite constituent parts (a departure and an arrival) 'would be a scandal' (Barthes 1973: 105). Is Barthes maintaining that only completeness can make the process of reading (or watching) pleasurable? Barthes' implied answer in the affirmative is not unlike Hayden White's assumption that history, in order to be meaningful, must be cogent and complete. In making a distinction between history and more rudimentary information-structuring forms such as annals and chronicles, White presumes that narrative is needed not only to give the events structure beyond the chronological (that is, to transform them into history), but to give them meaning, which 'they do not possess as mere sequence' (White 1987: 5). In White's estimation, the annals and the chronicle are merely components of a sophisticated history, insufficient in themselves. As proof of this, he lists the entries into the *Annals of Saint Gall* for the years 709–34, in which many years are left blank (years in which, one is left to deduce, nothing happened) and which appear to give equal weight to quite disparate events: in 722 'Great crops' is entered; in 731 'Blessed Bede, the presbyter, died' (White H. 1987: 6–7).

Such recording methods exasperate White because there is no causal logic and no hierarchy or prioritisation of information; accordingly, the 'importance' of the events recorded 'consists in nothing other than their having been recorded' (p. 7). Such non-narrative forms abound in documentary journey films. Many journey films – like a chronicle – are structured around what Edward Branigan (1992: 20) would term a 'focused chain':

> a series of cause and effects with a continuing centre. For example, the continuing adventures of a character, the events surrounding an object or place, or the elaboration of a theme.

Unlike more random categories such as the 'heap' or the 'unfocused chain', the 'focused chain' possesses an internal logic and cogency, whilst still failing to abide by the causal regularity of the conventional narrative in which the sequence of events is all-important and in which 'the ending situation can be traced back to the beginning' (p. 20).

Although much documentary practice and theory demonstrates this overriding need for total narrative cohesion, many journey films, ironically, do not. The city films cited by Winston possess a central location – the city – and frequently abide by a diurnal structure. The action therein contained, however, is almost invariably non-narrative; in both Dziga Vertov's *Man With a Movie Camera* or Alberto Cavalcanti's *Rien que les heures,* image association and not causal logic often determines the order of shots (Vertov's juxtaposition of eye lids closing and window shutters, Cavalcanti's compilation of kisses). Likewise the travelogue has a beginning and an end, but there is little sense that its participants have progressed in anything other than a physical way. Many documentaries are effectively chronicles or chains; it is not the case, therefore, that all potentially open documentaries seek to impose a narrative that will render them retrievable and comprehensible. An increasingly common observational documentary form developed through the 1990s was the diary form, exemplified by *Video Diaries.* The video diary, confessional or the compulsion to confide in a portable camera is now a mainstay of much documentary and a means of permitting the documentary subject to reflect upon the unfamiliar journey they are undertaking: it was there subliminally in docusoaps (Maureen getting agitated in the middle of the night about her looming theory exam) and it features in nearly every reality television series and formatted documentary (the room in *Big Brother* where contestants go to have a 'confidential' chat with 'Big Brother' and several million viewers, the end of the day video asides by family members in series from *The 1900 House* to *Wife Swap*). Diaries are journeys in the broadest sense of the term; they chart a progression through time of an individual to whom something happens or is happening and which, in turn, gives the diary a focal point beyond the details of daily existence. This rudimentary linking of the personal and the larger historical, political or formal considerations of the documentaries has become a pervasive documentary motif and journey films such as *Hoop Dreams* and *Seven Up* are essentially diaries.

Bill Nichols suggests that there has been a pervasive shift in our understanding of the very word 'documentary':

> Traditionally, the word *documentary* has suggested fullness, and completion, knowledge and fact, explanations of the social world and its motivating

mechanisms. More recently, though, documentary has come to suggest incompleteness and uncertainty, recollection and impression, images of personal worlds and their subjective construction.

(Nichols 1994: 1)

Nichols here is entirely correct to suggest that documentary no longer needs to seek out ways of controlling its own unpredictable elements and that, on the contrary, non-fiction films are now more likely to be constructed around such instabilities as memory, subjectivity and uncertainty. The journey film is indicative of this trend, taking the traditional documentary concerns of enquiry (itself a type of journey), travel and historical search to create a loose sub-genre of the observational mode, borrowing from direct cinema the key notion that a documentary and its thesis is dictated by events as they unfold in the present and in front of the camera.

The action the films represent is the result of a dynamic, dialectical relationship between fact, filmmaker and apparatus. In Patrick Keiller's *London* (as in *Robinson in Space*) the dialectics are somewhat ironic and take the form of an intellectual game (the films' narrator is omnipresent as a voice but is never seen, the purpose of his journey – Robinson's 'pilgrimage to the sources of English Romanticism' – constantly being forgotten in favour of the journeys he actually undertakes, nothing is a 'chance' encounter as the films are intricately scripted). Conversely, in the other films the encounters and their consequences are genuine, spontaneous and the resulting journeys open and unpredictable. However, even journeys as diverse as Lanzmann's in *Shoah* or the Narrator's in *London* are built on paradoxical foundations: on the one hand they are responsive journeys, Lanzmann or the Narrator being surprised and diverted by who and what information they meet; on the other, however, they both conform to a preconceived plan of what the journeys are setting out to discover. Perhaps this is a generic characteristic of journey documentaries, as all the films under discussion here contain both a sense of a grand narrative they are intent upon pursuing and a realisation that this narrative's specific conclusion cannot, at the outset of filming, be known. Lanzmann in *Shoah* and Ophuls in *Hotel Terminus* both set out, for example, to piece together an already established historical truth (the Holocaust; the guilt of Klaus Barbie, the 'butcher of Lyon'), while both *Seven Up* and *Hoop Dreams* are explorations of social truisms (that an individual's future is determined by their social origins or that sporting success offers African–American boys a route into college and away from social disadvantage). More elliptically, both *London* and *Sherman's March* set out on one pre-selected journey in order to actually undertake another more spontaneous one.

Making documentaries over time: *Seven Up; Hoop Dreams*

Formally and ideologically *Seven Up* (1964) and *Hoop Dreams* (1994) are similar. Most importantly, they are filmed over extended periods of time, although both were initially intended to be shorter. *Seven Up* only retrospectively became a series; the first programme selected and interviewed fourteen children from diverse social backgrounds (Neil, Peter, Nick, Sue, Lynn, Jackie, Tony, Simon, Paul, Bruce, Andrew, Charles, John and Suzy) and was intended only as a one-off documentary for Granada's current affairs strand *World in Action*. Subsequently, Michael Apted (the researcher on the original film and the one who, hastily, found and selected the children) has returned every seven years to interview them again (bar Peter and Charles, who have pulled out), charting their progress through to *49 Up* in 2005. *Hoop Dreams* also became a longer project once filming had begun. The final three-hour version took five years to shoot and two and a half to edit. Both *Seven Up* and *Hoop Dreams* also function as social documents, detailing specific aspects of the English and American class and racial systems respectively and although neither is an overtly political docu-mentary, both share an interest in the personal impact of politics and political issues. *Seven Up* articulates this explicitly as wanting to test the Jesuit maxim 'Give me a child until he is seven and I will give you the man' – the notion that an individual's future is shaped by the environment into which s/he is born; *Hoop Dreams*, with its focus on two black teenagers' bids to become professional basketball players, has similar sociological and political reference points.

They are also both open journeys in that their starting point is the selection of individuals whose lives the filmmakers are intent on following without knowing in detail where these individual stories will take them. In both there are surprises and both have aroused intense and extended public interest (*Seven Up* has diver-sified and has been produced in several countries outside the United Kingdom, including the United States and Russia; *Hoop Dreams* is still the subject of various websites and blogs). Another more recent documentary that superficially at least uses the same format is *Spellbound*, another (like *Hoop Dreams*) cinema-release documentary about the American national spelling bee competition; the essential difference; however, is that the interviews in *Spellbound* were allegedly conducted retrospectively. Because of their openness, *Seven Up* and *Hoop Dreams* are poised between certainty (surety of intention and motivation) and uncertainty (the unpredictability inevitably caused by the individual subjects), and the trajectory and conclusion of both of them is the result of a combination of imposed formal structure and unexpected changes in direction.

That these documentaries are filmed over time and are largely observational, places them readily within the tradition of American *cinéma vérité*, alongside the documentaries of Fred Wiseman, for instance. As Joe Moran suggests, *Seven Up* was another product of the technological changes that led to Direct Cinema, French *cinema vérité* and British Free Cinema at the end of the 1950s: the intro-duction of lightweight 16mm cameras, portable sound equipment and the increasing speed of films that facilitated filming using natural light (Moran, J. 2002: 389). Quintessentially, *Seven Up* and *Hoop Dreams* abide by the notion of documentary filmmaking as following action and argument rather than prompt-ing or creating them. As with many early Direct Cinema documentaries, the pleasure of the journeys they undertake derives from observing people change over time, getting to know them, observing their growing familiarity with the filmmakers, predicting the future and frequently having those predictions overturned.

Although early exponents of Direct Cinema such as Robert Drew and Richard Leacock (Wiseman, though related to this group, always stood apart from them) preferred and sought finality and closure, documentary history since the 1960s has suggested that structural fluidity can be liberating and positive. The equivocal attitudes to formal determinism demonstrated by the *Seven Up* series and *Hoop Dreams* recalls again the work on history and narrative by Hayden White. At the beginning of *The Content of the Form* White proposes that

> So natural is the impulse to narrate, so inevitable is the form of narrative for any report on the way things really happened, that narrativity could appear problematical only in a culture in which it was absent – or, as in some domains of contemporary Western intellectual and artistic culture, programmatically refused.
>
> (White H. 1987: 1)

To White this (presumably irresistible, illogical, suspiciously spontaneous) 'impulse' is perverse, although it is an inevitable hazard of much documentary filmmaking. For White the logical need is to solve the 'problem' of a lack of narrative. As he goes on to say:

> Far from being a problem, then, narrative might well be considered a solution to a problem of general human concern, namely, the problem of how to translate knowing into telling.
>
> (p. 1)

This idea of translating knowing into telling is helpful to our understanding of the *Seven Up* series and *Hoop Dreams* for both have constructed fluid narratives out of potentially fragmentary, disjointed material. In constructing a logical, linear story that gives an account of seven or five years respectively of their subjects' lives, both necessarily are forced to omit significant chunks of material. This omission is formalised in the later *Seven Up* films as Apted only films with his interviewees every seven years, never in between (although he did break this rule to film Bruce's wedding for *42 Up*); each interview obviously makes reference to what has happened in the seven years since his last visit, but is essentially about the point each interviewee has arrived at. These are documentary equivalents to the empty years in White's annals in which 'nothing happened'. As White says of such blank spaces: 'Every narrative, however seemingly "full", is constructed on the basis of a set of events that might have been included but were left out' (1987: 10). The portraits of the individuals in the two documentaries to be discussed here are assumed, in much the same way, to have assimilated and been partially formed by the events and details that have been omitted; like the narratives White cites here, they are 'seemingly "full"' and intimate, and yet highly selective.

White's view that we understand and process information through narrativising it can also be linked to the presence (referred to above) of a dual open-ended/determined structure in both *Seven Up* and *Hoop Dreams*. Not only do both documentaries possess social scripts,[2] which condition our responses to otherwise unpredictable material but they also share a tendency towards narrativising these scripts about social inequality into melodramas, fairytales, three-act structures and the like. The narrative of the *Seven Up* series changed at the time of *28 Up* as Apted started to tell the stories of individual interviewees separately, whereas before they had been edited together, often contrapuntally, to foreground distinctions between the children, often related to class. With this shift from social to individual came a more humanist emphasis but also a no less keen eye for effective narrative, Neil's circular journey to date from contentment to disillusionment to social exclusion to social rehabilitation and contentment being the most persistently memorable. Likewise *Hoop Dreams* couches its social script within familiar narrative structures, such as focusing on whichever protagonist is most successful at the time while sidelining the other (that this, in a rather insidious way, supports rather than criticises a belief in competitiveness and success contradicts the film's otherwise liberal social agenda and determinist social script).

In the *Seven Up* series the 'social script' Moran detects has either, over time, weakened or it has become so omnipresent that it does not need to be retold any more. Any social agenda the series might have is far more self-consciously articulated in the first programme, *Seven Up*. This *World in Action*'s stated intention was to test the theory that the environment into which a child is born and raised was the most important factor in shaping who s/he will become; as the 'Voice of God' narration says, the programme sets out to provide 'a glimpse of England in the year 2000'. Coupled with this specific intention was the perceived social agenda of *World in Action* as a strand: founded in 1963, it frequently 'fell foul of the Independent Television Authority for its alleged leftwing bias' (Moran, J. 2002: 388). Despite the presence of all these predictable determining factors, *Seven Up* as a series has not, since this first film, necessarily unfolded in entirely predictable ways.

In *Seven Up*, the children have been selected specifically as representatives of their social class and are subsequently introduced as such and often interviewed in pairs and batches that cement this initial and reductive image of them. As Moran observes, the manner in which the interviews were conducted – the 'leading questions' about money and schooling, for instance – 'reveal(s) the programme's class agenda' (p. 389), as does the way in which people are juxtaposed. Moran cites a key example of this editing style as the three posh public school boys (concluding with Charles Furneaux arguing for private education because otherwise 'all the poor people would come rushing in') are immediately followed by an interview with the trio of working class girls that includes Lynn saying she is 'going to work in Woolworth's' (Moran, J. 2002: 389–90). Almost every article about the *Seven Up* series mentions Apted's own position within the English class structure – that he is an ex-public schoolboy and Cambridge graduate; one writer emphasises the perceived similarities between Apted and Bruce, the least class-fixated and most socially conscious of the *Seven Up* posh boys, commenting that they share 'both upbringing and point of view' (Bigio 1986: 5). Apted himself has explained that his own background is bound to impinge on the way he puts the questions in *Seven Up*: 'I'm a pretty neurotic, ambitiously-driven, middle-class person from Ilford and I can't not be that when I ask these questions' (Moran, J. 2002: 394).

The emphasis on class in *Seven Up* has given the series rigidity, despite its fluid and open narrative structure. As issues of class still surface regularly, so it becomes clear that, in some respects at least, Apted has preconceived ideas of what each of his interviewees represent in terms of the British social system and how they will turn out. In *49 Up* issues of class are prominent and Apted's possible fixation with it are exposed by Jackie, always the least acquiescent of the 'East End girls' (when Apted in the same programme asks Sue, for example, if she has 'gone up a class' now that she and her partner have moved out of the East End and bought a house together, she answers his question without resentment or weariness). Conversely, Jackie recalls how she and Apted have argued in the past, particularly during *21 Up*, when Apted angered her by asking if she had known enough men before getting married (at 19). Jackie's belief is that Apted has got her wrong and has consistently asked her the wrong questions; she also queries the way in which he has simplified her in the past, accusing him in *42 Up* of having focused too much on sympathising with her because of her rheumatoid arthritis to the exclusion of other facets of her character. In *49 Up* Jackie gets Apted to ask the questions she wants asked, not the ones he wants to ask, so, for instance, she gets the opportunity to say that she hopes to 'start my education all over again'. Jackie's segment concludes with her challenging Apted's perception of her:

> I'm more intelligent than you thought I would be ... I enjoy being me, but I don't think you ever expected me to turn out the way I have.

With this, Jackie mounts a clear challenge to not only the British class system but also the Jesuit maxim which prompted *Seven Up*. However, as this attack on the foundations of *Seven Up* indicates, concerns with the British class system (and, to a certain extent, with its preservation) are endemic to the series, which may be a reason for it now being emphasised less strongly, but there are also formal and historical reasons for this shift away from the 'social script'. The decision at *28 Up* to begin telling each individual's story in turn, as opposed to cutting between them, was presumably at least partially made necessary by the increased volume of material Apted was working with; it also, however, signalled a change in emphasis. *28 Up* was also the first of the series to be taken to and be successful in the US. Apted was initially reluctant to introduce it to the Americans, claiming:

> I was very loathe to do it because I thought 'Here's a film based on the English class system which has as its reference a kind of esoteric knowledge

of the English education system' And I thought 'How is an American audience ever going to understand any of this?'.

(quoted in Nahra 1999: 22)

That *28 Up* proved, contrary to Apted's expectations, 'extraordinarily successful' in the US, made him 're-evaluate the whole thing' (p. 22). It is after the success of *28 Up* in the United States that Apted begins to consistently attach the terms 'humane', 'humanist' and 'humanitarian' to the series, commenting to me, for example, that

> It's stopped being a political document and has become more of a humanist document. The series honours the ordinary life; it deals with things we all deal with ... The series doesn't disown politics, but deals with politics via character.

(Apted 2006)

Rather like the question of whether the *vérité* films of the late 1950s and early 1960s came about because of advances in filmmaking technology or rather, as Kuhn suggests (Kuhn 1978), that the filmmakers prompted changes in technology by starting to make a different sort of documentary, whether *Seven Up* as a series changed or whether Apted's perception of it having changed following its reception in the US is ambiguous. The move away from more ideologically motivated intercutting to a more straightforward narration of the individual stories is the reason for a shift of emphasis having taken place, but this has not been referred to by Apted as a conscious move away from politics and towards humanism; instead, he now passes comment on the series' 'humanism' while at the same time regretting that it missed certain crucial political moments, such as 'the whole feminine revolution' (Apted in Bigio 1986: 20).

This transition from the overtly political message of *Seven Up* to the blend of political commentary via interviews and humanism of the programmes from *28 Up* onwards is arguably an inevitable symptom of the long-haul documentary journey. Any form of intellectual editing (editing to make a point as opposed to editing to tell a story) inevitably perhaps stems from a certain emotional detachment on the part of the filmmaker; documentaries in which the editing is not 'intellectual' seem much more likely to have a higher degree of personal, intimate and emotional content. Not that intellectual montage is not moving: it simply creates an intellectual response, which can be very emotional, but which is nevertheless intellectual in origin. The 'humanism' of the series thereby pertains both to Apted and to the responses of *Seven Up* audiences. Apted's relationship with his interviewees has altered and grown over time – as he comments, he has gone from being a young researcher on the series, to being a 'father figure' to now being, as he sees it, their 'colleague', as a mark of this collaborative relationship he has also established series ground rules that give interviewees the 'opportunity to see rough cuts and demand changes' (Apted 2006). He has been criticised for his soft questioning – that he 'does not probe enough' (Bigio 1986:

20), against which one could put Apted's own characterisation of his interviewing style when commenting 'I think it's a process of wearing them down and a process of interviewing through silence ... I just shut up and let them talk' (Robinson 2002: 37). This style of letting interviewees talk has always been a crucial, valid component of observational documentary.

As a series *Seven Up* has become progressively more moving as it has become more 'humanist' and focused on the individual stories. This, however, raises huge questions about the series as a journey, because the spectators' potentially emotional responses are inevitably bound up with their accumulated knowledge and attachment to it: each time a programme comes around we want to know what has happened to Neil, Lynn, Tony or Simon in the seven intervening years since the last one. The series would not work in the same way for people coming to it afresh. Apted indirectly has acknowledged the significance of his audiences' journey through his structuring and narrating of recent episodes, for example by putting the sections on Neil right at the end since *35 Up*, as this is the story to have most 'captured the public imagination' (Moran, J. 2002: 396).

Through this restructuring our viewing of *Seven Up* has become potentially vertical as opposed to linear in that we can choose to follow certain stories and not others (although I am not entirely sure that this is how people watch it; it is more likely to be how they re-view an episode if they choose to). The non-linear trajectory is also evident in how each individual's journey might or might not follow the series' putative 'social script'. Whereas Andrew said, at seven, that he would attend Charterhouse and then Cambridge and then go to the Bar – and then did just that, Neil's life cycle has been far more turbulent. At seven Neil (alongside Peter, the other state school boy who lived in a middle-class Liverpool suburb) wanted to be an astronaut or, failing that, a coach driver; in *Seven Plus Seven* he is serious and academically ambitious; by *21 Up* he has dropped out of the University of Aberdeen and is living in a squat in London (he had wanted to go to Oxford and anywhere else was 'second best'); by *28 Up* he is living in remote Scotland on social benefits; by *35 Up* he is still unemployed and in sheltered housing in the Shetlands; at *42 Up* he is living in London again (as he had predicted seven years earlier) but not in a squat and, though still unemployed, is a Liberal Democrat councillor for the Borough of Hackney; at *49 Up* he is living in Cumbria, still involved in local politics and a lay preacher.

Whilst Apted's questioning of all his interviewees repeatedly seeks to draw parallels between their individual lives and broader social issues, this imposed linking of the personal and the political only partly explains the impact of a story such as Neil's. In some respects Neil's biography tells us a lot about the last half century in Britain: the aspirations of the middle-classes, their inability at times to handle disappointment resulting from these aspirations not being fulfilled, the workings of the social benefits system, the shifts in party politics since the 1990s. And, as Moran observes, Neil has a tendency to 'place his own story within broader social narratives' (Moran, J. 2002: 395), although what Moran does not explore is the link between this tendency and Neil's intelligence and concomitant tendency – present from *Seven Plus Seven* – towards intellectualising and philosophising about his own predicament. Neil's narrative journey is cyclical as he has returned to the contentment seen in him at seven – a return Apted clearly feels and signals through the insertion of footage from *Seven Up* of Neil waving his arms about in an expressive movement class into the 49 year-old's description of taking pleasure in nature and the moment.

The series is attractive on the level of fantasy and fairytale. Its positive characters elicit both empathy and sympathy – we see ourselves in them or we want to know and help them; Neil has probably prompted both responses in a large number of viewers, certainly after *28 Up* Apted received several offers of employment on his behalf. Neil's story is the series' fairytale – these letters from viewers and the fantasy so many have obviously shared that they could help Neil is reminiscent of the mawkish romantic comedy *Sleepless in Seattle* in which thousands of women write to Tom Hanks after hearing him talk on a radio phone-in about how much he misses his dead wife. That it was in fact another of the *Seven Up* children – Bruce – who befriended Neil, offered him a home after *35 Up* and facilitated his social reintegration made *42 Up* deeply poignant television. When one then considers the possibility that, for the middle-class viewers at least, Bruce has been a positive point of identification as well as the one who most closely resembles Apted in terms of social background, in this fairytale various fantasies converge. It is therefore disappointing – strictly on the level of narrative fantasy – that, by *49 Up*, Neil and Bruce have lost touch and Bruce, ground down by his inner city teaching job, has taken up a position at a public school in Hertfordshire. Neil is still relatively happy (the fear between programmes for many viewers being, presumably, that Neil will once again revert to being depressive) and, as Apted remarks, looks at 49 more like he did at seven than he had done at 14 (Apted 2006).

Apted's comment about Neil was made in the context of what has changed over the course of this protracted series. Of his interviewees Apted observes:

> The core personality hasn't changed. In the seven-year-old faces you can see the adult … This isn't a determinist view but an observation about character – that the core character shines through.
>
> (Apted 2006)

Seven Up as a series has proved a great but typical documentary journey of this type: being filmed over such a long period of time has suggested both that some things are predictable (the Jesuit predictions that the adult can be seen in the child) whilst others are not. It is crucial to how dated the first programme now seems and how wrong its view of Britain in the year 2000 was. The programme makers could only guess at how things would pan out and the 1964 voice-over asks who will be the shop stewards of the future, for instance, not realising, obviously, that Margaret Thatcher and the Conservative government of the 1980s would quite so effectively dismantle the power of the Trade Unions. Likewise the technical and generic revolutions that have taken place between *42 Up* and *49 Up* have led to other changes. *49 Up* has been the first of the series to not be shot on 16mm film (that Apted was still shooting on film in the 1990s is, though, testament to the privileged status afforded the series as a whole), the greater length of digital tapes (40 as opposed to 10 minutes) allowing interviews to flow more freely (Apted 2006). Also, as the greater knowingness of the inter-viewees in *49 Up* suggests – that several of them argue with Apted or comment that they resent the intrusion into their lives every seven years – the impact of reality television has been immense. As Apted remarks:

> The big gorilla of recent years has been reality television, a development that made some of his *Seven Up* interviewees feel 'vulnerable' and fear that they might be being 'exploited.
>
> (Apted 2006)

But as he also says about the relationship of his series to reality: 'the whole essence of reality television is to contrive a situation, which may be illuminating or not, but this isn't what I do. I choose not to contrive; I take a chance' (Apted 2006).

This notion of taking a chance is the essence of long-term documentary film-making, because the doubt is always there that what unfolds might not work (Apted has remarked how *Seven Plus Seven* was 'terrible' but that what was inter-esting was the result of juxtaposing film of the children at fourteen with the footage of them at seven and that in this he saw 'the seed for the series' [Bigio 1986: 5]). Equally likely, though, is that all that shot footage is bound to throw up something interesting, which is perhaps the assumption that sustains Fred Wiseman. Steve James and the others who worked on *Hoop Dreams* (cameraman Peter Gilbert also shot the American *Seven Up*) limited the potential for chaos and meandering inherent within long-term filming by choosing only two black teenagers to follow as they gained sports scholarships to prestigious Chicago high school, St Joseph's in a bid to work their way up to being professional NBA basketball players. As the two protagonists are from similar backgrounds, the film's social script is simplified. The documentary proved extremely popular and although it did not achieve its preferred ending as neither Arthur Agee nor William Gates made it to the NBA, it remained a cult film and Agee in particu-lar has acquired some celebrity status since. As with *Seven Up*, the journey *Hoop Dreams* charted has an indissoluble relationship with the real world around it; not only is it, like *Seven Up*, a social document but also it serves as an example of a particular era of documentary filmmaking. Again, comparisons are now made between *Hoop Dreams* and reality television; in one newspaper article William Gates (now a pastor) comments: 'If you think about it, we were the first reality series … We just didn't bank in like everybody else. Nowadays even the *Survivor* losers go on TV and get paid' (Wise, M. 2004).

The comparison Gates makes between *Hoop Dreams* and later reality shows raises specific issues about winning and losing. Gates makes an assumption here that winners deserve their 15 minutes of fame more than losers do, but this is to misunderstand reality television, although it is not necessarily to misunderstand *Hoop Dreams*, whose underpinning preoccupation is with competition. It may be a way of rationalising otherwise sprawling material, but *Hoop Dreams* is, in its form as well as its content, imbued with simplified notions of success and failure. In a highly critical discussion of the film, bell hooks argues that, even though 'we see glimpses of camaraderie between the two black males, the film, constantly comparing and contrasting their fate, creates a symbolic competition' (hooks 1995: 23). hooks goes on to observe that *Hoop Dreams* is reactionary in its attitudes to competition, that it 'clearly argues that the context in which one "makes it" is within a nuclear family that prays together, works hard and completely and uncritically believes in the American dream' (p. 23). The film as well as many of those in it, she ultimately suggests, zealously upholds the ethic of competition, to the extent that William Gates' desire to be a good father at the end of *Hoop Dreams,* to have goals outside basketball 'is not represented as a positive shift in his thinking' (p. 23); likewise, after a series of injuries, hooks detects in the portrayal of Gates an emphasis on defeat and dejection.[3]

Hoop Dreams does not only have competition as its dominant subject, it also structures its narrative around competition, augmenting its theme by engineering a competitiveness between William and Arthur that otherwise would be minimal. At the outset both, having been spotted by talent scouts, are offered places at St Joseph's, a school with a strong basketball heritage. hooks and others – including Spike Lee in the film – question the emphasis placed on sport as a means to 'escape the poverty and crime that characterizes many African-American neighborhoods' (Cipriano 2005: 78), an escape route also cited in John Singleton's feature film *Boyz n the Hood.* As the boys are welcomed by St Joseph's coach Gene Pingatore, it immediately becomes apparent that he has higher hopes for William than he does for Arthur, thereby establishing a disparity between them that is not, for a while, dislodged. William and Arthur enter St Joseph's on similar academic grades (they have been singled out exclusively for their sporting prowess), but while Arthur continues at the same poor level, William works his way up and is demonstrably the better learner. Although William is brought up by a single mother, Arthur's family at this stage of the film is shown to be the more dysfunctional: his father – who supposedly lives with them – is a drug addict who is absent for stretches of time (including a spell in prison) while his mother is on welfare. Arthur's problems are compounded by him not progressing as quickly as Pingatore had hoped, so when both families hit financial difficulties, the coach finds William a scholarship to help with his fees but not Arthur, who is forced to leave St Joseph's, indirectly as a result of his relative failure on the basketball courts. Arthur transfers to a state inner city school, Marshall's, where he plays better. The 'script' at this juncture is manifestly that William is the 'hero of the story' (Arthos 1996: 87) while Arthur is the relative failure, a depiction strengthened by the surrounding familial problems.

Things change, however, as William suffers a serious knee injury, necessitating surgery and a lengthy period of convalescence; at this time Arthur too is at a low point, his new coach declaring him to be disappointing. That this criticism of Arthur is juxtaposed with a friend commenting in interview that his home life 'gets to him', is one of several indications that a calculating ethos of competition dominates the American sports scholarships system and that the exploitative nature of this system is here the ostensible subject of criticism. The middle section of *Hoop Dreams* runs contrary to expectations as William's knee problems persist, his school grades start to decline and he becomes a teenage father (that the filmmakers had not given any indication that this was imminent is a peculiar if telling omission for it suggests – wrongly as it turns out – that William's life revolves around basketball). Conversely, Arthur starts to play increasingly well and is the main reason why Marshall wins the end of year city trophy and comes third in the state finals, his mother Sheila is seen graduating top of her nursing assistant class and his father is home (although not for long) and has found religion. What is disturbing is not the unexpected reversals in this factual narrative but the filmmakers' responses to them: during Arthur's period of resurgence they effectively abandon William as a film subject, returning to him sporadically and only briefly, dedicating film time to Arthur's successes instead.

Hoop Dreams pursues a roughly three-act structure that internally presents the protagonists' journeys through the film as contrasting barometers of success or failure. The first 'act' centres on William as the successful one and Arthur as the troubled under-performer; the second 'act' shows a reversal in the fortunes of both, with William's knee injury and Arthur's success at Marshall; the third 'act' shows the two of them on the way to college. Placing Arthur and William as binary opposites is also a familiar narrative device (Hollywood's endless bad son, good son narratives; television's bad cop, good cop ones; the employee lower down the pecking order supplanting the one at the top in films such as *Working Girl*) that polarises experience and emotion. In 'Act Three' as he is leaving St Joseph's (at the fifth attempt he gets the scores he needs to enter Marquette University) William bids Pingatore an awkward farewell, the coach commenting to the cameras once his former protégé has left his office: 'Well … another walks out the door, another one comes in the door'. As Arthos observes, William has belatedly and only gradually learnt that the system for grooming future sportsmen 'regarded him as a commodity' (90); the documentary, though, far from critiquing the value of such a system has consistently mimicked it. William never disappears from *Hoop Dreams* but it is Arthur who concludes the film in the ascendancy, as if a film about the competitive basis for the 'American Dream' does not know what to do with 'failure' in these narrow terms. bell hooks criticises what the documentary depicts from a socio-political perspective, stating that

> it is precisely the institutionalised racism and white-supremacist attitudes in everyday American life that actively prohibit black male participation in more diverse cultural arenas and spheres of employment, while presenting sports as the one location where recognition, success and material reward can be attained.
>
> (hooks 1995: 22)

Hoop Dreams does little to dispel feelings of regret that neither William nor Arthur are destined to emulate Michael Jordan.

In his discussion of *Hoop Dreams* Arthos is more charitable than I am being here as he views positively the film's repeated process of building audience expectation and subsequently reversing it. Of the film's epilogue – in which the reversals of fortune are cemented as it is revealed that William has quit the basketball team at his prestigious conference school and dropped out of college altogether, while Arthur has been recruited from the more peripheral Mineral Area Junior College to a conference championship contender – he comments:

> This reversal subsumes the structure of the entire piece, and in great part accounts for its effect. It is a kind of jolting rather than pleasurable surprise. It does not so much provide the comforting traditional topos of the underdog as it upsets the standard moral that decency and hard work wins out in the end.
>
> (Arthos 1996: 88)

To Arthos's mind, the journey of *Hoop Dreams* is an unexpected, ambivalent but largely uplifting one as we are 'jolted' out of our belief in the value of hard work. This is, I think, to mistake *Hoop Dreams'* initial tenet – which is not faith in the protestant work ethic but a faith, as hooks identifies, in the ethic of competition, a faith that persists to the extent so that the film's final acknowledgement that neither William nor Arthur are, in Michael Jordan's terms, going to 'make it' is repressed by what hooks identifies as 'the thrill of victory'. As she concludes: 'Despite the costs, the American dream of conquest prevails and nothing changes' (hooks 1995: 23).

The journey of any documentary to an extent includes what happened next, and the impulse to discover what became of protagonists such as Arthur and William is strongest when the end of the film, as is the case with *Hoop Dreams,* is a possible beginning, not simply the end. Since *Hoop Dreams*, Agee and Gates have stayed in touch. Gates has become a pastor in Cabrini Green, the neighbourhood he lived in whilst making the film, while the Arthur Agee Role Model Foundation had been established in Arthur's honour to 'educate parents and all adults that they are role models for their children' (www.edgesportsintl.com/arthur.htm) and, in 2004, Arthur had launched a 'Hoop Dreams' clothing line whose slogan was 'Control your Destiny'. Gates, in the early 2000s, tried to make a comeback and was feted by Michael Jordan, only to then fracture a bone in his foot. Of this injury coming just as Jordan had promised him an NBA trial he said: 'That was my NBA dream ... I never put that uniform on, but I knew I was good enough to play' (Wise, M. 2004). Both men have four children (William's are all with Catherine, the mother of the infant daughter Alicia, seen in *Hoop Dreams* while Arthur's were unplanned and with four different women). When asking himself where he would have been if *Hoop Dreams* had never happened, Agee says 'I don't know. I'm very, very happy. It helped my family out. Not only financially, but emotionally. It put that love back – it put what was important first' (Wise, M. 2004). Gates is the one who has remained disappointed. Looking at their respective biographies, it becomes apparent that Arthur and William have both conformed to and defied the 'social script' suggested at the outset.

One final consideration when thinking about the long-term documentary journey is the question of personal involvement. Filming with the same people over a number of years or decades inevitably brings documentary filmmakers closer to their subjects. *Hoop Dreams* offers an interesting example of how this level of commitment can impinge upon the making of a film. When, as we see in *Hoop Dreams*, the Agees' electricity is cut off, Steve James *et al.* 'cobbled together some cash to help them get their lights back on.' James comments of this decision to intervene: 'We need to be more than just filmmakers. And it's a tough line to walk' (Leeman 2003: 15). In the same article Albert Maysles recalls how, when making *Lalee's Kin*, he did not help out when Lalee's granddaughter could not go to school because she did not have paper or a pencil. This scene is included in the film and, upon seeing it someone sent Maysles an email berating him. Maysles' view is a traditional one, namely that 'after filming' when he felt that 'it couldn't interfere with anything' he and his crew did help out by buying Lalee groceries, for example (Leeman 2003: 14). After Steve James and his partners had paid their bills, they reputedly shared their profits from *Hoop Dreams* with Arthur and William, giving them each around $175,000 (Wise, M. 2004). At the beginning of the documentary Arthur Agee had mused that, when he gets to the NBA, he is going to buy a house for his family; this he eventually does with James' generous gesture as they use the money to move out of West Garfield Park into the neighbouring suburb of Berwyn. In the light of the legal wrangling that followed *Être et avoir*,[4] James' decision to pay his contributors becomes a loaded issue: in the *Être et avoir* case, when the teacher's case for being paid a substantial portion of that film's profits was rejected in court (he had already been offered a not insubstantial sum but had rejected this as insufficient), the lawyer representing director Nicolas Philibert remarked that, had Philibert lost, it would have signalled the death of documentary filmmaking. Is it ethically different to share a film's profits with two socially disadvantaged contributors who have been dogged by cameras for a number of years? Probably most people would agree that it is, but this raises equally pertinent questions about celebrity based on documentary appearances. In *42 Up* Nick jokes that he would one day like to be more famous for his contribution to science (he is Professor of Physics at the University of Wisconsin) than for 'being in these programmes – although I probably never will be'. The journeys undertaken by documentaries such as *Seven Up* and *Hoop Dreams* that are filmed over years or decades will inevitably always remain 'open': questioning what it means to appear in them will change, as is occurring increasingly in the *Seven Up* series; the relationships between filmmakers and subjects will evolve, as will the interaction between the lives of the subjects as shown on film and their lives in the real world. In these examples the fluidity of the dialectical relationships between off-screen and on-screen spaces, between filmmakers and subjects are most pronounced. Our viewing of these texts will likewise evolve over time, mimicking the developments on screen.

Journeys towards the Final Solution: *Shoah and Hotel Terminus*

As Nichols suggests in his discussion of the epistemological shift away from documentary connoting completeness, fact or explanation, non-fiction films have become more intrigued by forms and subjects that challenge these certainties, so that 'History and memory intertwine; meaning and action, past and present, hinge on one another distinctively' (Nichols 1994: 1). For Linda Williams a similar coincidence existed in the 1980s/1990s between a renewed 'hunger for documentary truth', demonstrated by films such as *Shoah, Hotel Terminus, Roger and Me* and *The Thin Blue Line,* and 'the clear sense that this truth is subject to manipulation and construction by docu-auteurs who, whether on camera or behind, are forcefully calling the shots' (Williams 1993: 12). The renewed importance of the 'docu-auteur' is further exemplified in both *Shoah* and *Hotel Terminus* by the films' marginalisation of archival material which has become by default the normative, conventionalised way of representing the Holocaust (as Steven Spielberg commented about his choice to make *Schindler's List* in black and white: this is how we recall those events). *Shoah* (1985) is, in many ways, the antidote to the conventional, authoritative documentary representation of the Holocaust that preceded it and, considered alongside *Hotel Terminus,* made three years later, instigated an alternative, investigative and personalised way of tackling the Nazi past. Whereas previous films such as *Nuit et brouillard,* Ophuls' *The Sorrow and the Pity* or *The World at War* were dependent upon the power of archival images of Nazi atrocities, Lanzmann prioritised personal testimony and eschewed the need for archive because, as he has argued, the archive is too familiar and so has lost the impact to shock and to convey the truth of the Holocaust. In part through their focus on personal testimony and the relative absence of archive, both films bring the events of forty years ago into the present, so also constructing a further journey that links the past with the present. This preoccupation with enforcing the relevance of past events to the present is particularly evocatively expressed in *Hotel Terminus* in which Ophuls is ironic and critical of a tendency to view the events of the past and especially Barbie's role in the torture, murder and transportation of Jews and others during the German occupation of France as events that should be laid to rest, left alone because they had happened forty years before. Both *Shoah* and *Hotel Terminus* chart the process of un-forgetting this past.

Lanzmann himself, on screen for most of the film, is the focus of *Shoah's* journey, compelling survivors to speak, following in the tracks of the trains to the camps, reliving the Holocaust. His interaction with the people he meets forms the basis for the film and its argument, as he explains:

> The concept was built during the work. If I had had a concept at the beginning, the film would be very bad. It would be too abstract. No, I had an obsession. ... I have made the film and the film has made me.
>
> (Lanzmann 1985a: 322)

This obsessional quality is demonstrated by the sheer volume of material Lanzmann collated and the time *Shoah* took both to make (350 hours of film were shot in 14 different countries over 11 years and took four years to edit) and to watch (nine hours). Lanzmann has described the editing process as a journey towards certainty: when he got stuck he 'would stop until I could find the proper way. And there were not several ways, there was only one' (Lanzmann 1990: 83).

The film's power stems in part from the central journey being both metaphorical and actual, both concerned with the emotional and intellectual comprehension of the Holocaust and with its physical organisation and execution (a quality echoed by the arduous experiences of making and then watching it). The clearest symbol of the film's journey is the train and its concomitant paraphernalia of tracks, stations and steam. Trains, however, can only function symbolically as elucidations of less concrete journeys: the personal journeys of the interviewees compelled by Lanzmann to summon past memories into the present, descriptive domain; the identificatory and often equally personal journeys undertaken vicariously by Lanzmann and the spectator; the journey to the camps and to extermination; the journey towards a cumulative knowledge of the detail of the Holocaust assimilated through a meticulous amassing of facts, numbers and evidence; the journey encircling absent archival images. The effect of the multiple journeys in *Shoah* is to bring into the present a series of events that, principally relayed through archive, hitherto has been contained within the past.

The multiple journeys *Shoah* undertakes are, in part, the expression of this struggle between the possibility and the impossibility of representation. *Shoah* is not linearly structured, although it features – obsessively – the linear, repetitive journeys of the trains that dissected Europe and took millions of prisoners to the death camps. These incessant, regular journeys scarred the landscape of Europe; the actual modes of transportation are thus instrumental in conveying to the spectator the arduousness of the film's journeys. *Shoah* emphasises both trains and rail tracks. The repetition of image and event is significant, but so is the realisation (that only comes with such repetition) that the Final Solution necessitated quite so much hardware and covered quite so much ground. Most documentaries focus on the rounding up of the Jews and on the camps – that is, the trains' departures and destinations; the journeys themselves are frequently cut. The trains are emblematic of the Jewish journeys across Europe and convey a collective experience; conventionally they are generic, emotionally rather than specifically meaningful. As Lanzmann comments the collective experience is of travelling towards death: 'I built a structure, a gestalt! I didn't tell one personal story – the subject of the film is the extermination of the Jews, not the handful of survivors' (Lanzmann 1985a: 324).

One train journey in *Shoah* that is intrinsically meaningful is that of the steam locomotive driven by Henrik Gawkowski, which re-enacts the transportation of Jews to Treblinka. Coming only 48 minutes into *Shoah,* this sequence is the first to give the spectator a point of view parallel to that of the victims. The camera looks forward at Gawkowski, the steam and the tracks ahead; as the train slows and pulls into the station, it holds a shot of the sign stating the destination:

Figure 3.1   Shoah
Source: Courtesy of BFI Stills, Posters and Designs

Treblinka. Proximity to the original events is important, and Lanzmann hired an engine (though no wagons) comparable to the one Gawkowski would have driven. Consolidating this, Gawkowski, unsolicited by Lanzmann, makes a gesture of cutting his throat – the final greeting he gave the Jews as they filed off the train; a gesture that is later repeated by other Poles in Chelmno.[5] The trains in *Shoah* are linked to both death (that they re-enact journeys that had an end) and to the desire to keep alive and perpetuate the memory of those the original trains transported.

Despite its focus on the intended annihilation of all the Jews in Europe, *Shoah* does not conform to conventional notions of closure, and in Lanzmann's film Simone de Beauvoir finds a far more fluid structure:

> The fact that many times they [the witnesses] speak about the same events does not tire you. To the contrary. You think of the intentional repetition of a musical phrase or leitmotiv. For, with its moments of intense horror, peaceful landscapes, laments and resting places, what Shoah's subtle construction calls to mind is a musical composition. And the whole work is punctuated by the almost intolerable din of trains rushing towards the camps.
>
> (de Beauvoir 1985: iv)

De Beauvoir is touched here by *Shoah*'s surprising lyricism (considering its subject matter), a lyricism that finds an echo in its overall narrative structure. To return to Winston's assumption that a journey necessarily implies finality and a coherent trajectory: *Shoah* both affirms and denies this. Intellectually,

Lanzmann's mammoth exploration possesses an inherent coherence that is articulated by historian Raul Hilberg's proposition (during his interview for *Shoah*)
that the Final Solution, though a radical 'turning point' or a moment of 'closure', remains a continuation rather than a break with the past. As Lanzmann
himself comments: 'The film is the abolition of all distances between past and
present; I have relived the whole story in the present' (Colombat 1993: 302).

The process of 'reliving' the Holocaust and of eliminating the distance
between past and present, centres on the interaction between Lanzmann and the
interviewees he pursues. These encounters are intensely physical: Claude
Lanzmann travels to them, walks with them, asks them to re-enact as opposed to
merely relate events and gestures from the past, sometimes in locations that
directly recall them. It is the concreteness of these encounters that ostensibly
belies Lanzmann's contention that the story is impossible to show. Two interviews that illustrate the physicality and presentness of Lanzmann's pursuit of personal recollection are those he conducts with Jan Karski and Abraham Bomba.

Karski, a Professor in America, is extremely reluctant to re-summon the memories of being a courier for the Polish government, of visiting the Warsaw ghetto
and of being asked, by his Jewish guides, to tell the Allies what he had seen, with
the intention of precipitating an official denunciation of the confinement and
extermination of the Jews. Initially he terminates the interview. Karski has
repressed his Holocaust memories for 35 years, so when he eventually agrees to
'go back' and recount – and so relive – the events, he is doing so publicly for the
first time. In Lanzmann's words, 'one must know and see, and one must see and
know. Indissolubly' (Colombat 1993: 301); Karski's 'testimony' is unusually
compelling in its ability to do this because of its frequent use of the present tense
('every day counts'; 'perhaps it will shake their [the Allies'] conscience').[6]
Bomba's 'reliving' of the past is more literal than Karski's. When in Treblinka, he
cut the hair of women and children just before they were taken into the gas
chamber; after the war he continued to be a barber in the basement of New
York's Pennsylvania station, but was retired by the time Lanzmann found him.
Bomba is interviewed whilst cutting hair in an Israeli barbershop Lanzmann
hired specially. Conducting the interview as Bomba is in the act of cutting a
man's hair is brutal, although the sequence is not mimesis but re-enactment as
Bomba refers only to cutting the hair of naked women and children inside the
gas chamber, not men (as he is doing in *Shoah*). He strove to make them 'believe
they were getting a nice haircut' as well as cutting 'as fast as we could' because
there were 60–70 women in the chamber at any one time (Lanzmann 1985b:
115), a vacillation between care and efficiency that is echoed by the way in which
Bomba cuts the hair of the man whilst being filmed: his client's hair is dry and
the cuts are small – delicate but ineffectual. As Lanzmann has remarked:

> I think he [Bomba] would not have agreed to do this with women, and I
> think that I would not have agreed. I think that would have been unbearable.
> It would not have been transmitted, I am sure. It would have been obscene.
> (Lanzmann 1985b: 97)

Lanzmann concludes the Yale seminar on *Shoah* by evoking what would have been the most graphic archive of all – a film of 'three thousand people dying together in a gas chamber' (Lanzmann 1985b: 99). Bomba's testimony is the last stage of the journey to this hypothetical endpoint:

> no one human being would have been able to look at this. Anyhow, I would have never included this in my film. I would have preferred to destroy it. It is not visible. You cannot look at this. And if the customers of Bomba in the barbershop had been women, it would have been, for me, of the same kind of impossibility as that of the gas chamber.
>
> (p. 99)

Shoah's journey is ultimately impossible: the conclusion of Lanzmann's encounters, all the film's tracks and trains will inevitably stop short of their historical destination, the moment of extermination.

Both the journey Lanzmann physically undertakes in *Shoah* and the way in which that journey is filmed enact the entrapment within a perpetual present. As Marcel Ophuls observes in his discussion of the film:

> This constant blending of the past and present, rather than a mere juxta-position, this constant effort to erase time in order to re-create a continuous reality, is, as far as I can see, the basic principle on which the whole film is constructed.
>
> (Ophuls 1985: 19)

This stasis is heavily ironic in a film visually dominated by movement and a permanently restless camera. The cinematic apparatus is probing, questioning, it leaves nothing alone and in this, the presentness of the film image incessantly relives the experiences evoked through the witnesses' testimonies. Complementing this and often graphically demonstrated is Lanzmann's own physical journey through this perpetual present, wanting to relive it himself. He recalls, for instance, whilst walking, during filming, from the gates to crematorium of Auschwitz-Birkenau, how he asked himself 'At which moment did it start to be too late? ... How to transmit these questions? How to transmit these feelings to the spectators, to the viewers?' (Lanzmann 1990: 89). Within *Shoah* Lanzmann actually marks out the journeys the Jews took, his aim being to 'relive all of it, to retrace the steps', to thus cross the 'imaginary line' so that the experience as well as the boundary 'becomes real' (quoted in Insdorf 1989: 252). It is thereby logical that Lanzmann's own involvement extended to pushing the dolly for the tracking shot into Auschwitz; he needed to cross and redraw these lines himself.

The camera – the apparatus through which the questions Lanzmann raises concerning how the present effect of such actions and images can be transmuted – becomes the focal point of his filmic quest, the juncture between emotional or intellectual intention and practicality and, appropriately, *Shoah*'s visual style is dominated by tracking shots or 'travelling shots' as Lanzmann refers to them (Lanzmann 1990: 91–2), evoking the actual journey of millions to their deaths. *Shoah's* camera, whether hand-held or mounted, becomes its tool of re-enactment: its steady pace, the frequent use of 'excruciatingly long takes' (Kellman 1988: 24); except in rare instances, such as the zoom into the Treblinka station sign which Lanzmann refers to as 'a violent act' (Insdorf 1989: 252), there is a pervasive eschewal of disruptive cinematic techniques for denoting elisions of time and thought such as jump cuts, montage, rapid zooms or pans.

The insistent apparatus is linked to the film's personal journeys by conveying the sense of bearing witness. Lanzmann compels all his interviewees, whether Jews or those implicated in their extermination, to lay down a testimony for others; the restless camera is the acknowledgement, often, that this is being done. Lanzmann too is bearing witness by visiting the sites of atrocities, and the camera is most closely affiliated to him. During Filip Müller's testimony, the two types of journey – the physical/technical journey and the personal – coalesce. Müller, a Czech Jew and survivor of five liquidations of the Auschwitz 'special detail', recounts the first time he entered the Auschwitz 1 crematorium. His words emphasise his incomprehension at what he saw:

> I couldn't understand any of it. It was like a blow to the head, as if I'd been stunned. I didn't even know where I was. Above all, I couldn't understand how they managed to kill so many people.
>
> (Lanzmann 1985b: 59)

Müller's look (on his face in interview as he recounts this sequence as well as the look of the camera) is, as he says, one of incomprehension. The accompanying visuals function as ways of explicating, making real Müller's responses. This is, in large part, due to the characteristic slowness, persistence and length of the 'travelling shots' that start with a slow track out from Auschwitz 1's Black Wall (against which prisoners were rounded up and shot) before progressing to hand-held shots for Block 11, the new chimney, and finally the ovens. This sequence, like many others, has the camera mimic the movements of the individual describing the scene, travelling at walking pace to the crematorium and inserting rare whip pans as if looking around the dark oven chambers. Another journey is the sequence's mirroring of the evolution of the Nazis' methods of extermination. However contextualised, the look of the camera in *Shoah* is linked to the film's lack of archive, to Lanzmann's argument that we no longer look meaningfully at archive images of the Holocaust because we have become inured to their effect and meaning.

The various textual elements of *Shoah* coalesce: the movement of the camera echoes the trains and in turn functions as a visual metonym for Lanzmann's search for witnesses and truth. *Shoah* is characterised by a repeated oscillation between the steady fluidity of movement (the camera, the moving trains) and the act of grinding to a halt. These halting journeys, combined with the film's disquietingly mesmerising rhythm are the reasons, perhaps, for the spectator, as de

Beauvoir observes, not tiring of watching the film. (Herein lies the fundamental irony of *Shoah*: that it is easier to watch than the archive of the Final Solution that Lanzmann is so convinced we have become immune to).

De Beauvoir also says of *Shoah*, 'I should add that I would never have imagined such a combination of beauty and horror. True, the one does not help to conceal the other' (de Beauvoir 1985: vi). *Shoah's* pleasure, I'd posit, stems from its identification of and play upon a quite specific form of masochism. Firstly, there is the effect of nine hours of repetition not being dull but totally absorbing, no doubt because of its content. But having said this poses a problem of its own; although I have not noted the amount of time given to interviews and words in *Shoah* relative to trains, tracking shots and pans, that the film's complete text is so short (200 small, not densely packed pages) suggests that the latter group predominate. The repetitiveness of *Shoah* as a visual, cinematic experience is masochistic, in that the length of our journey as spectators is so long and also so aesthetically minimalist. *Shoah* is not like *Nuit et brouillard*, which offers an at times uncomfortably aestheticised representation of the Holocaust with its juxtaposition of black and white archive and colour, its use of Cayrol's poetic voice-over and Eisner's contrapuntal music. Lanzmann's film centres on lack as opposed to gratification: the lack of archive images (themselves a conventional source of catharsis), the lack of satisfying closure. To embark upon a journey that can never end (but which nevertheless takes us nine hours and Lanzmann several years) is inherently masochistic; the fact that this denial then gives us pleasure of sorts makes it indubitably so.

The journey becomes especially masochistic when the conflict between the implied, preferred resolution and the film's actual irresolution is considered. *Shoah* ends ambivalently: Simha Rottem, as he recalls re-entering a deserted Warsaw Ghetto, remembers thinking to himself: 'I'm the last Jew. I'll wait for morning and for the Germans'. Rottem's belief that he would bear witness to the total extermination of the Jews is followed by another procession of rumbling train carriages. Although the conclusion to *Shoah* is ostensibly open and despite comprising the words of survivors and the living, it contains narrative closure and finality of sorts as it is – as Lanzmann's often brutal insistence that his witnesses must speak on behalf of the dead attests – about the Jews who died. The uncomfortable fact remains that the narrative's preferred ending is encapsulated within Rottem's fearful, but false conclusion that he is the last Jew left alive. This is, in turn, suppressed in favour of the film's actual inconclusiveness. In direct contrast to the multitude of renditions of the Holocaust that could be termed 'survival myths' because they prioritise survival and escape such as *Playing for Time, Escape from Sobibor, Schindler's List* and *La vita è bella (Life is Beautiful)*, *Shoah's* suppressed logical ending remains total annihilation. The survivors of the Final Solution survived by chance.

Marcel Ophuls' *Hotel Terminus* shares many things with *Shoah*: it is made only three years after, it too has at its core a filmmaker-investigator who goes in search of the truth about the Final Solution (in this instance, the war crimes of the head of the Gestapo in Lyon, Klaus Barbie), it too charts a physical as well as a historical and intellectual journey as Ophuls goes from one location to another and from one interview to another and it too is a long and painstaking film, although at four and a half hours it is roughly half the length of *Shoah*. *Hotel Terminus*, however, is a less elliptical and lyrical film, perhaps because the reason for making the film when Ophuls did was more pressing: namely that Barbie, having eluded capture for 40 years, had finally been extradited to France to face trial, an event around which the film is shaped. Ophuls' original intention had been to use the trial 'as a dramatic device', but the trial was delayed and so he had to look for other approaches. However, he adds: 'I admit that if there had *never* been a trial I could never have finished the film ... Certainly the film could not have been a *substitute* for that judgement' (Ciment 1988: 39). The action or journey at the centre of *Hotel Terminus*, necessarily incomplete when Ophuls started filming, was resolved at the time of filming itself – and not entirely as Ophuls had predicted. He admits, for instance, to being 'quite convinced for a long time that the trial would not take place ... and that the French were afraid of their past and did not have the political courage to face the consequences of the trial. I was very happy to be proven wrong' (Ciment 1988: 40). *Hotel Terminus* is characterised by this open-mindedness.

The journey the film follows is, to once more adopt Branigan's narrative categories, a 'focused chain'. The dual focus of this 'chain' is Barbie and Ophuls' corresponding search for evidence of his guilt. How the 'chain' then operates is to go from one location, subject or theme to another as the film pursues a path dictated by Barbie's narrative trajectory and the interviewees Ophuls finds. The link between each element is not arbitrary but causal – although the causality is generally factual and historical rather than thematic, and the derivative thematic links between each section of the film (what they tell us about Barbie, the French Resistance, the reasons for Barbie to successfully evade capture for so long, etc.) emerge cumulatively and in a less linear fashion. Maybe it would be more accurate to talk about *Hotel Terminus* comprising parallel, interlocking chains that, if one works through the film, might go something like this:

Time/history	*Place*	*Barbie*
Wartime	**Lyon**	**Pre-war biography**
		Resistance
		Murder of Moulin
		Massacre of Lizieu

→ Link: Anti-semitism, a brief theme-led section that leads into:

1945–51	**Germany**	**Working for CIC**

→ Link: 'Rat line' out of Europe

	South America:	
1952→	**Bolivia**	**Works as interrogator**
		alias: Klaus Altmann
	Peru	1971: Barbie positively identified
		Murder of Moulin

1983	Bolivia	Arrested

→ Link: Barbie thinks he's going back to Germany

1983–7	Lyon	**Trial**
		Vergès +
		Barbie's defense
		Verdict

→ conclusion: Simone Lagrange visits the apartment block where her family lived and remembers the one neighbour who tried to intervene in her family's arrest.

As with *Shoah*, there is a Spartan relentlessness that characterises *Hotel Terminus*. Although Ophuls does not question the validity of archive as Lanzmann has done, unlike *The Sorrow and the Pity* (1970) – Ophuls' monumental film about the Nazi occupation of France – *Hotel Terminus* contains little archival material, instead using interviews with participants and eyewitnesses only. In one interview Ophuls exclaims: 'I avoid Historians and Scholars like the bubonic plague' although his subsequent reason for doing so is interesting: 'because they have no sense of the importance of Show Biz drama, and I do!'; he also uses very little voice-over narration because '"Voice of God commentary" was rightly discredited and ridiculed' (Ophuls 2004: 57). This means that the narrative broken down above is recounted using comparable elements to those found in *Shoah*: Ophuls (and other members of his film crew) and their encounters with eyewitnesses (principally Jewish survivors of Barbie's torture and the concentration camps, members of the French Resistance, members of the CIA and CIC, friends and associates of Barbie, Nazi hunters, Jacques Vergès).

The overall structure of *Hotel Terminus* is very simple and its narrative trajectory is working inextricably towards Barbie's return to Lyon to face trial; the film thus possesses a satisfying overall circularity, even if this dominant narrative comprises a series of intersecting, kaleidoscopic elements that, in constructing the big picture, also construct several smaller ones. Above, the principal narrative features are in bold while subsidiary elements are in normal typescript; the symbol → indicates the mechanism by which Ophuls goes from one section to another, in effect the link in the focused chain. These are by no means unpredictable and the use of a discussion of anti-Semitism to engineer a route back to Germany and then to Barbie's post-war period working in American counterintelligence is the least specific amongst them. The others are straightforward: a section on the 'rat line' which gave ex-Nazis safe passage out of Europe to get from an extended section on Europe to one on Bolivia and Peru, or Barbie's arrest to get the action to go back the other way. Ophuls himself, though, has argued:

> But I think that part of a documentary filmmaker's business is not to have any absolute principles, otherwise he closes too many doors in advance. So

you must always be prepared not only to surprise other people but to surprise yourself. Something might happen to you in the course of events that changes your mind about previous statements in previous interviews.

(Jacobsen 1996: 62)

But as Ophuls indicates slightly later in the same interview when discussing *The Sorrow and the Pity*, he does not make neutral films; just as *The Sorrow* 'comes down very squarely on the side of the Resistance' (p. 62) so *Hotel Terminus* is not going to dedicate too much time to sympathising with the CIC agents, for example, who refused to acknowledge or try to find out about Barbie's criminal past before employing him to do counterintelligence work for them. *Hotel Terminus* is a piece of determinist filmmaking inasmuch as its opinion of Klaus Barbie might be embellished as the film progresses, but remains essentially unaltered; the 'surprise' is in details, such as the fact that so many people seemed to have liked or been impressed by Barbie. Unlike *Shoah* it also reaches a point of definite closure with Barbie's sentencing to life imprisonment (he died of cancer whilst serving this sentence in 1991). Ophuls does not, though, conclude *Hotel Terminus* with the announcement of Barbie's sentence; instead, the final sequence is of Simone Lagrange, one of the documentary's main spokespeople and the individual whose testimony does most to build up a picture of Barbie's brutality and sadism, revisiting her family home in Lyon and recounting the day of her family's arrest. Like so many Jews and members of the Resistance, Lagrange's family was betrayed by a French citizen wishing to curry favour with their Nazi occupiers. When she takes Ophuls back, there is an old woman leaning out of her window wanting to talk; she does not recognise Lagrange, but then remembers her family (and the fact that Simone was the only one to survive the war). Lagrange then recalls the one neighbour – not the woman leaning out of her window – who tried to intervene in the family's arrest. The film is dedicated to this neighbour.

As this conclusion suggests, inside the narrative skeleton of *Hotel Terminus* fit the more discursive and thematic concerns, the most significant of which is the conviction that, whether during the war or after, there was a silent complicity with the Nazis in their desire to bury the past – that French citizens and successive governments, American intelligence and others knew where to find Barbie and other Nazis, for example, but they turned a blind eye. As Ophuls suggests in a parody telephone conversation he enacts with another member of his production team: when making the documentary they repeatedly encountered the attitude that the events Ophuls was investigating took place 'forty years ago' and so were best left alone. The manner in which *Hotel Terminus* concludes reflects the underlying belief that we have not yet reached – and indeed will not reach – comfortable closure on the events that happened 'forty years ago'. Exemplifying this is the sandwiching of the film's logical conclusion – Barbie's sentence – between two crucial interviews that complicate the finality of this ending with Simone Lagrange, as cited above, and Julien Favet, an agricultural worker who witnessed the arrests of the children at Lizieu.

Just prior to the interview with Favet, there is an interview with Vergès and a piece of archive of Jean-Marie Le Pen, leader of the French National Front, referring to the Nazi death camps as a 'minor point' of World War Two history. Vergès denies Barbie had a role in the Final Solution, despite the existence amongst the prosecution's papers of a document stating otherwise. This, Vergès claims, had not been made available to him. The interview with Favet follows immediately after; Favet had been discredited as a witness by the courts (one suggestion was that he had been given a frontal lobotomy – his face is distorted through injury) and is here being given his time on the witness stand, as it were. He testifies to one of the two most significant acts of violence perpetrated and masterminded by Barbie: the rounding up of 44 mainly Jewish children at the refuge of Lizieu, which he witnessed. On 6 April 1944 several lorries arrived and took the children to a 'collection centre' in Drancy whence they were put on the first available train to the camps in the East. Not one child returned. Alongside the murder of Resistance leader Jean Moulin, upon which an earlier section of *Hotel Terminus* concentrates, the murder of the children at Lizieu was Barbie's most infamous crime. Favet's testimony is interrupted by footage of Vergès announcing the court's verdict of life imprisonment; after the last section of his interview comes Lagrange returning to her family's apartment block.

The literal encircling of Le Pen and Vergès by witnesses to Barbie's guilt and his complicity in the Final Solution becomes formally representative of both that guilt and the pervasive reluctance Ophuls has encountered to rake over or even acknowledge the events of the war. As with *Shoah*, *Hotel Terminus* charts an intensely personalised journey. Ophuls steers the film but his interventions, unlike Lanzmann's, are often (though not always) quite soft. Ophuls' performance is hugely important to the tone and effect of *Hotel Terminus*. For instance, during his interview with Robert Taylor, the American agent who initially hired Barbie for the CIC, Ophuls asks Taylor why he hired Barbie, to which the latter replies because he thought he was 'honest' and 'a Nazi idealist'; Ophuls asks the agent to expand upon what he meant by Barbie being a 'Nazi idealist', but Taylor no longer can. Ophuls functions here as a prompter rather than as an intervener or interpreter (it is Taylor's wife Leni, taciturn and looming over her husband as she sits behind him in an upright chair, who on occasion more forcefully intervenes on her husband's behalf).

When later, he interviews Alvaro de Castro, Barbie's bodyguard and friend in Bolivia, Ophuls still appears superficially vulnerable but he becomes far more aggressive: first, he keeps de Castro waiting (he is engaged in a conversation with American journalist Peter McFarren about de Castro, which is intercut with de Castro showing his annoyance at being kept waiting); second, when he does arrive, Ophuls – accompanied by McFarren – is in his dressing gown, stating that he is ill with altitude sickness. De Castro, who is particularly neatly turned out with his shimmering black hair and pressed shirt finished off with fetishistic, military-esque leather trim, appears disarmed by Ophuls. After Ophuls gets de Castro to talk about allegations that Barbie traded arms with a Bolivian drugs baron and de Castro maintaining that the roles of Eichmann,

Barbie and Mengele had been overstated, he then, in his shabby attire, asks de Castro if he realises he is Jewish. De Castro stumbles a bit at this confrontational move. As the introduction to one interview with Ophuls remarks: 'Ophuls aptly has been likened to TV's Columbo, a sly, perpetually rumpled detective who deftly manages, through deceptively simple queries, to pin his smug prey squirming to the nearest wall' (Jacobsen 1996: 61). (In an earlier interview, Ophuls admits to being 'a great *Columbo* fan, just as Truffaut was, and *Columbo* probably influenced me in the way that I constructed this film' [Ciment 1988: 41]). Ophuls makes use of this persona to discredit de Castro and undermine his slickness.

Whereas Lanzmann was altogether more aggressive, Ophuls steers *Hotel Terminus* far less overtly, instead using his Columbo persona (much as later Nick Broomfield would use his alter ego of the friendly man with a boom) to peel away the layers of deceit, forgetfulness and disinterest. Although Ophuls describes it as having been a difficult film to make because 'Klaus Barbie is a subject that has a tendency to make people want to shut up' (Ciment 1988: 41), it is hard to imagine Lanzmann raising a laugh with a broad parody of frustratingly inconsequential phone calls to old ladies who deny ever having known Barbie. In his use of humour and irony or in his wry smiles and shrugs to camera as the old Nazis he is doorstepping elude him, Ophuls is more modern in his interpretation of the on-camera encounter than Lanzmann. As he comments:

> There may be something entertaining even joyful in the fact that a filmmaker is able, with the camera, to turn the tables on the secret agents, the liars, the people who covered up for Barbie and make viewers laugh at them by ironic juxtaposition.
>
> (Ciment 1988: 38)

Exemplifying most of these recent journey films, *Hotel Terminus* also offers no 'final truth'; as Ophuls observes, while such 'complicated events' cannot yield a definitive answer, they '*can* give you a decent sense of what human justice should be about' (Ciment 1988: 43). *Hotel Terminus* is Barbie's alternative trial.

The reflexive journey: *London; Sherman's March*

The reflexive journey documentary is here defined as one that offers a commentary beyond the journey undertaken, frequently on the nature of filmmaking, as occurs in Wim Wenders' *Notebooks on Cities and Clothes,* his documentary about Japanese fashion designer Yohji Yamamoto. Concomitantly, the journeys themselves are not straightforward. Patrick Keiller's *London*, like its sequel *Robinson in Space*, is a mock travelogue, showing the travels and intellectual travails of two middle-aged men whom we never see: the Narrator, who has just returned from serving as a photographer on a cruise ship, and his friend and ex-lover Robinson who lives in a flat in Kennington and teaches part-time at the fictitious University of Barking. *Sherman's March* is Ross McElwee's quasi-autobiographical documentary journey that, alongside his decision to chart Sherman's march through the American South, positions McElwee's more personal and fervent search for a lasting romantic relationship. Keiller is a British avant-garde filmmaker, one of several filmmakers to have come to cinema from other professions (Keiller trained as an architect) and to conform to the tendency of such directors to bring to documentaries certain qualities of the avant-garde and to take issue with and confuse the boundaries between fictional and non-fictional filmmaking. *London* was Keiller's first full-length film; it was funded largely by the BFI (whereas a substantial proportion of British documentary emanates exclusively from television) and was produced by Keith Griffiths, who has also worked with Chris Petit. Many of Keiller's earlier films, such as *Stonebridge Park* (1981) or *Norwood* (1983), display, in miniature, the obsessions with place, history and architecture to be found in *London,* whose journey is part documentary (in that the places visited are real) and part fiction (in that the journey is undertaken by two fictional characters). As an example of how the values and conditions of direct cinema have both consolidated and developed, *London* and *Sherman's March* form part of another growing tradition that takes the attributes and ethos of observational cinema (its interest in contemporary life, detail, personalities, mannerisms) as the basis for reflexive films that simultaneously debate these observational foundations. A belief in the importance to documentary of spontaneity and in particular the unplanned encounter also link *London* and *Sherman's March,* although the films are tonally quite distinct. Whilst *London* is a detached film – one senses Keiller's passion in it, but viewing the film is not an emotional or passionate experience – *Sherman's March* is overtly about passion; yet both documentaries share a distrust of the linear, closed journey, and consequently imply a dynamic relationship with their respective spectators. Both films contain firstly a putative journey the Narrator or McElwee is endeavouring to complete and secondly an actual journey. Both subsequently focus narratively on the collisions and synergies between the two.

As the Narrator announces at the outset, the intended journey in *London* is Robinson's 'pilgrimage to the sources of English Romanticism'; however, the actual journey the friends undertake is less predictable and comprises a series of unplanned encounters that frequently send the men off course and frustrate their intended search. Their journey is divided into three 'Expeditions' with further subsections, of which some are explanatory ('Vauxhall' before a shot of the MI5 building next to Vauxhall Bridge), while others are cryptic or ironic ('Utopia' before a shot of the murky waters of the Thames). *London* juxtaposes a richly evocative, densely factual and cogitative voice-over (spoken by Paul Scofield) with a series of uniformally static, tripod-mounted shots of different images of London, not always logically linked to the narration. As with the dissonance created by the female voice-over in *Sunless,* the relationship of this narration to either Robinson or Keiller is ambiguous (is Robinson, the collator of images, really the Narrator – or is the Narrator, a ship's photographer, Robinson? Are either Keiller's alter ego?). The Narrator, however loquacious, is not given a 'character' as such, but is a site where ideas, observations and fact collation congregate. There are some similarities between him and Keiller (Barwell 1997b: 161), but to interpret him as a self-portrait would be wrong. Similarly there is no motivation afforded Robinson, with whom we become acquainted in far more depth through the Narrator's words, but who may only be a fantasy figure.

Such strategies are generally undermining of narrative equilibrium. Whilst the Expeditions enact a conflict between the cerebral, intellectual journey as planned and its reality, clearly evident is the film's lack of concern over its own 'incompleteness', owing much to Laurence Sterne's stream of consciousness novels such as *Tristram Shandy*, which comprises a perpetual struggle between its slim narrative line and the numerous exuberant digressions. As Sterne (who is referenced in *London*) mocks the novel, so Keiller parodies the non-fiction film's pursuit of developmental structure.

Like Peter Greenaway's obsession with numbers or the importance of Sei Shonagon's lists to Chris Marker's *Sunless*, Keiller is intrigued by non-narrative forms of grouping and structuring. In response to this, Mike Hodges calls *London* a 'film mosaic' made up of 'eighty-four minutes of memorable moments' (Hodges 1997: 166). London's collage of 'moments' is comparable to the *portmanteau* film's bracing together of internally coherent but often tenuously linked shorts (*Paris vu par*, for example). Lists permit alternative and extraneous associations to invade the completeness of a larger unit such as a journey and suggest associations that both complement and disrupt the overall structure.

Like the Surrealist game of consequences or the collation of facts about lightning in Greenaway's *Act of God*, a linking system or data organisation can coincidentally be logical but it will preclude such ordering factors as motive and determinism. Take the Strawberry Hill sequence of *London:*

> Over an image of Walpole's house the narrator relates that Robinson tells him that this is where Walpole wrote *The Castle of Otranto*, the first English gothic novel; then, simply because it is nearby, the two visit Teddington lock and then go on to Twickenham, which is illustrated by a sign for a pub named 'Pope's Grotto'. Though we might expect a mention of the poet, none is given. Over shots of Marble Hill, the Narrator tells us he and Robinson encountered some Peruvian musicians whom they stay with overnight and accompany to Brentford in the morning. The image then cuts to black and over the subsequent shot of a woody path the Narrator remarks cheerily, 'When we awoke it was spring'. Peruvian music then starts up over the image of a cow grazing at the base of Richmond Hill; over the same image, the Narrator then interjects 'he told me Turner used to walk along the river here' before cutting to the view down the same valley from Joshua Reynolds' house. After shots of West London bridges Robinson and the Narrator arrive in Isleworth, represented by another pub sign, this time for the 'Coach and Horses' on the old road to Bristol, 'a notorious haunt of highwaymen' the Narrator divulges, before recounting that he and Robinson are sworn at by the pub's landlord and go onto Kew.

A sequence such as this is comprehensible but it is not cumulative; the only logic is geographical. There is also the disruption of Robinson and the Narrator's excursion by the accidental encounter with the Peruvian musicians, who like most people in *London*, we do not see. This is a prime example of a list: the spectator accumulates facts, but these are fairly random except for being linked to both the characters we have been following and to a limited geographical area. The progression here is not causal, and the journey is further broken up by a number of formal devices, the most notable being the use of intertitles and black leader to separate images. A key feature of a list and of the journey undertaken in *London* is that no image is prioritised over any other, but similarly none is thrown away; a lingering close-up of the grubby Thames, overlaid with snatches of Rimbaud, is treated as reverentially as images of the last fragment of the London stone. Likewise, the framing of the actual images is consistent: few close-ups, precisely composed, detached and certainly unemotive as if emulating the impersonality of a tourist snapshot or picture postcard. A correlative of this non-hierarchical treatment of image is *London*'s editing style. Cuts appear at regular intervals, there are no excessively long takes, nor are there any strikingly rapid montage sequences.

London falls within the category of the city documentary; like many such films, it conforms to a chronological structure as the action takes place over a year (January–December 1992) and it notes several significant historical events, such as John Major's victory in the 1992 British General Election. For much of the time, however, *London* exhibits the more prominent traits of the city film: a disinterest in narrative cohesion except for the flimsiest kind coupled with an interest in non-narrative forms such as lists, catalogues, chains – forms that link material in casual rather than causal ways. This links Keiller to other British art cinema filmmakers such as Greenaway who, since his early documentaries, has been heavily preoccupied with lists and the collation of statistics (*Dear Phone, Act of God, Drowning by Numbers*). City films pursue a very characteristic type of journey: one that has a broad purpose (finding out about a city) but one which is prepared to embrace the accidental encounter or event. Consequently, they do not dwell on the most recognisable and familiar aspects of a city but rather tend to unearth its submerged and obscure outer reaches; as Iain Sinclair says about Keiller, he finds buildings that 'had no idea that they had been lost until Keiller nominated them' (Sinclair 1997: 300). Like Lanzmann, Ophuls and McElwee, Keiller is most intrigued by hidden, private history.

This hidden history is allied to the unpredictable events (for example the bomb on Wandsworth Common that prevents the Narrator and Robinson from getting to Strawberry Hill where they are bound, or the discovery in Stoke Newington of a Daniel Defoe landmark when they had set out to discover relics of Edgar Allen Poe) that endlessly undermine and assist in the suppression of the intended journey the two men have embarked upon. This collision between their actual and their intended course, in turn, poses questions of the feasibility of their predetermined endeavour. The digressions, however, are invariably more interesting than the journey set aside. This ironic treatment of the sensible, purposeful journey finds a parallel in *London*'s attachment to the false logic offered by a chronological structure. Instead, *London*'s circumlocutory style and its pre-occupation with the collation as opposed to linear organisation of images and experiences, suggests more that the journey's destination is of little significance except as a frustratingly unattainable ideal. Despite these frustrations, rather like Vertov's man with his movie camera, the Narrator in particular gives the impression of not being unduly demoralised or deterred by the difficulties he and Robinson encounter.

Parallel to this energy is the repressed but nevertheless evident passion of *London*'s subsidiary journeys through the city's cultural history (which is sorely missed by Robinson) and, more markedly, the political landscape of 1992. The whole journey in *London* is given a quaint but dynamic quality through the insinuation that it is being undertaken by two men who stubbornly refuse to rejoice in the modern city (although the film itself indubitably does), and who choose to continue their despairing rail at the replacement of a European cultural heritage by a grimy present in which Montaigne's name is given to a Soho school of English and an oppressively large, garish poster for the Chippendales now dominates the view from the window at the Savoy Hotel where Monet once stayed. It is ironic and bathetic that the film is obliged to dwell visually on the modern. This modern chronicle (which conceivably represents Keiller's alternative Expeditions) is subliminally critical of Robinson's lofty ambitions, exemplifying its fractious relationship between past and present.

In contrast to these historical amblings is *London*'s journey through the political events of 1992, the subtext that suggests Keiller's personal bias. Rather like the annals quoted from by Hayden White, *London* offers a selective as opposed to comprehensive skirt through the year's events. As befits this journey, it is as if Robinson and the Narrator are present only coincidentally at, for example, the Conservative's general election victory celebrations in Smith Square and John Major's return to Downing Street, the Queen Mother's unveiling of the statue to 'Bomber' Harris, or the Queen's official re-opening of Leicester Square. Of course, running counter to the notion that these events are recorded as if by chance, is the definite implication that none of *London* is accidental (it all being pre-scripted) and that, in these sequences, a consistent political viewpoint – conceivably commensurate with Keiller's – is clearly discernible. As with the rest of *London,* these sequences are shot mute. In these instances, narration is then imposed, some of which repeats verbatim comments that were being made at the time of filming. These focused moments of political and social commentary are not merely narrative digressions but tonal disruptions; the lush, honeyed tones of Paul Scofield uttering criticisms of the Royal family (the cry of 'pay your taxes, you scum' to the Queen Mother) becomes a deeply anarchic act.

This alienation extends to other features of the film. London in *London* is defined by its 'looked-at-ness', it is fetishised and made strange by even familiar images being looked at with such an obsessively static, photographic gaze. Keiller comments that, although the Narrator is pessimistic, 'the whole point of making the film is rather optimistic in that the idea is to make everybody value the place.

It is to say: LOOK' (Barwell 1997b: 165). This compulsion to look at each image afresh imbues *London* with a timeless quality and the lack of an underlying narrative context or a sense of development ensures that the journeys in *London* appear to have no depth or temporal logic, they lack priority or a sense of progression and thus inhabit a repetitive, ever-presentness. Each shot is unspontaneous, not reacting to its subject but framing, composing or confining it. Claire Barwell, Keiller's camera assistant on *London*, recalls how he took an entire morning to re-shoot a single shot, each element (a train, a flag, etc.) needing to be precisely as he had envisaged it (Barwell 1997a: 158).

The ultimate perversity is that *London*, a film that so assiduously maps out journeys, is composed of a series of tripod shots that never move, whether through tracking, panning or zooming. In contrast to *Shoah's* constantly moving, roaming camera or McElwee's fidgety point of view, one that, because McElwee shoots his own film and is forever attached to it, is integrated into *Sherman's March* as a person might be, *London* represses the motion any physical journey necessarily entails. There is much motion implied through the film, but never by the images; the stages of the physical journey occur only between the shots; there are not even any edits suggesting movement or the passage of time, just hard cuts between images and cuts to black or subtitles. A further ironic discordance is that Robinson and the Narrator most characteristically walk to places (another indication that they are out of touch); although *London* pictures every conceivable modern mode of transport except the underground – red Route Master buses, cars, boats, planes – these are only looked at, never mounted or used. We also never see the acts of departing, of going to or arriving at destinations, we are just given images connoting having stopped or having reached a destination. The very classification of *London* as a documentary is, as I have said, problematic and it is very different to other more straightforward documentaries of the 1980s and 1990s in that they are very frequently preoccupied with getting or being there – with sharing with their audience the journey of making a film.

This is quintessentially the case with Ross McElwee's *Sherman's March*, an intrinsically reflexive documentary whose journey is both physical and emotional. Although probably scripted and premeditated, *Sherman's March* does not come across as such. Compared to *London,* it possesses a rougher and more authentic thinking aloud quality, a more 'present-tense quality' as Bill Nichols terms it (Nichols 1991: 47), a genuine-seeming sense of McElwee going where his encounters and conversations take him, whereas *London* meticulously mimics such qualities using beautifully crafted sentences and fastidiously framed shots. Although *Sherman's March* is a classic 'interactive' documentary, to apply Nichols' categories, in that it prioritises interviews and conversational exchanges between its director and his 'social actors' as Nichols terms those who appear in documentaries, it complicates and goes beyond the moment of encounter. Nichols says of *Sherman's March* and *Hotel Terminus* specifically that the films are '*about* the interaction itself' (p. 45), later adding that such films as McElwee's are 'rooted' in this moment and that 'When heard, the voice of the filmmaker addresses the social actors on screen rather than the spectator' (p. 47). It is probably clear by now that this chapter, although focused on documentaries that all, in various ways, feature encounters between filmmakers and 'social actors' and so are 'interactive', has sought to explore beyond the moments of encounter and towards a discussion of what such moments suggest about the journey of making and watching a documentary.

It is the addition of this dimension that makes films such as *Sherman's March* reflexive: they offer a discursive analysis of the nature of documentary filmmaking itself via the mechanism of the encounter. The film's reflexivity is manifested first and foremost in its intertwining of several journeys: the actual journeys of Sherman's march and McElwee's pursuit of eligible Southern women as well as the emotional and intellectual journeys which centre on what making the film comes to mean to and reveal about Ross McElwee (his adoption of the camera as an extension of himself and as something perhaps to hide behind, his use of both narration and the camera – in the rare moments when he talks to it rather than looks through it – as vehicles for personal testimony and confession, his growing realisation that making a film in this manner is not the way to find a partner). In all of these journeys *Sherman's March* goes beyond the interactive mode as the interaction and camaraderie between McElwee and his spectator is crucial.

The full title of McElwee's film is *Sherman's March: A Meditation on the Possibility of Romantic Love in the South During an Era of Nuclear Weapons Proliferation* (McElwee's fear of nuclear war is discussed intermittently throughout). Sherman's March may be the motivation and underpinning metaphor for McElwee's documentary, but it is not its principal subject. As the director explains at the outset, the titular march of 1864 left in its wake a 'path of destruction' and ultimately forced the Confederates to surrender, in McElwee's hometown of Charlotte, North Carolina. At the end McElwee returns to the moment when Confederacy officially died just as he is explaining in voice-over the impact of making this multilayered film and how 'my real life has fallen into the crack between my life and my film'. Moments later he comes to the realisation that his active search for the perfect woman has not been helpful (although the film ends as McElwee has just arranged a date, this time in Boston). The notion of masculine conquest, historical or sexual, is suggested by the formal linking of Sherman's and McElwee's respective marches: Sherman's ransacking of Southern towns which, because they were away fighting the Civil War, were missing much of their male population and McElwee's introduction and attraction to a series of 'nice Southern girls'. But neither 'march' is treated predictably. Just as McElwee fails to proffer the conventional Southern view of Sherman, arguing instead that he was 'one of history's tragic figures' who, commanded to wage total warfare against the civilian population of the South, executed his duties successfully but nevertheless was dismissed by the North and vilified by the South, so his own quest for a suitable woman is tragicomic and notably lacking in sexism.

Despite his sister's suggestion that he use his camera (McElwee shoots as well as directs and edits this movie) as a courting tool, his omniscience is divested of

most conventional affiliations to voyeuristic potency, even when the act of filming is potentially genderised, as when he films an old school friend modelling a
dress at a genteel fashion show come toiletries-buying afternoon his stepmother
has taken him to. Later, McElwee films Pat (the woman with which he most
clearly falls in love) performing her bizarre exercises to reduce the cellulite on her
legs. His valorisation of the phallic camera is at the very least equivocal, despite
several of the women he encounters being filmed – like Pat – in superficially sexual ways: their flesh on show, exercising, swimming, getting dressed for a gig.
McElwee frequently draws attention to the potential eroticism of these encounters, but in so doing draws out their comedic potential at the same time as he
marginalizes their potential for objectification and exploitation. Often, he undercuts the sexualisation of the image by inserting a piece of self-deprecating or
humorous voice-over; as Pat completes a round of cellulite exercises, for
example, McElwee's voice-over states that she had told him she wasn't wearing
any underwear – 'it's not like she told me she wasn't wearing any socks'. At other
times it is the situation itself that nullifies the voyeurism as when he films Winnie
(a PhD student living an alternative lifestyle on a sparsely populated island off the
coast of Georgia) picking tics off her skin, before she roots around for tics on
McElwee's legs, but laughs because she cannot find any amidst the freckles.

As he signals directly his attraction for these women, so McElwee both draws
attention to and undermines the scenes' eroticism (filming Winnie, for instance,
sensuously milking a cow as she talks about her doctoral subject of linguistics and
commenting 'My interest in linguistics continued to grow'). His deadpan delivery and ironic, knowing attitude to the gender relationships he has set up necessarily complicate the simple potential for objectification of such exchanges and
are further accompanied by an impulse to prioritise the success of his movie, ultimately, over the potential success of any of these relationships (the twin desires
– to make a good documentary and to start a successful romantic relationship are
brought together as he says he tried to persuade Pat to stay and star in his film
rather than go to Los Angeles to pursue her acting career).

Such reflexivity serves to highlight McElwee's own position – as the weakened
onlooker, something that, because the women he is most clearly attracted to
leave him, makes the act of filming become sadly solitary and disempowering. We
do not see McElwee with these women, an absence that makes the attraction he
shows and the relationships he describes seem more imaginary (perhaps even illu-
sory) than credible. In fact, his camera (and his attachment to it) is more of a
hindrance than a weapon; frequently, as a spectator the camera becomes a palpable barrier as women strain to look round it at him or ask him to turn it off or
draw attention to the oddity of the situation, as his stepmother does, when she
enquires why he is squinting. As his old teacher Charlene tells him as she tries to
set McElwee up with a Mormon woman Deedee, he should stop filming if he
really wants to get to know her. Towards the end of the film McElwee himself
arrives at the same realisation when, in a final attempt to salvage his relationship
with Karen, he stops filming because he realises that this is ruining their friendship.

In undercutting predictable apparatus/gender relations, *Sherman's March* also undercuts traditional notions of masculinity and narrative; the very nature of the journey McElwee undertakes – that it is unpredictable, spontaneous (or purportedly so), meandering, that, bar a couple of asides, it comprises the unofficial romantic journey at the expense of the official Sherman's march one and includes McElwee's soul-searching, confessional narration and pieces to camera – is more conventionally 'feminine' than 'masculine' (or serves as an indication that such binary oppositions are meaningless). The recent Jim Jarmusch feature film *Broken Flowers* (2005) follows much the same narrative – and might well be in part derivative of *Sherman's March*. Don Johnston (Bill Murray) receives a pink letter from an anonymous ex-girlfriend informing him that he has a 19-year old son. A resolute bachelor, he does not know which of his early conquests might be the boy's mother and is persuaded by his amateur sleuth next door neighbour to make the journey to visit as many of his past girlfriends they can locate. As in *Sherman's March*, the women Don tracks down are, in different ways, cooky and eccentric. He does not find his son.

Broken Flowers is a simplified version of *Sherman's March* and in its straightforwardness (that it centres on Don's encounters with the ex-girlfriends) serves to highlight the relative complexity of the earlier documentary and to signal its own definitely masculine viewpoint. Whereas the women in *Broken Flowers* are looked at through Don's gaze (their objectification is complete as they become most interesting for what they reflect of Don), in *Sherman's March* the gaze is less assured. This is largely due to the layering of the documentary narrative and to the intermittent displacement of McElwee's romantic journey by its otherwise repressed titular counterpart. The two journeys, though compatible, get in each other's way and (to apply an apt metaphor for the situation) it is when he is at a crossroads that McElwee confronts this. One such point comes under half way through the film, just after McElwee returns from a costume ball. He recognises that he is still in love with Pat, and it is at this juncture that he decides (though not for very long) to resuscitate the Sherman idea. McElwee offers his eloquent defence and analysis of Sherman (in whispers for fear that his father, who is in the adjacent room, might hear and wonder about the sanity of his son – still dressed in his Confederates costume). The next stage of his journey, however, is to the island where Winnie lives. The next crossroads and the next time McElwee resolves to leave Charleston is after Charlene, despondent that it has not worked out between him and Deedee, assures Ross that she wants to set him up with another woman who is certainly not a Mormon – 'in fact, she sleeps around'. At this point McElwee goes in search of more shrines to Sherman's destruction of the South, but again his contemplation of his putative subject compels him to return to considering his romantic plight and the role his filming is playing in his own life as he muses: 'It seems I'm filming my life in order to have a life to film, like some primitive organism that somehow nourishes itself by devouring itself'. This introverted despondency – which characterises his obsessive filming not as a desire to look at others so much as a desire to look inside himself – leads McElwee to then agree with Charlene's assessment that the only way he can relate to women is through filming. It is at such critical personal junctures that McElwee decides to resume filming Sherman's march, although such resolutions are invariably short-lived. Moments later, McElwee finds himself sidetracked by and drawn to the singer Joy performing outside a shopping mall.

As the journeys in *Sherman's March* are so half-heartedly about reaching a conclusion, it is appropriate that it is the journey retracing Sherman's steps – the one that has been perpetually marginalized, forgotten – that reaches conventional closure as McElwee visits New York, a city that Sherman liked and returned to often on his public lecture tours. It is here that McElwee relates the circumstances of Sherman's death from pneumonia on St Valentine's Day, 1891. Here one comes to realise that McElwee, far more interested in Sherman's character than his march, returns to consider Sherman at times when the parallels with his own predicament (being undervalued, forever journeying across the United States) are particularly marked. The circularity and inconclusiveness combined of *Sherman's March* is confirmed at the end as McElwee finds Karen – the woman who abandoned him at the beginning of the filming process and who became the catalyst for his journey to meet a 'nice Southern girl', is rejected again by her and then moves to Boston, where he meets Pam, whom as the film ends he has asked out on a date. The struggle between the two narratives bidding for supremacy is resolved as Sherman's narrative concludes with his death (as his march had been concluded moments earlier as McElwee recounts the demise of the Confederacy at Charlotte, North Carolina) while the romantic narrative goes on. Because we do not know, McElwee's upbeat tone notwithstanding, how the relationship with Pam will turn out, the documentary's important narrative is left dominant but open.

Conclusion

This chapter has taken an essential ingredient of the observational documentary, namely the encounter, and developed this into a discussion of a fundamental component of many documentaries: the journey. The performative elements of the documentary journey are various, most obviously the fact that, when they begin, the end-point of a journey is unknown, defining the journey embarked upon as a fluid performative act. In their inherent performativity the films examined here extend and to a certain extent reinvent the parameters of traditional observational cinema and more specifically direct cinema. Whereas so much direct cinema sought narrative certainty, even when it could not predict the end-point of a film by seeking out a crisis or a sequence of events with an inbuilt conclusion, such as the election in *Primary*, journey films play with the notions of certainty and finality (journeys are, after all, going somewhere) and ultimately undermine them. The most apparent way in which films such as *Sherman's March, Seven Up, Hotel Terminus* or *Hoop Dreams* undermine the supposed purposefulness of the journey is by embarking upon one journey only to find themselves pursuing another, sometimes altogether different one. This sidetracking is a key generic feature and highlights the prioritisation of the act of journeying over the act of getting to a destination; the means justify the end. Several of these documentaries can appear ambling, even chaotic and can seem to have marginalized purposefulness, although their coherence tends to be cerebral, political or emotional rather than formal, as they frequently conclude ambiguously or their journeys left unresolved.

Despite the documentaries' indebtedness to the observational tradition, these journey films contrast directly with the areas of television documentary to be discussed in the following chapter. Docusoaps, reality television and formatted documentaries are all overly and overtly preoccupied with imposing a form, a structure, a narrative; an endpoint has been decided upon before their journey has begun. A good comparison with which to end this discussion and usher in the next is to be found in the differing approaches to interviewing in first journey documentaries and then reality-based shows. As Michael Apted indicated when talking about his reputedly soft interviewing techniques in *Seven Up*, his attitude has always been to let his interviewees talk, to 'take a chance'. Although similarly rooted in observation, the form the interviews and conversations in reality and formatted documentaries will take has already been prescribed: the chats with 'Big Brother', the judges' views of the challengers on *Faking It* or the round the table discussions between the families at the end of *Wife Swap*. Here little is left to chance, and the two extremes of early observational documentary – the desire to let the cameras roll and see what happens and the inclination to impose some kind of narrative order on events that might otherwise seem formless – are here enacted.

4　New observational documentary
From 'docusoaps' to reality television

Observational documentary has not been rendered obsolete by the advent of more interactive and reflexive modes of non-fiction television and film. Instead what has occurred is an evolution from within the parameters of observational documentary, so that the form, in all its permutations, remains recognisably 'observational', whilst incorporating many of the tactics and devices of its so-called interactive, reflexive and performative successors. Firstly, it is wrong to imply that observational documentary ceased to be popular once de Antonio and colleagues introduced more interventionist forms of filmmaking; within the observational mode's continuing popularity, especially in the US and the UK (where it is popularly known as 'fly-on-the-wall'), there has emerged a desire both to address the mode's shortcomings and to incorporate into the traditional observational framework other elements of documentary filmmaking. Since direct cinema, the Anglo-American observational tradition has gone through several stages: the later one-off films of Pennebaker, the Maysles brothers, Wiseman *et al.* (*Grey Gardens, The War Room, Hospital*) have stayed faithful to their tradition, modifications were introduced by such television series *An American Family* (Craig Gilbert, 1972), *The Family* (Paul Watson, BBC, 1974) and *Police* (Roger Graef, BBC, 1982) and the genre has since been more radically altered by the interventions of specific filmmakers such as Nick Broomfield, Molly Dineen and Michael Moore and popular series such as docusoaps and reality shows to have appeared on British television and around the globe from the late 1990s onwards.

The characteristics that have come to represent the docusoap and reality-based sub-genres of observational documentary (and affiliated formatted documentary series such as *Wife Swap* and *Faking It*) are their emphasis on entertainment, the importance of personalities who enjoy performing for the camera, fast editing and the intercutting between alternate stories or personalities, a prominent voice-over (although this is less the case in pure reality shows), a focus on the quotidian. These sub-genres are also linked by having been inconsistently received. Frequently scorned by critics, programmes such as *Driving School, Big Brother, I'm a Celebrity ... Get Me Out of Here!* and *Survivor* have garnered consistently high viewing figures. The progression from docusoaps to reality television can now be seen to have been a journey that has redefined observational television documentary. What these factual sub-genres helped the press, viewers and programme-makers formulate was the new category of 'factual entertainment'. Ironically, because there is now so little traditional documentary output on British television, a programme such as *Big Brother*, which used to be considered 'entertainment', is currently classified under 'Factual' in *Broadcast*'s weekly dissection of British television audience figures. The emergence of these strands signals the growing unhappiness with classic observational transparency and passivity, the absenting of an authorial voice and the abstention from any overt means of demonstrating the filmmakers' presence. Instead, what these sub-genres have responded to is the pervasive modern concern with the notion that documentary's most significant 'truth' is that which emerges through the inter-action between filmmaker and subject in front of the camera (classic direct cin-ema being predicated upon the different premise that documentary was simply the recording of events that would occur whether or not the cameras were pres-ent). As a result, there has been a relaxation of some of the boundaries between documentary and fiction – a reconfiguration of John Grierson's infamous defini-tion of documentary as the 'creative treatment of actuality' (Rotha 1952: 70) of which Grierson himself never would have dreamed. The intention of this discus-sion is to highlight the shifts that have occurred within the modern observational documentary tradition towards this more relaxed position, reflecting back to the perceived shortcomings of direct cinema in the 1960s before examining docu-soaps and their antecedents (such as the series *HMS Brilliant* and *The House*) and concluding with a consideration of reality television and formatted documen-taries, which have essentially globalised the documentary market.

As in the case of *cinéma vérité* and direct cinema in the early 1960s, the evo-lution and current extension of the parameters of observational film and televi-sion is in large part due to specific technological advances. Although Annette Kuhn, for one, resists the assumption that technology was a determining factor where *vérité* and direct cinema were concerned, positing instead that the oppo-site might be true – that 'certain types of equipment were developed and mar-keted expressly to make a specific type of filmmaking possible' (Kuhn 1978: 75), the most commonly held view of the technology-form relationship is that advances in sound and camera equipment had a radical effect upon the type of film (documentary or fiction) that was conceived or could be envisaged. Just as the wave of observational films at the beginning of the 1960s was made possible, it is argued, by the appearance of lightweight cameras and portable sound equip-ment that could record live, synchronous sound (see Mamber 1972a: 79), so the more recent interest in similarly observational styles of programme-making have been influenced by equivalent technological advances. The first significant factor has been the rise of non-linear editing systems such as Avid. Traditional linear video editing was slow and inflexible and non-linear systems have enabled film-makers to edit quickly and to experiment with sequences and cutting styles. Any documentary or series rooted in observation is, by being based upon observing action as opposed to dictating it, necessarily going to amass a higher than aver-age shooting ratio, and immediately prior to the arrival of Digicam, 16-mm film was getting too expensive as the documentary's medium of choice. Another important advance has been the introduction of small digital video cameras increasingly operated by directors who, whether because of taste or financial restrictions, are willing to experiment with 'multiskilling' and shoot their own material. The first high-profile UK series to use 'digicams' was Chris Terrill's *Soho Stories* (BBC2, 1996), for which Terrill operated both camera and sound. Yet another significant factor has been the incorporation of surveillance technology and footage (originally the defining feature of 'Reality TV') – the presence of cameras around the clock, recording the subjects' every move. Clearly there are financial benefits to contemporary modes of working. As Paul Hamann commented, while head of the BBC's documentary and history department, docusoaps cost on average only a third of the price of the equivalent amount of programming in light entertainment or situation comedy (Hamann 1998: 6). There are also, however, creative reasons for working in this way, such as the opportunity for greater intimacy and immediacy. Again, therefore, technological changes have enabled documentary to shift direction.

Docusoaps: the arrival of factual entertainment

Docusoaps were a phenomenon of British and other national televisions during the late 1990s. Although a few series such as *Airport* (BBC, 1996–) and *Airline* (ITV 1998–) have continued, by the early 2000s they had largely disappeared from the schedules in their 'pure' form. *Big Brother* first appeared on Dutch television in 1999; the format was bought in the UK by Bazal and the first series of *Big Brother* UK started in July 2000. 'Reality Television' as these game show- and surveillance-based programmes came collectively to be known, took over as the primetime 'factual entertainment' of choice. Paul Hamann offered a loose definition of docusoaps as series 'constructed around a small group of charismatic characters in a common endeavour' (Hamann 1998: 6). This definition is broad but nevertheless highlights two areas that are key to the sub-genre: 'characters' (that is personalities audiences respond to and who feature prominently throughout the series) and the grouping of such characters around work, pleasure or place. Both of these features have clear antecedents in the wider observational tradition, as the selection and prioritisation of 'characters' have been consistent ploys of the observational mode since the 1960s, and both have subsequently become central to the appeal of reality television. *Salesman,* with its focus upon Paul, testifies to this, and to the realisation that an entertaining and different 'character' is a useful narrative device. The concentration on a fixed place (or shared experience) has been another tactic deployed by traditional observational cinema, most notably in the institution-based films of Fred Wiseman, and has functioned as an additional means of lending coherence to a sequence of otherwise unplanned events.

The arrival of docusoaps proved a watershed moment in factual television output, and key to their importance was how they diverged from the observational tradition. Crucial was their marginalisation of issues (socio-political, historical, etc.); as important were their production values. Series such as *HMS Brilliant* (Chris Terrill, BBC1, 1995), *Nurse* (Jenny Abbott, BBC2, 1998) and *The House* (Andrew Bethell, BBC2, 1995) – made around the time that docusoaps started to emerge – were still shot on film and all incorporated, more or less explicitly, issues (women in the front line, the state of the nursing profession, grandiose over-spending at Covent Garden) that transcended the boundaries of their form and gave the series significance or direction beyond their entertainment value. Whether docusoaps ever possessed such weight or substance is debatable; some, like *Vets' School* and *Vets in Practice* or *Children's Hospital* proffered information in addition to character and plot, whilst others such as *Driving School, Pleasure Beach, Clampers* or *The Cruise* more blatantly elevated personalities over situation and ignored subsidiary 'issues'. Other generic features were the use of fast editing and the imposition of overt structuring devices more akin to those of soap operas (hence the coined term 'docusoap'). Docusoaps tended to comprise short sequences and to intercut different narrative strands, not necessarily to create a point through such juxtapositions, but rather to move the story along; they also frequently constructed opening sequences that introduced the audience to the 'characters' each episode would then focus upon, closing sequences that anticipated the next episode and functioned as hooks to maintain audience interest, and often gave each episode a title. Within this observational/soap framework, docusoaps also included elements such as narration, interviews and music conventionally excluded from traditional observational documentaries.

When talking about docusoaps, it is always the balance between entertainment and serious issues that divides people. Classical observational director Roger Graef vociferously defended docusoaps when he said 'I am pleased to see television recognises that ordinary lives are worth watching' (Graef 1998), while Paul Watson, who arrived at much the same time as Graef onto the observational documentary scene, condemned docusoaps for containing 'no analysis, no insight, no unexpected side to the story, no light shed ... their only function seems to have been to turn the rest of us into peeping toms' (McCann 1998). Graef, however, conflated docusoaps (somewhat erroneously) with the traditions of classic observational filmmaking, namely 'filming events as they happen, without lights, staging or interviews' and 'editing in chronological order' (Graef 1998), whilst Watson differentiated between that tradition (into which he placed his own pioneering series *The Family*) and the wave of 'cheap series' that merely '[point] a camera at someone wanting self-promotion' (Watson 1998).

The preoccupation Watson expresses here touches upon the basis for the very definition of 'documentary' as a discourse of sobriety, as Nichols has termed it, as if a natural affinity exists between factual representation and earnestness of endeavour. Docusoaps (and later reality television) questioned this affiliation in a manner that differentiated them from straightforward observational documentary, despite the common lineage, and it is the mounting of this challenge to traditional definitions that provoked Peter Dale, Channel 4 commissioning editor for documentaries until February 2005 (when he was made head of More4), to comment at the start of his tenure

> Documentaries were once cherished by broadcasters because they fascinated us and contributed to our understanding of the world. ... Today, documentaries are cherished because they entertain. ... It would be ironic if, at this time of greatest popularity, the documentary genre was dying for want of genuine curiosity and passion.
>
> (Dale 1998:17)

Like the documentaries he commissioned, Dale soon altered his opinion of what constituted a worthy documentary and presided over Channel 4's dominance of the 'factual entertainment' market with series such as *Wife Swap, Big Brother, Faking It* and all those programmes about weight and house-selling. In one interview from 2003 his interviewer reports that the first thing Dale said to her when they met was that he wanted to 'remove the word "documentary" from the English language because it carries so much baggage with it' (Hughes 2003: 15). After initially being worried that documentary might be 'dying' at just the time of its 'greatest popularity', Dale (who left the BBC during its docusoaps heyday) soon embraced 'factual entertainment', saying bullishly in 2003:

> There are some people who say that the kinds of films I used to make are dead and I say: 'The king is dead, long live the king'. There are many different forms to replace them that are more vivid and more interesting. That means you change the audience and the filmmakers' perception of what a documentary for Channel 4 in 2004 is. It isn't what it was when I arrived in 1998.
>
> (Hughes 2003: 15)

The emergence of docusoaps proved the catalyst for a fundamental reconceptualisation of factual broadcasting – to even use the word 'documentary' (as Peter Dale intimates) seems now to be endearingly quaint and anachronistic. With docusoaps, documentaries became what Nick Shearman, who initiated several of the key popular observational series to have come out of Bristol BBC (*Vets' School, Vets in Practice, Holiday Reps*) has called 'people-based documentaries' – documentaries in possession of a universality that enabled them to 'appeal to a broad range of people and to touch on common experiences' (Shearman 1998).

In terms of docuoaps' anecedents, *HMS Brilliant* and *The House* were unexpectedly successful observational series that paved the way for the renewed interest in the late 1990s/2000s in observational documentary. *HMS Brilliant* followed the crew of the first British Navy vessel to take Wrens as it patrols the coast of the ex-Yugoslavia (Terrill has returned to similar subject matter with his recent series *Shipmates* [BBC1, 2005] about HMS Chatham's time in the Gulf and then in Asia, where it went on a mercy mission after the tsunami struck in December 2004); *The House* infiltrated the Royal Opera House, Covent Garden, during the period before its closure for renovations prior to its re-opening in 1999. The two series exemplified the main routes observational documentary could take: Terrill's work has been more classically observational in that his films are largely examinations of institutions and the issues they illustrate (although *The Cruise* proved a notable exception), whilst *The House* had a more direct stylistic influence upon docusoaps with its use of ironic, pointed narration, its confrontational editing style and its pursuit of crises and star performers.

HMS Brilliant (six episodes of 50 minutes) was the first time the British Navy had permitted filming aboard a vessel on active deployment in a war zone, as well as the ship being the first (in October 1990) to take women to sea.[1] Terrill and his crew spent twelve weeks filming the series, living alongside and in similar circumstances to the crew of the ship. Terrill's immersion in navy life (he is a former cadet and his parents served in the Navy during World War Two) and his non-interventionist attitude to filming were paramount. As Terrill, in traditional observational vein, has remarked, a filmmaker should 'never be judgemental' nor should s/he 'distort the way those in the films see things' (Terrill 1998). An example of this method is Episode three of *HMS Brilliant,* 'Rocking the Boat', revolves around preparations for and the performance of 'The Sod's Opera', a revue show which resembles a traditional twelfth night entertainment during which the junior classes exchange places with their superiors. The episode is structured around this and the concomitant issue of Wrens on active duty, a fusion that culminates in a group of Wrens performing 'I Will Survive' and being drowned out by the jeers of their largely male audience. Towards the beginning of the episode, Lieutenant Commander Bob Hawkins, who throughout the series espouses a variety of patriotic and traditional views, gives an interview in which he intimates his unease with women on active duty, commenting that they are 'the fairer sex and we [men] are the people who should protect them'. He indicates how much he, 'a masculine guy', appreciated the ship's exclusively male environment, saying 'I enjoy the camaraderie, the aggression of a warship'. Hawkins' conflation of 'camaraderie' and 'aggression' illustrates succinctly the violent exclusivity of Eve Sedgwick's notion of 'homosocialism'; it also predicts the confrontational irony of Hawkins' own contribution to 'The Sod's Opera': a drag act. Following Hawkins' interview are a series of sequences that further the debate surrounding women on active duty: a brief montage of principally negative comments by other male crew members about the presence of the Wrens on board *HMS Brilliant;* an interview with Lieutenant Tracey Lovegrove during which she observes that the ship is 'very much a man's world' and that women are excluded from the 'male bonding'; an interview with Captain James Rapp in which he articulates the differences he perceives between the men and the 'girls' aboard his ship. This initial issue-focused sequence concludes with Hawkins suggesting that a country that chooses to send its women to the frontline is 'morally bankrupt'.

As voice-over is entirely absent from *HMS Brilliant,* during these ten minutes there is no intervening commentary. Intercutting alone between the various elements sets up the revue – the illustrative proof of the ideological argument, most overtly the Wrens' run through of 'I Will Survive' being sandwiched between one male crew member suggesting that Wrens on board are a temptation to married men and another saying that women lack the stamina of their male counterparts and are forever complaining. The final section of the film comprises last minute preparations and the revue proper. The men's contributions are: Leading Seaman Micky Goble telling crude jokes that are bleeped out, a close harmony quintet, a parody gay act and Hawkins in drag; the women's contribution comprises a mock thank you speech to the men and 'I Will Survive', which closes the film. As a woman, viewing the Wrens struggling defiantly through their rendition of Gloria Gaynor's feminist anthem is deeply moving, in part because the women sing quite badly; the booing from their male colleagues hardly comes as a surprise to them or us, and what the sequence cements is an implicit counter-bonding between the women on the screen and those watching. As Terrill himself observes, this climactic confrontation was 'sort of a stand off' (Terrill 1998).

Of this exemplary observational film Terrill commented: 'I was obviously trying to show that there are many attitudes to women and to women in the front line. All these people were also my friends, and its wasn't for me to agree or disagree with Bob Hawkins, who had a very particular line that women should not go to sea'. What comes as a surprise, perhaps, is Terrill's own attitude to the question of women in the armed forces, which is that he has 'difficulty relating to the idea of women in the front line', a view that he qualifies by saying, 'but that's a personal thing that has no part in a Chris Terrill film' (Terrill 1998). It is richly ironic that this episode's ideological sympathies are seen – through editing and juxtaposition – to lie with the Wrens, proof, in a sense, that observational documentary need not necessarily reflect the filmmakers' opinions and biases.

Within a discussion of non-fiction and objectivity, Noël Carroll examines the relationship between subjectivity, bias and selection. Carroll refutes Balazs' assumption that 'a personal point of view in every shot is unavoidable' (Carroll 1996a: 227), arguing instead that not only is this dubious, but that the premise upon which such a view is founded is flawed. The crux of Carroll's argument is that the brandishing of the term 'subjectivity' to signify 'everything that doesn't suit the criteria of the objective' (p. 230) is to misinterpret the 'objectivity' itself. Just as scientific research can be classified 'objective', Carroll maintains, despite its selectivity, so can documentary. Terrill's desire not to impose his own point of view onto his documentaries now seems rather old school. First docusoaps then the reality shows and formatted documentaries that followed in their wake all show to a greater or lesser degree how the manipulation and intrusion of their production teams, whether through voice-over (often condescending, nearly always directional) or other means such as editing style, the contributors talking to camera or the presence of a presenter.

The House seemed at the time to be a comparable observational series to *HMS Brilliant*, but with hindsight it has become obvious that it was a more direct precursor to docusoaps. Firstly, its production team was far more directly involved in illustrating and manufacturing the confrontations and issues raised by its content, most concretely through Jancis Robinson's arch and critical voice-over. *The House* was actively not passively observational; the filmmakers (though falling short of directly engineering crises) were, for example, forewarned of looming conflicts, such as the imminent sacking of the Box Office manager, which subsequently features in Episode 1, 'Star Struck'. The whole nature of the series was to pursue such crises and to structure episodes around them, and in so doing the significance of the institution was inevitably marginalized in favour of the individuals involved, as were any related issues. As Andrew Bethell has commented, *The House* was not really about the arts, but about 'fear and loathing in the work place' (Bishop 1996: 13); it was not institution-specific but universal in its appeal. Much about the style of *The House* – the hand-held camera's furtive pursuit of people and its presence at crucial moments of tension – seems relatively traditional; the series, however, was also generally credited with being the immediate precursor to docusoaps (which the BBC pioneered) and 'factual entertainment'.

A discernible pattern emerged through the series, so that each episode comprised one major and several minor crises, some of which were resolved by the end of the episode, while others remained open, to be resumed in later weeks. In Episode 2, 'Horse Trading', the major crisis was the phenomenal overspend caused by simultaneous last minute alterations to the designs for the Royal Ballet's production of *Sleeping Beauty* and the Royal Opera's *Katya Kabanova* (in excess of £60,000 on each and overtime expenses of £117,000). Linked to this central structuring device were various subsidiary arguments, problems and rivalries: a horse slipping on the shiny *Kabanova* set (necessitating yet more modifications); the rivalry between Royal Ballet ballerina Darcy Bussell and guest star Sylvie Guillem for the most prestigious dates of the forthcoming American tour of *Beauty*; another slippery floor, this time causing Bussell to slip several times during the ballet's final London rehearsal. The significant aspect of *The House*'s 'crisis structure' (itself a mode of storytelling attributed by Stephen Mamber to direct cinema) was the lack of discrimination or hierarchical placement; all major and minor crises were valued according to their narrative as opposed to their political, social or ideological importance (a notable departure from direct cinema's use of a similar device). Thus the laying off in the final episode of established older Royal Ballet dancers in order to save money, or the protracted pay discussions between personnel and unions in Episode 4, were given comparable weight to the dispute between traditionalists and modernists over the Opera House's revival of Harrison Birtwhistle's *Gawain*. This uniformity clearly anticipated docusoaps' underpinning desire to entertain. Likewise the very use of (mini)crisis structure became a characteristic of docusoaps, as did the fast editing between different but interlinked strands within one episode. What, however, set *The House* apart from the series it manifestly influenced were its production values. At a cost of £150,000 per episode and with a nine-month shoot and a twelve-week editing period for every one-hour episode (from a shooting ratio of 1:28), *The House* – like *HMS Brilliant* – proved a costly venture.

Within the evolutionary process, the use of 'crisis structure' and other implicitly entertaining narrative devices are important to the recent reconfigurations of observational documentary. 'Crisis structure' was discernible in *The House* and also in early docusoaps such as *Airport* (1996–2002) and *Vets' School/Vets in*

Practice (1996–2002). The pursuit of events with an in-built narrative structure rapidly became one of the mainstays of early direct cinema, as this circumvented the problem of feeling compelled to impose a narrative on events to render a documentary comprehensible and digestible. The aim of Robert Drew and others was also, however, to find and film events that were monumental; events that were so significant in themselves (such as a closely contested presidential primary election or the integration of the University of Alabama) that their filming seemed, to the participants in the crisis, unimportant by comparison. The docusoap's 'crisis structure' is more to do with creating narrative tension than capturing a significant moment. Michael Waldman, series director on *The House,* commented at the time of making the series that, 'getting narrative from observational documentary is hard. We had to impose a structure [during editing] and that is what took the time' (Bishop 1996: 13). Waldman then explains how this need came to affect the shooting process, that, for the early weeks of filming, they cast their net wide and filmed what material they could, whilst by the last two months the direction in which the series was going had emerged, so they 'had a shopping list' (*ibid.*).

Blithely perhaps, Waldman re-opened one of the most contested areas of documentary practice – the right and need of the filmmaker to intervene in the direction of material he or she is filming. Many subsequent docusoaps depended upon similar moments of crisis (*The Clampers, Driving School, Airline, Airport, Hotel*) and inserted such confrontations in varying degrees. *Hotel,* in fact, was concerned with the structuring of tension almost to the exclusion of anything else. In one episode (which even begins mid-crisis), one confrontation – the Duty Manager on the telephone to the wife of the hotel dishwasher who has failed to turn up for work – gives way immediately to another crisis – two guests complaining about the rudeness of one of the waitresses at breakfast – which, in turn, gives way to the fractious preparations for two major functions. Editing is here used for the accumulation of a *Fawlty Towers*-like farcical tension.

Finding a strong narrative thread is all about entertainment and the exemplary docusoap was structured and edited to maximise entertainment value. Unlike comparable 'crises' in direct cinema, docusoap crises were primarily concerned with the mundane and the non-monumental, and so the creation of a structure performed the very different function of making everyday events coherent and entertaining. In Mark Fielder's opinion (Fielder was Series Producer on *Driving School*) the fast editing, short sequences style of docusoaps served to divert attention away from their lightweight material: 'It's like running on lilies floating on a pond, you can't spend too long on each [scene] because the story will sink ... so what you have to do is keep moving, keep offering flashes of excitement, a bit of colour, a bit of a joke, an emotional moment – nothing too heavy' (Fielder 1998). This entailed editing documentary material along the lines of popular fiction, in particular the soap. Whereas the media derogatorily coined the term 'docusoap', there are real parallels to be drawn between the fictional and non-fictional soaps that in part serve to explicate the latter's appeal to audiences. Traditional soaps cut between a pool of relatively stable characters, focusing on a limited group within each individual episode. Shearman noted how *Vets in Practice* tended, from very early on, to juxtapose three stories per episode, frequently intercutting two (because parallel editing usually works better) and inserting a third half way through. This continued to be the structuring format used on later series of *Vets* and, if anything, the scenes became progressively shorter over the series' long run (Bell 1998). The prevalent tendency in later docusoaps was towards accentuating such parallels with soap operas. *Lakesiders* (Hart Ryan for BBC1, 1998), for example, was transmitted immediately after *EastEnders* and directly mimicked the BBC soap opera in its title sequence and music.[2] The fast editing was a feature that categorically differentiated the docusoap from both traditional observational documentaries (more likely to be renowned for their long takes and minimal editing) and from contemporaneous observational documentaries such as *HMS Brilliant* or *Nurse*. Editing has two primary functions: to forward narrative and to create argument; in a docusoap the former was dominant. Unlike a comparable theme at the centre of a Fred Wiseman film or an institution-based observational series, any 'big theme' around which a docusoap could have been structured tended to be marginalized in favour of narrative concerns.

The overriding factor that differentiated docusoaps from other forms of observational documentary was thus entertainment. They were more popular with viewers than previous forms of documentary programming (*The Cruise* achieved approximately 11 million viewers, *Driving School* peaked at 12.45 million and even long-running series such as *Vets' School* and *Vets in Practice* remained stable at around 8 million) and whether or not they were broadcast pre- or post-watershed (9pm) was a crucial issue. The docusoap, on the whole, was thought to appeal to a mass, family audience, and there were relatively few subjects that fitted naturally post-watershed, although with *Estate Agents* (Shearman Productions for ITV, 1998), *Jailbirds* (Chris Terrill, BBC, 1999) and *Paddington Green* (Lion Television for BBC, 1999), docusoaps also infiltrated the post-9pm slots. The target audiences and the concomitant emphasis on entertainment were the most plausible reasons for the nature of docusoap subjects – animals, hospitals, the police and related jobs, shopping – and for the rapid, short concentration span editing. The programmes' universality was thereby an essential component of their success, much as it is a reason for the success of so many children-centred documentaries in the twenty-first century (*Little Angels, The House of Tiny Tearaways*). Albert Maysles remarked that 'our films very much proceed from particulars to generalities' (Levin 1971: 280–1), ostensibly functioning, therefore, in much the same way: manoeuvring universal points from individualised situations, creating an identificatory bond between spectator and subject. The important distinction between old and new methodologies, though, resided in how this 'universality' was effected. *Salesman* possessed grandiloquence beyond its superficial mundanity and functioned as a 'tragedy of the common man' comparable to Arthur Miller's *Death of a Salesman* to which it was, at the time, readily likened. Conversely, docusoaps aspired merely to represent a life more ordinary. This emphasis on the ordinary individual and the interest of mundane events persists into reality TV and format-ted documentaries. Even in reality shows that feature celebrities (*I'm a Celebrity ... Get Me out of Here!, Celebrity Big Brother*) the celebrities are rendered ordi-nary – or brought down to earth – by the televisual environment in which they temporarily find themselves.

Underlying the issue of entertainment is the spectre of falsification. The ques-tion of 'honesty' was paramount to docusoaps, and it was questions over their 'honesty' that arguably contributed to their demise. Similarly, by being dubbed 'reality television', subsequent observational output raises comparable questions about verisimilitude, accuracy and authenticity. Some of the issues surrounding docusoaps and honesty were factual, others were aesthetic. For example, in 1998 several allegations were made in the press that Ray Brown, the 'star' clamper of *The Clampers,* was not, except in emergencies, a clamper at all but a desk-bound supervisor who had last been a regular on the beat at least two years before the series was transmitted, rumours subsequently confirmed by Southwark council. The honesty of *Driving School* was likewise challenged. The sequence most fre-quently cited was that in which Maureen Rees, on the eve of another attempt at her theory exam, wakes in the middle of the night and asks her husband Dave to test her on the Highway Code. The sequence is a reconstruction, and Jeremy Gibson (then head of BBC Television Features, Bristol) and others have gone on record exonerating themselves from blame, commenting that, having gleaned that Maureen *did* get up at night through panic, it was perfectly legitimate to recreate such a sequence without the film crew having to camp out in her bed-room for an entire night. Another such instance of reconstruction occurs in *Pleasure Beach* (Andrew Bethell, BBC1, 1998), during a bomb alert. The alert is real and filmed as it happened, as are the telephone calls concerning it; these scenes are then juxtaposed with shots of security staff searching Blackpool pleas-ure beach. The bomb alert is an authentic individual action, but the subsequent search is, like Maureen's night-time panic, a representative typical one (although the search in *Pleasure Beach* is not a reconstruction, but the filming of a subse-quent bomb alert). Andrew Bethell maintained that taking such a liberty was, once again, legitimate. One of the problems with such a presumption is that the audience's awareness of this kind of conduct is likewise presumed. Jeremy Gibson and Grant Mansfield (Executive Producer, *Driving School*) both argued that audiences would have been able to pick up the signs that a sequence such as Maureen revising her Highway Code were reconstructed, but is this sufficient?

Mark Fielder problematised the issue further when he described another set up sequence from *Driving School*. This 'fabrication' is more contentious as it involves actually altering the course of the series' narrative. The producers on *Driving School* were concerned that Maureen, the series' 'star' subject, would not pass her manual driving test, an event they felt would be the series' natural and desired conclusion, and so suggested that she learn instead in an automatic car. Maureen agreed, having indicated that this was an option she had already con-sidered. As Maureen's instructor in Cardiff did not have an automatic vehicle, the producers intervened to effect this switch, putting Linda (the instructor in

Cardiff) in touch with Pam (one of the Bristol instructors also featured in the series) and having them enact a scene on Clifton Downs in Episode 2 in which they discuss Maureen's case, the result of which is that Pam agrees to take Maureen on and to pass her on to her colleague Paul. As Fielder asks, 'How do you tell that story in reality? You can tell it in voice-over and no one would quite believe it. ... The ... reality is that Linda and Pam didn't know each other, so we had to make the introduction. That was our intervention into the story' (Fielder 1998). Clearly the actions of the producers in this case directly altered the course of events as they would have in all probability unfolded (although Maureen subsequently passed her manual test as well). Yet Fielder's justification for this is that he personally did not think 'it was critically important, because in the end what was important about Maureen's story was how she dealt with driving, the pressures on her, her relationship with her husband, which we didn't alter, and finally whether or not she was going to pass which is what people really cared about' (Fielder 1998).

This is an interesting defence of manipulation within a documentary, but one that many are bound to find troublesome. On 8 December 1998 the BBC held an editorial policy meeting at which new guidelines were issued concerning 'Staging and re-staging in factual programmes'. Having acknowledged that 'there are few factual films which do not involve some intervention from the director, even those which are commonly described as "fly on the wall" or observational documentaries' (BBC 1998: 2), the guidelines proceeded to identify certain 'production methods' (specifically single camera set ups) that 'make it impossible to record all events exactly as they happen' and to then single out the accepted techniques (such as cut-aways) commonly deployed to combat this (BBC 1998:2). This section of the document concludes with a series of bullet points itemising 'acceptable and unacceptable practice in factual programmes', many of which pertain directly to instances of overt intervention on the part of the producers:

- Programmes should truthfully and fairly depict what has happened.
- Programmes should never do anything to mislead audiences.
- While it may, on occasions, be legitimate to re-shoot something that is a routine or insignificant action, it is not legitimate to state or re-stage action which is *significant to the development of the action or narrative, without clearly signalling this to the audience.*
- Contributors should *not* be asked to re-enact *significant* events, without this being made clear in the film. ...
- If significant events have been arranged for the cameras that would not have taken place *at all* without the intervention of the programme-makers, then this must be made clear to the audience.
- Shots and sequences should never be intercut to suggest that they were happening at the same time if the resulting juxtaposition of material leads to a distorted and misleading impression of events.

(BBC 1998: 3)

Both *The Clampers* and *Driving School* would have been flouting such rules, despite arguments such as the ones mounted by Fielder. In this instance, the producers' intervention altered the subsequent path of the narrative and – even acknowledging the argument of Mansfield and Gibson in defence of the night-time swotting scene from *Driving School* – in the absence of any categorical signals, the audience remained ignorant of the fact that such scenes had been staged specifically for the cameras. Arguably, the meeting between Linda and Pam on Clifton Downs signalled its constructedness via the stilted performances of the two driving instructors. The exchange between two instructors who live in different cities but happen to know each other and happen to bump into each other is indeed (with hindsight) too neat and uncomplicated: Linda says 'I'm glad I've seen you, Pam – I've got a pupil for you', Pam mentions Paul, Linda concludes 'he sounds ideal, Pam' and they exchange cards. In more recent documentary or reality series (*Wife Swap, Hell's Kitchen, Survivor, Big Brother, Ladette to Lady*) the artifice and staging are announced very clearly at the outset and through the series' style – from the specially created settings for the series (a swanky restaurant, a remote island, a jungle, the *Big Brother* house, a re-opened finishing school) to the microphone each contestant has pinned visibly to her/his clothes. These people, unlike the 'characters' in docusoaps, are quite manifestly not being filmed 'being themselves', that is: doing what they usually do when there are no cameras present. Issues of performance abound even here, but one fundamental confusion has been eliminated.

Was it the docusoap's bias towards entertainment value and audience ratings that compromised the sub-genre's potential for honesty? The arguments that drive this book are: that documentaries inevitably fall short of being able to reproduce authentically the actuality they film; that the notional grail of the non-fiction tradition – that a mode of representation exists that can break down the barrier between reality and illusion – is a false utopian ideal. Many modern observational documentaries start from a premise that implicitly supports this theoretical position, indicating that all documentary is circumscribed by its technical and theoretical limitations and can only present a mutable truth – the truth that comes into being as the documentary is being filmed. This is a departure from early direct cinema and Chris Terrill (1998) has articulated a new (arguably more realistic) approach to observational filmmaking when he says:

> Our stock in trade [in documentaries] has to be honesty; not necessarily truth, whatever truth is – truth is a construct. We deal in perceptual truth, personal truth, not absolute truth. Who deals in absolute truth? Nobody does. It's continually an interpretation, a relating of events as we see them to our audience.

This opinion is very similar to Emile de Antonio's observation that honesty and objectivity are not even closely related and recalls Dai Vaughan's critical observation (made in the 1970s): 'for those who bewail its absence, honesty is a moral problem. For those who try to achieve it, it is a technical one' (Vaughan 1974:

73). Terrill's own progression from relatively classical observational documentaries through to single camera series signals the increased importance of technology to the manufacturing of 'honesty'. Terrill remarked that docusoaps particularly offered 'much more room for creativity and bias' (1998) than their more traditional predecessors, that, paradoxically, the sub-genre's affiliation to dramatic methods ensured, in his estimation, its increased honesty, if indeed honesty is equated with the expression of a personal and perceptual truth. The flaw in this idea is that most docusoaps did not employ such overt methods as authorial intervention to signal their interpretative as opposed to categorical truth, except for standardised devices such as interview. Terrill, in his later documentaries, can often be heard from behind his camera conversing with the subjects of his films – just as Molly Dineen or Lucy Blakstad can (this does seem to be a more female trait) – a trope that necessarily identifies the specificity of the situation represented. For all the use of emotive music (sad for Maureen's test failure or the death of a pet, for example), fast editing, guiding narration and packaging, the docusoap retains one feature of the direct cinema legacy: the anonymous camera and filmmaker. In the absence of such straightforward devices as speaking in one's own film or appearing in it, both the BBC guidelines and Chris Terrill, from differing perspectives, proposed that additional measures should be enforced to ensure the mutability of the truth being represented is understood by those watching. (Whether or not such direct forms of intervention are more 'honest' than their less visible counterparts is examined more extensively in Chapter 6.)

The issue that most clearly and consistently highlights the question of artificiality within the context of observational documentary is that of performance – both the performance of the filmmaker and that of the subject in front of the camera. At times, performance, lying and documentary ethics are linked, as in the case of Carlton's documentary *The Connection* (Marc de Beaufort, 1997) in which several participants in a documentary reputedly about a drug run from Colombia to Britain assumed roles or faked actions. Likewise, in the pulled Channel 4 documentary *Fathers and Daughters* (1998), it was discovered, on the eve of transmission, that one of the father and daughter pairs interviewed for the series were, in real life, partners (the television company only realising this when the woman's actual father contacted them after seeing the programme's trailer). In both these cases, subjects of a documentary were deliberately pretending to be someone they were not – in *The Connection* with the full knowledge of the filmmakers. Performance in observational documentaries is normally a more nebulous issue. As they had actively pursued events with an in-built 'crisis structure', so the exponents of direct cinema also pursued subjects who were professional performers, thinking that this would once again reduce to a minimum the distorting effect of the cinematic apparatus on the subjects' behaviour. In *Meet Marlon Brando* or *Don't Look Back,* neither Brando nor Dylan drops his guard for the camera or stops performing; the filming process becomes an extension of their public personae. Clearly, performance within an 'ordinary lives' observational film or a docusoap is a very different matter, as the 'characters' who become familiar through the programmes – with exceptions such as *The Cruise's* Jane McDonald who was already a professional singer or the various performers in *The House* – do not have a history of professional performance and are thereby enacting themselves exclusively for the benefit of the cameras. In a tangible sense, Maureen Rees and others only come into being as performers through and at the point of filming, which is an artificiality that the direct cinema directors sought not to confront.

The immediate response to the notion of performance in documentary is to criticise it as a falsification – an element not to be trusted. The journalist Allison Pearson, for instance, has commented about performance in docusoap:

> In the hands of its most serious practitioners – directors such as Molly Dineen and Roger Graef – documentary aspires to tell us something about the human condition. The docu-soap, by contrast, tells us something only about the condition of human beings who know they're on television.
>
> (Pearson 1998)

Pearson's dismissiveness also stems from her perception of performance as an obstacle to serious documentary endeavour; she fails to equate it, as Terrill did when referring to his interventionist style that utilised the interaction between filmmaker and subject, with 'a new honesty' (Bishop 1998: 17). Terrill's opinion is compatible with Jean Rouch's suggestion that, in *cinéma vérité*, people's reactions are 'infinitely more sincere' on camera than off *because* 'they begin to play a role' (Levin, 1971: 288). Sincerity is thus equated with an acknowledgement of the filming process. 'A camera's a camera, an object which you can't not notice' (Fielder 1998) and a documentary is inevitably built around its presence – and the concomitant presence of a crew. In docusoaps, however, there was very little engagement with the theoretical permutations of such awareness as they remained programmes that largely circumvented the overt acknowledgement of performance.

Hotel was an exception to this rule. If one briefly compares *Hotel* to *HMS Brilliant* a substantial discrepancy emerges between the two approaches. Whereas *HMS Brilliant* was about observing life on a Royal Navy vessel and offering as many viewpoints of this as possible, *Hotel* was not about the Adelphi Hotel in Liverpool, as much as it was about those who worked there. In *Hotel*, the routine of working in a hotel is marginalized in favour of character development, unless the everyday details supplied an argument, a confrontation or a crisis. The majority of the series revolved around its protagonists (notably manageress Eileen Downey, chef Dave Smith and operations manager Brian Birchall) and their interaction with the camera and with each other. A familiar device was to have a character turning to confide in the camera, to put his or her side of a story in the immediate aftermath of a quarrel or crisis point (a trope also adopted by Jane McDonald in *The Cruise*). In one episode there occurred a running argument (much of which was bleeped out, despite the post-watershed transmission slot) between the chef and the operations manager. The underlying reason for this confrontation – that the kitchens were over-stretched, catering for two large Saturday night functions – was sidelined in favour of the protracted slanging match that ensued between the two men. We never did find out precisely how the chef coped with the catering problem, and instead were offered personal insights into how the men viewed each other. It was almost as if the fact that Dave and Brian worked in a hotel was an incidental detail not a defining factor in how they came to be represented. Conversely, *HMS Brilliant* was overtly concerned with the workings of the ship and with the contextualisation within that environment of the person-nel, a difference that is most clearly signalled by the series' identification of those featured by rank and full name, whereas *Hotel* (like other docusoaps before and since) identifies its 'characters' by their first names alone.

Another significant aspect of the docusoap's use of performance was its pre-occupation with the star performer. The defining paradox of docusoaps was that they purported to be interested in the excessively ordinary, whilst at the same time having reached the level of success and notoriety they did by the discovery and promotion of 'stars' – individuals who, more than those around them, tran-scended and achieved an identity beyond the series that created them. The cast-ing of documentaries has always been commonplace, but docusoaps took this a stage further. Maureen in *Driving School* proved crucial to the series' popularity, so much so that without her it 'would have been virtually impossible' (Fielder 1998), and after it ended she starred in a follow-up *Driving School* special, acquired an agent, made copious independent television appearances and released a single (a cover version of 'Driving in my Car'). Likewise, Trude from *Vets' School* and *Vets in Practice* stopped working full-time as a vet as her televi-sion career took off. It became evident with later docusoaps such as *The Clampers* or *Lakesiders* that the series were no longer merely focusing on charac-ters the producers thought the public might like, but were inviting subjects to perform exclusively with the camera in mind. In *Clampers at Christmas* (BBC1, 1998) the series' seasonal 'special', Ray Brown, already known as a character who sings whilst on clamping duty, halted the progress of the narrative to perform fes-tive numbers (at the end of his day, for example), with arms swaying and a decid-edly embarrassed colleague by his side cajoled into joining in. This was no longer something Ray did whilst clamping, it had become an activity that replaced it.

There are two separate issues here that, with the rise in the docusoap's popu-larity, became blurred: the acknowledgement that the more engaging and like-able subjects should be prioritised, and the threat posed to a documentary's intentions by the independently lucrative career of one or more of its protago-nists. Both Maureen and Trude are significant because they became stars as a result of the viewing public liking them, suggesting that one crucial element of the star/audience rapport is the potential for identification. According to Nick Shearman (1998), Trude had 'no concept of acting up' for the cameras; similarly, Mark Fielder stresses that Maureen and Dave Rees just happened to be less affected by the presence of the cameras than the others featured in *Driving School*. The accidental popularity of Trude and Maureen conformed to one ideal of documentary: that it 'has to feel slightly effortless and as if bits fall into place'

(Shearman 1998) without too much manipulation. The comparable popularity of Ray Brown or the wannabe singer Emma in *Lakesiders* was more manufactured, less an accident than an actively sought addition to the respective docusoap narratives. Despite Trude's success without resorting to 'acting up' for the cameras, Shearman noticed that, particularly in a long running series such as *Vets,* the subjects eventually 'start to give you what they think you want' (Shearman 1998) – that is, they produce performances with the end television product already in mind.

The series 'special' emerged directly from the docusoaps' success and its concomitant creation of successful stars. In addition to *Clampers at Christmas,* Jane McDonald's wedding to her long-term partner Henrik was featured in *Jane Ties the Knot* and in 1998 a *Cruise Christmas Special* was broadcast. Maureen Rees was featured in a follow-up programme and the wedding of vets Joe and Emma was given a dedicated episode. This emphasis on the single performer, despite its possible derivation from direct cinema, ran counter to the establishing ethos of observational documentary; it did not simply observe the moment at which the performance is produced, but rather invited the stars to exist as separate entities from the documentaries they had been affiliated with. From this perspective, performance interferes with rather than enhances reality because the presence of the cameras has irrevocably altered what documentary subjects might be like if they were not being filmed. Most observational style documentaries retain a keen sense of off-screen space, an existence that will not be terminated when the cameras are switched off; *Nurse,* for instance, shows the trainee nurses to have altered substantially through the series without the audience having been party to the primary causes for those changes. With many of the docusoaps and particularly the later ones, there was, conversely, the feeling that the documentary set-up created the situation, that the off-screen space was, if not empty, then not the predecessor or an adjunct of its on-screen counterpart.

Reality television and formats: 'Hell is other people'

Nick Shearman has illuminatingly likened the formatted documentaries (*Holiday Showdown, Wife Swap*) he and his fellow executive producers at RDF Media now oversee to Jean-Paul Sartre's bleak play *Huis Clos* and the misanthropic notion that 'hell is other people'. The hell that is other people forms the basis for much of the factual output on television at the moment: a group of strangers all competing with each other for celebrity status and (by modern television standards) a modest cash prize under the omniscient eye of 'Big Brother' and the cynical gaze of five million viewers; the wives who have to swap places with their binary opposite or the families who swap holidays with theirs; the minor celebrities being mauled and taught to cook by Gordon Ramsay; or the wannabes who ingratiate themselves with Donald Trump or Alan Sugar with as much brittle gusto as they pile blame for any mistakes onto their team-mates. In the team-based reality shows such as *The Apprentice, Survivor* and *Big Brother,* the 'hell' stems specifically from a shared duality: a need to forge alliances with just those people you are in direct competition with. Although there are important distinctions to be drawn between reality television series and formatted documentaries, an essential component they share is the artificiality of their setting. Whereas docusoaps – however much they emphasised and constructed (via editing, music and visual style) their entertainment potential – were essentially observational documentaries that followed people 'being themselves', the subsequent batch of reality shows and format-driven documentaries manufacture a situation 'that wouldn't have come about if we hadn't created it' (Lambert 2005). As Stephen Lambert, Chief Creative Officer at RDF, goes on to point out, this common basis for these programmes should not mask their differences. Although reality television is rapidly becoming a catch-all term, Lambert observes that it should only apply to 'a handful' of programmes (in the UK: *Big Brother*, *I'm a Celebrity … Get Me Out of Here*, *Celebrity Love Island* and *Hell's Kitchen*) which take place in a wholly artificial environment where things are broadcast live or almost live (within 24 hours) and over which the viewer exerts some influence, 'usually through voting people out' (Lambert 2005). Conversely, for the formatted documentary – which RDF has 'probably led the way in … you create a situation in the real world as opposed to a kind of artificial world like the *Big Brother* house … and then you let it run its course' (Lambert 2005). The imposition of a format (two wives swapping lives, mothers going on strike and leaving the men to cope alone, two families sampling each other's holidays, a 'ladette' being sent to finishing school to become a lady) does not preclude the spontaneity of traditional observation but, by definition, 'means that certain things are going to happen' (Lambert 2005), a narrative certainty that in turn makes the documentaries commercially viable and valuable.

These programmes, like docusoaps, can be classified as 'factual entertainment', although they do not occupy the same slots in the television schedules (they are broadcast later and tend to be longer – at least an hour in length). Docusoaps were also parochial and their format – of following the 'little dramas' (Lambert 2005) of individuals as they go about their work – was limited and ran out relatively quickly. Reality shows and formats, by contrast, have hastened the globalisation of popular factual television as formats are sold from country to country, modified and repackaged. The most obvious example of the market value of formatted factual entertainment is *Big Brother*: originally broadcast in Holland in 1999, it has since been sold by its Dutch originators Endemol all over the world and is still going strong (despite protestations in the media that audiences are beginning to tire of it). The success of this branch of factual television has both limited and extended the appeal of documentary. Just as it has arguably hastened the homogenisation of mainstream, main channel television documentary output, its proliferation has also expanded the exploration of celebrity within observational documentary, an interest in the famous performing themselves that has been an obsession since the direct cinema movement. Now, 'ordinary' people become celebrities through their participation in *Big Brother* or *Wife Swap* and celebrities are rendered 'ordinary' as they forego makeup and glamour to be in the jungle for *I'm a Celebrity …*, in the kitchens of *Hell's Kitchen* or on

Celebrity Big Brother. The impact of this cross-fertilisation on issues of documentary and performance will be returned to at the end of this chapter.

An essential ingredient of both reality television and formatted documentaries is conflict. The inherently dialectical structure of many of these formats (the notion of swapping or becoming someone else so as to learn more about yourself) leads naturally to conflict: personalities clash, individuals argue and assert themselves, reconciliations are reached and often broken. Conflict is also an important factor in the programmes' broad appeal and series such as *Wife Swap, Holiday Showdown, Big Brother, Survivor, The Apprentice* or *Hell's Kitchen* are structured around a formalised series of collisions, whether these are merely engineered (incompatible contestants) or built into how each series functions (the weekly confrontation between the losing team and Donald Trump or Alan Sugar in *The Apprentice,* having to devise signature dishes for a critical Gordon Ramsay, families finding they have entirely incompatible ideas of what makes a good holiday). The dialectical structure of several of these series also encompasses the audience; not only do audiences enjoy the spectacle on-screen conflict offers, but as they are invited to vote off contestants from the reality shows, for example, they become active generators of conflict and disagreement.

The value of personal conflict to factual entertainment had already been signalled by a series such as *The House* or *Hotel.* Simply because it possesses residual entertainment value does not inevitably mean, however, that conflict and its prioritisation within factual entertainment is devoid of seriousness. Although not strictly a formatted documentary, the BBC2 one-off documentary *Michael Portillo Becomes a Single Mum* (2004) – in which the then Conservative MP took on the role of a working-class Liverpudlian mother for a week, living on her part-time salary and benefits – mimicked and modified the format of *Wife Swap* and other derivative series such as *Mum's on Strike* (ITV, 2004–5) or *When the Women Went* (BBC3, 2005) and illustrated the potential documentary value of conflict. *Michael Portillo Becomes a Single Mum* shared many features with the formatted documentaries, such as a video link from the house through which the absent mother can observe how her surrogate and her children are faring. The clash of cultures so much a feature of regular *Wife Swaps* was here extended as Portillo was not only from a far more privileged background than the mother whose life he was living for a week (he remarks at one point, as he realises that he is going to find it extremely hard to get the money he has to last the week, that he is not used to having to pay attention to the price of each item he puts in his shopping trolley) but he was also childless. Such a documentary is constructed around a series of dialectics (mother/Portillo, children/Portillo, poor/rich, woman/man), which ultimately result in enlightenment and change. The programme was made towards the end of Portillo's political career and so well into his renaissance period and well after he had shed his hard-right image in favour of a more liberal, caring 'I've had gay experiences' one. Through coming into conflict with an unfamiliar way of life Portillo – via the quotidian mechanisms of having to cook for and look after a brood of lippy and unruly children – earns a deep respect for working single mothers.

To return to Allison Pearson's criticism of docusoaps (that the 'serious' documentary 'aspires to tell us something about the human condition' whilst the docusoap merely 'tells us something about the condition of human beings who know they're on television') one could extrapolate that the intention behind the engineered conflicts in the Portillo documentary differs from and is weightier than similar conflicts in less politically or ideologically motivated factual entertainment. A midpoint between the Portillo or an equally serious piece of factual entertainment such as *The Monastery* (also on BBC2 – and indicative of that channel's burgeoning desire to produce the thinking person's version of reality and formats) could arguably be something like the *Wife Swap USA* (2005) that featured a lesbian mother swapping with the mother of a conservative, black, Christian family. Although the children and husband of the latter grow to like the greater freedom brought to their home by the former, during the inevitable showdown (a feature of all *Wife Swaps*), the hard-line Christian makes the lesbian mother cry as she calls her way of life perverted and degenerate. The fact that no extended ideological message is explicitly extrapolated from this finale does not detract from the significant ideological conflict that is taking place here. A curious ambivalence permeates the more popular and populist of these programmes, the conflicts they film are at once notably unsubtle and predictable (neither the homophobic abuse nor the waves of tears come as a surprise) and yet, in the best programmes, they are seldom over-emphasised or milked by, for instance, the voice-over. In the established tradition of observational documentary, even the brashest, newest traits of its most recent reincarnations leave something to the collective imagination of the audience.

In much contemporary factual entertainment, however, conflict is highlighted purely for the sake of entertainment. Where the conflict works best is obviously when it retains some vestige of spontaneity. Manufactured conflict is transparently contrived. Two examples from *Big Brother* serve to illustrate this. Series One of *Big Brother UK* yielded the case of 'Nasty' Nick and his argument with Craig, the likeable Liverpudlian who went on to win that first series, by beating Anna, the lesbian ex-nun. Nick Bateman became the first *Big Brother* (2000) celebrity after he was evicted for attempting to influence the voting of his fellow housemates. He was found out and arguments ensued, notably one with Craig Phillips. Murray and Ouellette remark that the confrontation between public school-educated Bateman and working-class Phillips, which generated the highest ratings for Channel Four since 1995, made the two into 'emblematic stereotypes of contrasting English masculinities' (2004: 31). Not only was their argument interesting because it featured such opposing personalities, but it also stood out because it was spontaneous. Channel Four saw the potential of 'Nasty' Nick, extending the Friday night broadcast of 24 August 2000 to show Nick's expulsion in full. At its peak, this programme had an audience share of 30 per cent and 7.5 million viewers, roughly double the viewers it had been averaging across the previous four weeks and the significance of the argument between Nick and Craig was that it cemented *Big Brother's* appeal. The viewing figures dropped after 'Nasty Nick Week', but at roughly 5 million they remained substantially higher than they had been before it.

A very different sort of *Big Brother* fight occurred in UK Series Five. Two evicted housemates (Emma and Michelle) were put in a flat together, able to watch events in the house via a video feed and hear the unfavourable comments about them made by the remaining *Big Brother* housemates. The two were then controversially reintroduced 'into a booze-fuelled atmosphere and, surprise surprise, a furious row ensued' (Wood D. 2004: 21) as Emma threatened to kill Victor. Viewers responded negatively to the violence and the television regulators Ofcom received 328 complaints about the fracas of 17 June 2004. Many also criticised Endemol for engineering the conflict (seen as an intervention to ensure this series was less boring than its immediate predecessor had been deemed to be). Ofcom did not uphold complaints that Channel Four had been exploitative, although it did find the live coverage of the fight on E4 'exceeded viewers' expectations' and had 'breached programme codes' (*Broadcast* 22 October 2004, 6). Pre-show publicity had emphasised how *Big Brother* was going to get 'evil'; subsequently, Channel Four are believed to have thought that their campaign had backfired, even though viewing figures were up slightly on *BB4*.

The important difference between these two infamous conflicts is that one was not engineered whilst the other was. An intriguing feature of the enduring appeal of reality and formats is that, for all their generic consistency and familiarity, what audiences manifestly like about them is their *un*predictability, the potential they offer for spontaneity amidst and despite the heavy formatting. Five, for instance, poured £4.7m into *Back to Reality*, a reflexive reality series in which 12 stars of past reality shows had to live in a studio-based house for three weeks, the winner receiving £75,000 to donate to charity. They were convinced presumably that a series featuring the stars of past hit shows (Nick Bateman among them) would be a hit for them, but the series flopped, shedding over 1 million viewers after the first transmission, forcing Five to move it from its 8pm slot to 9pm (*Broadcast* 20 February 2004: 5). What *Back to Reality* lacked was the unexpected – and indeed its live transmission at 11pm did consistently better than its edited shows. As Stephen Lambert comments about formatted documentaries, despite the formats giving directors a 'very clear sense of where you're going and what you're trying to get' it is always 'more important to keep the spontaneity of things going' (Lambert 2005). This is why the reconstructed sequences in *Driving School* or the sing-along in *Clampers at Christmas* also seemed forced and lifeless.

A brief comparison between the 2004 and 2005 UK series of *Hell's Kitchen* serve as good examples here. The first featured Gordon Ramsay, well known for his volatility, his swearing and his macho posturing as well as his Michelin starred restaurants. The second featured two other chefs, Gary Rhodes and Jean Christophe Novelli. Ramsay is effortlessly aggressive and confrontational, a factor that made both the first UK series and the US version in 2005 so compelling, particularly as he took on the wilfully stroppy and slow Edwina Currie. Looking at the early episodes of *Hell's Kitchen 2*, it seemed suspiciously as if some executive from ITV had told Rhodes and Novelli that what worked about Series One was Ramsay's aggression, and so this is what they should emulate. What one subsequently got was two less volatile chefs working hard at being something that did not seem to come naturally – there was much posturing, much criticism of the other chef and the dishes he had devised and yet, to British viewers at least, Gary Rhodes was a familiar TV cook who had always worked quite hard at projecting a smiling, cheeky-chappy image entirely at odds with his mean persona for *Hell's Kitchen*. Maybe it was not the aggression per se that worked in the first series, but the fact that it was coming from Gordon Ramsay. Devising a successful reality show is not merely a matter of cherry-picking the key ingredients of previously successful reality shows and putting them together.

Another factor of reality and formatted documentaries is the importance given to emotion and character, once again building on how docusoaps had worked. The juxtaposition between the artificiality of the settings of these programmes and the generation of supposedly authentic emotions is a defining feature. The selection process for the shows is convoluted and thorough: individuals are chosen first and foremost for their personality, but then they are vetted and subjected to a series of checks. All potential participants are seen by psychologists and production companies run police checks to unearth any criminal records; in the United States, they are also tested for contagious diseases and given blood tests (to screen for drug use, for example, which would automatically disqualify them from taking part). In terms of character, the format of each show can dictate the sort of people the production company want to find: for the swap programmes the producers need clear opposites, for the big household programmes they seek out an entertaining social cross-section (as one anonymous celebrity booker for reality shows has put it: 'You have to have a pretty one, a funny one, a thick one and a mad one ... That is a mix that works. It's a bit like being a psychiatrist' [see Freeman 2005]). Nick Shearman adds how, for RDF's shows, 'We're looking for people who are emotionally articulate' and who can 'say what they think and feel pretty frankly and openly... I think all we're asking people to do in these situations is to be frank and open and honest because you're trying to observe people going through a sequence of events and you need their responses to those events all the way down the line, so when they bottle things up it can become problematic' (Shearman 2005). Within the parameters of docusoap, the participants were visibly able to be themselves in many ways: they were leading their own lives and doing their own jobs, albeit temporarily for the benefit of television cameras. In reality shows and formatted documentaries, the boundaries have been redrawn so that the individuals taking part have been transported into an unfamiliar environment and into a situation of their choosing (they have applied to be on the programmes) but not of their own making – and over which they have limited control. This, ironically, heightens the importance of personality, as a person's character is circumscribed by and has to transcend the alien situation it has been propelled into.

A further irony is the use of the term 'reality' in conjunction with these shows. Critic and filmmaker Bernard Clark suggests that 'a lot of "Reality TV" is now no more authentic than a take-away hamburger meal and even less nutritious' (Clark 2002: 1), but this, to many of its producers and promoters, is an essential component. As Gary Carter of Endemol UK posited in a speech delivered 25 February 2002 to BAFTA (British Academy of Film and Television Arts), modern audiences 'take it for granted that documentaries are subjective', which in turn 'reflects a broader shift in the way that we understand reality'. Carter goes on:

> It is not simply that people are more sophisticated now, and therefore less inclined to believe everything they see on TV, though this many well be true. Today it is no longer taken for granted that there even is such a thing as objective reality.
>
> (Quoted in Cummings 2002: xiii)

Character within this artificial framework is no longer allied to authenticity (as Allison Pearson presumed occurred naturally in traditional documentaries) but has become a key adjunct of the imposed inuauthenticity of 'reality television'. Character becomes how you react to being asked to masturbate a pig on *The Farm* (as happened to Rebecca Loos) or how you respond after finding yourself the mother of eight children when you only have two of your own (as happened to Emma on *Wife Swap*). The rules of the game dictate that 'character' is inherently unstable and necessarily performative.

Linked to this is the part played by emotion in contemporary factual entertainment. Producers seek out personalities because they will deliver emotion, a prerequisite to finding suitable characters who can, in turn, function as points of identification for members of the audience. Factual entertainment is no longer confined to the slots in the television schedules previously and traditionally taken by documentaries. Docusoaps (episodes of which generally lasted 30 minutes, more like popular dramas such as sitcoms than documentaries) came to be put into pre-9pm slots and so took on some of the expectations and characteristics of the dramas they usurped, most importantly the generation of conflict and emotion. Stephen Lambert makes a convincing case for 'the big story' being the collapse of the sitcom on American network television. Compared to 'more realistic drama' or 'entertaining factual programming like … *Wife Swap* … the sitcom has to struggle a lot to cope with the fact that it's so artificial' (Lambert 2005). Once again, it is the reality of modern factual entertainment that is crucial, Lambert's point being that audiences would rather watch real characters emoting than purely fictional ones approximating similar emotions. The commissioning by US network channels of factual and documentary series is in itself a new departure for, as Lambert observes, 'until recently, they didn't have anything other than scripted television'; this changed when ABC and CBS commissioned respectively *Who Wants to be a Millionaire* and *Survivor* (both British formats) and 'suddenly, almost anything seems possible in terms of what you can have on a network' (Lambert 2005). Reality television and formats have thus fundamentally altered the balance of programmes within American network television. Unlike the UK where, as Lambert notes, because 'we have had 30 years of observing people and observing natural dialogue' a novel format such as *Big*

Brother feels 'like an extension' of something we are already familiar with (Lambert 2005), US network television had never had anything like *Survivor.* Although *Survivor* falls under the term 'reality', it is in fact a recorded event, much more like the formatted documentaries; it lacks the looseness and unpredictability of *Big Brother.*

To return to the question of emotion: it is key that these new factual series fill a slot vacated by drama. Whether manufactured for the cameras or not, the emotions they show possess a credibility that comparable displays in most dramas lack. The emotion in factual entertainment is deeply ambivalent. When a person shouts, cries, argues, it is convenient to label such moments as 'authentic', moments when generic restraints and imposed artificiality are ruptured. However, these moments of extreme emotional articulation are now so predictable, even necessary, to the success of a series that they do just the opposite, signalling as opposed to masking their formal rigidity. There is often, for instance, the person in reality or formatted shows who cries very easily: the mother in *The 1900 House* who starts to cry at the thought of having to do the family washing by hand, the wife in *Wife Swap* who fights back tears when confronted with the state of house she has to manage for the next few days or Lionel Blair who blubbers when told, as a reward after only a couple of days on *The Farm*, that he can telephone his wife. Blair has presumably toured with a pantomime in the past and so been away from his wife for weeks on end, with no ill effects. Reality's suspension of disbelief is that it has become a requirement amongst those – particularly the celebrities – co-opted onto the shows that they forget how to cope with being away from home and signal repeatedly that each series is an endurance test and not merely a piece of light entertainment (a need for sufferance exemplified by several participants of *Castaway 2000*, many of whom complained about the unbearable primitiveness of their existence – didn't they read the fine print before signing up?). A crucial facet of this highly wrought reality is that the guinea pigs who inhabit it have to temporarily forswear any knowledge that, just outside the gates or walls of their artificial home, is the real real world. The emotions displayed stem largely from a desire to underline the conviction that the world of reality television is the one that matters. Why else would Germaine Greer snivel as she packed her bags and prepared to leave the *Celebrity Big Brother* house? Or why would Vanessa Feltz and Anthea Turner weep in unison as they were threatened with eviction on two series previously?[3] As with many of these outbursts, Feltz and Turner reached breaking point very early in the proceedings and as Victoria Mapplebeck comments: '*Big Brother* had got its money shot without the usual foreplay … The tears seemed such a formulaic *Big Brother* moment, you couldn't help but wonder whether this was an elaborate mock documentary parody' (Mapplebeck 2002: 31).

The emotions displayed in reality and formatted documentaries are frequently disproportionately intense. In the last of four episodes of *Ladette to Lady*, for example, being declared the overall winner of a finishing school diploma at Egglestone Hall (an ex-finishing school specifically reopened for the series) seemed to be disproportionately important – as was getting expelled, as happened to another finalist, after an evening in the pub. When it comes to the plausibility of these emotions, reality television and formats are forever playing with the presumed ingenuousness of its audience, and often in the ways that a drama might. In the sequence in which the ladette gets drunk, the final four contestants have been allowed out on Saturday night to test the depth or otherwise of their conversion to gentility. They do not know this, although they might have guessed, as they were being filmed throughout. Did the cavorting ladette forget the presence of the cameras, or were the audience being asked to forget the presence of the cameras so as to believe that her bad behaviour was as unpremeditated as her tears upon being expelled were spontaneous? As Mapplebeck stresses about reality television in general:

> This is not *The Truman Show*. These subjects haven't discovered the cameras, they have actively sought them out. The access these subjects have provided is consensual.
>
> (Mapplebeck 2002: 23)

However, it is in part due to the neutralising effect of these convolutions that examples of truly unexpected emotional outpourings are so powerful. In *The Monastery* (2005) five outsiders are invited into a community of Benedictine monks and made to forsake the outside world for forty days and forty nights. The men selected from hundreds of volunteers have a significant relationship with religion, from Gary an ex-member of the UDA put in prison for his part in a bombing to Peter a retired teacher and poet who is the most sceptical. Towards the end of the second episode Tony, who works in advertising and is eager from the outset to be immersed in religious life, explains how, when in church one day, he had what he can only term a religious experience, overcome by feelings of weightlessness and of heaviness being lifted from him. Tony explains that he is still a long way from embracing God, but he does sense that he has felt His presence. In a series dedicated to engineering a dialogue between a monastic order and a bunch of guys who have difficulty abandoning their mobile phones and personal stereos, this is the consummate moment when *The Monastery* becomes more than factual *entertainment*. Television perpetually hopes it can be in attendance at just such an accidental, spontaneous utterance, but even in the live, uncut broadcasts of *Big Brother*, the private moments we gain access to are almost invariably interesting because of their banality, not because of their momentousness.

This brings the argument round to the putative seriousness of much reality television and many formatted documentaries. In the opening voiceover of *The Monastery* the narrator declares that the five participants have been invited to 'take part in a *unique social experiment*'. The exact same words had been used to introduce *Castaway 2000*, in which 35 volunteers were sent by the BBC to the remote Outer Hebridian island of Taransay for twelve months like the Swiss Family Robinson and they were used again to usher in *The Nightmares Next Door* (RDF for Channel Four, 2005) in which five households deemed to be bad neighbours are brought together in a remote caravan village under the supervision of a lecturer in psychology. RDF had already used a variation of this terminology for *Ladette to Lady* when the voiceover defined the subject of that series as 'an extraordinary social experiment'. In an essay entitled 'It's not new and it's not clever' critic Chris Dunkley names the televisual antecedents to reality television which conducted similar social experiments, such as the BBC's *Surviving the Iron Age* and *Living in the Past*. What has been cited as another touchstone for current factual entertainment's obsession with social experiments is the Stanford County Prison Experiment, conducted by social psychologist Philip Zimbardo in 1971 in which the Palo Alto Police Department arrested nine men on charges of armed robbery and burglary and took them to Stanford County Jail, known to be a harsh prison. This was all part of a two-week experiment which, as it turned out, had to finish after only six days as the prisoners turned on each other, 'evincing signs of concentration camp or gulag inmate behaviour' (Zimbardo quoted in Brenton and Cohen 2003: 89). Such experiments have since largely been discredited by psychologists, although they have found a new home in popular television, interested in their voyeuristic, exploitative potential perhaps? In 2000 the BBC broadcast *The Experiment,* an unsuccessful re-run of Zimbardo's prison experiment. During the few days of the Stanford experiment, everybody seemed to be changed by it for the worse and one of the clearer links between contemporary factual entertainment and this experiment is the cruelty inflicted on the participants in each. As Brenton and Reuben mention, fear and deprivation are primary motivations in several reality shows: contestants of *The Chair* are administered shocks to get their heart rates up, in *Big Brother* and *I'm a Celebrity … Get Me Out of Here!* the contestants have to perform revolting or humiliating tasks. As Dunkley remarks, 'if anything sets apart reality television from previous television series, which were otherwise very similar, it is the significance of the part played by humiliation' (Dunkley 2002: 42).

The role of psychology in reality television and formats is ordinarily a nominal one: contestants are vetted by a psychologist and there is a psychologist who observes them whilst a series is on air (such as *Big Brother*), but the level of real experimentation is low. On *The Nightmares Next Door*, the resident psychologist imposes simple and fairly transparent psychological tests to make the bad neighbours become more neighbourly. These include rationing food and utilities and, at the end, depriving the community of their last party as a means of gauging whether or not their camaraderie was genuine. Those involved might have learnt something about themselves, but the 'experiment' being conducted served television not psychology. Once again, the issue is one of motivation: in the Stanford experiment Zimbardo devised the experiment for professional reasons; when it comes to the reality shows of the new millennium, the experiments are for the benefit of the participants (who might want to change an aspect of their lives but more than likely volunteer because they want to be on television) and of the audiences (who find such mild experimentation and self-reflection as the programmes offer entertaining). Sometimes the changes experienced by the subjects of factual entertainment are relatively profound: after appearing on *Faking It,* some people have 'completely changed their lives' (Lambert 2005) and after being on *Wife Swap* others have 'fundamentally changed how they relate to their children and their partners' (Lambert 2005). Lambert maintains that, both sides of the Atlantic, people take part in *Wife Swap* 'out of a sense of there's something about their relationship that they would like to change', hoping that 'taking part in the programme might have that effect' (2005). The psychological support given to these programmes was not, however, equipped to prevent the suicide of the first contestant to be voted off the Swedish version of *Survivor – Expedition: Robinson* – in 1997, nor to foresee the threat posed by a male contestant on American *Big Brother* who threatened a fellow female contestant with a knife, maintaining afterwards that this was just a joke (Brenton and Cohen 2003: 129–30).

The fundamental difference between these contemporary experiments and Stanford is television: that these latter day inmates have chosen to participate in an experiment that might or might not change their lives ... that is being filmed for television. Bill Nichols' insight that traditional observational documentary 'appears to leave the driving to us' now seems slightly naïve even in respect of the *vérité* films of the 1960s; such a comment, however, certainly no longer holds for the contemporary factual entertainment that has observation at its core, as these television series are far more knowing, self-conscious and cynical than either films or filmmakers were in the 1960s. Stephen Mamber subtitled his book on direct cinema '*Studies in Uncontrolled Documentary*'. Whereas some of the films of the 60s to which he refers might arguably have *appeared* uncontrolled (they clearly were nothing of the sort, although they were more leisurely and relaxed than most documentaries had hitherto been), reality television and formatted documentaries are, despite their predilection for observation as a means of getting to know subjects in front of the camera, excessively controlled: their structure is predetermined, their subjects are carefully selected and their audiences know what to expect when they sit down to watch them.

Even for the one person in the UK who might not have come across any such factual entertainment, the form would become transparent pretty quickly via a narrator or presenter who recaps endlessly what has happened and what is going to happen or the teasers before advert breaks. Again, the antecedents for these are the key documentaries of the 1990s such as *The House*, alongside the success of both Jeremy Clarkson and the new, ironic *Top Gear* presenter style he spawned and Angus Deayton, the first presenter of *Have I Got News For You* and latterly the presenter of *Hell's Kitchen*. Quentin Willson (who joined *Top Gear* after Clarkson) narrated *Driving School*, and since then the patronising, ironic, laddish voice-over has proved a mainstay of factual entertainment. Exemplary in this respect is *Mum's on Strike*, a daytime formatted documentary by Lion TV for ITV (2005), narrated by comedian Rory McGrath. The format here is simple: each episode features two fathers whose wives have left them to cope with the home and children for three days while they pamper themselves at a health spa. The wives are able (as always) to view how their husbands are getting on via a video link. Each father is given a challenge (in one episode, for example, he has to make a cake for a group of mothers who are on a diet) and the fathers are expected to do the cooking and housework themselves rather than cheat and use ready cooked meals or meals previously prepared by their wives and put in the freezer. An added ingredient is the presence of Anna Raeburn, the series' parenting advisor who comments on how the dads are doing and at the end awards the better dad with a certificate. Rory McGrath's job is to make the dads left behind by the mums' 'strike' appear even more incompetent than they would of their own volition. Often McGrath's comments precede an action, telling us in advance that the father in question is about to manifest such incompetence. In *Hell's Kitchen*, Deayton's role is very similar: he mocks the efforts of the novice celebrity chefs, reminds us how long the diners are having to wait for their meals, feigns incredulity at how the public are voting and stokes the flames of the ongoing arguments between Gordon Ramsay and the chefs. A notable victim in the first series was ex-MP turned romantic novelist Edwina Currie. She and Ramsay went head to head early on and Currie made it known that she wanted to be voted off the show, but the audience refused for several nights to oblige, no doubt finding themselves entertained by the spat with Ramsay. Deayton announced the results of the votes with disbelief, although the triangular discordance between Currie, Deayton and Ramsay presumably delighted the producers.

This overt signposting for the benefit of the audience alters fundamentally the notion of performance offered by factual entertainment. Any attempt or pretence at 'being oneself' in such a situation is inevitably circumscribed by form: what the audience know to expect, what they are told, what the format dictates. The spectator/text relationship is thus fundamentally different in a reality series or a formatted documentary from the comparable relationship in a traditional observational documentary; to pursue Bill Nichols' driving metaphor, we are chauffeured to where we already know we are going. Although in the current climate, reality television offers a certain celebrity status to all its performers, the performers of these series are, broadly, of two types: the celebrity and the ordinary person. The 'real' celebrities are as manifestly cast as the non-celebrities, as indicated by the celebrity Casting Director earlier. Sometimes it becomes apparent that the reality culture itself has given rise to a certain casting necessity. Several shows in the UK have featured the grumpy middle-aged woman – someone who is a respected and intelligent professional whose partial role it is to formulate a critique of the reality genre and the situation in which she and her fellow celebrities find themselves. Three such grumpy middle-aged women have been Janet Street Porter (*I'm a Celebrity* …), Germaine Greer (*Celebrity Big Brother*) and Edwina Currie. They all stand up to both those (more often than not men) around them and the rules of the game by which they are supposed to abide. Through questioning why they are there they question the reality format itself, although the sub-genre rarely seems damaged by such reflexive commentary. In these instances, an individual performance becomes one means through which the highly wrought and artificial mechanics of reality television are acknowledged and rendered transparent.

Whether celebrities or non-celebrities, different issues of performance are raised by reality television and formatted series. In the former, where the action is live or transmitted almost live, the events occurring on the screen are taking place in the present or the virtual present and are, by their very nature, open-ended. Although this liveness does not necessarily alter the nature of the performances themselves, it alters how we the audience observe these performances: these are not finished actions – Edwina Currie, for instance, could have changed overnight into an eager cook and dutiful protégé. A series such as *Survivor,* like formatted documentaries, is a recorded event, a game whose outcome is known before transmission starts. All the events onscreen have already occurred by the time they are aired and watching it is 'a bit like watching the recording of a football match or a horse race: it never has quite the same feel about it when you know the outcome has already happened' (Lambert 2005). Watching a live/nearly live *Big Brother* or *Hell's Kitchen* offers the audience the thrill of knowing that events and characters are infinitely changeable and fluid; therein lies the thrill, the camaraderie of watching a piece of genuine reality television: things could change very rapidly and things could change as a result of interaction (via voting, emails etc.) between audience and programme. *Survivor* or *The Apprentice* (both bigger in the US than the UK) both offer weekly digests of events that have already been processed and concluded; this gives the series a slicker, more heavily produced feel. This in turn lends the performances a more studied, self-conscious quality, presumably resulting from the fact that each episode is edited in full knowledge of the outcome (which team wins, who is fired) and is so paced to build up to this (in *Apprentice USA,* for example, the number of cutaways – to anxious faces on the losing team particularly – are far more frequent than in reality shows). When considering the reception of these shows, both reality and formatted documentaries enact the same dialectical struggle at the heart of observational documentary between who these people are off screen and who they become when the cameras are on them. With the formatted documentaries, there is the added factor that what the onscreen subjects become has been made predictable by their framing within an established format: everyone has been chosen for a reason (that they complement the others around them) and the structural format itself has drawn the boundaries within which their performances must necessarily function. Once a series is established, the form dictates performances to an extent. A wife invited onto *Wife Swap* after the first series will understand – even if she does not know the exact situation that awaits her – what is expected of her and her performance will to a degree reflect this awareness of generic expectations and restraints.

An arresting and infamous performance comes from Lizzie Bardsley in the first series of *Wife Swap.* Lizzie is a mother of eight from Rochdale who lives on benefits (as does her husband Mark); she swaps with Emma, a mother of two from Devon who on more than one occasion mentions that she and her husband Colin are 'aspirational'. Emma describes herself as such in the 'Household Manual' she has to leave for Lizzie and, despite having a lower (by £10,000) joint post-tax income than the Bardsleys, gives Lizzie the immediate impression that she is a snob and would look down on Lizzie and Mark. The motivating conflict of this episode is thereby established; Lizzie's role has been prescribed from the outset and continues to be defined throughout the swap (which only lasts three days out of an intended two weeks, due to Lizzie's irrational jealousy of Emma). Despite the structuredness of *Wife Swap*, Lizzie's performance is erratic. At times (although this is not what she is remembered for) she comes across as quite tender, particularly when, during the final meeting with the other family, she starts to cry after describing how the swap has made her realise how precious her children are to her. However, this closing moment is not consistent with Lizzie Bardsley elsewhere and even Mark is ready to acknowledge this as he remarks how, upon seeing his wife cry, 'she is normal' after all. The audience do not know whether or not this is a moment of 'realness': the tears make it look spontaneous, but then Lizzie's performance prior to this point had been marked by equally spontaneous-seeming outbursts of anger and irrationality. The programme's turning point comes when Colin, Emma's husband, takes Lizzie out for a meal, as he and Emma are wont to do on a regular basis. *Othello* it is not, but Colin has sown the seeds of doubt in Lizzie's mind by showing her photos of Emma and remarking how attractive she is, then asking Lizzie what she thinks of Mark being with her. Lizzie holds conventional views on gender (early on she describes Colin as 'all man', a comment that is juxtaposed with Mark belching after taking a swig from a can of lager during his end of the day piece to camera) and she sees any woman as a potential threat. She then interrupts Colin and explodes: 'You think I'm picking, you think I'm obnoxious, you think I'm arrogant. And you don't like me doing that. Well hey, life's a bitch'. She then goes outside for a cigarette. This type of performance is repeated for much of the final meeting, and the producers were so worried by this point that Lizzie might attack Emma (she had threatened to go for her earlier) that they planted two security guards in the room, posing as crew members. Here, Lizzie shouts over people, interrupts, gets up and shakes her breasts at Emma, and all Emma and Colin can do is look on in disbelief and amusement. Conversely, at other times Lizzie shows the tenderness she displays right at the end, particularly after she has been allowed (against normal *Wife Swap* rules) to phone home on her twins' first birthday and Mark has assured her Emma is not his type. Her complex personality, though, has to some extent to be interpreted against the earlier insight offered by Lizzie's mother, who drops in to see how Emma is coping: contrary to what is said in the Household Manual, Lizzie's mother maintains that her daughter does not do the ironing and cleaning and that Mark does a substantial amount of the cooking as well. In this context it becomes futile to speculate which – if any – is Lizzie's 'real' self; she seems genuinely upset by the idea of Emma stealing Mark, but then the implied mendacity in the Household Manual suggests that the whole performance is a multiple charade.

Stephen Lambert and Nick Shearman of RDF both believe that people who put themselves forward for shows such *Wife Swap* and *Holiday Showdown* do so because they want to change something in their lives, whether they are clear what this is or not. Of *Wife Swap* Lambert says 'there are some people who have fundamentally changed how they relate to their children and their partners as a result of taking part in the programme. It's amazing how big an effect it seems to have had on them given what a limited period of time it is' (Lambert 2005). In *Faking It* (2001–present) or *Ladette to Lady* the desire to change is built into the series' format. Shearman puts the success of such programmes at this particular moment to 'a general sense of malaise'; he perceives a link between the swap documentaries, the no going back documentaries and the going to live abroad documentaries, all of which feature and appeal to 'people wanting to try something different' (Shearman 2005). This trying something different extends maybe to how the characters in these documentaries perform themselves: just as Lizzie Bardsley jokes that attaching a hair piece completely transforms her, so the rules of *Wife Swap* or *Holiday Showdown* dictate that character is mutable and dependent on circumstance and the responses of others.

The problem, as some of the sub-genre's critics perceive it, is that these are potentially serious issues treated too lightly. The issue in *Ladette to Lady* is only subliminally the class conflict exposed by the exercise; the daily conflicts are smaller and, much of the time, played for laughs, as when an instructor demands 'I don't want Table Mountain, I want the Matterhorn', upon being confronted with one pupil's failed attempt at making a pointed tower out of choux pastry balls. In his 2004 James MacTaggart lecture at the Edinburgh Television Festival BBC broadcaster John Humphrys criticised reality television for turning 'human beings into freaks for us to gawp at' (Humphrys 2005: 268), then going on to argue:

> It is frankly outrageous even to think of it in the same terms as the sort of reality television pioneered by Roger Graef with his fly-on-the-wall documentaries.
>
> (Humphrys 2005: 268)

Within his critique of the programmes, lies concern for television audiences. Humphrys talks as if, even after 'this reality genre eventually exhausts itself', it will leave behind an audience 'that has been de-sensitised' (p. 269): the 'sheer vulgarity' (p. 268) of the programmes will have rubbed off on them. Humphrys' perception is that it will be impossible to return television and its audiences to the innocent state they knew before.

This state of innocence was characterised in Humphrys' mind, one could surmise, by documentaries possessing clear sobriety and seriousness. Humphrys probably believes in the 'proper documentary'. In a discussion of *Big Brother* and recent factual broadcasting John Corner offers an argument for the revision of documentary as a filmic and televisual category, suggesting that something like *Big Brother* problematises the notions of the 'proper documentary' and functions within what he terms 'the "postdocumentary" culture of television' a culture within which 'the legacy of documentary is still at work, albeit in partial and revised form' (Corner 2002: 257). *Big Brother*, Corner maintains, 'operates its claims to the real within a fully managed artificiality' (p. 256) and turns the 'living space' into a 'performance space' (p. 257). Although Corner refutes the idea that the 'proper' documentary and reality television are mutually exclusive, he does still hold onto the notion that 'living' and 'performance' are two entirely separate states. Perhaps what reality television and formatted documentary series instead suggest is that performance is an integral part of living, that when Suzie in *49 Up* (2005) tells Michael Apted that she dreads taking part in *Seven Up* every seven years and hopes that by the next time she will have the courage to turn Apted away, this gives us no more of an insight into the 'real' Suzie than do Lizzie Bardsley's on-screen outbursts. Modern factual entertainment does not signal its constructedness, nor does it forefront any serious subtext. It also fails to make a definitive distinction between the 'real' person and the 'performance', a slippage that troubles critics and prompts accusations of trivialisation and making 'human beings into freaks for us to gawp at'. It is a sub-genre based upon generating conflict and big emotions and it is probably the Pandora's Box of factual broadcasting in that reality and formats might run their course but what they have brought to documentary – notably entertainment and drama – will linger.

Part III

Performance

The logical extension to an analysis preoccupied with the idea that a documentary film can never simply represent the real, that instead it is a dialectical conjunction of a real space and the filmmakers that invade it, is the non-fiction film explicitly focused on issues of performance. The two chapters that follow – a discussion of the American presidential image in documentaries and television broadcasts and the companion discussion of performative documentaries, principally in Britain in the 1990s – tackle the issue of performance from different angles. Performance has always been at the heart of documentary filmmaking and yet it has been treated with suspicion because it carries connotations of falsification and fictionalisation, traits that traditionally destabilise the non-fiction pursuit. This suspicion – as so many problems with documentary history and its theorisation – stems largely from the advent of observational cinema in America in the early 1960s (direct cinema), a movement that denied – except in its performer-based documentaries – the role performance played in their films. The essential dilemmas posed by direct cinema have been examined at greater length in the Introduction to Part II of this book, but this marginalisation of the issue of performance within documentary is fundamental to how non-fiction film has been and is to be interpreted. As this book's Introduction suggests, direct cinema practitioners were misguided when they ignored the issue of how their intervention into real situations altered those situations irrevocably. Despite this, it is precisely this intervention that continues to be one of the most enduring aspects of observational documentary and why, as a mode, it has continued to be influential: that it can capture the moment at which subjects make the transition to performer for the sake of the cameras.

Because the advocates of direct cinema persisted in making the unrealisable claim for observational documentary that the filmmakers' intrusion made a negligible difference to how the films' subjects acted, the previously more relaxed acceptance of the role performance has always played in documentary has been sidelined. It is not just Robert Flaherty, the founding father of dramatic reconstruction, who incorporated performance into documentaries; in the work of filmmakers as diverse as Dziga Vertov, Georges Franju, Emile de Antonio, Chris Marker, Claude Lanzmann and Marcel Ophuls repeated use is made of performance, not as a means of invalidating the documentary pursuit but of getting to the truth each filmmaker is searching for. The historical and theoretical perception of documentary would, one feels, have been different if the French counterpart of direct cinema – the *cinéma vérité* of Jean Rouch (*cinéma vérité* itself being a term coined by Vertov) – had prevailed instead. *Chronique d'un été* is an exemplary performative text, one whose truth is enacted for and by the filmmakers' encounters with their subjects for the benefit of the camera. This remains the essence of the documentaries and broadcasts to be examined in the following two chapters.

An additional intention of these discussions of the performative possibilities of the factual image is to bring to bear upon the area of documentary more contemporary and heterogeneous theoretical perspectives than is usually the case, to bring documentary up to date, for instance, with the concept of gender and identity as mutable rather than fixed states. In his final autobiographical documentary, *Mr Hoover and I,* Emile de Antonio comments to the camera filming him: 'Who am I? I suppose I'm the ultimate document.' These two chapters examine and extend this notion of the performance for the camera as the 'ultimate document', as the truth around which a documentary is built.

5   The president and the image

The focus of this chapter will be the role of performance in the realm of mainstream politics with specific reference to the performances in documentaries and factual television broadcasts of American Presidents Kennedy, Nixon, Clinton and George Bush Jr. There is, however, a fluidity of definition and a variety of material available when it comes to considering the presidential image, and this discussion will encompass the *faux* documentary *Tanner '88* and will make passing reference to relevant fiction films and drama-documentaries. The role played by performance in the realm of American presidential politics has been crucial, from John Kennedy's affinity with the observational camera, to Nixon's manipulation and suspicion of broadcast television and to the creation of Clinton's image by spin doctors and media advisers in an era when the media has increasingly sought and managed to dominate presidential politics. Elsewhere I have argued that this shift is due to a lessening of respect for the incumbent president (and this would hold for Michael Moore's satirical treatment of George Bush Jr. in *Fahrenheit 9/11*, for example) but it is not the only reason (see Bruzzi 1998); as the influence of the image makers has grown, so the individual politician has become more detached and distanced from us. There is also a discernible developing relationship between each incumbent president and documentary; it is no coincidence that John Kennedy's image was cemented by his real appearances in early direct cinema films such as *Primary* and *Crisis,* appearances that made him both accessible and idealised. Conversely, Nixon, though associated very much with the live television broadcast, was suspicious of media representations not under his control and, as a consequence, did not willingly become the subject of documentaries. Although many documentaries, from *Millhouse* to the series *Watergate,* have been made about Nixon, they form part of the political tradition of assembling critical portraits of politicians by editing together out-takes and juxtaposing, for ironic effect, official and unofficial pieces of film, a tradition illustrated by Santiago Alvarez's *LBJ* and Kevin Rafferty's and James Ridgeway's *Feed,* about the 1992 Clinton campaign. An instructive point of comparison with Kennedy's championing of documentary in the early 1960s can be found in another documentary about the 1992 campaign, *The War Room* – an observational film made by Donn Pennebaker and Chris Hegedus in which Clinton appears, but only fleetingly. The absence of Clinton from official documentary texts came at a time when, primarily after the Monica Lewinsky scandal, the public's veneration of the actual president was diminished but its desire for a mythic, idealised presidential image was just as strong as it always had been, hence the number of Hollywood films (such as *Air Force One*) made in the Clinton era to feature larger-than-life presidents.

John Kennedy: the positive influence of television and film

John F. Kennedy's presidential career could be charted via images, from the direct cinema film *Primary* (Drew Associates, 1960) following him and his rival for the Democratic nomination, Hubert Humphrey, through the Wisconsin primary to Abraham Zapruder's film of his assassination in November 1963. The end result of this close relationship between the president and the image is the accrediting of Kennedy, despite the attempts of historians to reveal the tawdriness of his 'Camelot', with mythic status,[1] made more significant by such idealisation being the result of real rather than fictional representations of him. The moment that cemented this image of Kennedy in the public consciousness was, after having secured the Democratic nomination, the first of his televised debates with the Republican candidate, Richard Nixon. By 1960, nine out of ten American families had a television set, so the live debates were bound to be influential. Oddly, despite his previous use of the direct television address (notably for his career saving Checkers speech of 1952) Nixon, in 1960, underestimated its power and, despite being the more experienced politician, seemed unable to gauge the requirements of the medium. Infamously, Nixon – who had been in hospital for three weeks and so was pasty and had lost a substantial amount of weight – looked awful: he refused make-up because Kennedy (who conversely had been campaigning in the California sun and so did not need make-up) had, he sweated under the television lights and he wore a slightly crumpled and ill-fitting grey suit. In contrast to this, Kennedy was bronzed and, in the gushing words of the CBS director, 'tanned, tall, lean, well tailored in a dark suit ... he looked like an Adonis' (Matthews 1996: 148). The majority of those who saw the debate thought that Kennedy had won on points (some 43 per cent to 29 per cent), whereas those, such as Lyndon Johnson the Democratic vice-presidential nominee, who had only heard the encounter on the radio, gave it to Nixon. As one Nixon aide muttered at the time 'the son of a bitch just lost the election' (Matthews 1996: 155), a view confirmed by Nixon, who refused to ever look at the tapes again. In terms of poll figures, after this first debate (on domestic policy) Kennedy had climbed from 47 per cent to 49 per cent, whilst Nixon had dropped from 47 per cent to 46 per cent. The margin remained tight and the first debate disproportionately significant, as Kennedy went on to win the presidential election by a very narrow margin.[2]

This first debate now functions as shorthand for the importance of the image to any aspirant to public office. Theodore White comments that 'American politics and television are now so completely locked together that it is impossible to tell the story of the one without the other' (White J. 1982: 165). The image of the American president, probably more than any other political figure, has been forged and circumscribed by what have been termed 'medialities': 'events that take place mainly to be shown on television – events that, in the absence of television, would not take place at all or would take place in a different manner' (Ranney 1983: 23). The relationship between 'medialities' and politics is, however, complex. During a televised debate in 1976 against Jimmy Carter, President Gerald Ford made a significant gaffe when he claimed that Poland and Eastern Europe were not then under Soviet military domination. Whilst a poll taken immediately after the debate suggested that, despite this mistake, Ford was still considered to have won it, polls taken after extended media coverage emphasising his error indicated that voters switched allegiance to Carter, giving Ford's statements on Eastern Europe as the major reason (Ranney 1983: 25–6). In 1980, Carter's repeated decision not to debate his main rival for the Democratic nomination, Edward Kennedy, was vindicated by his victories in the primaries, whilst his decision to challenge Reagan, the eventual Republican candidate, to a debate only seven days before the 1984 election was considered to have been the event that converted a slender Reagan lead into a 10 per cent victory margin (Ranney 1983: 27). The significance of this move away from more traditional forms of electioneering signals the shift towards a more performative idea of the politician: one who is constructed with the spectator in mind and whose media image is not automatically presumed to be a direct correlative of his off-screen personality.

As the chief of staff in Rob Reiner's Hollywood film *The American President* (1995) speculates to the fictional President Andrew Shepherd, the wheelchair-bound Franklin D. Roosevelt – a radio President – would not have been voted in if the American electorate had been confronted with daily reminders on television of his disability.[3] There is thus a direct correlation to be found between John Kennedy's astute manipulation of the media and the mythic significance attributed to his image both during his presidency and after his death. The very endurance of the Kennedy image-ideal suggests a serious dislocation between fact and desire. Despite the debatable accomplishments of his three-year administration – the Bay of Pigs, the collapse of the Vienna conference with Krushchev, the US entry into Vietnam – and the subsequent revelations about his private life, it is still the case that 'If there is any enduring monument on the ever-changing landscape of contemporary American politics, it is the people's affection and esteem for John F. Kennedy' (Brown, T. 1988: 1). This veneration is not rational but emotive. As Brown argues, Kennedy's canonisation was in part due to his being 'cut down in the prime of manhood' (Brown, T. 1988: 44), but it was also due to the diversity of his appeal so that Americans 'have projected upon him their deepest beliefs, hopes and even fears' (p. 5).

This is in direct contrast to the way in which both Kennedy's immediate successor, Lyndon Johnson, and his most enduring rival, Nixon, have been perceived. Although there was considerable continuity between the Kennedy administration and the Johnson years, and despite Johnson's very tangible successes in implementing a liberal and enduring domestic programme during his years in office,[4] he is largely remembered as the usurper, the intruder. Santiago

Alvarez's *LBJ* (1968) epitomises the discrepancy between the public perceptions of Johnson and Kennedy. This short avant-garde film constructed out of photographs, archive film, cartoons and movies, casts Johnson as the villain of the 1960s and John and Robert Kennedy, Martin Luther King and Malcolm X as his martyred adversaries. Although he falls short of direct accusation, Alvarez's hatred for Johnson is evident in many of the film's montage sequences, the most vitriolic of which depicts JFK's funeral through a series of images, the clear inference of which is that Johnson was not only indifferent to Kennedy's death but was implicated in it: stills of the funeral procession to Johnson on a horse to archive film and more stills of the funeral to Johnson digging a hole in the ground, smiling. That this is the 'right' point of view is repeatedly implied by *LBJ*'s use of a close-up of an owl (symbolising wisdom and omniscience presumably) observing all the key deaths that are catalogued through the film. The most protracted sequences in *LBJ* to feature Johnson himself are the opening montage of stills showing his daughter Luci's wedding and its concluding counterpart which focuses on him as a doting grandfather, both of which serve to trivialise and undermine their subject when juxtaposed with Vietnam and assassinations. Conversely, goodness in the documentary is represented by the Kennedy brothers and the Civil Rights leaders, particularly Robert Kennedy whose 1968 assassination was a recent event. The contrasting responses to Kennedy (and his brother) and to Johnson are more emotional than rational; JFK is a figure of desire, LBJ a figure of hatred.

As mentioned, the durability of the Kennedy myth is in part the result of Kennedy's own skilful use of the media and his ease in front of the camera compared to either Johnson or Nixon. John Kennedy learnt to entrust the glorification of his image to documentary following his perceived success of *Primary*. Although the film fails to give a rounded account of the election and the electoral process as Theodore White, Jean Luc Godard and others have observed (Mamber 1974: 40), it nevertheless captured the essence of campaigning and elicits from its audience an emotional identification with the candidates. The film's most expressive image, 'the *locus classicus* of the direct cinema "follow-the-subject" shot' (Winston 1995: 152), is Albert Maysles' 75-second hand-held tracking shot following Kennedy through a dense crowd and into a packed hall where he and Jackie address a gathering of Polish voters. The fluidity and casualness of this shot mirrors Kennedy's apparent ease and, like many others in the film, serves to forge a strongly empathetic relationship between spectator and 'star'. Indeed, despite dedicating equal time to each candidate, *Primary* forges a greater affinity with Kennedy than it does with Humphrey. Whilst Richard Leacock's camera[5] observes with tangible closeness the tension and fatigue in the Kennedy camp on election night, the parallel sequences following Humphrey are (with the notable exception of Leacock's shot of Humphrey falling asleep in his car) more formal and reserved. *Primary* invites those watching to take sides, to engage with one 'character' over another. This process of identification detracts from *Primary*'s political bite (although it is debatable that this is what the film is after). Brian Winston (1995: 153) comments that

Rather than representing a breakthrough in the cinema's ability to illumi-
nate the nature of the 'real' world, *Primary* flags the onset of one of the
most significant media failures of our time, certainly in the USA – the
failure to control, and effectively explicate, the political image.

For Winston, *Primary* demonstrates the need for 'spin', indicating that, whilst
some politicians (like Kennedy) are adept in front of the camera and effectively
wrest control of their image from the filmmakers, others, like Nixon or
Humphrey, are controlled by the medium. It was John Kennedy's ability to look
as if such a struggle was not taking place, as if nothing could be further from his
mind, which cements the power of his performance.

Although eschewing any conventional notion of performance (acknowledging the deceit, playing a part or acting up for the cameras), direct cinema establishes an alternative: the documentary about performance. In performance-based
observational documentaries (*Meet Marlon Brando, Don't Look Back,* even
Salesman), the subjects' rapport with the camera is vital, and their success as film
performers predicated upon their ability to appear natural and at ease when being
filmed. This was John Kennedy's greatest asset. Despite the lack of analysis or
direct political commentary in a film such as *Primary,* the benefit to the photo-
genic or 'cinegenic' subject is that he or she becomes accessible to the spectator,
to the electorate through an ability to turn in a non-performance, to affect a
casual disregard for the camera that just happens to be pursuing them. Towards
the end of *Primary,* there is a lengthy election night sequence in which the film
intercuts footage of both candidates awaiting the early returns and projected
results. The Humphrey material is much tighter, more formal and coldly edited,
as if the crew are no closer to him now than they were at the outset. The
Kennedy sequences are considerably looser, the editing is more relaxed, the camera focuses on him not only doing things, but also observing and listening to
others. Far from coming across as 'uncontrolled', the relaxed quality displayed in
this footage serves to establish control with the subject, in this instance John
Kennedy, whose responsive and engaged style mirrors that of observational documentary itself.

Likewise in *Crisis: Behind a Presidential Commitment* (1963), Kennedy, the
then president, exudes a measure of authority and calm as he is captured on camera in long, reactive close-ups not doing very much except absorbing the advice
being proffered by others and rocking gently in his familiar Oval Office chair.
Crisis is another Drew Associates film, this time charting the build up to the integration of the University of Alabama, a move that Robert Kennedy, then
Attorney General, supports and which George Wallace, the Governor of
Alabama, opposes. *Crisis* sides with Robert Kennedy over Wallace, just as
Primary sided with John Kennedy over Humphrey. Characteristic of this
inequality are the two opening 'politicians at home in the morning' sequences.
Whilst Bobby Kennedy is followed gently by a hand-held camera as he eats
breakfast with his children, urging his daughter Kerry to drink up her milk,
answering the telephone, George Wallace is, quite literally, kept at a distance, as

a far more static camera captures him greeting his child (who has just left the arms of the black maid) and then is led by Wallace on a grudging, formal tour of his collection of oil paintings of Civil War leaders.[6] Not only does this shift in style display bias on the part of Drew Associates (but then, contrary to conventional opinion, the exponents of direct cinema were never entirely averse to or oblivious of subjectivity),[7] it demonstrates again the power that stems from establishing an affinity with the documentary camera, something the British Prime Minister Tony Blair had clearly learnt by the time he commissioned Molly Dineen to make Labour's most memorable broadcast of the 1997 election: a relaxed, informal interview with him in a car and his family kitchen. *Crisis* makes one wonder to what extent Robert Kennedy's casualness in particular is contrived. Towards the conclusion of the film, as the crisis is coming to a head and as the Attorney General's office is still facing the very real possibility of having to arrest the Governor of Alabama for stopping two black students from enrolling at university, Robert Kennedy has been visited in his office by three of his children, all running around freely. When on the telephone to his deputy Nick Katzenbach, Kennedy is pestered by Kerry, to whom he then hands the receiver so she can say hello to (a surprised) Katzenbach. The implications of this one action are several: that Robert Kennedy is cool in a crisis; that he is a tender, loving father, that he can focus on more than one thing at once; that he treats his colleagues as friends. Because of all these inferences, the effect of this sequence is highly beneficial to Robert Kennedy, but to what extent was the situation orchestrated to subtly enhance his image? (In a recent documentary about Robert Kennedy,[8] journalist Anthony Lewis recalls, however, the informality of the Attorney General's office – that Kennedy himself was usually to be found in shirtsleeves and loosened tie, that his children visited him frequently and his walls were adorned with their artwork).

In both *Primary* and *Crisis,* the films' emphasis on character and personality over issues ironically enhances rather than detracts from the successful politicians' credibility. The Kennedys' non-performances in front of the cameras project a naturalness that makes them appear accessible and, as their counterparts in fictional narrative film, to behave as if there are no cameras present. John and Robert Kennedy become automatic points of identification, the documentaries' emotional focuses and 'characters' imbued with an amalgam of fictional and historical significance. It is worth proposing that this ability to appear 'natural' in front of camera complicates the commonly held opinion of direct cinema's overwhelming significance to the evolution of documentary filmmaking. It could be that the chosen subjects in these early documentaries (films that, in turn, made the filmmakers' reputations) happened to be so at ease with the filmmaking process that they simply reflected well upon the new observational style. Perhaps it is these ground-breaking performances and not merely the arrival of lightweight cameras and portable sound recording equipment that revolutionised documentary; if the direct cinema crews had only had Wallace and Humphrey at their disposal, the course of documentary history might have been quite different.

Aware that he could make the media work for him, John Kennedy consolidated this image of the controlled, effective, accessible politician by allowing subsequent crews to film at the White House and by initiating such things as the regular presidential press conference. He embraced image-makers. A concomitant of this (and of his untimely death) was that he as a figure became mythic in his own right, symbolic (however erroneously) of a successful, liberal presidency. If one looks briefly at the fiction films that appeared in the 1960–3 period or later features that invoke Kennedy as an ideal presidential figure, the extent of the veneration of his image becomes clear. Apart from *PT 109*, a fictional account of Kennedy's wartime experiences which he endorsed (even intervening to suggest Warren Beatty for the part),[9] other feature films being made or released during the Kennedy administration (*Advise and Consent, Dr Strangelove, Or: How I Learnt to Stop Worrying and Love the Bomb, Fail Safe* and *Seven Days in May*) present fictional presidents of lesser romantic stature than Kennedy himself. Although liberal and 'good', these fictional presidents are ineffectual, weakened or ageing. Kennedy's own abilities as a charismatic performer likewise explain why the many posthumous fictionalisations of his own life (as in the television movies *Missiles of October, Kennedy* or *A Woman Named Jackie*) seem particularly deficient.

In the spate of presidential films to appear in the 1990s, Kennedy was again idealised, made into a national ego ideal. J. Michael Riva, the production designer on *Dave*, comments that, in reconstructing the White House, he 'wanted to mirror the Kennedy administration as much as possible, because he was my favourite recent president' (Glitz 1993: 35), using primarily the absurdly genteel Jackie Kennedy-narrated guided tours as research material. Likewise, Lilly Kilvert, production designer on *The American President*, 'picked the White House of the JFK years' (McGregor 1995: 84). Reiner's film further mythologises JFK by twice using the pensive portrait of Kennedy that hangs in the White House (significantly more informal than those commemorating the majority of his fellows), once in the opening title sequence in which images of presidents past are intercut with symbols of Washington power, and once when a dejected President Shepherd walks past it at the film's final moment of crisis. The latter makes explicit the desire to forge an identificatory pattern with the dead JFK. In Oliver Stone's *Nixon* the same JFK portrait figures more ostentatiously as a quasi-relic, the destroyed Nixon musing as he contemplates the image: 'When they look at you, they see what they want to be; when they look at me, they see what they are.' Here, the gulf between ego and ideal is clumsily enacted on the screen; Kennedy, *Nixon* suggests, remains the one president to have successfully integrated the two. People are still prepared, in Kennedy's case, to invest even the real image with positive connotations, so the image is activated in order to suppress any knowledge of the negative aspects of the Kennedy history. The glorified image of John Kennedy is thus mobilised to mask the lack that both the filmmakers and the audience are potentially aware of, and becomes a performance of a falsifying history.

The president's image is an effective metaphor for the state of the presidency within public consciousness, and the Kennedy–Nixon binary that has come to dominate the representation of American political history exemplifies the essential opposition. Whereas Kennedy's image symbolises cohesion and stability, Nixon's more ambivalent image symbolises disunity and instability. The essence of this differentiation lies in the relationship between performance and the narrative of history. In an essay on Oliver Stone's *JFK*, Robert Burgoyne discusses the 'tension between the film's formal innovations and its explicit aim to articulate a narrative of national cohesion' (Burgoyne 1996: 113). Although Burgoyne's analysis of Stone's tortuously inconsistent style as expressive of 'the fracturing of historical identity' (p. 113) is predictable, he rightly identifies the enduring significance of John Kennedy as representative of a nostalgic desire for the refiguration of a 'unified national identity' (p. 115). Burgoyne's argument is in part based on Timothy Brennan's analysis of nations as 'imaginary constructs that depend for their existence on an apparatus of cultural fictions' (Brennan 1990: 49), the idea of nations as mythic, allegoric entities invented as a social necessity rather than being the inevitable result of historical events. In his discussion, Burgoyne pins these ideas onto the nation's 'nostalgic desire ... for a unified national culture' destroyed by 'the memory of discontinuity emblematically figured in the death of Kennedy' (p. 123). Is it not conversely possible that the death of Kennedy - far from destroying the illusion of national cohesion – was the point at which this illusion became cemented in the social consciousness? If the link between nationhood and cultural fictions is to be sustained, the determining factor in Kennedy's continued symbolic presence as icon for national stability seems to be that, by remaining perpetually a figure of tragedy fixed in the memory by the real images of him up to and including his assassination, he represents the moment at which the myth of national unity took hold rather than the moment at which it was destroyed. It is due to his untimely death that Kennedy's image has become so consistent, unchangeable; his real persona has become synonymous with the mythic significance it is fancifully identified with.

Richard Nixon and the dangers of television

Whereas Kennedy's composite image has been assembled through documentary, live broadcasts, home movies (his own family's as well as Zapruder's) and fiction films, Nixon's image is forever associated with his televised appearances. Although he has featured in a multitude of films, documentaries such as *Millhouse* or *Watergate* make extensive use of Nixon's televised images. Nixon chose the television broadcast as his preferred mode of address because he assumed he would find it easy to control; he was not intent upon giving the public unprecedented access to him as an individual as Kennedy had done, but on addressing them in a more confrontational manner, often in times of crisis. Unlike Kennedy's rather deftly understated performances in *Primary* and *Crisis*, in Nixon's more carefully orchestrated appearances one sees a severance as opposed to a reinforcement of the ties between reality and fiction, between the image and the ideal. Instead of posing as the embodiment of a mythic presidency, Nixon represents the moment at which a belief in such a myth became untenable. While JFK has become part of American and Hollywood mythology, Nixon has been airbrushed out of the picture, and is conspicuously absent from the montage of past presidents at the beginning of *The American President*. This negativity is not simply the result of Watergate, it was innately linked to Nixon's own public persona, his inability to mask convincingly the cracks between who he was and what he sought to represent. Although he understood the media, Nixon never won it over, seeking the approbation of an institution that he distrusted and knew would never like him (see his self-pitying acknowledgement to the press upon his defeat in the 1962 Gubernatorial race in California and his supposed resignation that he is a national joke: 'Just remember, you won't have Dick Nixon to kick around any more').

Nixon's media performances exemplified a growing disillusionment with the unproblematic representation of truth. An early example is the Checkers speech, Nixon's 30-minutes long televised plea (transmitted 23 September 1952 on NBC and funded by the Republican National Committee) to persuade Eisenhower to keep him on as his running mate for the forthcoming presidential elections following revelations that he had accepted illegal gifts and misdirected party funds. The Checkers speech (so called because of the family dog Checkers Nixon cites as being the one unsolicited gift that he will admit to and intends to keep) has had a complex history. At the time of its broadcast it was deemed successful, as Republicans called in droves asking for Nixon to be retained as the party's vice-presidential nominee. The television station's copy was subsequently buried, assumed lost, until it was delivered anonymously to Emile de Antonio, after which it was used at length in his satirical documentary *Millhouse: A White Comedy* and acquired sufficient cult status to be released as a short to accompany Robert Altman's *Secret Honor* (1984). Similarly, the Checkers speech is open to analysis from various different perspectives: as an example of a primitive political use of television; as illustrative of Nixon's pervasive phoniness and corruption; as an example, post-Watergate, of how his career was based on sleaze, rule-bending and getting out of scrapes by adopting desperate measures, often the televised broadcast. Now, it is hard to see how the Checkers speech was ever a success. Nixon himself later admitted that the entire broadcast was staged, that Pat (who sat beside him) was as much a prop as the American flag in the background. Hollywood producer Darryl F. Zanuck reputedly told Nixon that the Checkers speech was 'the greatest performance I have ever seen' (Monsell 1998: 18). Nixon's tactic was to evoke (as he often did subsequently) his 'poor man made good' alter ego and to prove his innocence through an excess of detail, offering his viewers a 'complete financial history' and itemising with preposterous precision his meagre inheritance. With a flourish Nixon adds that Pat does not own a mink coat but instead wears, with pride, her 'respectable Republican cloth coat'.

Nixon's quality of performance is very different to that of the Kennedy brothers. It now seems inconceivable that the Checkers speech saved Nixon's career because, as an American journalist commented in 1972, Nixon is always an actor, 'he is conscious of the role he is playing and he has tried to train himself to his needs' (Walter Kerr quoted in Monsell 1998: 9). Perhaps it is easy to say this

Figure 5.1   Millhouse: A White Comedy
Source: Courtesy of BFI Stills, Posters and Designs

with hindsight but in the Checkers speech Nixon's performance, unlike those of either Robert or John Kennedy at comparable moments of crisis, appears fraught with conflicts and barely concealed strains. His mannerisms are brittle, the mock conviviality and informality – as, for example, he comes round to the front of his desk to deliver his protestations of innocence – are unconvincing, so obviously rehearsed; to a modern viewer, they convey precisely what Nixon wants to mask, namely his untrustworthiness. An essential component of this masquerade is Pat, hovering rigidly and precariously on the edge of a sofa, her expression stiffened into the weary, wary grimace we came to recognise from Watergate and the period of her husband's ignominious departure from the White House in 1974. Although Nixon survives repeated 'crises'[10] throughout his political career, it was often touch and go, and a means of exerting some control over his fate Nixon sought broadcast situations that he and his aides could control.

As a result of both this and his 'trickiness', Nixon came to symbolise the decline of any idealistic belief in the credibility of the presidential image. These schisms are most evident in the appearances during the Watergate period. On 30 April 1973 Nixon made a televised address in which he announced the resignations of his key aides John Dean, John Ehrlichman and Bob Haldeman and countered rumours of his own implication in the Watergate scandal. Umberto Eco's 'Strategies of lying' offers a semiotic analysis of this speech, accounting for the strategies Nixon adopts to exonerate himself from blame for his administration's corruption. Most significant for Eco is Nixon's equivocation, that he can admit to the 'imprudence' of Watergate (p.8) and so acknowledge a generalised guilt whilst simultaneously exonerating himself from blame. This strategy of equivocation was the tactic Nixon consistently deployed throughout his 'crisis' speeches: he used it in the Checkers speech and continued to use it until he finally resigned from office. In this 1973 speech he portrayed himself as at the mercy of the so-called 'collaborators' – Dean, Ehrlichman and Haldeman – to Nixon's mind the representatives of a system over which he, the little man, had no control. Eco's analysis concludes with the observation that 'Before the televised speech, a small percentage of Americans distrusted Nixon, yet after it the figure increased enormously and exceeded 50 per cent' (Eco 1985: 11); Nixon's otherwise masterful use of narrative was undermined by how it had been visually conveyed:

> Every muscle on Nixon's face betrayed embarrassment, fear, tension. Such a fine story, with the benefit of a happy ending, told by a frightened man. Frightened from start to finish. Nixon's speech was the visual representation of insecurity, acted out by the 'guarantor of security'.
>
> (p. 11)

It was Nixon's performance, his clumsy body language rather than his laborious self-justifications that exposed his lack of integrity.

The speech in which the discrepancy between words and implied truth is most acutely manifested is Nixon's resignation speech of the following year, 9 August 1974. A defiant Nixon (reputedly willing to face impeachment rather than accept Gerald Ford's promise of a pardon, who maintained he did not fear jail as Gandhi and Lenin had done much of their writing there[11]) stands flanked by his faithful family as he addresses the assembled White House staff. Once again Nixon constructs a grand narrative around himself as the tragic figure. At the outset, the identification of himself as a flawed but great man is merely implied in an impersonal dialogue with those watching:

> When the greatness comes and you're really tested, when you take some knocks, some disappointments, when sadness comes – because only if you've been in the deepest valley can you ever know how magnificent it is to be on the highest mountain.

Through this grandiloquent portion of the speech Nixon avoids the direct gaze of both audience and cameras, until he reaches the description of the 'highest mountain', at which point he looks up and half smiles, as if recalling the feeling of reaching such a peak. The manner in which he delivers this obscure dramatisation of his fall and rise (it is interesting how the sentence's structure puts the two in that order, as if the misdemeanour is already in the past) both mirrors his words and exposes the denial inherent within this formulation. Nixon, by transporting himself to the 'highest mountain', denies that he is in the 'deepest valley'; his rhetoric distancing his immediate situation from the parabolic transition he evokes. Having thus perked up, he continues:

> always give of your best, never get discouraged, never be petty, always remember others may hate you, but those who hate you don't win unless you hate them, and then you destroy yourself.

Once more this achingly inelegant sentence contains a double narrative. Superficially, this presents a buoyed Nixon issuing wise words to those listening (another defiant disavowal of the predicament he is in), and suggests that he himself has acknowledged the obstacles cited and has learnt how to surmount them. This renewed surety is confirmed by Nixon's more confident smile and a greater engagement with those present; he has deployed the characteristic tactic of detaching himself from the negative connotations of what he is saying by deflecting guilt onto something else, in this instance the impersonal narrative.[12] Nixon then resorts to the narrative he knows and performs best:

> I remember my old man, I think they would have called him a sort of little man, a common man. He didn't consider himself that way. You know what he was? He was a streetcar motorman first, and then he was a farmer, and then he had a lemon ranch. It was the poorest lemon ranch in California, I can assure you. He sold it before they found oil on it. ... Nobody will ever write a book, probably, about my mother. Well, I guess all of you would say this about your mother: my mother was a saint. ...

This piece of sub-Arthur Miller contains Nixon's classic emergency exit, the diversion he takes when refusing to admit he is wrong: to talk about life before he entered politics. Paradoxically, it is sections such as this that most manifestly signal Nixon's failure to achieve his aim. Emile de Antonio comments that, 'the real history of the United States in the Cold War is the out-takes' (Weiner 1971: 4). In fact, history arguably exists in the tension between the official and unofficial histories it comprises, and Nixon (whose specific television out-takes de Antonio is discussing) is revealed through a similar conflict between how he ostensibly presents himself through words and gesture, and the very different connotations these mannerisms betray.

Nixon's lack of straightforwardness has meant that he has become not a hero like Kennedy but a symbol of untrustworthiness and instability, Watergate still being the most ignominious moment in American presidential history. As an event, it engendered scepticism on a widespread scale, and has resulted in two oppositional approaches to the issue of the presidential image in general and to Nixon's image in particular: the impulse to reinstate a historical continuum via narrative and representation, and the acknowledgement that such a continuum is irretrievably lost. As George Herbert Mead, writing in 1929, notes, 'When a society is confronted with a seemingly novel event that disrupts the meaningful flow of events, the past must be rewritten to repair the discontinuity' (Johnson

1995: 37, 38). The former tendency is epitomised by Oliver Stone's *Nixon* which, for all its emphasis upon Watergate and Nixon's demise, nevertheless offers the view that Nixon was misguided rather than evil, a view sustained only by the prioritisation of personal and psychological character analysis over political scrutiny. To cement this view, the film concludes with real archive of Nixon's funeral (which all living ex-presidents attended) over which a voice-over lists his achievements since Watergate: his pardon, his six books, his work as an 'elder statesman', his view that, if he had not been 'driven from office', North Vietnam would not have overwhelmed the South in 1975. *Nixon* is an exercise in the collective recollection and forgiveness of a moment of national trauma, as Stone's Nixon becomes one who loves not wisely but too well, a strange metamorphosis indeed for Tricky Dickey. Rather than excise Nixon from American political history, Stone conforms to the revisionist trend to reinvent him as a quasi-hero and concomitantly to impose historical stability onto the very events that ruptured the illusion of a continuum in the first place.[13]

In the immediate aftermath of Watergate, there was a spate of diverse texts all of which criticised the Nixon administration and displayed a deep-rooted cynicism about presidential politics: films such as Altman's *Secret Honor* and Pakula's *All the President's Men* (1976) or books such as the entirely blank *The Wit and Wisdom of Spiro Agnew*. A more recent documentary series to tackle the corruption of Nixon and his administration is Norma Percy's *Watergate* (Brian Lapping Associates/BBC, 1994). *Watergate* has, as its opening premise, Nixon's unquestionable guilt and accountability, placing right at the start of its first episode Ehrlichman's comment that White House staff always 'carrying out Richard Nixon's instructions, day to day'. The five-part series unpicks in great detail the events that made up Watergate, from the establishing of Nixon's own paranoid political intelligence and surveillance systems to his departure from office. Perhaps it is because for so long we had been subjected, especially through the 1980s, to a romantic reassessment of Nixon's career that Percy's intricate series is refreshing: it reminds us – through the replaying of the White House tapes, through interviews with all the main Watergate protagonists and through archive – of the infinite corruption of the Nixon administration. The series gains extensive interviews with key figures: Haldeman, Nixon's Chief of Staff (who died very soon after), Ehrlichman, his chief domestic adviser, Dean, his counsel, and the White House Intelligence organisers, Howard Hunt and Gordon Liddy. (The interview that stands out is the one with Liddy in front of a highly polished table on which is carefully arranged his gun collection). The sense, particularly as Nixon's illegal tapes are played and memos (many assumed destroyed) get passed from one witness to another, is of reliving Watergate. Although the series concludes with the comment that Nixon died in April 1994, still denying he had broken the law, *Watergate* testifies against this. For example, John Dean (with the palpable relish of Nixon's scapegoat exacting his revenge) talks of how he plucked from the air (assuming Nixon would balk at this) the figure of $1 million to hush up Hunt and Liddy once the break-in had gone wrong. To Dean's amazement, Nixon said he could find the money. Likewise there is the replaying of the 'smoking gun' tape of 23 June 1972 on which Nixon blatantly orders a cover-up and from which someone in the White House erased 18 minutes. Nixon may deny his guilt, but the historical documents do not. *Watergate* painstakingly enacts the development of what John Dean, on a tape recorded 21 March 1973, terms a 'cancer ... close to the presidency that's growing'. Unlike *Nixon,* which buries the unpalatable truths of these recordings under the romantic notion of fluid political progression, *Watergate* does not let us forget that this was the event that most conclusively wrecked the ideal of not only a historical continuum, but also the myth of the good president. In the words of Jonathan Rauch in *The New Republic,* Nixon was 'easily the worst president of the post-war era, and probably of the century' (Johnson 1995: 7).

Tanner '88 and Clinton

Robert Altman's *Tanner '88,* a fictional six part television series in which fictional and real political figures intermingle, exemplifies the post-Nixon shift towards distrust of the idea that truthfulness and politics are in any way closely related. *Tanner '88* was written by political cartoonist Garry Trudeau and broadcast by HBO concurrently with the 1988 presidential campaign. The series' focus is an idealistic but ineffectual democrat candidate, Jack Tanner. Like much of Altman's work, it is shot (this time on video) in a fly-on-the-wall style reminiscent of direct cinema, pasting the fictional Tanner into the events of the real campaign. The blurring of the distinction between real and fictional presidential politics has since been much copied, most directly by *Bob Roberts* (Tim Robbins, 1992) which is a virtual homage to *Tanner '88* and the later film *Dave,* in which a fictional president is seen to meet actual politicians (among them Thomas P. 'Tip' O'Neill, Speaker of the House of Representatives from 1977–87 and Senator Paul Simon) whilst going about his fictional duties. In some of his films since *Tanner* (for instance *The Player* [1992] and *Pret-à- Porter* [1994]) Altman has again pasted real people into fictional situations and his visual style throughout his career has been characterised by a use of traditionally documentary or documentary-derived techniques such as hand-held camera, overlapping dialogue and sound and improvisation (see Roscoe and Hight 2001: 86–8). Jack Tanner is an innocent abroad whose image is created, distorted, used by the sassy throng that surrounds him. In the opening episode, 'Dark Horse', his first campaign video is shown to a group of sample New Hampshire voters who unanimously declare it to be disastrous. The only aspect of the video these punters like is Tanner's face. They adamantly reject such plausible campaign ploys as the woolly fireside address to camera in which Tanner (a single father) – dressed in a chunky cardigan – talks about having to interrupt his political career because of his daughter's Hodgkin's disease, just as they dislike the montage that positions Tanner within the liberal 1960s, juxtaposing Kennedy's 1961 inaugural speech ('Ask not what your country can do for you ...'), his assassination, Neil Armstrong's 'Giant leap for mankind' and the album cover of The Beatles' *Sgt. Pepper.* To replace this unsuccessful video Deak, the uncontrollable maverick

Figure 5.2 Tanner '88
Source: Courtesy of BFI Stills, Posters and Designs

cameraman of the Tanner entourage, makes a new one out of secretly shot footage of the spontaneous, impassioned monologue that closes the first episode in which Tanner admits, 'real leaders have always stepped forward ... it's time for that leadership now. I'm not sure it's me, but I'd like the chance to find out'. Filmed through a glass table and thus hard to decipher, this new video is aired on television at the outset of Episode 2 and concludes with the new campaign slogan in the corner of the screen: 'For Reel' crossed out and replaced by 'For Real'. However, although this might please the party workers, the response from the barmen watching this bemusing exercise in hidden camera technique is to ask: 'What the fuck was that?'

The replacement of the first derivative attempt to the 'For Real' video is representative of Tanner's metamorphosis from a carefully constructed candidate overly aware of the correlation between political success and image manipulation, to one who recognises the power of naturalness and honesty; as one aide comments, 'Tanner is about as real as Reagan is unreal'. This is, of course, out of step with the times and fatal to Tanner's credibility as a presidential candidate. Between 1968 and 1992, Jimmy Carter was the Democrat party's only president, and it is to the maligned Carter that Tanner is compared. In a piece of fake news footage, he is seen carrying his own bags, after which an aide remonstrates with him that this signals 'you can't or won't delegate. It says Jimmy Carter. People may want you to be for real Jack, but that doesn't mean they want you to be like him.' It was not until Clinton's victory in 1992 – when even Dan Quayle, the Republican nominee for Vice-President, remarked that, if Clinton runs the country the way he ran his campaign, things will be all right – that the Democrats fully engaged with the importance of slick image-making. Tanner is an eminently plausible 1980s Democrat loser who could be readily compared to George McGovern as well as to Carter, woven seamlessly into the 1988 campaign. (Discussed at the end of this chapter is the more recent *Staffers*, a film very like *Tanner '88* but a 'real' documentary charting the Democrats' 2004 campaign to select their presidential nomination. By this point, however, the expected conclusion was victory to John Kerry, which of course did not happen).

The fictional Jack Tanner is integrated seamlessly into the actual 1988 campaign. He is shown meeting a wary Bob Dole, a real Republican contender, and declares, in a speech at a Waylon Jennings-led gala evening, 'I've become Al Gore's worst nightmare'. (Gore, obviously, was later to be another losing Democrat contender, losing the closest election of them all to George W. Bush in 2000). Even Tanner's partner Joanna is seen in conversation with her 'friend' Kitty Dukakis after the Democrat convention, being asked whether or not Jack will come out in support of her husband Michael, the real Democrat nominee. At the convention itself, Tanner goes to the floor (the first candidate – however unreal – to do this during the vote itself), canvassing support after taking a stance (alongside Jesse Jackson) against the system of block 'super delegate' voting.[14] Tanner's invasion of the real political arena does two notable things: it problematises the boundaries between the factual and the fictitious and it makes one view with great cynicism the values of real presidential politics. Unlike *Forrest Gump* or *Zelig*, films that graft the documentary onto the fictional for essentially comic effect, Tanner's realness is equivocal. *Tanner '88* draws attention to the distinction between the composite, pastiche character of Jack Tanner and his real counterparts, at the same time as it renders *him* a highly plausible Democrat candidate and *them* equally credible fictional entities. The struggle within Tanner is the struggle between possessing and relinquishing an identity, and so functions as a metaphor for the ailing, compromised Democrats of the 1970s and 1980s. Tanner's progressive pro-environmentalist, anti-racist stance is at odds with his shameless promotion as the unknown outsider who attends small town barbecues and drops in on a Ladies Auxiliary quilt-making afternoon. Inevitably it is his progressiveness that is repressed.

Tanner '88 has a perpetually accidental quality that mirrors the meandering nature of the Democratic Party at the time. In terms of its narrative structuring, apart from generally leading up to the convention and the conclusion of Tanner's failed bid for the presidential nomination, the series maintains a veneer of formlessness – journalists get stranded on the press bus on the way to the Waylon Jennings evening and so miss the bungled assassination attempt on Tanner; Tanner unwittingly gets arrested at a 'Free South Africa' rally. This formlessness is in turn mimicked by the observational filming style, exemplified by Deak's progressively extreme and clandestine shooting for his alternative campaign film. Tanner's campaign is pursued by a lazy, unbothered and uncritical observational camera that all too frequently gets diverted, at times onto something interesting, such as Tanner emerging with Joanna from a room when no one yet knows they are an item. This filming style is an inherent component of the series' pretence at realness, its eavesdropping quality replicating the essential direct cinema paradox of constructed, ordered chaos. The filmmaking style pioneered by the direct cinema exponents of the 1960s has become the common shorthand mechanism for giving a piece of fiction a documentary edge, of legitimating its claim to reality. In *Tanner '88*, Altman utilises this technique ironically, overemphasising and so complicating the notion of the real, both through Deak and through the persistent references to Tanner or his image as real.

Tanner '88 is an ambiguous, hybrid text: both in its visual style and its narrative it advocates truthfulness; it also signals that, in the 1980s' political climate, Tanner's attachment to such values lacks political credibility. What the appositely named Jack Tanner lacks is Kennedy's ability to perform naturalness, to be both politician and real at the same time. This deficiency has altered by the time another Jack – Stanton in *Primary Colors* – appears in another semi-fictional campaign film. Altman's series, rather than merely accept the necessity of the Kennedy paradox, ridicules the political allegiance to a concept of fabricated realness, within this undermining the idea of 'a cinema of truth'. The transition from natural idealistic candidate to victorious politician is more straightforwardly made in an earlier film, *The Candidate;* in *Tanner '88* the neat progression is substituted by a polemic on realness. Within the very different documentary context of Jennie Livingston's *Paris is Burning*, realness is understood as a performance that cannot be 'read' or deciphered as false by others. Tanner's dilemma, and the one that Altman's unflinchingly observational style underlines, is that he can too easily be 'read'. By the 1980s we no longer believed the transparency of observational documentary, nor could we any longer, in the aftermath of Nixon, believe that the politician and his image are meaningfully correlated. A gag that runs through *Tanner '88* is that no one knows who he is; from an early encounter with a pair of New Hampshire autograph hunters who enquire 'Jack Tanner, who's he?', to the perplexed responses to the 'For Real' campaign film, Tanner the candidate is a nonentity, epitomised by the bemused, uncertain smile that perpetually adorns his face.

Jack Tanner exemplifies the liberal Democrat who loses elections to wilier conservative opposition – not just McGovern and Carter but Al Gore in 2000 and John Kerry in 2004 (during whose campaign against George W. Bush *Tanner '88* was, in the UK, rerun). Bill Clinton was a successful version of

Tanner: a child of the 60s whose liberalism, however, was endlessly compromised by both politics and scandal. There are various formal similarities between *Tanner '88* and actual documentary accounts of the 1992 campaign, such as *Feed* (Kevin Rafferty and James Ridgeway, 1992) and *The War Room* (Chris Hegedus and Donn Pennebaker, 1993), both of which depict a similar blend of hypertension and boredom. By the time of Clinton's election in 1992, the cynicism that pervaded *Tanner '88* had come to dominate representations of both the real and fictional presidential image. Whereas *Primary* was elegant and evocative, suggesting that there was still a mystique surrounding the presidential fight and that the filmmakers had been granted privileged, unprecedented access to the candidates, a modern equivalent such as *Feed* indicates that now there is limitless media access to the American electoral process, that the candidates are mere cogs in a system represented by dull and trivial television images. As if acknowledging this loss, the anonymous novel *Primary Colors* (later identified as the work of journalist Joe Klein), a thinly veiled fictionalisation of Clinton's 1992 election campaign, opens with a conversation between the idealistic Henry Burton and Susan Stanton (assumed to be George Stephanopoulos, Clinton's communications director, and Hillary Rodham Clinton respectively). Burton, contemplating joining Jack Stanton's presidential campaign, says:

> The thing is, I'd kind of like to know how it feels when you're fighting over ... y'know – historic stuff. I'm not like you. I didn't have Kennedy. I got him from books, from TV. But I can't get enough of him, y'know? Can't stop looking at pictures of him, listening to him speak. I've never heard a president use words like 'destiny' or 'sacrifice' and it wasn't bullshit. So, I want to be part of something a moment, like that. When it's real, when it's history ...
>
> (Anonymous 1996: 24)

Susan Stanton simply replies: 'It's good. History's what we're about, too. What else is there?' Reading or watching (in Mike Nichols' film of *Primary Colors*) Burton's naïve vision of what is real and what is history gives voice to our collective awareness that such mythologisation is 'bullshit' anyway.

The War Room, made in a comparable observational style to *Primary* and *Crisis* (especially the loose, eaves-dropping camera work much of which is Pennebaker's own), illustrates the shift that has taken place between the Kennedy and the Clinton campaigns: that, by the time of the latter, the mythologisation of the candidate is manufactured by spin doctors and their artful manipulation of the media. As suggested by its title, which refers to the Arkansas 'war room' from which Stephanopoulos and James Carville, campaign manager, masterminded Clinton's victory, the documentary observes the entourage responsible for that victory. Clinton himself is marginal; foregrounded is the relationship with the media covering the campaign. *The War Room* contains a few inevitable but somewhat sardonic echoes of *Primary* (on which Pennebaker worked as a cameraperson), for instance two lengthy hand-held tracking shots in pursuit of George

Stephanopoulos, reminiscent of Albert Maysles' shot following John Kennedy in 1960. The second is particularly emblematic of the shift in political representation that has taken place. Following the first televised debate (of which we only see bites on the television sets that Stephanopoulos, Carville and others are fixated upon) Stephanopoulos runs out clapping, his arms in the air, convinced that Clinton has won the night. The jubilant communications manager is not running to congratulate his candidate (in fact, any communication between the two is strictly limited to telephone conversations in which Stephanopoulos imparts information to Clinton) but towards the press to reiterate his point that Bush has lost.

Whereas *Primary* draws us in and forges an affinity with the candidates, *The War Room* invites its audience to experience electioneering vicariously: we are doubly removed from Clinton by gaining access to him second and third hand from, firstly, the media and, secondly, his campaign team who are constantly analysing that media coverage. Direct cinema in the 1960s emphasised and followed individuals – *Primary* boiled down to a contest between the two candidates with party politics taking a back seat, *Crisis* offered a portrait of how a political crisis impinges on the people involved – *The War Room*, with its twin stress upon process and party politics, lacks the emotive pull of the earlier films precisely because it lacks Clinton. Throughout the film there is an overwhelming sense of Clinton engulfed by throngs of people or being coached and guided by a string of minders; once he has gained the nomination, he becomes even more marginal, effectively disappearing altogether whilst Carville and Stephanopoulos think up soundbites and evolve strategy. Clinton is depicted as the team's figure-head, in itself a necessary comment upon the manner in which power has shifted away from the individual candidate – of Clinton's victory address to the Democratic convention, for instance, the film includes only the last phrase ('I still believe in a place called Hope'). The real power resides with Carville and Stephanopoulos. Stephanopoulos' role, more than anything else, is to patch up Clinton's fragile image, to stem leaks, to divert dangerous exposés. On the eve of victory he is shown aggressively fielding a call concerning allegations (later disproved) that Clinton fathered an illegitimate mixed-race child. The culmination of his and Carville's success is Clinton's emphatic victory, and yet, dressed in evening wear, Stephanopoulos is still amending the now President's victory speech and, just before we cut to the party, there is a final phone conversation between the two in which he advises the president-elect to 'say what you wanna say – this is your night'. In this context, such deference to the President becomes ironic, as the whole documentary has stressed Clinton's lack of power and independence. This is a documentary about the team that manufactured Clinton's victory and its downbeat conclusion (two shots of the empty 'war room') serves as a reminder that the political process is ongoing, that, unlike the romantic 'crisis' narratives of direct cinema, closure is not granted by the victory celebrations as those celebrations are simply part of the process.

It is tempting to agree that *The War Room* reveals simply 'the amoral and ultimately apolitical attitude of approaching political communications solely as a battle of images, waged through the mass media' (Diamond and Silverman 1997: 108), although it is more complex than this. What it signals, more than pure cynicism, is a sense of what has been lost by this inevitable shift towards media-dominated politics. *The War Room* does not only offer evidence that Carville and Stephanopoulos created the electable candidate Bill Clinton through their dual manipulation of his image and the media, it raises the suspicion that the main task of the two advisers, having saturated the media with pictures of their candidate, is perversely to shield him from view. Despite its direct cinema pedigree, *The War Room* does not (and presumably was not permitted to) show Clinton or the others in many undirected situations (although there is what looks like a hidden camera shot of Carville fixing a date with Mary Matalin, deputy manager of the Bush campaign). Towards the beginning of the documentary, there is a brief sequence showing Clinton on the telephone in baseball cap, T-shirt and shorts, he looks at ease and comfortable. As *The War Room* progresses, there are fewer and fewer glimpses of him, the implication being that the spin doctors do not want to run the risk of exposing their candidate to unpredictable encounters with a documentary crew. The motto of modern politics is 'always be on your guard'.

The observation that politics has become solely a battle of images could more legitimately be made about *Feed,* a documentary that appeared in arthouse cinemas on the eve of the 1992 election and comprises unofficially collated footage from the campaign. Punctuating *Feed* from start to finish is a series of shots of George Bush Sr. waiting behind his desk to begin a television address; Bush looks bored and vacant, and the most interesting question raised by this material is what precisely is he doing with the hand that repeatedly drops behind his desk? Although as de Antonio remarks the real history of post-war America is to be found in television out-takes, *Feed* appears to be quite consciously unanalytical of its 'collage junk' potential and insufficiently discriminating as it covers all aspects of the opening Primary campaign. Much of this (such as the press conference at which Gennifer Flowers repeats her allegations of a 12-year affair with Bill Clinton) is highly familiar, but is juxtaposed with plenty of material that is less so and funnier for it, such as Paul Tsongas (recently recovered from cancer and keen to prove his fitness) posing for the cameras in his swimming trunks. Elsewhere, Jerry Brown lectures college students for not knowing who Marshall McLuhan was before offering a rather inept account of his ideas himself and Bill Clinton suppresses giggles as he is about to go on air.

Feed achieves two notable things: it demonstrates that presidential politics is so image-dependent that the candidates are (in terms of character, the man behind the mask, etc.) all but interchangeable; it also suggests that the business of politics has become a puerile joke. The film's use of unofficial footage ultimately leads to a reassessment of its official corollaries such as the televised address or the documentary, both of which remain environments the politician can, to some extent, control. What *Feed,* through its intercutting of the official with the unofficial image, proceeds to focus upon is the moment of transition between waiting to go on air and commencing the public performance. Through this juxtaposition, *Feed* questions the belief in the 'real' person as opposed to the 'performance'.

Is the 1992 presidential election to be remembered as the one that admitted that standing for office is a performative act? At a White House dinner to commemorate the Hollywood version of *Primary Colors,* Bill Clinton invited John Travolta, who in the film plays his fictional doppelganger Jack Stanton, to impersonate him for the assembled guests. Travolta declined, but both Clinton's action and the accuracy of Travolta's rendition of Clinton's mannerisms in Nichols' film demonstrate the corrosion of the distinction between the real and the performed. *Primary Colors,* the film, is a historical enactment, a narrative representation so close to the actual events and individuals portrayed that it, on several occasions, collapses the differences between them. Included in it is a quasi-re-enactment, or re-presentation of the Gennifer Flowers episode, although Flowers' name has been altered to Cashmere McLeod – now Susan Stanton's hairdresser rather than a nightclub singer. The fictionalised version of events shares many components with the original news story: Cashmere sells her story to a magazine, the Stantons go on television to deny the allegations and Cashmere retaliates with a press conference at which she plays a tape (later discovered to be faked) of an alleged conversation between her and Stanton. Although not a verbatim rendition of the Clintons' appearance on *60 Minutes* to refute Flowers' claims, the version in *Primary Colors* is an accurate paraphrase, simulating not just the narrative situation but also the couple's deliberate and studied body language (sitting very close to each other, clasping hands, Hillary/Susan gazing fixedly at her husband as he admits there have been problems in their marriage). The proximity of reconstruction to historical original renders the performance transparent. *Primary Colors* lacks the critical distance of *Tanner '88;* whilst Jack Tanner was a credible pastiche of an 1980s Democrat, Jack Stanton is merely a pseudonym for Clinton, a 'readable' but accurate citation.

If it was the corruption and collective mendacity of Nixon's administration that paved the way for the cynicism and disillusionment with presidential politics of Robert Altman's *Tanner '88* and *Secret Honor* or *All the President's Men,* discrepancies between the actual president and his fictionalised counterparts became even more pronounced during the Clinton years. Although loved for his liberalism and charm, scandal dogged Clinton's two terms in office, no more so than his affair with White House intern Monica Lewinsky. The nadir for Clinton during this period was his videoed testimony to the Grand Jury on 17 August 1998 in which he was cross-examined about his sexual liaison with Lewinsky and his alleged perjury in denying the affair whilst testifying under oath during the 1994 Paula Jones hearing.[15] The video was intended for private Grand Jury use only, but copies were soon leaked and a commercial edited version quickly became available. The quality of the four-hour video is poor, with Clinton just to the left of the fixed camera looking towards a screen that links him to Special Prosecutor, Kenneth Starr. It is, however, compelling, in large part because of the tenor and subject of the questions (Clinton is forced to answer questions about cherry chocolates, the sexual potential of cigars and what constitutes sexual relations) and the crude quality of the video (this is another instance, like the Zapruder film, of technically unrefined footage proving particularly compulsive). The corollary of this fusion of exaggeratedly enticing content and inelegant visual style is that the disparity between Clinton's unrehearsed performance here and his usually slick performances in situations such as press conferences where his image is more clearly controlled becomes exaggerated. For most of the time Clinton manages to be composed and sympathetic; the one time he looks genuinely shocked is when Starr asks him whether or not he used a cigar as a sexual aid, at which point Clinton's eyebrows arch and his eyes widen. Several factors here intersect: the voyeuristic pleasure granted by the incumbent President of the United States being asked in detail about his intimate sexual conduct; that this treatment of the president is unprecedented; that Clinton is momentarily disempowered. As such, this moment is the antidote to the intensively mediated image created by Clinton's spin-doctors and strategists, its spontaneity signalling the inherent precariousness of the manufactured political image.

This problem is compounded by the number of feature films about American presidents produced during the Clinton years, which collectively functioned as an indirect commentary on Clinton's 'for real' performances. Between 1993 and 1997, Hollywood released seven major president films – *Dave* (1993), *Clear and Present Danger* (1994), *The American President* (1995), *Independence Day* (1996), *Absolute Power, Air Force One* and *Wag the Dog* (all 1997) – and in 1998 two more satirical films about the electoral process in general – *Primary Colors* and *Bulworth* – joined *Wag the Dog*. A deep-rooted political alienation set in and, in turn, spawned the Clinton era's public investment in fictive presidents. As the presidency lost its iconic status, so the figure of the president became a palimpsest onto which could be transferred multiple and contrasting fantasies of his putative narrative and symbolic potential. In a film such as *Wag the Dog*, the president is even more exaggeratedly marginal to the electoral process than Clinton is portrayed as being in *The War Room*; in *Dave* or *The American President* he is implausibly idealised – liberal, politically effective and personally charming; in *Independence Day* and *Air Force One* he becomes an action movie hero and in both *Absolute Power* and *Clear and Present Danger* he is portrayed as ruthlessly villainous. These films contain covert references to real politics, such as the obvious parallels with the Lewinsky scandal in *Wag the Dog* or, more obliquely, the echoes in *Air Force One* of Lloyd Bentsen's admonishment of Dan Quayle during their 1988 vice-presidential televised debate as President Marshall's daughter says to the head of the terrorist group which has hijacked the presidential aircraft: 'You are a monster, and my father is a great man. You're nothing like my father'.[16] These fictional renditions are more fanciful but eminently plausible.

George W. Bush, *Fahrenheit 9/11*

Since I first wrote this chapter, disillusionment with the office of president under Clinton has been superseded by direct contempt in some quarters for George W.

Bush, elected in 2000 and again in 2004. One potent vestige of the Clinton era, though, remains in the (originally) Aaron Sorkin-scripted *West Wing,* which has run since its first pilot in 1999. President Josiah Bartlet is a liberal idealist and an extended version of Andrew Shepherd (Michael Douglas) in *The American President,* for which Sorkin also wrote the screenplay. Bartlet is a composite president who incorporates the best traits of Kennedy, Carter, Clinton and noble losing Democrats such as Al Gore and frequently his actions echo those of these past Democrat icons – his decision in 'The Birnam Wood', Episode Two of Season 6 to secretly barter with the Palestinian leader, who he is trying to get to the negotiating table with the Israeli premier at Camp David, is very reminiscent, for example, of Kennedy's conduct during the Cuban Missile Crisis of October 1962 as he equally secretly and contentiously agreed to withdraw US missiles from Turkey in exchange for Kruschev's removal of Soviet missiles from Cuba. Bartlet is the embodiment of what Americans might have had as their president had they not tended, over the past five years, to gravitate quite so consistently to the Right, a fantasy figure as different from George W. Bush – the incumbent his fictional tenure in the White House has mirrored – as it is possible to conceive.

The shift from disillusionment with the presidency to contempt for it is illustrated by Michael Moore's quintessential cinema documentary *Fahrenheit 9/11* (released to coincide with the elections of 2004), although more generalised contempt for the electoral system also manifested itself in a documentary such as *Last Party 2000* (Donovan Leitch, 2002). The latter, fronted by actor Philip Seymour Hoffman (an impassioned but frustratingly inarticulate spokesman for disillusioned and disenfranchised left of centre Americans) is an election campaign film, vaguely in the mould of *Primary* and *The War Room,* although, rather than getting close to one of the candidates in 2000, it follows the campaign from a distance. *Last Party 2000* is clearly anti-Republican and – slightly less clearly – anti-establishment and by extension anti-Democrat (Michael Moore is interviewed at one point expressing his familiar view that very little divides the two main political parties. However Hoffman counters this at the close when he remarks that he could discern a difference between the delegates at the Republican and the Democrat conventions, that those at the latter were more culturally and ethnically mixed). Its climactic moment is, inevitably, the vote in the state of Florida, which was originally called for Al Gore, then – controversially – for Bush and which, after a few weeks of recounts, demonstrations, allegations and counter-allegations, in the end won the election for Bush with a margin of only 527 votes. (This was also one of very few elections when the president won despite losing the nationwide popular vote). *Last Party 2000* is rather shambolic and unfocused, but it does rally at the end as it invites its audience to relive those strange weeks of dimpled chads, recounts and allegations against Governor Jeb Bush that he rigged the election for his brother by disenfranchising swathes of African-Americans and felons (who turned out not to be felons at all).

The 2000 vote in Florida is the starting point for Michael Moore's *Fahrenheit 9/11,* which opens with Moore in voice-over wondering whether the state's voting debacle was 'all a dream'. The declared intention of *Fahrenheit 9/11* was to mobilise the American public into voting against Bush (as Moore has said: 'I hope that people go see this movie and throw the bastards out of office' [Smith 2004: 22]); to this end, the documentary did not succeed, as Bush beat John Kerry in 2004 just as he had beaten Gore in 2000. Republicans, however, still sought to minimise its impact by pressuring theatre chains not to screen the film, trying to have any advertising of it banned and doing what they could to cancel or foil Moore's scheduled appearances on college campuses (see O'Connor 2005: 7). As with its immediate predecessor *Bowling for Columbine* (2003), *Fahrenheit 9/11* is stridently polemical; not a piece of agit-prop in the way it looks (as *LBJ* is, for example) but agitational in sentiment. As with Moore's other cinema documentaries, *Fahrenheit 9/11* is manifestly subjective, an essay film with a clearly delineated and personalised point of view. Any discussion of performance in relation to Michael Moore's films is necessarily complicated by Moore's visibility, the fact he is a dominant physical presence as well as an intellectual one. Gary Crowdus's often cited criticism of Michael Moore's debut documentary *Roger and Me* (1989) – that it 'might have acquired a little more political bite if it had focused a little more on "Roger" and somewhat less on "Me"' (Crowdus 1990: 30) – cannot, however, be levelled at *Fahrenheit 9/11*, which is, as Kent Jones argues, 'genuinely incendiary' (Jones 2004: 20) as opposed to a film that relies on the 'questionable and even shameful moves' Jones detected in his earlier films (p. 20) or adopts the 'cheap shot' strategies that Crowdus specifically found in *Roger and Me* (Crowdus 1990: 29). Individuals are used in a familiarly auteurist way (Lila Lipscomb, for instance, the mother from Flint whose son has been killed on military duty in Iraq is one of several 'victims' Moore latches onto in his documentaries and through whom he dramatises the emotional, personal aspects of his anti-establishment cause). However, whereas in previous films (for example, the two teenage boy victims of the Columbine massacre who Moore takes with him to Kmart – where the bullets used in the massacre had been purchased – to get them to stop selling handgun bullets) Moore has used 'victims' of the injustices he is exposing as vehicles for bringing the focus back onto himself, usually by sidelining their pain in deference to showing on camera his responses to their pain, in Lipscomb's case Moore stays off camera and in the shadows (although there is the moment when the familiar pan across after Lipscomb has walked off crying begins. In previous films this would have been the moment when Moore's reactions were put on screen. Here, it is as if Moore considered using the same tactic but then thought better of it).

This sidelining of 'Me' in *Fahrenheit 9/11* does serve expressly to sharpen the focus onto George W. Bush, who is portrayed not just as an untrustworthy politician in his own right but also as a figurehead for a larger, more powerful regime. There is some mention of Bush's perceived stupidity – the inelegancies of speech, stumbles and malapropisms lampooned in the satirical British radio and television series *Dead Ringers* or which feature in Chris Cooper's portrayal of a fumblingly challenged state governor in John Sayles' fiction film *Silver City*, interpreted by many critics (perhaps because, like *Fahrenheit 9/11* it was released around the time of the 2004 election) as a reference to Bush. *Fahrenheit 9/11*, however, is a departure for Moore in that, along with Moore's onscreen appearances, Bush's gag potential is minimised in favour of a more sober emphasis upon the political impact of his actions and policies. For the same reasons that *The Leader, His Driver and the Driver's Wife* remains to date Nick Broomfield's most effective documentary, *Fahrenheit 9/11* has probably had more of a political impact than its predecessors because in it Moore has made his tendency towards what Crowdus has termed a 'scattershot satirical approach' that makes everyone 'fair game' (Crowdus 1990: 29) serve a more serious ideological message. The first twenty minutes of *Fahrenheit 9/11* are potently exemplary of Moore's style and of the manner in which he reigns in his penchant for cheap jibes to suit his subject matter. They will be used as the basis for this discussion of Moore's method. This opening section goes like this:

- Pre-titles: Bush pulls off an unlikely victory in Florida in 2000.
- Still pre-titles: moving footage of Al Gore, in his capacity as outgoing Vice President of Leader of the Senate, presiding over a long line of principally African-American Representatives bringing signed objections to the way in which the voting was conducted in Florida before a joint sitting of both houses. In order to be considered and debated these objections needed to have been signed by at least one member of the Senate; none of these were, but as one Representative states as Gore asks for the umpteenth time if her petition has been signed by a Senator, her face glistening with indignation and defiance: 'I don't care if it's not signed by a Senator'.
- Bush's inauguration, January 2001: as his car is pelted with eggs, Bush's motorcade speeds up and Bush declines the opportunity to get out of his car and walk part of the way, as is traditional.
- Voice-over accompanied by archive conveys that, during the first months of his presidency, Bush's approval ratings dropped and that he spent 42% of his time on vacation.
- Titles intercut with a preparatory sequence of images: Paul Wolfowitz (Deputy Secretary of Defense) preparing himself for a television appearance by licking his comb before running it through his hair in an attempt to get it to lie flat. An aide – or the interviewer – then lends a helping hand and Wolfowitz grins; Bush likewise preparing for a broadcast, having his face brushed and flipping a cocky, sly smile and a wink to someone to the side of frame.
- After titles: the screen cuts to black and stays black, accompanied by sound archive of the attack on the World Trade Centre, September 11 2001; the black then runs into footage of devastated New Yorkers in the streets at the time crying, praying and in shock.
- Moore's voice-over and archive tell us that the President, as the first plane struck, was on his way to visit a school in Florida. Moore's voice-over comments that Bush 'just decided to go ahead with his photo opportunity' despite this.

- The voice-over states that the second plane strikes whilst Bush is observing a class. Bush's Chief of Staff comes in and, Moore informs us, tells the President 'the nation is under attack'. Bush looks perplexed. Moore comments on the fact that he just sat there 'and continued to read *My Pet Goat* with the children'. Seven minutes passed (the timings are shown in the bottom left-hand corner of the screen) as the voice-over speculates that Bush failed to do anything because no one had told him what to do.

- This heralds the most incriminatory portion of these opening minutes as Moore accuses Bush of having cut the CIA's terrorism budget since coming to office and having ignored their 6 August 2001 report that 'Osama bin Laden was planning to attack America by hijacking airplanes'. To accompanying archive of jovial meetings and the like, Moore then details the close ties between the Bush family, the Saudis, the bin Ladens and the Taliban, culminating in the accusation that, while all other flights in and out of the US had been grounded, the bin Laden family and other prominent Saudis had been given clearance to fly out of the country.

The dominant tone at the outset of this introductory section of *Fahrenheit 9/11* is humorous and relatively light, with the exception of the sequence in the Senate. The pre-titles sequence includes classic Moore 'cheap shots' of Wolfowitz licking his comb and Bush sniggering, throwaway jibes reminiscent of *Feed* and other satirical movies and television series that derive amusement from simply cutting together out-takes of public figures caught off-guard or before cameras have officially started to roll. This is a key satirist's tactic and in an interview Moore Gavin Smith asks the director about 'showing us what precedes or follows a piece of footage' (Smith 2004: 25), to which Moore explains that the usual agreement is that the White House press office will dictate when a camera is turned on and off, the press person often standing in front of the lens immediately after the official business has been completed so as to render the out-takes unusable. Later in *Fahrenheit 9/11* comes its most infamous out-take: Bush speaking earnestly about how 'we must stop the terror' before turning round to resume his game of golf and inviting the assembled press to 'now watch this drive'. As Moore comments to Smith: Bush rightly assumed that the networks would not use this.

Moore's signature tactics are most clearly in evidence during the vacation sequence. A recurrent rhetorical flourish adopted by Moore here and in previous films is to give a sequence exit velocity, to build up its argument, its level of noise, the seriousness of its allegations until a punch-line is reached, commonly accompanied by a loud, catchy music track, in this instance 'Vacation' by The Go-Go's. The culmination is then a rapidly edited montage – often, as here, ushered in by an irreverent remark in the voice-over (such as the quip that 'With everything going wrong, he [Bush] did what any of us would do – he went on vacation') – offering a potted version of the argument that has been building: here, that Bush is innately lazy and unwilling to face his troubles. This is not unlike Eisenstein's tactic, exemplified by the Odessa Steps sequence of *Battleship Potemkin*, of concluding a montage sequence with a brief series of shots whose meaning might, on the surface, appear elusive and abstract but which have been rendered logical of what has gone before.

As the most significant trauma of modern American history, the events of 9/11 altered everything, and in his response to those events Moore demonstrates the underlying seriousness of his filmic endeavours. To mark the difference of those events *Fahrenheit 9/11* represents them via a black screen accompanied by archival sound; the break with the tone of the pre-titles and title sequence is clear, as is the break with the use, primarily on television, of images that have become so familiar and iconic (the latter being the term I have given to archive material that has become not only over-familiar but emotionally charged [see pp. 21–22). Quite simply, Moore is requiring his audience to look at 9/11 in a different way and so perhaps to contextualise it differently too and to examine its wider repercussions, principally the subsequent war against Iraq.

Moore then reverts to focusing on Bush's behaviour as he is told the news of the attacks. As Bush sits in the classroom looking both panicked and blank it might seem as if Moore is also reverting to type by falling back on his favoured method of criticising through ridicule. Instead, coming after the 9/11 sequence, the account of Bush's actions in the classroom display a similar dialectic to that found in good Nick Broomfield, namely that ostensibly puerile humour (finding Bush's facial expressions, mannerisms and ineffectuality funny) is being mobilised to serious ends, namely that Bush responded slowly to 9/11, a tardiness that, Moore believes, stemmed from his family ties with the bin Ladens. In an article about essay documentaries Paul Arthur suggests that 'It's tempting to cite the deployment of found footage and collage as endemic to the essay' (Arthur 2003a: 59). He goes on:

> However, if essays are not invariably heterogeneous in materials, their segmental and sound-image relationships tend to entail collision or dialectical critique. The emphasis is on converging angles of inquiry rather than historical nostalgia or pastiche.
>
> (p. 59)

Moore's use of found footage has always been based on collision, but in *Fahrenheit 9/11* it is also dialectical: through the juxtaposition of his voice-over and archival images Moore reaches a conclusion that is not only confrontational towards George Bush but also historically and politically valid. As with the vacation sequence, the portion of *Fahrenheit 9/11* that presents its most serious allegations against Bush (that his family has long-established links to the Saudis and the bin Ladens, based on a shared desire to protect oil production) culminates in a faster, more hard-hitting section in which the professional affiliations of cabinet members such as Dick Cheney are brought into question and the view that companies to whom they are affiliated indirectly benefited from the war against Iraq. As when Emile de Antonio rejoiced in the fact that Senator Joseph McCarthy's lawyer, Roy Cohn, failed to find any lies in *Point of Order*, despite dedicating years of effort to this, Moore similarly relishes the challenge of proving the validity of his accusations on his website (www.michaelmoore.com) and elsewhere. As historian Robert Brent Toplin points out, although 'the film-maker's angry detractors argue that he employed facts incorrectly', in fact the *major* disagreements between admirers and detractors of *Fahrenheit 9/11* are primarily over the *interpretation* of facts, not whether the facts are, themselves, true'. Toplin concludes: 'Moore's principal evidence is not inherently incorrect, but what one makes of it can, of course, excite animated disagreement' (Toplin 2005: 8). A whole section of Moore's website and a recent book (*The Official Fahrenheit 9/11 Reader*) are dedicated to detailing his sources for his more contentious allegations and his facts are not often disputed, even if his interpretation of them frequently is.

Unlike Emile de Antonio, Moore does not formulate his arguments via the juxtaposition of archive alone, but through a mixture of archive and voice-over. *Fahrenheit 9/11*, however, is an example of contemporary agitational cinema: it tried to influence viewers and voters, it sought to disrupt a political regime. At its core is the dialectical collision with George W. Bush. *Fahrenheit 9/11* ends where it started – poking fun at an inarticulate president – as Bush recounts a Southern motto: 'There's an old saying of Texas and I'm sure Tennessee … fool me once, shame on … shame on you. A fool can't be fooled again'. As Bush pauses between 'once' and 'shame' and then again between the first 'shame on' and the second, the sense of this saying appears to be lost on Bush as well as his audience and he sinks into the quicksand of inarticulacy once more, seeming fleetingly aware, though, of the painful relevance of his glossing of this saying ('A fool can't get fooled again'). Moore's voice-over makes sure no one else misses this as he concludes *Fahrenheit 9/11* with a familiar triumphant put down: 'For once we agreed'. Within the framework of such a clearly targeted, directional film the image created of George W. Bush, though not a fabrication, is entirely subservient to and dictated by Michael Moore's point of view, his perspective reflecting his thwarted desire to assist in the removal of Bush from office.

Conclusion

It perhaps comes as no big surprise that consensual documentaries (in which politicians have consented to being filmed) are invariably about Democrat candidates whilst we are only granted glimpses of Republicans and their campaigns in films based on outtakes and stolen footage (*Millhouse: A White Comedy; Feed; Fahrenheit 9/11*). Following in this tradition is *Staffers* (Steven Rosenbaum, 2005), a recent documentary (or documentary series, as it is divided into six discrete episodes) following the ultimately unsuccessful Democratic presidential campaign of 2004. As its title suggests, *Staffers* focuses on the campaign teams of the various candidates, not – as did *Primary* – on the candidates themselves.

Like *The War Room*, *Staffers* treats the candidates (and ironically what they stand for) as peripheral to its drama, although unlike Pennebaker and Hegedus's fly-on-the-wall observation of the first Clinton campaign, Rosenbaum's film suffers greatly from being about a series of defeated candidates, as ultimately George Bush was returned for a second time, defeating Democrat nominee John Kerry. Although the Kerry team contains two important and charismatic members, *Staffers* suffers from being about too many people (until later, when the number of candidates has been whittled down, *Staffers* spends too little time following one individual before cutting to the next) – and too many people who, by the end of it, are all on the losing side. That *Staffers* ends up telling the story of a bunch of hopeful losers is a drawback illustrated by a sequence in 'Episode 2' in which Joe Lieberman, who is performing badly in the early primaries, is caught on camera discussing with his assistant Chris the issue of who should carry his bags, on the night of the New Hampshire primary. Lieberman draws attention to the fact that Chris is carrying several bags onto a plane, to which the staffer replies 'Jimmy Carter carried his own', Lieberman then remarking directly to Rosenbaum's camera that 'it would be appropriate to the night' if he did carry his own bags. (Lieberman has just come a dismal fifth in New Hampshire and a week later withdraws from the race). Carter carrying his own bags has clearly become among Democrats iconic shorthand for 'loser', and has also been mentioned in *Tanner '88*. Whereas *Tanner '88*, however, formulated a comic pastiche of the boredoms and tensions of a losing presidential campaign, *Staffers* – in part because Rosenbaum presumed that Kerry would ultimately defeat Bush and so that this would be a documentary about a winner – has no such comedic bite and becomes boring in earnest, a problem exacerbated by Rosenbaum having missed or not having been given access to the real dramas of the Democrat campaign. Firstly, there is hardly a mention of John Edwards (Kerry's nearest rival and his eventual running mate) who, we are left to assume, would not allow cameras to follow his campaign and so is virtually airbrushed out of the documentary until the latter stages; secondly, *Staffers* ends on the only big up-note it has: the confirmation of Kerry as the Democratic candidate. This, though, means that it inevitably ends before the more important conclusion we all know: that Kerry, in another tight race, eventually loses the election to Bush. Rosenbaum commented on *Newsnight* that Kerry's loss deprived *Staffers* of its script. Having been deprived of its grand narrative *Staffers* can only conclude with a false, apologetic victory – Kerry's acceptance of the Democratic nomination, thanking his workers for their 'team effort'. As a night-time motorcade arrives at an airfield (the film's final shot) it is as if, as the credits roll, the interesting story is about to start. The same footage, however, would have looked quite different had Kerry eventually won the presidency as any evaluation of his campaign several months on is automatically coloured by the defeat that followed: Kerry's hang-dog face looks lugubrious and nervous, his staffers seem idiotically optimistic, the Democrats are all Carters. Kerry is Jack Tanner, even his campaign slogan 'The Real Deal' resembles Tanner's 'For Real'. As the real blends into the parody so the performative aspect of documentary again surfaces: that the truth any image holds is

perpetually unstable, vulnerable to interpretation and forever being recontextualised and reassessed. Within this framework, the performances by the presidents
and candidates themselves are comparably performative and serve as reminders
that to try to enforce the distinction between the 'real' person and the performance is futile; the politician is necessarily performative. In the next chapter, this
notion will be discussed in relation not merely to those in front of the camera
but also to the performative documentary, films that in and of themselves
acknowledge the inherent instability of representing reality.

6 The performative documentary

This chapter will discuss the performative documentary, a mode which emphasises – and indeed constructs a film around – the often hidden aspect of performance, whether on the part of the documentary subjects or the filmmakers. When
one discusses performance and the real event, this fusion has more usually been
applied to documentary drama, where a masquerade of spontaneity can be seen
to function at an overt level. It is useful to note the discrepancy between performative documentaries and dramas that adopt the style of a documentary by
using, for instance, hand-held camera work, scratchy synch sound recording and
ad-libbed dialogue as one finds in Ken Loach's *Cathy Come Home*. Loach, the
exponents of Free Cinema at the end of the 1950s (Lyndsay Anderson, Karel
Reisz and others) and the British tradition of gritty drama that ensued – for
instance BBC social issue dramas such as *The Spongers* (1978, directed by Roland
Joffé, written by Jim Allen) or Granada Television's docudrama output of the
1970s to early 1990s – all approach 'realness' from the opposite perspective to
the filmmakers to be discussed here, assuming proximity to the real to reside in
an intensely observational style. The docudrama output of the past 30 years is
predicated upon the assumption that drama can legitimately tackle documentary
issues and uncontentiously use non-fiction techniques to achieve its aims. It thus
becomes possible for drama to perform a comparable function to documentary:
Cathy Come Home raised public awareness of homelessness and prompted the
founding of Shelter, whilst Granada's *Who Bombed Birmingham?* (1990) led
directly to the re-opening of the case of the Birmingham Six. Continuing in this
tradition, Jimmy McGovern's *Dockers* (1999), about the Liverpool dockers'
strike, confused the boundaries between fact and fiction further: dockers and
their wives collaborated with McGovern on the script and some appeared alongside actors in the cast.[1]

Within such a realist aesthetic, the role of performance is, paradoxically, to
draw the audience into the reality of the situations being dramatised, to authen-
ticate the fictionalisation. In contrast to this, the performative documentary uses
performance within a non-fiction context to draw attention to the impossibilities
of authentic documentary representation. The performative element within the
framework of non-fiction is thereby an alienating, distancing device, not one
which actively promotes identification and a straightforward response to a film's

content. There is, however, an essential difference between films that are performative in themselves and those that concern performative subject matter, frequently in conjunction (as in the work of Errol Morris and Nicholas Barker, to be discussed here), with an elaborate and ostentatiously inauthentic visual style. The argument posited throughout this book has been that documentaries are a negotiation between filmmaker and reality and, at heart, a performance. It is thereby in the films of Nick Broomfield, Molly Dineen, Errol Morris or Nicholas Barker that this underlying thesis finds its clearest expression.

Bill Nichols in *Blurred Boundaries,* a little confusingly (considering the familiarity of the term 'performative' since Judith Butler's *Gender Trouble* was published in 1990) uses the term the 'performative mode' (following the didactic, the observational, the interactive and the reflexive modes)[2] to describe films that 'stress subjective aspects of a classically objective discourse' (Nichols 1994: 95). Conversely, this discussion will focus upon documentaries that are performative in the manner identified by Butler and others after J. L. Austin – namely that they function as utterances that simultaneously both describe and perform an action. Austin's radical differentiation between the constative and performative aspects of language (the former simply refers to or describes, the latter performs what it alludes to) has been expanded upon and relocated many times in recent years, but rarely with reference to documentary.[3] Examples of words that Austin identifies as being 'performative utterances' are 'I do', said within the context of the marriage ceremony, or 'I name this ship the Queen Elizabeth', said whilst smashing a bottle of champagne against the vessel's side, his reasoning being that 'in saying what I do, I actually perform that action' (Austin 1970: 235). A parallel is to be found between these linguistic examples and the performative documentary which – whether built around the intrusive presence of the filmmaker or self-conscious performances by its subjects – is the enactment of the notion that a documentary only comes into being as it is performed, that although its factual basis (or document) can pre-date any recording or representation of it, the film itself is necessarily performative because it is given meaning by the interaction between performance and reality. Unlike Nichols, who finds it hard to disguise his latent wariness of the performative documentary mode, supposing that the more a documentary 'draws attention to itself', the further it gets from 'what it represents' (Nichols 1994: 97), this chapter will view the performative positively.

The traditional concept of documentary as striving to represent reality as faithfully as possible is predicated upon the realist assumption that the production process must be disguised, as was the case with direct cinema. Conversely, the new performative documentaries herald a different notion of documentary 'truth' that acknowledges the construction and artificiality of even the non-fiction film. Many theorists would view this reflexivity as breaking with documentary tradition – but this is only valid if one takes as representative of the documentary 'canon' films that seek to hide the modes of production. This, largely, has been the way in which the documentary family tree has evolved, with the relative marginalisation of the more reflexive documentary tradition exemplified by early films such as *Man with a Movie Camera, A propos de Nice, Land Without Bread* and continuing into the work of Emile de Antonio, Jean Rouch and French *cinéma vérité,* Chris Marker. Just as legitimate is the view that the new performative documentaries are simply the most recent articulation of the filmmakers' unease at this very assumption of what documentaries are about, that, like the previous films discussed in this book, the films of Broomfield, Michael Moore and others have sought to accentuate, not mask, the means of production because they realise that such a masquerade is impossibly utopian. The erroneous assumption that documentaries aspire to be referential or 'constative' to adopt Austin's terminology (that is, to represent an uncomplicated, descriptive relationship between subject and text), is being specifically targeted in performative films, which are thus not breaking with the factual filmmaking tradition, but are a logical extension of that tradition's aims, as much concerned with representing reality as their predecessors, but more aware of the inevitable falsification or subjectification such representation entails.

A prerequisite of the performative documentary as here defined is the inclusion of a notable performance component, and it is the insertion of such a performance element into a non-fictional context that has hitherto proved problematic. If, however, one returns to Austin's speech models, then the presumed diminution of the films' believability becomes less of an issue: what a filmmaker such as Nick Broomfield is doing when he appears on camera and in voice-over, is acting out a documentary. This performativity is based on the idea of disavowal, that simultaneously signals a desire to make a conventional documentary (that is, to give an accurate account of a series of factual events) whilst also indicating, through the mechanisms of performance and Broomfield's obtrusive presence, the impossibility of the documentary's cognitive function. Nick Broomfield's films do this quite literally, as the conventional documentary disintegrates through the course of the film and the performative one takes over. The fundamental issue here is honesty. The performative element could be seen to undermine the conventional documentary pursuit of representing the real because the elements of performance, dramatisation and acting for the camera are intrusive and alienating factors. Alternatively, the use of performance tactics could be viewed as a means of suggesting that perhaps documentaries should admit the defeat of their utopian aim and elect instead to present an alternative 'honesty' that does not seek to mask their inherent instability but rather to acknowledge that performance – the enactment of the documentary specifically for the cameras – will always be the heart of the non-fiction film. Documentaries, like Austin's performatives, perform the actions they name.

Style, meaning and the performative subject

As indicated earlier, there are two broad categories of documentary that could be termed performative: films that feature performative subjects and which visually are heavily stylised and those that are inherently performative and feature the intrusive presence of the filmmaker. Following Judith Butler's discussion of it in

Bodies that Matter, the most notable single film to fall within the former category is Jennie Livingston's *Paris is Burning* (1990), a documentary about the New York black and Latino drag balls of the late 1980s. As a result of its subject matter, the issue of performativity has dogged *Paris is Burning,* and the film itself has been (wrongly) viewed as performative. For the most part, Butler's own discussion of the film focuses on content, above all the issue of drag and gender problematisation, only touching upon the issue of filmmaking at the end (Butler 1993: 136). Caryl Flinn goes one step further in her analysis when commenting:

> Recent documentaries like Jennie Livingston's *Paris is Burning* (1990) and documentary criticism – influenced by poststructuralist and postmodernist theory – have cast the concept of pre-existing 'reality' and its attendant notions of authenticity, truth and objectivity into permanent question (e.g., Allen, McGarry, Nichols, Rosenthal). In fact, it is no stretch to say that documentary films, in many ways more so than other cinematic forms, reveal the constructed – indeed, performative – nature of the world around us.
>
> (Flinn 1998: 429)

Flinn is here conflating form and content and is asking *Paris is Burning* to perform a dual function: to be both a documentary concerned with performativity and to be a performative documentary, which, in the main, it is not. Flinn then unproblematically lists parallels between *Paris* and Michael Moore's *Roger and Me* such as the manner in which both 'send up ... images and behaviour supported by corporate America' (p. 432), without negotiating the issue that in *Roger* it is Moore and thereby the film that are sending up corporate America, whilst in *Paris* it is the subjects of Livingston's film that are doing so. As Butler observes, *Paris is Burning* would have been a markedly different film had Livingston reflexively intruded upon her subject or implicated the camera in the film's 'trajectory of desire' (Butler 1993: 136) – that is, had it been a performative film in the Moore mould instead of remaining a film observing performative actions.

Paris is Burning remains a documentary about the issues of drag, and as such offers a useful discussion of performativity. Livingston's technique is to juxtapose images of the balls with commentary and interviews with drag queen 'walkers' (those who participate in the balls). The interviewees are aspirational, they dress up under various categories of chic whiteness ('Executive Realness', 'High Fashion Eveningwear', 'Town and Country') which they seek to emulate and be mistaken for. Throughout, there is an ongoing discussion about 'realness' which, in the words of Dorian Corey, one of the more senior drag queens, is 'to look as much as possible like your straight counterpart ... not a take off or a satire, no – it's actually being able to be this'. To be real, therefore, is to pass for straight and to not be open to 'reading' or 'shade' which are differing levels of critical repartee engaged in after having detected and found fault in the 'realness' of someone's performance. The successful performance is that which cannot be read. On this level, *Paris is Burning* plays a game with its audience inasmuch as its interviewees, however convincing, will always be open to 'reading' because we know, by virtue of the interview/performance juxtaposition, that they are perform-ing/taking on another identity when at the drag balls. As a result, the more sig-nificant episodes of the film as far as an examination of performativity is concerned are those which occur beyond the parameters of the balls. There are fleeting moments in *Paris is Burning* when the film itself becomes performative, expressing the notion that the documentary – like the drag performances it cap-tures – is ephemeral, fluid and in an unstable state of redefinition and change. One such episode (although rather clumsily self-reflexive) is the film's first inter-view with Pepper Labeija. Pepper is filmed asking 'Do you want me to say who I am and all that?' to which one hears Livingston reply 'I'm Pepper Labeija ... ', a command which is in turn mimicked by Pepper himself as he begins again 'I'm Pepper Labeija ..'. with a roll of the eyes. More significantly performative are the couple of forays Livingston makes onto the 'real' streets of Manhattan to film 'real' rich, privileged whites in their designer attire. These sequences, by being intercut with the balls and inserted into the ongoing dialogue about realness and drag, take on a strange, performative quality of their own, throwing into disar-ray the notion – upheld by the majority of the film – of a 'realness' that can be 'read'. The rich whites (who, in contrast to the interviewees, do not appear to know they are being filmed), through their contextualisation within the dis-course of drag, start to look no more authentic than their black and Latino imi-tators; the difference between originals and mimics becomes hard to 'read' in a film where performing is the norm. For the most part, however, *Paris is Burning* is a conventional film that espouses such stability but just happens to be about a group of individuals who do not.

The performative potential of documentary can be interestingly introduced with reference to its other: the *faux* documentary, fictions which emulate and are stylistically interchangeable with nonfictional texts. *Faux* documentaries such as *This is Spinal Tap* and subsequent films directed by Christopher Guest (who in *Tap* plays guitarist Nigel Tufnel) such as *Best in Show* and *A Mighty Wind*, Robert Altman's *Tanner '88* (discussed in the previous chapter) or *Man Bites Dog* draw attention to the potentially entertaining realisation that fact and fiction can be indistinguishable. This essential performativity is exemplified most horrifically by the last of these, *Man Bites Dog*, a film about a film crew making a documentary about a serial killer; as the filming progresses, members of the crew get sucked into participating in the killings (including a particularly obscene gang rape which functions as a prelude to yet more murders) as opposed to merely filming them. It would take a Martian who knows nothing about cinema and satire to now mistake *Spinal Tap* for an authentic documentary as the Guest 'school' has become a significant comic sub-genre in itself, although these films are superfi-cially more authentic than *Man Bites Dog*, which, as if warning against its horri-bleness, intimates in its very first scene (the murder of a woman in a train carriage) that it is not to be believed. Filmed as a standard fictional sequence, the scene shows the woman – though pleading for her life – not pleading directly (as one surely would do in such a situation) to the characters supposedly shooting this snuff movie of her imminent murder. This is the converse of the moment in *The Truman Show* when we realise the characters are inhabiting a set as, like a character in a standard fiction film, the first victim in *Man Bites Dog* maintains the pretence that this is for real and that the apparatus and crew are not there. That the rules of the *faux* documentary are only superficially adhered to in *Man Bites Dog* by this lack of awareness of the camera distances it from other films in the genre, which are almost invariably built upon an acknowledgement of the filming process (through interview, for example, or the deployment of 'wobbly cam' *vérité* techniques) and which are, as a result, more closely affiliated in terms of style to 'real' documentaries. Just as the dog shows in *Best In Show* are only distinguishable from Crufts and other actual dog shows by virtue of being included in a Christopher Guest movie in which interviews such as that with the dog owner who has two left feet have served to indicate that this is a piece of comic fiction, so the folk acts in *A Mighty Wind* are frequently 'unreadable' renditions of the real folk acts featured in *No Direction Home*, for example, Scorsese's documentary about Bob Dylan's early career.

This reflexivity is an important synergy between the *faux* documentary and the performative documentary. As with the performer-based direct cinema films, which many recent performative documentarists cite as influential on their work, performative documentaries feature individuals who are performers and/or comfortable with the idea of performing on film, but whereas the ethos behind the earlier observational films was to use subjects so used to performing that they would not notice the potentially intrusive documentary cameras, the ethos behind the modern performative documentary is to present subjects in such a way as to accentuate the fact that the camera and crew are inevitable intrusions that alter any situation they enter. It is significant that several of the filmmakers to be discussed here have cited as primary influences the chief exponents of direct cinema or their successors; Nick Broomfield, answering questions at the NFT during a season of his films (in 1996) singled out Donn Pennebaker and Fred Wiseman as major influences on his work (the former being formally thanked at the end of *Soldier Girls*), and Nicholas Barker, when researching *Signs of the Times*, said the series would be an extension of the observational mode. In fact what happened in the cases of both Broomfield and Barker is that they evolved radically different and innovative styles of documentary that replaced the observational with the performative.[4]

The performative element of Nicholas Barker's work stems from the correlation of a minimalist visual style and the self-consciously constructed performances he elicits from his subjects. At the front of the feature film *Unmade Beds* (1997) there is the apparent oxymoron 'the characters in this film are real', a literalness that arose out of necessity, as those who attended the film's London and New York test screenings 'were convinced they were watching highly naturalistic fiction' (Barker 1999). The ambiguity created by this residual complexity around the nature of performance is a development of Barker's earlier series *Signs of the Times* (BBC, 1992) about interior design and personal taste. Each of the five parts abides by much the same format: a pre-title montage of images and comments, followed by a series of seven or eight interviews with individuals or couples about their homes. The films are episodic and non-narrative; the interviewees are loosely grouped around a theme (couples, mothers and daughters, singletons, those who see themselves as being a 'little bit different'), but are not subsequently used to develop a cumulative argument. In this, *Signs of the Times* is quintessentially observational, and yet it differs markedly from the style of classic observational documentary. Whereas observational documentaries traditionally remain unreflexive, *Signs of the Times* is analytical of the voyeuristic impulse close observation prompts in its audience and, in its self-conscious visual style, also reflects its subjectivity and authorship. The series proved hugely influential in terms of the development of British television documentary, BBC2's *Modern Times* (the channel's replacement for the more conventional, people-based *40 Minutes*) being one such 'slavish imitation' (Barker 1999).[5]

Signs of the Times abided by a manifesto of rules that included:

> minimal artifice in lighting; where possible shooting everything frontally and at the height of observation so you never looked down or up at anything; no arty angles, no angles that screamed elegance or style; very few close-ups; no dissolves; everything had to be shot on widescreen; no music.
>
> (Barker 1999)

As Barker now admits, 'whenever anyone gets into manifesto mode they are generally protesting too much' (Barker 1999), but his forensic approach to documentary achieved two notable things: the dissection of his subject matter and the dissection of documentary convention. *Signs of the Times* is minimalist, stylised and possesses a stylistic uniformity that gives it a clear identity and lends it a fetishistic intensity, mesmerised by superficialities, appearance and detail. In that it challenges notions of fixed identity or truth and prioritises the moments of interaction between filmmakers, camera and subjects, *Signs of the Times* is performative, repeatedly capturing the tension between the realness of the documentary situation and its artificialisation by the camera. Just as it is somewhat perverse to alienate the spectator through the dislocation of sound and image (Barker adopted a technique whereby he 'would either give you too much to look at and nothing to listen to ... or I would give you something spectacularly banal and a rich display of words' [1999]), so it is equally perverse to maintain a distance from the series' 'characters'. These 'characters' are performative on two counts: they are performing their words by being the embodiments of their identified tastes and attitudes, and they perform their interviews in such a way as to raise questions about spontaneity and documentary authenticity. These alienating performances stem from how they are eventually filmed and from the interviewing methods employed. In the first instance, Barker would record his subjects using a digital video or High 8-mm camera from which he made detailed transcripts, he would then distil those transcripts and selecting passages he wanted his subjects to repeat when it came to the actual recording, returning to them (with Super 16-mm cameras) for the filming and coaxing them into 're-articulating something they had said before' (Barker 1999). This is not a completely unusual technique, but one that is, in *Signs of the Times,* taken to an extreme, in that the characters clearly signal this lack of spontaneity through how they interact with each other, look at the camera and pose for it. In this, the subjects in *Signs of the Times* are, like the walkers in *Paris is Burning,* playing with concepts of 'realness', giving an approximation of themselves; the difference being, however, that the scripting is done very much by Barker, the overtly controlling director.

The duality at the heart of the series' fetishistic involvement with the image and its subjects revolves around both engrossing us in the subjects' narratives and distancing us from its characters by imposing a heightened, reflexive visual style. The close-ups of accessories, ornaments and fabrics function as weighty metaphors for the conflicts they symbolise: in one of the mini-narratives of the opening film 'Marie-Louise collects bric-a-brac', one woman (Tricia) is accused by her partner of spoiling his spartan mansion flat with her clutter, an invasion illustrated by a montage sequence of Tricia's ornaments gradually encroaching upon the surfaces of an empty shelf unit. Like Freud's concept of the fetish as the indirect purveyor of sexual desire, the series' way of revealing the characters of its subjects is via a perverse interest in minutiae – many interviews start, for example, with close-ups of details such as the subjects' shoes. This fetishistic eye is, by association, applied to the people's performances: the mannered and rehearsed way in which they speak, their direct address to camera and their painterly poses. We are invited not to observe but to scrutinise them, their mannerisms, their words; the effect of this scrutiny functioning as an indication that each time these people speak they are doing so with their audience very much in mind. Just as they are putting their houses on display, so they are presenting themselves for assessment. These subjects are not caught unawares or merely talking about themselves in an unpremeditated fashion, rather they are conscious of their involvement in a performative event, one that is simultaneously a description and an enactment of their lives and lifestyles.

This challenge to preconceived notions of realness is taken further in *Unmade Beds,* Barker's feature film following, over the course of several months, four single New Yorkers (two men, Michael and Mikey; two women, Aimee and Brenda) in their pursuit of relationships. Barker takes the preparatory techniques used in *Signs of the Times* much further, ending up with 'a formal script which was then negotiated with the principal characters who were then directed under more or less feature film conditions to perform it pretty much as we'd agreed' (Barker 1999). With the performances from the characters he sought an 'illusion of spontaneity' (Barker 1999), thus imposing another perverse marriage between seemingly incompatible elements that, in turn, are reflected in the film's equivocal tone: warm and interested on the one hand, distant and analytical on the other. The structure of *Unmade Beds* is episodic and non-cumulative in that, by the end, although we have gained intimate insights into the four characters, their stories lack conventional closure. Instead the film offered a detailed composite portrait of not just four individuals but also the generalised issue of dating.

Unmade Beds is less brittle than *Signs of the Times* and builds up empathy between spectators and the characters, all of whom have a preoccupation with which we can sympathise: weight, stature, age, financial insecurity. Although Barker consciously refuses to furnish his spectators with traditional biographical information about the four characters (maintaining that 'as soon as I give you that information, I provide an easy handle for your prejudices' [Barker 1999]) he shows their vulnerabilities and invites us to sympathise with them. *Unmade Beds* is less obsessed with its own style and more responsive to the personalities of the characters being filmed. The younger Michael, for example, who seems particularly self-conscious (about his height) and angry at the world, is often kept at a greater distance than Brenda, who, from the outset, is more than happy to confide in the camera, discuss her maturing body whilst scrutinising it in the mirror or admitting that money is her sole motivation for wanting a man.

Interspersed throughout *Unmade Beds* and functioning as counterpoints to these long interviews are sequences shot, from a distance, through windows, looking in at anonymous New Yorkers as they go about their intimate, daily routines. These montage episodes make explicit the film's voyeurism. Barker restaged scenes that, 'with or without binoculars' he had witnessed over the seven or eight months he spent in New York researching *Unmade Beds*, scenes that he 'only half understood' (Barker 1999). These scenes (reminiscent of *Rear Window* and similarly receptive to fantasy and reinterpretation) were then reconstructed using people who were not those Barker had originally watched. Clearly directed (using walkie-talkies, lights) and filmed over long periods of time Barker maintains that at the times these subsidiary characters forgot they were being filmed. This idea of seeing the details of an intimate scene unfold without fully comprehending their significance is crucial to *Unmade Beds* and to the voyeuristic impulse it enacts. The strangeness of these interludes makes us reassess (rather like the 'real' Manhattan sequences in *Paris is Burning* do) the remainder of the film. What is being played out here is Barker's discovery of the role windows play in New York:

> The thing about New York is that most people in the city share a window with another window, and one of the really interesting things I discovered when I first started living there, was that there was a social contract between the people who looked onto one another, so that people would be entirely happy to share their nakedness or their daily toilet rituals with the window opposite, because that intimacy was reciprocated, but they all felt that if anybody else should see their daily pattern that it would be a violation of their privacy.
>
> (Barker 1999)

Windows grant access but they also alienate; this duality provides the temptation to construct, out of detailed fragments of people's lives, the fantasy of who they are because 'you don't have enough information to assemble your narrative and so fill in the gaps with your own imaginings and fantasies' (Barker 1999). This has repercussions for how *Unmade Beds* suggests we look at and assimilate the more conventional documentary image: out of snippets we construct whole stories and characters we can identify with and whose 'realness' we find credible.

The formalised use of the camera, framing and self-conscious performances by all the four protagonists in *Unmade Beds* might yield intimate and revealing details, but our knowledge remains compromised by the alienation imposed by such stylistic mannerisms. The performative aspects of *Unmade Beds* suggest that some things will forever be withheld from us. Although Barker describes himself as a portraitist, remarking that the scrutiny of the 'surface texture' can reveal 'certain underlying psychological truths', he does not give an interpretation of those 'psychological truths' and in fact intentionally represses them by, for example, withholding conventional biographical information pertaining to his characters such as age and profession or by keeping back, until late in the film, discussions of issues (such as Aimee's weight) that might touch on such 'truths'. This alienation is echoed directly in *Unmade Beds'* style and narrative form. What we retain immediately from watching the film are details of the characters' appearance, sartorial taste and verbal or physical mannerisms. Because Barker himself does not then mould these ostensibly superficial observations into a more rounded portrait, we as spectators are left to manage the contextualising for ourselves and imagine, as Barker describes he did as he watched strangers through windows, what these details tell us about the characters as a whole. We will never know whether or not our suppositions are correct.

There is a linear logic to the way in which time passes in *Unmade Beds* that can be correlated with the consistency of the film's visual style. Although less rigidly conceived than *Signs of the Times* (there is, for example, a richly evocative use of music), *Unmade Beds* still demonstrates a uniformity of style, using a static camera, getting the characters to pose, framing them so our awareness that these people are being filmed is never lost. The paradox of this regularity is that it accentuates the film's fragmentary nature – that it remains most intrigued by surface texture, and elects not to construct out of its assembled detail either a traditionally closed narrative or conventional portraits of its protagonists. Judith Butler articulates in her introductory discussion to *Paris is Burning,* 'There is no subject prior to its constructions' (Butler 1993: 124). *Unmade Beds* avoids being this dogmatic, and instead suggests that what we see in the film is a composite of what the characters bring to the film (much of which might remain hidden) and what the film itself can reveal.

From a very different standpoint the same could be said of Errol Morris's documentaries, documentaries that, like Barker's, have been thought to prioritise style over content (discussed in the following chapter, for instance, is J. Hoberman's evaluation of *The Fog of War,* of which he says, rather bitchily: 'McNamara's bad teeth and liver spots notwithstanding, the beauty of *The Fog of War* is entirely skin deep' (Hoberman 2004: 21 and 22). In fact, like Barker's, Morris's stylistic excess and visual refinement do not merely display a heightened aesthetic sense but become in themselves elements of a performative documentary discourse, the visual flourishes not being mobilised to dismantle in order to shed doubt upon the documentary endeavour but in order to uphold it. Linda

Williams offers Morris's *The Thin Blue Line* (1988) as a prime example of what she terms the 'postmodern documentary approach', namely the desire to access 'traumatic historical truths inaccessible to representation by any simple or single "mirror with memory" – in the vérité sense of capturing events as they happen' (Williams 1993: 12). The event under scrutiny in *The Thin Blue Line* is traditional investigative terrain – the 'true' story of Randall Adams, convicted of the murder of Dallas police officer Robert Wood in 1976. Morris's research led him to interview David Harris, Adams' principal accuser and also in prison for murder, and to the eventual extraction of his 'cryptic but dramatic' (p. 12) telephone confession to Wood's murder, played at the conclusion to *The Thin Blue Line*. As a direct result of the documentary, Adams was released, although he brought a court case against Morris.[6] As *Signs of the Times* altered the subsequent course of British television documentary, so *The Thin Blue Line* has proved hugely influential over documentaries in both cinema and television, primarily because of what Williams defines as its 'film-noirish beauty, its apparent abandonment of cinema- vérité realism for studied, often slow-motion, and highly expressionistic reenactments of different witnesses' version of the murder to the tune of Philip Glass's hypnotic score' (p. 12). Williams twice refers to something in *The Thin Blue Line* as 'hypnotic' – Glass's score and later Morris's pace (p. 13). In fact, much of *The Thin Blue Line* does not appear particularly 'hypnotic': the interviews are interestingly framed and atmospherically lit, but they are largely eyewitness accounts that impart classic documentary information; what Williams and others have made much of in relation to Morris's documentary is its use of 'filler' reconstructions of these eyewitness accounts that re-enact the various and contradictory accounts of Wood's murder. The stylisation of these – their extreme chiaroscuro lighting, their slowed pace, the use of Glass's portentous music – all serve to underline both the importance of the contradictory accounts and their possible affiliation to fiction, as Morris has created a *mise-en-scène* closely allied to feature films. (The closest reference points for Morris's *mise-en-scène* and use of music are probably to be found in the work of David Lynch).

In *The Thin Blue Line* and Morris's subsequent documentaries the slipperiness and indeterminacy of 'the truth' is principally signalled by how this overwrought visual style becomes linked to a scepticism concerning the capability or not of the documentary to represent such a truth. In *The Thin Blue Line* this scepticism is enacted via the multiple and contradictory dramatisations of eyewitness accounts; in a later film such as *Mr Death* (1999) it emerges through Fred Leuchter's obsession with the evidence he thinks he fails to find amidst the ruins of the crematoria and gas chambers at Auschwitz. Leuchter's painstaking research – taking scrapings from the walls of these ruins and analysing them for evidence of extermination etc. – leads him towards a conclusion that goes against received historical fact: that the death camps existed and that they killed in excess of six million Jews. The parallels between Leuchter's search and documentary are many. Most importantly for an understanding of Morris's films is the supposition that what you see only partially serves as an indicator for what a documentary can reveal about a subject. The tension between what Morris and we 'know' to have been the case at Auschwitz and Leuchter's denial of this using as 'evidence' the findings *Mr Death* has filmed him garnering is the same tension that underpins all of Morris's films, namely the often contradictory relationship between what individuals think they know/would like to believe and what actually occurred. To complicate matters, the latter it is frequently impossible to demonstrate with any certainty.

The qualities inherent within Morris's style proclaim his documentaries' essential performativity. As a director he is endlessly, obsessively preoccupied with how we (Morris and the audiences of his films) look at and are shown images; that we can bring to them fantasy and prejudice and can think we fathom them with only incomplete knowledge of the events they depict. The conclusion from watching Morris's films can only be that the image and/or the documentary can reveal a truth but not all the truth(s) of a story and one that is, if what we desire from a documentary is an answer to all the questions we might have brought to the documentary before we started viewing, mutable and complex as well as imperfect or incomplete. Several factors in Morris's visual style proclaim his films' performativity. There are his frequent cuts to black during interviews (he does not mask his edits with 'noddies' or cut aways to hands) and other devices that serve as distanciation techniques. Through his stylisation he also confirms the artificiality of the documentary production process, thereby confirming the existence of a life beyond the image and beyond the figure who might be talking, a confirmation that, rather tautologically, affirms the centrality to this process of the performative masquerade. Morris's documentaries are characterised by a feeling of 'presentness', a feeling that we are witnessing the events as they are at the moment of filming, with the suggestion that, had the film been made at a different time, then the representation of these events might have been different. A trait shared with the much more overtly 'present' documentaries of filmmakers such as Nick Broomfield, Molly Dineen or Michael Moore whose films mimic the act of following individuals and subjects in order to make films about them is the fact that Morris's films also chart the process of discovery that many retrospective documentaries omit.

Morris's films, in that they not only mimic the act of following a subject but also enact the process of factual and intellectual discovery that goes into completing a documentary, are performative. Morris's best documentaries are characterised by this intellectual unfurling: they are built around sometimes elliptical images and the links between sequences only truly become clear as the spectator is invited to re-assess images already viewed in the light of later revelations and events. Through *Mr Death*, Fred Leuchter – as he becomes more convinced that Auschwitz was not a death camp – appears himself to change, but it could be that our interpretation of him, altered by the film's gradually expanding portrait, imposes a change on him. Towards the end of the film, there is a sequence in which Leuchter reveals to camera that he was not paid for his revolutionary lethal injection machine and that it is still for sale for the price of maintaining it. His smile by now seems far more diffident, less brazen than it has been, as if he has been affected by how he now understands himself to be perceived.

In Morris's documentaries revelation exists in tandem with self-revelation; they do not start from an immediately perceptible, determined point of view and instead enact their subjects' and Morris's twin process of discovery and understanding. They often contain a surprise piece of knowledge that changes everything: from the course the film's investigation takes to the spectators' responses. Just such a moment occurs when David Harris, during an interview in *The Thin Blue Line,* raises a hand to scratch his head, revealing that he is handcuffed and in prison himself. This accidental revelation transforms and makes us reconsider everything that has preceded it (it is not so dramatic, but this casual indicator of Harris's situation is a shock tactic not unlike the late revelation of the drag singer's 'true' sex in *The Crying Game*). As with the Neil Jordan film, being told finally that Harris is being interviewed in prison makes us wonder whether we should have understood this earlier – whether his orange shirt might have alerted us to his incarceration – and wonder why Morris's strategy had been to light these interviews in such a stagy, colourful way as to deflect attention from this (the reddish lighting in particular complements Harris's shirt and so deflects attention from it). Morris's documentaries are unpredictable and a conventional sense of closure is rarely imposed; he saves Harris's confession for the very end of *The Thin Blue Line* in the same way as he saves until the final sequence of *The Fog of War* Robert McNamara's most shaming, shameful refusal to answer awkward questions about his political career. If they had come earlier, both Harris's confession and McNamara's most emphatic evasion would have determined our responses to whatever followed, a causality that would have run counter to Morris's performative desire to maintain his films' presentness and flexibility.

Issues of authorship in the performative documentary

What has occurred within the last decade (and performative documentaries are at the forefront of this) is a shift towards more self-consciously 'arty' and expressive modes of documentary filmmaking. Reflexive documentaries, as they challenge the notion of film's 'transparency' and highlight the performative quality of documentary, will emphasise issues of authorship and construction. Both Barker and Morris make their authorship explicit, not through personalisation but through formulating a consistent and flamboyant visual style. The question of authorship has traditionally proved a thorny problem for the documentary, as the recognised intervention of an *auteur* disrupts the non-fiction film's supposed allegiance to transparency and truthfulness. As, however, this book has argued against the uncompromised rendition of the real being an attainable goal for non-fiction, the presence of the *auteur* is not so problematic, for one of the corollaries of accepting that documentary cannot but perform the interaction between reality and its representation is the acknowledgement that documentary, like fiction, is authored. As with the theorisation of the *auteur* in the realm of narrative fiction film, what appears to pose particular difficulties where documentaries are concerned is the author-director. A familiar charge levelled at documentary directors – who, through a variety of means such as voice-over, appearance on camera and overt stylisation have signalled their control over their work – is that they are needlessly egotistical in not allowing the subject matter to 'speak for itself'. But as Nick Broomfield has countered, no one accuses Alan Whicker (or other presenter-reporters) of being egotistical. The signposting of the documentary author-director or his or her overt intrusion crystallises documentary's fundamental conflict between subjectivity and objectivity. One repercussion of the establishment of a documentary canon that has historically marginalised films emphasising the author's presence is that it has been too readily assumed that the repression of the author has been necessary to the implementation of objectivity.

Culminating in the recent work of filmmakers such as Michael Moore, Molly Dineen and Nick Broomfield, who are active participants in their films, documentary has an established tradition of the performer-director. These filmmakers, to varying degrees, participate in their films because they are interested in discovering alternative and less formally restrictive ways of getting to what they perceive to be the essence of their subjects. The means by which they achieve this are not those conventionally associated with truth-finding post-direct cinema as they entail breaking the illusion of film, thereby interrupting the privileged relationship between the filmed subjects and the spectator. Recently, many more documentaries are emerging that take for granted the existence and inevitable presence of their filmmakers, directly demonstrating the inherent performativity of the non-fiction film. The overt intervention of the filmmaker definitively signals the death of documentary theory's idealisation of the unbiased film by asking, categorically and from within the documentary itself: what else is a documentary but a dialogue between a filmmaker, a crew and a situation that, although in existence prior to their arrival, has irrevocably been changed by that arrival? What author-performer-based documentaries reiterate are the twin notions that a documentary is its own document and that the interventionist documentary filmmaker is a fluid entity defined and redefined by every context in which he or she appears. The author-performer is thereby one constituent of a film's ongoing dialectical analysis. As Broomfield comments in an interview about *Biggie and Tupac* (2002), in *vérité* films the audience is not granted any information about the filmmakers behind the cameras, going on to conclude about why he abandoned that way of filmmaking that 'it's not the presence of the camera that changes people's behaviour, it's the relationship they have with the people behind it' (Wise, D. 2002: 18). In Broomfield's films the relationship with the people behind the camera is explicit. Before discussing the rise of the 'star director' with specific reference to Nick Broomfield, this chapter will focus on the work of Molly Dineen, a filmmaker (director and cameraperson) who signals her presence through the persistent use of her voice off-camera, but who nevertheless works in a more straightforward observational way and leaves her subjects to visually dominate her films.

The second chapter of this book examined the historical rarity of the female voice-over, with particular reference to *Sunless*, a documentary that creates a complex dialectic around its woman narrator. Since *Sunless* (1982) or *Handsworth*

Songs (1986) – a documentary by members of the Black Audio Film Collective that is also noted for its use of female narration[7] – the female voice-over has become more commonplace, and yet it is more in the realm of the female authorial narration that a major shift has occurred. In late 1990s British television documentary, the presence of the woman director's voice is widespread (a vogue that probably would not have started had it not been for Dineen); the presence of Dineen's voice indicates a desire to use the voice as commentary, as a means of claiming control of the film.[8] Class and gender issues are particularly significant factors within Dineen's work, hence the interweaving of herself into the concerns of her documentaries. Bill Nichols' use of the word 'voice' to signal both the physical voice and the filmmaker's authorial imprint is strikingly pertinent to the work of contemporary women filmmakers such as Dineen, as what this trend towards the inclusion of their own commentaries and interjections most forcefully suggests is a growing desire to reinstate the personal, subjective aspect of the physical voice.[9] The films of Molly Dineen are manifestly personal visions, inscribed with her subjective presence via the physical intervention of her voice.

With this intervention, a filmmaker like Dineen is also signalling the constructedness (a preferable term to inauthenticity) of all documentary by formulating an alternative 'realness' around her desire to show the nuts and bolts of documentary-making. This standpoint is actually enacted towards the beginning of *Geri* (1999), Dineen's documentary about Geri Halliwell following her departure from the Spice Girls. Soon after she has agreed to make the film, Dineen travels by train with Halliwell from Paris to England. During the course of the journey, Dineen films Geri on the telephone to her lawyers offering assurances that she has 'complete control' over the documentary. Dineen immediately contradicts this, asking Halliwell why she should 'spend months following you round' only to relinquish control of the documentary, subsequently explaining, after Halliwell has interjected that she would stop herself being shown in too much of a 'bad light', that any film is a negotiation between filmmaker and subject. Since *Home from the Hill*, her first full-length documentary which she made whilst still at the National Film and Television School, Dineen's work has been predicated upon this understanding of documentary as a dialogue, although Dineen herself has argued that her documentaries are dictated entirely by the people in them, constructed around her intrusion into their lives. This mutuality is illustrated by Colonel Hilary Hook in *Home from the Hill* (BBC2, 1985), after Dineen has asked him whether or not he is happy. Hook replies: 'Blissfully, in your presence; otherwise I represent divine discontent'. What so many of Dineen's subjects acknowledge is that however well the filmmaker gets to know them (and Dineen, like Chris Terrill, 'goes native' for the long research/shooting period), the difference between them (without her camera and with it) will remain. Dineen's work is consistently illustrative of this dilemma, although between *Home from the Hill* and *Geri* her approach to the twin issues of performance and authorial control has altered substantially.

Dineen's early style – very much indebted to observational cinema – is exemplified by *Heart of the Angel* (BBC, 1989), a film about the Angel Underground station in London, prior to its temporary closure and modernisation. The film has no explanatory voice-over and elects, in spite of the station's decrepit state, to remain apolitical and to focus on the characters Dineen encounters. Because *Heart of the Angel* sidelines political issues (later series such as *The Ark*, *In the Company of Men* and *The Lords' Tale* tackle bigger establishments and themes) it is exemplary of Dineen's method of interacting with her subjects. Dineen's intrusiveness is kept to a minimum whilst the performances of her subjects are maximised; her authorial control, therefore, remains covert. As with many 1960s direct cinema films such as *Salesman*, *Heart of the Angel* is reliant upon the subjects' performances for and to the camera; as Dineen says, 'People know that they're quirky and eccentric. They *feel* different. It's why we all like watching each other' (Cleave 1991: 26). It is also why we like performing ourselves for others. *Heart of the Angel* opens with one such performance (deeply reminiscent of Paul's monologues in *Salesman*) by the ticket collector in the Angel's lift proclaiming to the customers that they are 'all gonna die – the exhaust fumes from cars are getting very serious'. Unlike the Maysles' film, however, a sense of irony permeates *Heart of the Angel*, and the subjects – including the ticket collector – knowingly act up to and for Dineen and her camera: a group of 'Fluffers' (the women who clean the Underground tunnels at night) sing whilst taking the lift down to the platforms; another 'Fluffer' parodies a striptease whilst changing into her overalls. Likewise Dineen does not hide her own presence, using her characteristic coaxing questions from behind the camera throughout all her films. Whereas some of her contemporaries use similar techniques aggressively, perhaps to catch their subjects unaware (Moore, Broomfield), Dineen does so to enable her subjects to talk more expansively about themselves, asking broad and ostensibly flimsy questions just to get her subjects to open up. Because of this, her films will seldom be political and sometimes her questions appear slightly inane: for example, after the Angel's foreman has said he likes Yorkshire because 'it's so wild', Dineen adds 'do you like wild places?'; she is responsive rather than proactive, and elicits, in this instance, a further description from the foreman of his paintings of Yorkshire landscapes.

The most memorable and emotive of Dineen's conversations in *Heart of the Angel* is with the man in the ticket office who, throughout the film, has been prickly and argumentative, having asked Dineen early on: 'Do you think God put you on this earth to point that stupid little camera?' Dineen could be said to specialise in the mollification of leathery men (most obviously in *Home from the Hill*). Here the ticket man reaches the stage when he too is forthcoming on camera, initiating a dialogue with Dineen by stating, ostensibly unprompted, 'I could do with a change'. Dineen's gentle, general questions subsequently try to coax the ticket seller into expanding upon the significance of 'change' and what he would have liked to have been different. Although he denies being depressed, the ticket man ruminates on death and the meaninglessness of life: 'No-one asks to be born ... you're born, you live, you die'. Dineen's role in this conversation is ambiguous; partly she manoeuvres the situation so the spectator forms a strong identification with the ticket seller (always easier to engineer if universal emotions and desires are being discussed), and partly she maintains her (and our) distance. The mechanism that enforces this equivocation is Dineen's use of her voice. Whilst her voice establishes notions of friendship and intimacy, it remains the tool with which to signal the essential artificiality of the filming situation. The realisation that this moment of revelation takes place in an inherently artificial environment likewise imbues the performances of Dineen's subjects. In the case of the ticket office man, juxtaposed against curious and personal revelations (Dineen: 'What would you actually like to achieve?'; ticket man: 'I don't really know ... I'd like to have been taller ... had a better education') are ironically informal exchanges with Dineen that once again emphasise the formality of the set-up. This conversation (interview being too formal a term) concludes with a short chat that does just this:

> *Ticket man:* 'You think I'm gorgeous'.
> *Dineen:* 'I think you're wonderful'.
> *Ticket man:* 'Can I drink my water now?'
> *Dineen:* 'Yes'.
> *Ticket man:* 'Thank you'.

The ticket man is here doing several things: he is reflecting back at Dineen her use of flirtation to elicit good answers to her questions from male subjects; he is indicating that Dineen is ultimately in control of what he says and does in front of the camera and that he, at times, doubts her sincerity; he is, through this knowingness, shedding doubt on the authenticity of his previous words, prompting us to ponder the multiple levels of his performance. Dineen's documentaries, more clearly than many, are negotiations between the reality before she arrived and intruded and the artificial environment generated by her presence. Within this, Dineen is perpetually oscillating between relinquishing and asserting control.

This is a problem that becomes more apparent in *The Ark* (BBC2, 1993), a series following events at London Zoo at a time when they are threatened with closure, because it is also an issue-led, institution-focused film that ostensibly demands more than a sensitive interaction with personable and eccentric characters. Unlike the comparable BBC series *The House,* that similarly features a grand organisation at a moment of crisis and threat, Dineen does not approach her subject with a critical eye and objects to 'the modern trend for trying to catch people with their trousers down' (Lawson 1995: 10). *The Ark* is less overtly critical of its subjects than *The House* and lacks a voice-over comparable to Jancis Robinson's arch commentary. Although the last of *The Ark's* three parts is a beautiful, subtle piece of documentary filmmaking, there is a slight listlessness about the series as a whole, stemming from the more pronounced absence of Dineen's actual and metaphoric voice. Subsequently in her career, a significant stylistic shift occurs, as she begins to introduce more of her own voice-over and thereby begins to overtly structure her work around her own sensibilities and observations, a change that becomes very noticeable with *In the Company of Men*

(BBC2, 1995), her series about the Prince of Wales regiment during their tour of duty in Northern Ireland. Besides personalising the films to a greater extent, this increased voice has the effect also of making *In the Company of Men* more conventional, not a loose, non-didactic observational documentary series of which Dineen is an instrumental part, but a structured observational series (more in keeping with the 1990s shift towards the formalised formats such as docu-soaps) that does the thinking for us. The transition to a more authoritative style with *In the Company of Men* makes Dineen into the series' principal subject as well as its *auteur*, and marks the shift towards a more concrete embodiment of the director-performer. It is significant that with this increased presence comes an increased focus on gender and difference. Still Dineen nudges the soldiers to respond to questions that are personal and apolitical, despite the regiment's role in guarding a border police station and despite Dineen's first bit of voice-over locating the action within the period around the first Northern Ireland cease-fire.

The opening interview is with the regiment's commander, Major Crispin Black.[10] He holds up a copy of *The Tatler* ('just to conform to stereotype') and, in one of his many reflexive references, urges Dineen to put on weight 'so that we can at least have sexual fantasies about you'. *In the Company of Men* is another of Dineen's elaborate flirtations with a band of unlikely men who, until *Geri*, have been the most prominent points of interest in her work. Contentiously (particularly considering the time given to the 'Fluffers') Dineen has referred to *Heart of the Angel* as 'a very political film, about male slavery. They'd give over their unopened pay packets to their wives, especially the Irish ones' (Billen 1995: 9). Such an unguarded comment encapsulates her work's essential tendency (epitomised by *In the Company of Men*) towards glorifying and exonerating masculinity. This is so in *Home from the Hill* with its essentially soft treatment of Hilary Hook, *Heart of the Angel,* in particular the interview with the ticket office man and the night-time sequence with the underground maintenance men, and *The Ark* in its uncritical attitude towards David Jones. Dineen, who also operates the camera in her documentaries and creates films that are intensely attuned to issues of sexual difference, clearly does not wish to repress her male subjects' flirtatious references to her, just as she rather obviously in *Heart of the Angel* treats with greater sensuality and warmth than she does their female counterparts the 'Fluffers' the male Underground night workers. Dineen's films are not often self-consciously stylised, but the use of carefully directed lighting to emphasise the contours of the men's grubby torsos in this tunnel sequence is marked, as is the men's boss's comment to Dineen 'Do you have to stop my blokes from working, eh?' Dineen explains this concentration on men as 'an ego thing – you want to be accepted by the most unlikely people' (Lawson 1995: 11), which makes filming sound like a series of conquests (she did go out with one of the maintenance workers for a time), but is not entirely accurate. She also enjoys engaging with men, not women – which is what makes *Geri* a surprising film.

The self-reflexive referencing of Dineen, her wispy though persistent middle-class voice, her increased presence as the narrator of her films and the fact that she will never (as the cameraperson) appear on screen, have specific gender connotations. Dineen remains an absent, fetishised body constantly evoked by her on-screen (usually male) subjects; she makes use of the camera to forge an intimacy with people, but also to preclude closeness; her subjects are always seen through her eyes and her apparatus, whilst Dineen is represented only by her voice. Whereas this has, at times, been treated as a position of weakness, here it connotes strength. Dineen performs an archetypal femininity that is concerned and curious, coaxing an intimacy and camaraderie out of her willing male subjects whilst never relinquishing her omniscient, camouflaged position. Ironically, however, because Dineen's films are largely driven by her desire to extract compelling performances from her subjects, the audience finds itself compelled to focus upon Dineen's performance as well. As she later also takes on the role of narrator, the flirtatious, feminine voice from behind the camera seems less genuinely curious and more scheming.

Flirting with crotchety old men returns as a central point of interest in *The Lords' Tale,* whilst in between is *Geri,* in which the hierarchical relationship between Dineen and her subject, Geri Halliwell is not so much about gender difference as about class. In Dineen's need to spell out that she is in control of the documentary, she is partly compensating for the fact that *Geri* is about a female subject who is far more famous than she is. *Geri* is not simply a biography of an individual, but an examination of celebrity, which includes a certain amount of dialogue concerning Halliwell's image. Dineen has a very definite, simple view of Halliwell, namely that behind her exterior performance as the recently rejected Ginger Spice, there is the 'real' Geri accessible to the filming process. When she films and questions a tearful Spice Girls fan looking over Ginger memorabilia on the eve of an auction at Sotheby's, Dineen asks the girl why she is mourning the effects of Ginger who, after all, was not the real person Geri Halliwell. The girl is sad and confused: to her, Ginger is real. Halliwell herself wants to believe in this basic split between real and fake, forever promoting her 'real', minimally made up self-image and contrasting this with her previous alter ego Ginger, a character she says was 'based on my wild-cat days'. Halliwell comes across as likeable but wholly unaware of the multiplicity of her performances and of the fragility of her distinction between the real and the fake. As a film, *Geri* substantiates Halliwell's self-perception, treating the post-Ginger Halliwell – whether she be at home with her mum or at a UN press conference following her instatement as ambassador for birth control – as unproblematically 'real'. This places Halliwell in a subordinate position, which, despite her command of the visual image, Dineen does little to dispel or qualify. Instead, Halliwell's inarticulacy concerning her image and her desire for fame is shown in the context of her having lost control to Dineen (the person who is now manipulating her image). Preceding the conversation about control on the train, Dineen comments in voice-over:

> I was becoming intrigued by the situation. I should have realised there'd be complications, though. Geri got on the phone to her lawyer, to tell him that I was taking over the film.

The ostensible purpose of this piece of voice-over is to locate the subsequent conversation; because, however, that conversation is about the struggle for control between filmmaker and subject, the very fact that Dineen prefaces it by telling us what to expect, ensures that the sequence is illustrative of Geri's lack of control over the film. So, Geri's performance of herself and her obsession with how others perceive her is more a manifestation of fragility than of strength. This is deeply ironic, considering Dineen's own preoccupation with how the men in her films view *her*.

Despite her fame, Halliwell's image is filtered through Dineen's perception of it. Geri's relative weakness is, in substantial part, the result of the imposition of a social hierarchy. Through the middle-class tone of her voice, the demonstration of her own articulacy and the critical use of narration, Dineen emphasises her intellectual superiority over Halliwell. *Geri* is equivocally both a celebration and a snobbish criticism of inarticulacy as it pursues a liberated Halliwell fervently seeking a serious role for herself and trying to define her aspirations, but not having the vocabulary with which to express them. Dineen's focus on this struggle is, in itself, far from generous and Halliwell is set up on several occasions only to be shot down. *Geri* is a smug ambush documentary, intent upon wresting control from its subject without telling her – and flaunting the fact that it has succeeded.

The Lords' Tale (2002), a documentary charting and commemorating the abolition of the hereditary peers from the House of Lords, offers a quintessential example of Dineen's developing authorial style: it features several crusty old men, it offers a humanist portrait of the peers' demise rather than a political critique of it and it is constructed around both Dineen's observational camerawork and her persistent narration. The compatibility between these latter two formal elements is becoming strained, as the unobtrusive, responsive camerawork still conforms to the conventions of observational documentary whereas her voice-over has become even more intrusive. The beginning of *The Lords' Tale* is extremely voice-over-heavy as Dineen elects to tell the story of the Blair government's decision to abolish the hereditaries through words and not through the juxtaposition of images. This is in contrast to earlier films such as *Heart of the Angel* and it makes *The Lords' Tale* far more didactic. True, as the narration says at the beginning, the government refused to take part in *The Lords' Tale* and urged its members to do the same, but it is clear from the outset that Dineen has taken rather a liking to these old buffers and does not believe, as she intimates early on, that their abolition will necessarily be 'any guarantee of democracy'.

As a testament to a significant political moment, Dineen's languid, gentle film stands up as an important one, not only because of what it is about, but also because of how it is made. Despite its heavy narration, *The Lords' Tale* is still an intensely old-fashioned, traditional observational documentary and as such, in the era of reality television, it is part of a marginalized – if not disappearing – sub-genre. In an interview given a year after the documentary's release (as she is preparing for the Grierson British Documentary Awards, 2003 where she received the trustees' award) Dineen draws attention to the specific impact of reality television on documentary output as she comments, 'I think reality television is fantastic', although its success she realises has meant that authored documentaries like hers are now fighting over 'only a few slots' (Brown, M. 2003). In the same interview Dineen also remarks that 'I have made the same film most of my career, about institutional change' (Brown, M. 2003). Focusing on institutional change has been an important strand within the observational tradition, linking Dineen's work to that of Wiseman and Broomfield, for example. The consistency within Dineen's work, whilst giving her oeuvre its identifiable auteurist stamp, is another reason for *The Lords' Tale* seeming quaint and old-fashioned: it is produced by Edward Mirzoeff, editor of *40 Minutes* and Dineen's early champion, and, despite being broadcast by Channel 4, bears all the hallmarks – with the addition of narration – of Dineen's work for that quintessential 1980s strand. The style, however, fits the subject matter, particularly as Dineen is – as she is in all her institutional documentaries in one way or another – manifestly sympathetic to the old guard about to be replaced by the new.

Dineen's admiration for and tenderness towards the hereditary peers is signalled by her proximity to two peers in particular: the Earl of Romney and Lord Westbury. The former rapidly becomes a sort of confidant who tells Dineen the names of some of his fellow peers, who invites Dineen to his (relatively humble) home and who talks her through elements of the abolition process, for example showing her 'the leaving photograph' of all the hereditaries together for the last time. In general Dineen films Romney – as well as some of the other peers – in extreme close-up, so his face takes up the whole screen, the effect of which is to suggest, alongside the twinkle in Romney's eye as he whispers things to the side of Dineen's camera, a strongly conspiratorial camaraderie between filmmaker and subject.

As Dineen informs us in voice-over, a deal had been struck between the hereditary peers and the government whereby 92 of the 750 hereditaries in the Lords would be allowed to stay in the House for the time being, until the government finally decided how to replace them. The 92 were selected by ballot, and Lord Westbury was one of those who stood for election, but lost. There is one sequence with Westbury in particular that is exemplary of Dineen's method, filmed in his office as he is clearing his desk and preparing to leave the House of Lords, extremely reluctantly. Dineen is talking to Westbury in front of his desk, now covered in removals boxes. A fellow peer (Lord Mowbray) comes in and Westbury calls over to him: 'Have you met this heavenly bird, she wants to interview you because you're one of the fortunate' (Mowbray is staying). Despite a brief exchange with Mowbray, it is extremely clear that Dineen is not interested in interviewing him at all, and is far more interested in scrutinising the inconsistencies between Westbury's feigned detachment and the fact that he is really sad at having to leave (and interested, it has to be said, in retaining yet another example of a male subject flirting with her). After his farewell drinks and after having assured Dineen that he will shed no tears because 'this is much too serious', Dineen edits together a sequence of Westbury leaving his office, one is led to believe for the last time. There has just been a short exchange between Westbury and his wife, who tells him how to turn on the video recorder at home for *Coronation Street* (the implications here are various: that Westbury never goes home; that his wife does everything for him; that he will be lost without his office, bar and cronies and Lady Westbury wants to make sure his comfort blanket is there for him). As Westbury goes, Dineen films him from behind, holding a static shot of this elegant old man trudging up some steps and along a corridor. There is a long pause as she holds the image before cutting it. As with the equally lingering shot of Paul at the end of *Salesman*, this shot of Westbury is pregnant with poignancy and signification. The greatness of observational documentary often lies in its ability to use one shot or sequence as the emotional distillation of a film's overall meaning. This shot of Westbury is just that representative moment, as the old institution finally gives way. Underscoring this are the film's concluding shots of preparations for the forthcoming Queen's speech (at which the abolition of the hereditaries is to be announced) and of Tony Blair and members of his cabinet striding into their chamber with brusque purposefulness. In this juxtaposition not only does *The Lords' Tale* signal the changing of the guard but it suggests the brutality and mediocrity of the new order that has triumphed over the experience and kindliness of the old. Dineen might not set out to make political films, but her documentaries always manage to convey an archaic, humanist, conservative political message. In tone as well as in subject matter she has continued to make the same film.

With Dineen's recent move towards claiming her films by adding her own authoritative voice-over to her already prominent conversations from behind the camera, she has moved towards becoming a 'star director'. It is ironic that Dineen's most overt bid for stardom came with *Geri,* a film about stardom, for this is a common factor among star directors of documentaries. The more famous Nick Broomfield becomes, for instance, the more famous the subjects of his films. Although they are frequently bracketed together (both British, National Film and Television School graduates, both direct and perform a technical role in their films, both 'author' those films through direct interventions that are not edited out), Dineen and Broomfield offer different types of documentary performances and elicit different performances out of their subjects. Ironically, considering her implied opposition to Labour policy in *The Lords' Tale,* during the 1997 British general election, Dineen was brought in to direct the Labour Party's most distinctive campaign film: a casual portrait of Tony Blair, chatting with Dineen and spending time with his kids. Tony Blair comes across as a 'Good Thing', an urbane, intelligent guy who has done ordinary things like play in a band but who now just happens to want to run the country. As Dineen has often stated in interviews, her aim is not to embarrass her subjects or stitch them up, but to take a mediatory stand: 'What I like to do is get people who are fair game and then not make them fair game at all' (Billen 1995: 9). It seems legitimate to speculate that the image- and media-obsessed 'new' Labour Party would have viewed this conciliatory tone (and her femininity) as Dineen's most significant credential: she offers a kind, witty portrait of Blair, but one that is ultimately not threatening, critical or undermining. One senses that 'new' Labour would not have commissioned Nick Broomfield to make a campaign film for them.

The 'star director': Nick Broomfield

BBC2's *The Late Show* ran an item entitled 'How to make a Peter Greenaway film' in which mundane clips from *Nationwide* were transformed into meaning-ful, choreographed moments once they had been set to insistent Michael Nyman music. Greenaway's style is formulaic, so too, it could now be argued, is Nick Broomfield's – so much so that in 1999/2000 he (with the assistance of his orig-inal cameraperson/collaborator Joan Churchill) starred in a series of Volkswagen Passat television ads brandishing his distinctive boom and asking his generic awk-ward questions. Broomfield is British documentary's 'star director', he is a recog-nisable face, has had a season of films at the National Film Theatre (1997) and has been a topic for discussion in gossip columns. His trademarks are films built around the tortuous chase after elusive subjects and the collapsed interview that sometimes, as in *Tracking Down Maggie,* fails to materialise. When *Kurt and Courtney* was released in 1998, several journalists expressed their disillusionment with 'the Broomfield film' (see Spencer 1999: 63).[11] The simple fact that there has been a Broomfield backlash – arguably concluded after *Biggie and Tupac* (2002) with the release of the more politically significant and serious *Aileen: The Life and Death of a Serial Killer* (2003; co-directed with Joan Churchill) – is tes-tament to his star status. Since *Driving Me Crazy* (1988), Broomfield has appeared in his films as the hassling director enacting the process of making a documentary, hounding his subjects and wearing them down until they finally give him a story. Broomfield's films (despite his indebtedness to direct cinema) have become supreme examples of the director-performer model; he is the undoubted *auteur* of his films and their very structure proclaims that, without his intervention, there would be no films.

The central issue in how one perceives Broomfield's work is the specific per-sona he performs on camera. Towards the end of *Driving Me Crazy* – a docu-mentary following the rehearsal period and performance of the all-black musical *Body and Soul* – scriptwriter Joe Hindy exclaims 'I don't think you're adorable any more, Nick', a sentiment echoed in *Heidi Fleiss: Hollywood Madam* (1995) when, once again after some time, Madam Alex, one of the film's three protag-onists, shouts at Broomfield down the telephone: 'You're such a greedy f****** pig. I'm so sick of you'. Broomfield's on-screen persona is the sweet, ingratiat-ing, slightly gullible buffoon; it is only late in the proceedings (if ever) that his subjects realise that this is an act, a ploy on Broomfield's part to get the material he wants. In one interview, Broomfield cites an unlikely precursor in Pier Paolo Pasolini, whom he met during the filming of *The Canterbury Tales* in England in 1971. He saw in Pasolini someone who, though ostensibly reserved himself, generated chaos around him, observing that, whilst other film crews 'were always incredibly ordered, almost military, with a clear chain of command', Pasolini's 'seemed to operate with a purposeful anarchy' (Broomfield 1993: 46).

Broomfield's particular admiration for Pasolini's 'ability to use chaos to a creative advantage' (p. 46) could be describing his own post-*Driving Me Crazy* films, for all the documentaries that revolve around his on-screen performance are exercises in controlled chaos. The 'control' aspect relates directly to Broomfield's performance of himself: he remains sweet, dogged, usually unflustered, whilst around him his films almost implode. The anger of Joe Hindy and Madam Alex stems from their belated realisation that Nick Broomfield the documentary film-maker is not synonymous with 'Nick Broomfield' the charming man with Mickey Mouse earphones and boom who extracts information from them. An interesting aspect of how critics and spectators relate to Broomfield's work is that they too sometimes find it hard to accept the dichotomy: after the screening of *Heidi Fleiss* at the 1995 London Film Festival, one member of the audience during the ensuing Q&A session asked Broomfield to expand upon the fact that, whilst he appears a little stupid on screen, he seems intelligent in real life. Broomfield's tactful response was to reiterate that his smiley persona has proved most useful in getting his subjects to open up on camera.

Broomfield's self-performance fuels the debate around 'realness'. Peter Wollen in 1974 used a formula to specifically illustrate this schism in relation to authorship and the fiction film, arguing – from an *auteur*-structuralist perspective – that the *auteur* is only the identity discovered within the text and does not pertain to the individual beyond its parameters.[12] Adopting Wollen's equation, Nick Broomfield ≠ 'Nick Broomfield', the inverted commas signifying the version of the *auteur* to be found within the films. It is over-simplistic to argue that Nick Broomfield, the author beyond the frame, is irrelevant to how one views and interprets the films in which 'Nick Broomfield' appears; rather it is the dialectic between the two that motivates the documentaries and informs our responses to them. The subject 'Nick Broomfield' is constructed on screen from within the documentary frame, whereas Nick Broomfield the *auteur* remains omniscient and detached (a role that is partly articulated through Broomfield's own narration for his films). Complicating matters is that the two are indisputably the same person, they just perform different functions for the purposes of making a documentary and it is this difference and the dialogue that ensues which informs the films. Quite graphically, Broomfield's dual presence articulates the idea that documentaries are the result of a dialectical negotiation between the reality that existed before he arrived and that which subsequently becomes the subject of his films. Why is the performative documentary problematic? Most importantly, it is problematic because it throws into sharp relief previously held notions of fixity of meaning and documentary 'truth'; in a film in which all reliable significance is generated by and through 'Nick Broomfield' the performer-director, there is necessarily a tension between the subjects before and after his arrival that is never fully resolved. The true stories upon which Broomfield's documentaries are based are compromised, filtered through the structured chaos on the screen.

Nick Broomfield's films could not always be characterised thus, and it is illuminating to compare the later documentaries with those he made with Joan

Churchill. Although it is in *Driving Me Crazy* that Broomfield first appears on-screen as his films' *agent provocateur*, it is the earlier *Lily Tomlin: The Film Behind the Show* (1986) about the American comedienne which proved to be the catalyst for a change of approach. Despite its title, *Lily Tomlin* is a straightforward film in the direct cinema mould that follows a performer, in this case Tomlin, preparing her one-woman Broadway show *The Search for Signs of Life in the Universe*. Subsequently Broomfield describes the 'nightmare' that filming *Lily Tomlin* became when, following an exchange of writs, the resulting film was severely compromised:

> The film was a very pale reflection of what had been a very miserable experience. But it occurred to me that if we'd had the miserable experience on film it would have at least been amusing.
>
> (Brown M. 1996: 42)

Prior to this, Broomfield had collaborated on several observational documentaries, many of which – such as *Tattooed Tears* (1978), about the California Youth Training School, and *Soldier Girls* (1981), about women US Army recruits of Charlie Company, Fort Gordon, Georgia – followed in the Fred Wiseman mould of showing the workings of institutions and official organisations. The films are serious, politically motivated and subject-driven, concentrating on material that is still the standard fare of observational documentaries. Even though (as in both films cited above) Broomfield and Churchill single out a handful of individuals to focus upon, such figures are used as representative characters through whom the workings of the institution/organisation can best be conveyed, so – in a generic sequence repeated 18 years later in *Soldiers To Be* – a brutal, aggressive Sergeant shouts at new recruits for making their bunks sloppily. As with Molly Dineen's early films, the Broomfield– Churchill collaborations use interventionist mechanisms only sparingly and functionally – for example, conveying factual information that assists the spectators' understanding of a sequence through short subtitles. The films' emphasis is on the subjects to such an extent that, at the end of *Soldier Girls* when Private Johnson (one of the film's principal characters) is leaving, she spontaneously turns and bids farewell to Churchill and Broomfield. Although the image of Private Johnson embracing Nick Broomfield is caught on camera and is not omitted from the finished film, he is only glimpsed fleetingly in the corner of a frame as if signalling the filmmakers' surprise and self-consciousness at this violation of a key observational rule. For the most part, *Soldier Girls* and *Tattooed Tears* serve as exemplary illustrations of the *vérité*-derived tradition: they feature personalised situations that carry with them more general political connotations; they make statements through observation as opposed to through intervention; they sublimate the filmmakers' opinions to those of the people they pursue, although elements such as editing, a greater identification with the 'victims' rather than the figures in authority and the subjective camera work serve to implicitly convey what those opinions might be.

Both early films contain several moments that could legitimately be termed 'classic *vérité*', when observation becomes synonymous with insight and the acquisition of knowledge. Sequences that dwell upon Ronnie, one of the youthful prisoners in *Tattooed Tears,* being forcibly restrained or Private Alvez in *Soldier Girls* being punished for lack of motivation by having to dig, well into the night, an ostensibly useless grave-like hole both manage to imply criticism of the actions they show simply by the length of time that is dedicated to each and the by the manner in which the filmmakers focus upon the suffering, victimised Ronnie and Private Alvez. Both sequences offer covert commentary on the events they depict.

Broomfield's subsequent style evolved out of a frustrated awareness of the limitations of the observational mode. He articulates this most directly in relation to *Driving Me Crazy* when commenting 'I'd always wanted to examine the documentary form and I'd become sort of disenchanted with the narrow parameters of this style of filmmaking. All too often what you look at on TV is very cleaned up and dishonest' (Paterson 1989: 53). In a later interview he adds: 'There's no point in pretending the camera's not there. I think what's important is the interaction between the film-makers and those being filmed, and the audience is aware of that interaction so they can make decision of their own' (Wise, D. 2002: 18). If one examines even the much earlier work, the tensions are visible within the films themselves. During the restraint sequence in *Tattooed Tears,* Ronnie snatches a quick, furtive glance to camera, this transgressive look highlighting the immutable wall between the subjects and the filmmakers of observational films. Similarly throughout *Soldier Girls* there is the suggestion that the film's protagonists are knowingly acting up for the camera and hence unable to mask the film process's lack of spontaneity. Part of the power of *Soldier Girls* results from its enactment of this tension between what should and should not be included in an observational documentary – moments such as Private Hall learning how to perform the role of Sergeant by joining in Sergeant Abing's sustained, personalised attack on Private Alvez following her fit of screaming after being made to dig the hole. Abing begins with the groundless intimidation 'you don't deserve to be out there in society, you might kill someone out there, Alvez' (Alvez, after all, was originally accused of lacking motivation as a recruit) to which Hall adds:

> You know Alvez there's something about you that tells me you might be the type that would take a weapon and go up on top of a building and start just picking off people in the street just for the heck of it, because you're so apathetic, sooner or later it's bound to turn to hate.

Besides contradicting herself, Hall delivers this fanciful diatribe in the deliberate, slow manner of someone who is both assuming an unfamiliar role that she is eager to perfect (in this case the part of the brutalising sergeant) and is trying to sound convincing despite having to make up what she is saying as she goes along. This and other similar performances in *Soldier Girls* imply, through their very awkwardness, that they are striving to seem unaware of the film-makers' presence but are finding this impossible. It is moments such as these that substantiate Broomfield's contention about 'dishonesty'. Not only are his and Churchill's films characterised by such textual cracks and tensions, but they illustrate the unworkability of the observational ideal by striving too hard to mask the necessity for more formally structuring devices such as voice-over or direct authorial intervention.

Broomfield's transition to a more openly authored style also coincides with the termination of his partnership (both personal and professional) with Joan Churchill, although she has continued to operate the camera on some of his later films such as *Tracking Down Maggie* and *Kurt and Courtney* and ultimately returns as co-director of *Aileen: The Life and Death of a Serial Killer.* If one returns to Broomfield's statement about his growing disillusionment with his methods at the time of *Driving Me Crazy,* what also becomes evident is his frustration at not having been able to show (in *Lily Tomlin,* for example) the mechanics and practicalities of documentary filmmaking. An indispensable corollary of making the shift towards appearing on camera is Broomfield's now proven desire to 'examine the documentary form' by dismantling it. From being good genre films, Broomfield's documentaries become anti-documentaries in which an analysis of the non-fiction film takes the form of a perverse enactment of what a documentary should not be: a film made up of telephone conversations, arguments before and after interviews, discussions between director and crew, chats with incidental characters. In this sense Broomfield's post-*Driving Me Crazy* films, with their formal and physical marginalisation of their central subjects, come to echo the dichotomy between director and performer that Nick Broomfield embodies when appearing in his films. Just as there is a fundamental distinction to be drawn between Nick Broomfield and 'Nick Broomfield', so there is an equally significant differentiation to be made between the documentary and 'the documentary', the former signifying the films' putative subject and the latter the resulting film. The contrast is most graphically illustrated by an unsuccessful film such as *Tracking Down Maggie,* a film, ostensibly about Margaret Thatcher, which contains very little of Thatcher (and certainly no proper access to her) and becomes instead a film about – not just featuring – the peripheral characters such as the neighbour on Flood Street who took Thatcher's old lavatory from the skip in front of her house. *Tracking Down Maggie,* despite amusingly self-deprecating moments like Broomfield's piece of parody documentary commentary 'I'd almost given up when, in a remote spot in the heart of the Essex countryside, we found Francis Wheen', fails because it cannot bring together the two components of the dialectic. The success of Broomfield's performative documentaries is directly dependent upon the collision at some point between the proposed conventional documentary subject (Eileen Wuornos, Eugene Terreblanche, Heidi Fleiss, Madams and clients of a New York fetish parlour) and the unconventional, ostensibly shambolic performance of that subject on film; the documentary and the 'documentary' must meet as must Nick Broomfield and 'Nick Broomfield'. The interview situation is the usual place for these meetings to occur, and films that lack a substantial interview with their pivotal figures (*Maggie* or *Kurt and Courtney*) prove unsatisfying because any serious intent behind the films is lost altogether.

Broomfield's most cohesive and powerful film is *The Leader, His Driver and the Driver's Wife* (1991), a documentary about Eugene Terreblanche, the leader of the neo-Nazi Afrikaner Resistance Movement (the AWB) in South Africa, made at a time when apartheid was crumbling. Still reminiscent of the earlier, more obviously committed films, *The Leader* is the apotheosis of Broomfield's amalgamation of political content and performative style, and so represents another turning point in his career. In subsequent documentaries the balance has shifted more (some would say too far) towards the performative, any serious commentary becoming quite clearly the films' secondary element. Like all of Broomfield's later *auteur*-performer films, *The Leader* parallels the amassing of the documentary story about Terreblanche with the experience of making the film; inevitably, much of the action revolves around travelling and establishing contact with Terreblanche and a variety of intermediaries, most notably his driver 'JP' and JP's wife Anita. Like Michael Moore's performance at the centre of *Roger and Me* (1989) in which he unsuccessfully tries to get Roger Smith, the chairman of General Motors, to come to Flint, Michigan to confront company workers whose jobs are being cut, Broomfield's performance in *The Leader* is successful because it appears rooted in earnest commitment rather than simple egomania. Despite flaunting the comic detail of the story (like so many trophies), *The Leader* powerfully enacts, through the mechanisms of the performative documentary, the real decline of the AWB from sinister, sizeable power to impotent political sideshow. The documentary opens with Barry Ackroyd, Broomfield's cameraman, being floored by a punch from an angry AWB member at a packed rally, but ends with a counter sequence at an AWB parade that was expected to attract 5,000 but which is attended only by a meagre few (Figure 6.1); it contains several incidental travelling sequences during which Broomfield's voice-over catalogues episodes of AWB brutality, whilst the body of the film shows Terreblanche unable to control his horse, getting angry when Anita points a loaded gun at him and JP leaving the party. The performative elements of *The Leader* ostensibly marginalise the documentary's substantive material, only to reflexively re-invoke it.

This correlation would not have occurred if the interview with Terreblanche had not taken place – if, that is, the conventional documentary had not met its performative counterpart. Although Broomfield encounters Terreblanche on a couple of occasions prior to this interview, these meetings are insubstantial; the interview itself (which comes two-thirds of the way through the film) likewise appears, on the surface, to be inadequate, a 'non-interview' in the words of many critics. To back this up, the interview (in JP's estimation, 'the worst he's ever seen') comprises an argument between Terreblanche and Broomfield concerning the latter's lateness for an earlier appointment and Terreblanche's repeated misunderstanding of one simple question: when had he decided that the AWB would have to go to war against the blacks? Turning up a few minutes late for

Figure 6.1 The Leader, His Driver and the Driver's Wife (True Stories)
Source: Courtesy of BFI Stills, Posters and Designs

the previous appointment was a deliberate ploy to anger Terreblanche, for 'Nick Broomfield' the *provocateur* is heard to mumble sweetly that the reason he and the crew were late was that they were 'having a cup of tea'. Throughout this argument, Ackroyd holds the camera steady on Terreblanche (from a low angle, ironically suggestive of power and superiority). Secondly, whilst the interview may not yield very much substantial discussion of the AWB's policy, it shows Terreblanche, not Broomfield, to be the buffoon of the encounter (it is significant that, for this sequence, Broomfield remains out of frame), as the leader misinterprets the only question the director is heard to put to him, understanding him to have asked when he will go to war, not when he decided he would have to go to war. Broomfield rephrases the question several times, each time laboriously making it clearer, but Terreblanche obtusely misses the nuances. The essential performative power of *The Leader* is that it spontaneously captures and plays out the disintegration of Terreblanche's power and concomitantly that of the AWB, for however manipulated and preconceived the film might be, Broomfield's way of making films ensures that 'there is never an opportunity to do a second take' (Broomfield quoted in Macdonald and Cousins 1996: 364).

The issue of 'realness' as it pertains to *The Leader, His Driver and the Driver's Wife* is, from the audience's perspective, relatively unproblematic, as the distinction between Nick Broomfield the director and 'Nick Broomfield' the enactment of himself for the benefit of the documentary, appears clear cut. The latter functions as a tool of the former, working to manipulate the figures of the documentary, notably Terreblanche; the persona in inverted commas, therefore, is an accurate simulation that nevertheless remains separate from his real counterpart. If one turns to the performative film as created by the juxtaposition of these two figures, then the identities of the documentary and the 'documentary' are likewise intact. A documentary is deemed performative if it formally illustrates the notion that a documentary is an unpredictable act. The way in which the performative works in *The Leader*, however, ultimately suggests that the pre-existing facts upon which it is based – like the actual Nick Broomfield – do exist. Certain of Broomfield's later films (most notably *Heidi Fleiss*) problematise this simple, reflective interpretation of the performative by not abiding by the simple binary oppositions examined above. Concomitantly, these later films show a move towards the clichéd Nick Broomfield film that is more about him than about his subjects. As the films become more fixated on the 'Nick Broomfield' persona and as that persona increasingly dominates the documentaries' action, so the films subjugate their proposed subject matter to a more focused, insistent interest in the issues of performance and 'realness'. It is also significant that the subjects and situations of these latest films are similarly preoccupied with performance and 'realness': Fleiss is a hooker and madam, the mistresses of Pandora's Box in *Fetishes* enact sadomasochistic scenarios, Courtney Love is an actress. In tandem with these complications, the previously straightforward Nick Broomfield ≠ 'Nick Broomfield' distinction is itself (irretrievably perhaps) problematised.

In *Heidi Fleiss: Hollywood Madam* (1995) all definitions of reality, of what is the truth are thrown into confusion; it is far from clear, by the end, where the boundary between the director and his persona lies (if anywhere), and it is likewise entirely unclear whether the film succeeds in revealing any even superficial truths about its three protagonists: Heidi Fleiss, Madam Alex (for whom Heidi first worked) and Ivan Nagy (her lover and maybe erstwhile pimp). As the confusion mounts, the documentary becomes fixated on this triangular relationship and on Fleiss in particular, leaving virtually untouched the facts surrounding Hollywood's 'Madam to the stars' – the catalysts, essentially, for her arrest (on pandering and narcotics charges) and also for the film. At the outset, and for much of the film, Broomfield appears in control; similarly we, his audience – upon seeing the familiar, formulaic mechanisms in place (the telephone calls, the schmoozing, the dogged pursuit of his subjects, the obtaining of significant access and interviews) – are lulled into a sense that we are indeed, once more, to occupy the privileged position of those whom Broomfield lets in on the act. The chain (one element leading to the next until the filmmaker gets close to his or her main subject) is a fundamental characteristic of the investigative documentary, and the feeling of security remains intact in *Heidi Fleiss* while Broomfield is able to follow leads that take him from one friend or ex-employee to another in his successful endeavour to build up a portrait of Fleiss. Likewise, the manner in which Broomfield subsequently intercuts interviews with two of his protagonists,

Nagy and Alex, suggests that he (as puppet master) is playing one off against the other, thereby controlling them and how they are perceived. If this is suggestive of Broomfield getting to the heart of his documentary subject, then this confidence is validated by his arrival at Heidi Fleiss, whom he interviews extensively whilst she is out on bail and in rehab.

However, in *Heidi Fleiss* the Pasolini analogy of the controlling director surrounded by orchestrated chaos crumbles, so that the inverse becomes true: that Broomfield is thrown into chaos as control is seen to reside with the subjects he has sought to manipulate. The film's final interviews with Nagy and Fleiss both suggest that it is they who have been stringing Broomfield along rather than *vice versa*. Nagy mocks him for being 'an idiot' who 'is not in the club' and maintains that he is still seeing Fleiss (a statement he substantiates with a smoochy telephone call to her); Fleiss, whilst denying her and Nagy are still together, likewise taunts Broomfield by saying 'you're missing something, Nick ... you're way off, Nick. Bye'. Broomfield adopts a particularly flirtatious manner with Fleiss, maintaining that 'We had a very flirtatious game-playing relationship; and if we hadn't I don't think I'd have got the interview' (Brown, M. 1996: 42), also saying that, by the end of filming, he had 'a problem with Ivan' and that it was the film's exposure of their relationship that ultimately precipitated Fleiss' break up with him (p. 42). Is a relationship based on faked flirtation, however, likely to be won by the filmmaker or the madam?[13]

Broomfield's more recent work has been unimpressive and increasingly slight and self-centred, that is, until the release of his second documentary about Aileen Wuornos, the notorious serial killer who was finally executed in Florida at the behest of Governor Jeb Bush on 9 October 2002. Since making *Aileen Wuornos: The Selling of a Serial Killer* in 1993, Broomfield had kept in touch with Wuornos, principally via her best friend Dawn Botkins (Wood J. 2005: 228), who wrote to Wuornos every day and to whom (as shown at the end of the second film) her ashes are returned after execution and cremation. The catalyst for this second documentary was Broomfield being served with a subpoena to appear at Wuornos's pre-execution trial, after she had changed her plea for the murders she had committed from self-defence to murder in cold blood. This documentary, which Broomfield made in collaboration with Joan Churchill, strongly implies that Wuornos in part changed her plea in order to bring closer her day of execution and categorically states that their informed belief is that Aileen Wuornos was insane and should never have been executed. As Broomfield says outside the jail to the assembled press reporting the execution: 'We're executing a person who's mad'.

Having arguably spent eight years making films (*Heidi Fleiss, Fetishes, Kurt and Courtney, Biggie and Tupac*) that were amusing and clever more than they were either politically significant or even personally involving, with *The Life and Death of a Serial Killer* Broomfield returned to documentary filmmaking with a sober purpose. Two – manifestly intertwined – features mark out the second Aileen Wuornos film out from its immediate predecessors: Broomfield's keenness to voice his own opinions on the issues raised by the case and his diminished physical presence in front of Churchill's camera. As with Michael Moore's films (for example his relatively restrained and peripheral performance in *Fahrenheit 9/11*) there is, crudely speaking, an inverse correlation between the extent of Broomfield's serious involvement in his subject matter (and indeed the seriousness of the subject matter itself) and the amount he appears on screen; the less he features the more seriously we should take the documentary. In *Aileen: The Life and Death of a Serial Killer* Broomfield's appearances are further validated by his actual role as a key defence witness in Wuornos's pre-execution trial. Broomfield at first does not realise why exactly he was issued with a subpoena, but it soon becomes clear that the prosecuting attorney is keen to discredit Broomfield's first film about Wuornos as it contained, if believed, evidence that she had been so badly represented in the first instance by her lawyer Steve Glazer that her initial conviction for murder could be found to be unsound. The prosecution play on a video monitor the 'seven joint ride' to visit Wuornos in prison, during which Glazer (who is driving) is shown to smoke seven joints of marijuana. Glazer at some point has changed shirt and the prosecuting lawyer makes much of this, insinuating that Broomfield pasted together two different sequences, an allegation that Broomfield on film denies and later refutes outright, after checking his rushes. Broomfield's presence as a witness adds yet another performative layer and consolidates the sense of his own personal investment in the film's argument that Aileen Wuornos was insane and so should not have been executed.

It was Wuornos's wish that Broomfield be granted her final interview before execution. As he is when on the witness stand, Broomfield (in keeping with his low profile through this film relatively) is nervous as he begins by asking Wuornos how she feels, to which she replies 'I'm prepared. I'm alright with it'. Broomfield has clearly sought to put on record three things: that Wuornos believed that she killed in self defence (illustrated during an earlier interview when he asks Wuornos – who thinks he has stopped filming – whether or not she murdered in self defence, to which she is heard to reply 'Yes'); that the abuse she suffered as a child – abandoned by her biological mother, beaten by her grandfather and probable biological father and sent to live in the woods near her hometown following the birth of a child when she was just 13 – had a direct impact on her later actions and mental health; and finally that, as a consequence of her life and her time in prison, she was not sane. Although Wuornos in this final interview refuses to answer Broomfield's questions about the killings, she reveals the extent of her paranoid obsession with the police who handled her case: that they knew about her after the first murder, but hushed this up as they wanted to let her become a high profile and lucrative serial killer; how they placed her under surveillance from before she started killing; and how, in jail, the guards had controlled and tortured her using sonic radio waves boomed into her cell via the intercom system. Aileen Wuornos cuts short this interview after Broomfield (who had just interviewed Aileen's mother Diane) tells Aileen that her mother had asked for her daughter's forgiveness. Later he maintains that 'I thought, in a way, asking her for forgiveness might be of some solace to Aileen' (Wood J. 2005: 231), but the film shows Aileen turning on Broomfield, her mad, intensely dark eyes staring accusingly into the camera lens as she asks for the interview to be terminated and walks away, giving Broomfield the finger. As Wuornos leaves the interview room, Broomfield is heard to utter an apologetic, timid 'I'm so sorry' – an attempt to bring her back? To exonerate himself? When asked what prompted him to say this, Broomfield answers:

> Because I felt that the interview was such a disappointment for her ... Obviously she was disturbed by the fact that she was going to be executed the next day and, frankly, who wouldn't be? But I felt that maybe she thought that I'd let her down, and it just seemed such a sad way to be saying goodbye to somebody.
>
> (Wood J. 2005: 231)

This is yet another shambolic and, in conventional terms, unsatisfactory Broomfield interview, but what it also conveys, extremely strongly, is that, on the day prior to her execution, Wuornos was not of sound mind. *Aileen: The Life and Death of a Serial Killer* is Broomfield's least showy film since he began appearing in them, but it is also his most sincere and motivating film at least since *The Leader, His Driver and the Driver's Wife*. The two documentaries are tonally quite distinct, but they serve as oppositional reminders of how effective and affecting Broomfield's authorial involvement can be. Whereas *The Leader* charted the demise of the white supremacist movement in South Africa through irony and humour, the second Aileen Wuornos film offers a more sombre indictment of a justice system that Broomfield has labelled 'primitive' and 'barbaric' (Wood J. 2005: 229). The latter, though superficially imposing narrative closure at the end with Wuornos's death and burial, also remains open as it raises the whole issue of whether or not a documentary can actually change the course of events; it clearly matters to Broomfield that he failed to prevent Wuornos's execution and so the film's attack on Jeb Bush and the legal system he sanctions continues.

Conclusion

Broomfield's very technique encapsulates the idea of documentaries as not necessarily determined or closed, but rather as dialectical and open to reinterpretation. This remains a constant factor linking all the documentaries here discussed. The performative documentary is the clearest contemporary exponent of this book's underpinning thesis that the documentary as prescribed by advocates of observational realism is an unrealisable fantasy, that documentary will forever be circumscribed by the fact that it is a mode of representation and thus can never elide the distance between image and event. It is imperative, however, to acknowledge that this deficiency does not invalidate the notion of the non-fiction film, merely that the non-fiction film is (and largely always has been) aware of the limitations of the audio-visual media. With this acknowledgement, what ensues when examining documentary output is an awareness that it is predicated upon a dialectical relationship between aspiration and potential, that the text itself reveals the tensions between the documentary pursuit of the most authentic mode of factual representation and the impossibility of this aim. The documentaries examined in this chapter express these tendencies through the use of multiple dualities: in *Unmade Beds,* there is the conflict between the invocation of the furtive, unpredictable act of secretly peeping in at strangers' windows represented via a series of precisely framed, lit and performed cameo sequences; in *The Thin Blue Line,* there is the shock caused by juxtaposing beautifully crafted noir-ish images with details of a murder; in *Geri,* Molly Dineen and her subject Geri Halliwell dispute the question of control of the film ostensibly freely; in *The Leader, His Driver and the Driver's Wife,* Nick Broomfield performs the role of sweet, chaotic investigative reporter as a means of undermining and controlling Eugene Terreblanche's image. From within such a performative framework, the very notion of a complete, finite documentary is continually challenged and reassessed.

Part IV
New directions

7 Contemporary documentaries
Performance and success

Être et avoir (Nicolas Philibert, 2002), *The Fog of War* (Errol Morris, 2003), *Capturing the Friedmans* (Andrew Jarecki, 2003), *Touching the Void* (Kevin Macdonald, 2003)

The majority of the documentaries discussed in the previous chapter, although many were premiered at film festivals, were funded and made for television. The films under discussion here were released in the cinema (although part-funded by television companies such as Channel Four's FilmFour, which produced *Touching the Void*) and were all relatively financially successful big-screen movies. There has always been a tradition of the theatrical release documentary, primarily from the United States where network television has been historically reluctant to fund documentary output,[1] and occasionally, when these cinema documentaries are released in groups, critics have written about there being a rebirth of interest in the genre. Linda Williams in 1993, for example, headily wrote about 'their unprecedented popularity among general audiences, who now line up for documentaries as eagerly as for fiction films', citing *Village Voice* critic Amy Taubin who had noted that, in 1991, a handful of documentaries made it onto the *Variety* charts (Williams 1993: 12). A little later, around the time of *Hoop Dreams, Crumb, Martha and Ethel, Unzipped,* there was another resurgence of interest in documentaries among cinema audiences. The post-millennium group of cinema release documentaries includes two films by Michael Moore – *Bowling for Columbine* and *Fahrenheit 9/11, Spellbound* (Jeffrey Blitz's film about the annual US Spelling Bee competition), *The Kid Stays in the Picture* (Brett Morgen and Nanette Burstein's stylistically innovative film about Hollywood Producer Robert Evans), *Supersize Me* (Morgan Spurlock's 30-day experiment of eating nothing but McDonald's food to demonstrate how bad for you fast food actually is), *Tarnation* (Jonathan Caouette's autobiographical account of his upbringing and his schizophrenic mother) and *The Corporation* (Jennifer Abbott and Mark Achbar, 2003). This discussion is included in this revised edition as a means of signalling the directions in which documentary film has gone recently, selecting out of the many documentaries to have been theatrically released a broadly representative cross-section in terms of style and subject matter. With the arguable exception of *The Fog of War*, which has achieved more critical than financial success, these documentaries have become particularly popular in financial terms. *Touching the Void*, when it opened in the UK and Ireland made a screen average of over £4,000, which was, as Mark Cousins remarked, 'within spitting distance of feel-good juggernaut *Love Actually*'s takings per screening' (Cousins 2004: 5). Kevin Macdonald's film is (to date) the second top-grossing documentary in the UK of all time, behind *Fahrenheit 9/11* (by a huge margin of more than £4 million) and in front of *Bowling for Columbine*, the film credited by many in the press with this recent revival of interest in documentary (see Gant 2005 for the top 10 documentaries).

The post-millennium years have produced an interesting moment in the annals of documentary, as much if not more important as a historical juncture than as a theoretical one – except inasmuch as the hugely diverse films collectively demonstrate that the performative aspects of documentary have by now become relatively commonplace. The divergence between on-screen and off-screen personae, the use of reconstruction as a tool for representing and reinvigorating the past, a sustained interest in subjects whose lives seem built around layers of performance are all performative elements that feature strongly amongst these post-millennium documentaries. The move away from traditional observational documentary was becoming evident in 2000, when the first edition of *New Documentary* came out; however, this shift has gained pace and has now become more of a systematic rejection of the observational form. The roots of observation are present in reality television and formatted documentaries, for example, but the imposition of a highly structured format such as *Big Brother* or *Wife Swap* necessarily conflicts with the more strictly observational aims of direct cinema or later British practitioners Roger Graef and Paul Watson. The marginalisation of traditional observational documentary is one reason for choosing to discuss *Être et avoir*, as Philibert's film is a by now rare and refreshing example of the observational form (the other, just as important, motive for discussing *Être et avoir* is its litigious post-production history, which reflects upon and complicates no end its more straightforward observational tone). The other three documentaries – *The Fog of War, Capturing the Friedmans, Touching the Void* – are all historical and so by definition non-observational, and *The Fog of War* and *Touching the Void* are also stylistically innovative in ways that mark them out as contemporary. This book has sought to argue that all documentaries, including observational ones, are performative in that the 'truth' depicted on screen only comes into being at the moment of filming and that, far from being equivalent to or a substitute for the truth that existed before filming began, all documentaries are the products of a dialectical as opposed to synchronous relationship between these two 'truths'. What has occurred recently is that documentaries that foreground this performative dynamic – usually formally – have become the most popular and pervasive, hence the relative sidelining of the observational mode. A quintessential example of this is *The Kid Stays in the Picture*, the hugely entertaining and financially successful cinema adaptation of Robert Evans's autobiography. The material is largely archival and, in this respect, conventional: excerpts from films Evans appeared in or produced, snippets of interviews with

Evans, newspaper headlines and photographs. Although the documentary is largely sustained through nearly two hours by Evan's eventful life story, what ensures that it remains visually memorable is its treatment of the stills – what, on the surface, appears to be the dullest of its archive materials. Morgen and Burstein frequently superimpose one photographic image onto another (in a similar way Errol Morris in *The Fog of War* merges two bits of moving archive) and use multi-planing, which detaches the foreground of photos from their backgrounds and exaggerates the distance between the two. The effect of this – like any technique when it first appears – is to activate the act of looking, to make one take note of these still images rather than treat them as merely illustrative wallpaper for Evans' rather flat narration. There is no particularly clever reason for the multi-planing in that it does not, as and of itself, bring to the surface any otherwise suppressed meaning. What it does is to make us look differently and through this act of looking differently the content as well as the formal qualities of *The Kid Stays in the Picture* remain memorable; our engrossment in the multi-planing sharpens as opposed to diminishes our attention towards the film's other elements.

Être et avoir

Nicolas Philibert's *Être et avoir* is almost the binary opposite of *The Kid Stays in the Picture*: a low key observational film about a tiny one-class primary school in Saint-Etienne-sur-Usson, Auvergne. Philibert is the film's director, cinematographer and editor. Upon its release *Être et avoir* was an unexpected success both in France and abroad, like many documentaries before it making a small-scale star of its protagonist, teacher Georges Lopez. The issues to dominate any retrospective contemplation of the documentary, however, are bound to centre on the subsequent legal wrangles between Lopez and the film's producers. Once *Être et avoir* had become a huge international success (earning 10 million in France alone) Lopez elected to sue Philibert and his producers for a share of the film's profits. He demanded €250,000, claiming that he had been treated as an actor in the film and asserting 'intellectual property rights' over his teaching methods, so prominently featured in the film. Lopez refused a one-off payment offered by the documentary makers of €37,000, preferring to pursue his case for proper remuneration as he saw it, also demanding that he be considered the film's 'co-author'. Lopez allied himself clearly with the parents of some of the children featured in *Être et avoir* as seven of the families involved have also gone to court, demanding €20,000 each as recompense for their part in it. Lopez's case has twice been defeated, once in the Court of Appeal in Montpellier and once in the Court of Bankruptcy in Paris. The second of these defeats (in Paris) occurred in September 2004, at which point Lopez was set to appeal. He has repeatedly argued that his motives for bringing this case against Philibert and his producers were not financial, that 'the trial for me [is] not about money' but rather stemmed from a desire to seek remuneration for 'a year's worth of investment' on the part of himself and the children and to set a precedent whereby children are protected 'from this sort of exploitation in the future' (Groskop 2005: 42). Lopez acknowledges that the general view of him is that 'he just wants money because it has been successful' (Groskop 2005: 41) – and indeed Kees Bakker, writing about *Être et avoir* in an essay about the ethics of interpretation, makes the sweeping assumption that 'Greed is the root to all attacks on documentary' (Bakker 2005: 27) – but he has repeatedly refuted this. If not motivated by greed, then why did Lopez reject the filmmakers' offer of €37,000 for his work in promoting the film (they did not want to set a precedent by paying so much for someone to participate in a documentary)? Why did he suddenly start accusing Philibert and his producers of exploitation after he and the children had tirelessly supported the film's promotion at Cannes and elsewhere? More than anything, perhaps, the responses to Lopez since embarking upon this legal battle are motivated in turn by disillusionment: that our collective idealisation of a 'national hero' dedicated to his teaching 'ended abruptly' once he started to stake his claim to be considered *Être et avoir*'s 'co-author' or principle 'actor' (Gentleman 2004b).

The ethics of this case are interesting in themselves – the issue of whether or not documentary filmmakers should have to pay those who participate in their films more than the usual nominal contributors' fee has, in a sense, been won by the filmmakers and their unions. As Claire Hocquet, who represented Philibert in court said after the Parisian court had ruled in their favour: 'To pay someone who appears in a documentary would be to treat them as an actor, and that would be the death of documentary filmmaking' (Gentleman 2004a). Concurring with this, an editorial in *Sight and Sound* argued that 'A rash of such interventions would soon see the end of the serious feature-film documentary' (*Sight and Sound* 2004: 3). Frequently, in documentary's revitalistion lies the threat and fear of the genre's imminent demise: Brian Winston commented, for example, about the docusoap that 'It is therefore something of an irony that these, the first documentaries really appreciated by the masses, seemed to many observers to be killing off the Griersonian tradition' (Winston 2000: 56), whilst journalists have periodically been declaring the death of reality television for several years now.

Rather than focus exclusively on the popularity of *Être et avoir* and the issues subsequently raised by Lopez's battles in the French courts, what I also intend to concentrate on here are the aesthetic, ethical and theoretical ramifications of his actions, in particular the issue of how these actions illustrate and emphasise the performative nature of the film, as what Lopez is like in *Être et avoir* clashes awkwardly with what he seems to be like in light of his claims in court. As a means of understanding its performative elements, it is pertinent to outline elements of the film's production history. Philibert's method is observational and akin to old-school direct cinema, although he himself denies this, maintaining that his method 'has nothing to do with the "fly-on-the-wall" approach. It is not a matter of people forgetting you, of being transparent … Hiding is contradictory to trust' (cited in Barneveld 2003: 16). *Être et avoir* is not a political film, a film (like Wiseman's *High School*) that focuses on an educational institution in order to formulate a critique of it; instead, in the words of Amy Taubin, it is 'an unabashedly humanist film, more concerned with teacher and pupils as individuals than with the pedagogical system within which they function' (Taubin 2003: 74).

Expressive of this tendency is the documentary's intricate and painstaking style: that it tells its story through images and editing instead of through a potentially directional, didactic voice-over, that it romanticises Georges Lopez and the tiny village school he has been the sole teacher at for 20 years at the same time as it is mindful not to idealise French rural life, instead punctuating the long scenes of idyllic learning with insights into the hard work and lack of affluence of the farming communities it serves. The pace of *Être et avoir* and its lack of voice-over are the features that immediately set it apart from most contemporaneous documentaries. Philibert's method is exemplified by the film's opening:

- A farmer steers his cows into a field during a blizzard.
- This action is replaced by a sequence made up of long, silent shots of an empty classroom.
- We finally notice two tortoises ambling along the floor.
- There is then a cut to a series of low angle shots of trees and the introduction of nondiegetic music (which is used sparingly through the film to mark the transition from one season to the next).
- These images then give way to various shots (interior and exterior) of a school bus driving along the wintry country roads, picking up children.
- Philibert here holds a shot of an empty road for a few seconds before cutting to Marie, one of the younger pupils, looking out of her window.
- There are then various shots from inside the bus of other pupils getting on; there are some shots of the driver and a point of view shot through the front windscreen at the white road winding in front of him.
- Finally, the children arrive at their school to be greeted warmly by Lopez; the first lesson is handwriting, for the younger pupils.

The pace of *Être et avoir* might appear slow but in fact this opening section is quite economical. In a little over five minutes it has conveyed quite a lot of information about what season it is, what sort of community the film is going to feature, the type and size of school the children attend and what kind of relationship Lopez has with his class. There is no voice-over used in *Être et avoir* and only one interview, so the only overt means Philibert has of telling his story is the juxtaposition of images and during this opening sequence it is through the accumulation of shots rather than through narration that the film's simple story is builds up. The collage of images cited above, however, does more than simply set the scene, it also establishes the film's tone by suggesting links between how the school and community function and the residual attitudes towards his subjects of its director. We are invited to infer the old-fashionedness of Lopez's teaching style from the prominence given to handwriting; we are also given an indication of Lopez's patience through the subsequent scene showing Jojo painstakingly, clumsily pinning a poster to the classroom wall.

Despite this being, in an intensely auteurist sense, Philibert's film, *Être et avoir* is collaborative in that there exists an almost conspiratorial collusion between Philibert's filming style, Lopez's personal style and the nature of the teaching he undertakes: all are low key and quiet, all in terms of genealogy belong to a traditional way of doing things – cinematic (observational, responsive), behavioural (gentle, quietly spoken, firm), pedagogical (handwriting classes, dictation, colouring in). *Être et avoir* is driven by synchronicity. There is a comforting smoothness about how it makes transitions from one sequence to another, from one class to another, from one action to another. There is a sweet moment, for instance, when Jojo (clearly Philibert's favourite pupil and – it is implied – Lopez's) is told by his teacher to go and wash the paint off his hands. He returns having done this and Lopez finishes off the job by cleaning Jojo's forehead for him, the transition from instruction to pastoral care having been seamlessly made. This seamlessness is demonstrably enhanced by the observational style – long takes, slow editing, the absence of narration – and is only sporadically broken, for example when Lopez is interviewed.

An hour into *Être et avoir* Philibert conducts a straightforward interview with his main subject during which Lopez fills in some biographical details and offers his reasons for going into teaching. This interview comes from a different documentary aesthetic and whereas elsewhere Lopez looks confident, at ease with the omnipresent camera, here he looks awkward and shifty, as if he would like to get back to the other realm. He is talking it appears, rather formally to camera, which is in itself uncomfortable within the context of an observational film in which elsewhere any acknowledgement of the apparatus has been limited to children looking into the lens and giggling a little or looking away self-consciously. What this sequence also does is to furnish us with conventional information about Lopez – that his father was a Spanish immigrant but is now dead, that Lopez going into teaching was socially a step up for them – in a manner not previously embarked upon. When, for example, Lopez talks to Natalie's mother about her eldest daughter's virtual muteness, Philibert never feels the need to spell out why she is marginally less reserved with Lopez than she is with her own parents. Perhaps this is tantalizing, but the lack of information makes the final conversation between teacher and pupil (Natalie is among the oldest children in the class and will soon be going on to Middle School) intriguing. In dappled sun on the school steps Lopez gently presses Natalie to tell him why she does not talk. She cries. He asks her if she is worried about leaving him. Natalie replies in the affirmative to this and other similar questions, although the fact that Lopez is always prompting her and that she never says directly that she will miss him suggests that a certain amount of projection is going on between Lopez and his pupils. Maybe Lopez is projecting onto them his need to be needed. Open-endedness is one of the many delights of observational cinema; the possibilities for what Lopez's classroom tells us (about the people in it, about modern day rural France) are various, but equally *Être et avoir* invites us to relish the detail it observes.

There is scope to observational cinema and if one was to search for additional meaning in *Être et avoir*, then Lopez's classroom in which he teaches a handful of children of different ages could be seen as representative of the small country school which, in France, is under threat (in 1960 there were 19,000 of these schools; now there are fewer than 5,000 [Groskop 2005: 41]). The links between school and environment are accentuated through the film – the mapping out of its narrative via shots that convey the passing of the seasons – as if, in turn, this school is further representative of a traditional type of Frenchness. *Être et avoir* is inherently conservative and offers a whimsical and idealised vision of what education could be; the film also centres on and is, to a large extent, dependent upon the teaching manner and dedication of Lopez. As Taubin again remarks, 'One can imagine, however, how different school would have been for these children if their only teacher for six years had been mean and unresponsive' (Taubin 2003: 74). Lopez makes the film, but he also fits conveniently into Philibert's vision. The director did not, for instance, go in search of a multi-cultural inner city school, instead he contacted over 300 rural schools while researching *Être et avoir* and visited more than 100 of them before being introduced to Lopez (whom he first met in October 2000) and seeing his school in the Auvergne. Over the course of four months Philibert shot about 60 hours of film, edited down to 100 minutes; the 'stars' he picks out are again compatible with the underpinning sentimentality: Jojo, the cheeky but cute little boy who is nevertheless eager to learn, Natalie the withdrawn and virtually mute older girl and Olivier, whose father is ill and who is coaxed by Lopez into divulging his fears for his father's health. The film deals empathetically with its subjects and makes us, via our strong identification as adults with Lopez, want to nurture these children.

As the film's pivotal figure Georges Lopez comes across as an inspired, patient, somewhat old-fashioned, slightly stern but hugely supportive teacher. Despite everything that has occurred since and despite no longer being on speaking terms with Philibert, Lopez still likes the film because it 'showed me what kind of teacher I was ... It was a surprise for me, but a good one. It was a portrait of an ideal teacher' (Groskop 2005: 41). To subsequently claim intellectual property rights over his teaching methods as Lopez did throws up intriguing questions of image-ownership. In Lopez's statement above he comments that Philibert constructed a portrait of 'an ideal teacher' which was, in turn, a pleasant 'surprise'. The very nature of this comment – that Lopez's observation admits there might be a difference between how he perceives himself and how *Être et avoir* depicts him – undermines his claims to the intellectual property rights of his teaching methods, for the teacher and his teaching as featured in the film (idealised as these are) are composites, grounded in Lopez and the way he instructs, but not exclusively defined by him or his methods. Lopez's assertion of his rights and his requests for remuneration throw up interesting and difficult questions about the nature of documentary filmmaking, but they also reveal a lack of understanding of the genre: that a documentary film (particularly one not made for ethnographic purposes) is not straightforwardly reflective of its subject but is, like Georges Lopez the screen persona, the meeting point for several distinct and perhaps divergent forces, in this instance: Georges Lopez as he was prior to meeting

Philibert, 'Georges Lopez' the 'ideal' teacher as performed by Lopez and shot and edited by Philibert, the schoolchildren and how they respond to Lopez onscreen, Philibert himself and what he was striving so painstakingly to discover through filming for seven months in Lopez's school and lastly the spectator. To break this down further, the act of watching *Être et avoir* could generate for the spectator multiple levels of meaning and recognition, for example: that this was what school was actually like, that this is what school should be, that Philibert is peddling an essentially nostalgic and quaint portrait of rural France and rural education or that this is first and foremost a piece of cinema and thus more naturally affiliated to the image of school and youth in a film such as François Truffaut's first feature *Les 400 Coups* than other documentaries.

There is a further divergence between the kind of film *Être et avoir* became and the kind of film Lopez and certain of the children's parents say they thought it was going to be. The 'problem' at the heart of the *Être et avoir* case has persistently been its success; whether or not greed was indeed the trigger for either Lopez's legal action or the subsequent action of the parents on their children's behalf, the effects of the film on Lopez or the children seemed of little interest until it became lucrative. Undoubtedly, the success of *Être et avoir* altered any effect the film might have had on the lives of Lopez and his pupils to the extent that the police had to be called to restrain the press who had descended on the school around the time of the film's release. As Valerie Roches, one of the mothers claiming that their children should be paid as actors for their participation, has said: 'We were not prepared for it; they (the press) just landed us with it. I suppose it was good and bad at the same time' (Groskop 2005: 43). Once Lopez had initiated proceedings against the filmmakers, the children's lives were further disrupted; some of them, Roches maintains, became afraid of the dark whilst one older boy 'was so distressed he started wetting the bed again' (p. 43). The older children were teased at school about their 'star status' and 'there was a lot of jealousy and misunderstanding' (p. 43).

A further 'misunderstanding' arose over the nature of the film itself. Philibert insists that he was at pains to make clear to the parents (who obviously had to formally consent to their children being filmed in the first place, something they all did enthusiastically by all accounts) that the film would be for cinema distribution. Roches, a spokesperson and representative for the parental group taking Philibert to court, has since stated that 'From the beginning, we were told that the film was *just a documentary* ... Now we find that it is a cinema film, which is a commercial success. And we have nothing out of it' (my italics; Lichfield 2004: 5). In a later interview Roches argues that 'she always thought it was an educational documentary for distribution in schools' (Groskop 2005: 42); ditto Lopez who claims not to have realised that people 'would be paying money to go into cinemas to see it' (p. 43) and that this 'small documentary about a one-teacher village school' was never discussed as a potential 'commercial venture' (Gentleman 2004b). This begs the question: what did Lopez and the children think they were doing smiling and holding hands on the red carpet at Cannes: promoting an educational film? What they were doing was offering their services to 'a documentary', and it is Roches's (and perhaps Lopez's) misinterpretation of documentary – as a genre unrelated to the inherently more financially viable 'cinema film' – that arguably lies at the heart of this prolonged and unseemly legal tussle. Documentaries, in Roches's estimation, are not meant to be financially successful.

Meanings and interpretations of 'success' have become confused in the aftermath of *Être et avoir*'s release. 'Success' as attributed to the film by Lopez and Roches refers to its ability to make money (and the film has been highly successful in this respect); within the framework of documentary history, however, *Être et avoir* has proved successful on an aesthetic level as well, and these opposing value systems – the monetary and the aesthetic – have inevitably collided. Whether motivated by greed or not, Lopez has confused himself with 'Georges Lopez', a performative rendition of Georges Lopez captured on screen, a rendition comprising several elements: aesthetic, factual, imaginative etc. This is not an item of news, so the moment Lopez enters the aesthetic domain he relinquishes overall control of his image; not that Philibert, as the film's director, abused Lopez's trust it would seem, having built up a friendship with his protagonist, his pupils and their parents. In an interview granted before Lopez embarked on his legal case, Philibert outlined the rapport he established with all involved and that he discussed with the parents, prior to filming, how 'he was not going to film their children only in beautiful situations, as then he would not have a film' and that in return for the parents trusting him, 'Everyone could come into the editing room at any time, but nobody would be allowed to ask him to remove a scene'. If just one of the parents had not agreed to these conditions, Philibert would have looked for another school (Barneveld 2003: 17). This is a contract of sorts, but also an explanation of documentary methods.

Although Philibert argues against comparisons with the 'fly-on-the-wall' approach (Barneveld 2003: 16), Lopez in *Être et avoir* is reminiscent of the memorable protagonists of direct cinema, such as John Kennedy in *Primary* or Paul in *Salesman*. The vital ambivalence of these past observational documentary protagonists is there, as Lopez is both realistic (in that the portrait of him is detailed and plausible) and undeniably idealised (in that he displays no negative traits whatsoever). As with previous heroes of observational documentary, Lopez in *Être et avoir* is a representative figure, a signifier of more than what he immediately stands for, in this instance his role as a schoolteacher. His fundamental role is to represent a set of values and to evoke a way of life that is inherently old-fashioned and, in contemporary France, under threat. He is a representative, trusted adult whose traditional teaching methods are coupled with his pastoral responsibilities (the sequence in which Lopez talks to Olivier about his sick father is one of the most moving of the film), his relative strictness (making Jojo stay in during breaktime, for example, because he has failed to finish his colouring in) and his role as parental surrogate. When a prospective pupil comes to spend a few hours in the school, he starts to cry repeatedly for 'maman'; Lopez hugs him but in a perfunctory if tender way, soon making it plain that this is a moment of transition and that the boy has to adapt to a world without 'maman' there all the time.

The idealisation of Lopez stems from the compatibility of this portrayal of him with *Être et avoir*'s aesthetic values. The documentary's underpinning style is – in an era of reality television or *auteur*-fronted films – appropriately old-fashioned in its observational approach. There is no voice-over to tell the story or guide the spectator through (although Lopez's voice is used at times over shots from which he is absent); instead, Philibert constructs sequences through editing, such as in the film's linking sequences that indicate the changes in season. It is partly as a result of appreciating – and having appreciated, when it was first released – the simplicity and pastoral beauty of *Être et avoir*'s aesthetic sense that makes the viewing of this film now, after the court cases, a far more complex affair than it had been. It is because Lopez was so idealised and inhabited such an idyllic land-scape (*Être et avoir* makes its spectator fall in love with not just the implied mean-ing of the French arable landscape but the farmed land itself) that his subsequent actions have had such an impact. It is now impossible to view *Être et avoir* with-out being disappointed in Lopez and interpreting him as, at the very least, a con-tradictory figure. It is ironic that a film so preoccupied with innocence and the transition from innocence to experience (childhood → adulthood; being at home with 'maman' → going to school; leaving primary school → going to middle school; leaving a one-teacher classroom → becoming relatively anonymous in a multi-classroom school) should now have added another coupling to this binary opposition: that of Lopez pre- and post- his fall from grace. Even if his perform-ance in *Être et avoir* is not fraudulent (he was not pretending to be something he was not), Lopez's persona both within and outside the film is somewhat akin to a masquerade, as he offers and makes use of different ways of being himself, the dedicated teacher and the avaricious 'star' being the two obvious polarities. The post-release history of *Être et avoir* has permanently altered our previously inno-cent relationship to the film's nostalgia – its own depiction of innocence. Just as Lopez's presence has become performative in its complexity, with any notion of permanence and stability now being abandoned, so the documentary itself is ren-dered performative through the inherent instability of its rich images of innocence now seeming an equally unstable masquerade.

The Fog of War: eleven lessons from the life of Robert S. McNamara

Errol Morris's documentary about Robert McNamara (infamous for being Secretary for Defense under Presidents Kennedy and Johnson and so inextricably and negatively linked in the eyes of many to the Vietnam War) could not be more different in scope, tone and subject to *Être et avoir*. Whereas Philibert's film illus-trates audiences' enduring attraction to traditional documentaries, Morris's doc-umentary conversely exemplifies the more expressly contemporary nonfictional trends. Morris is an unmistakeable *auteur,* and many of the tropes used in *The Fog of War* are, by now, familiar and generic: the Philip Glass score (his 'angst-drone' as J. Hoberman unflatteringly puts it [Hoberman 2004: 21]), stylised dramatic reconstruction, the insertion of representative, expressive images and sequences that function as visual metaphors for the arguments of the film, the use of the 'Interrotron' for the interviews with McNamara.[2] A common view of Morris has become that he spends his time making immensely stylish films about lightweight figures and subjects (to quote Gary Indiana: 'Much of Morris's oeuvre to date ... has consisted of a geek's-eye view of subjects only slightly geekier than the director himself' [Indiana 2004]). This is only partially the case,[3] and *The Fog of War*, through its focus on McNamara, tackles particularly monumental, iconographic historical events: the firebombing of Tokyo and other Japanese cities in World War Two, the Cuban Missile Crisis, the Vietnam War. Morris's aim is consistently to marry individual testimony with historical events; as Nunn observes: 'He focuses frequently on individual memories and places these within a tapestry of archival, poetic and reconstructed scenes' (Nunn 2004: 415).

The Fog of War's production values are high and the moral, historical, political, intellectual and philosophical questions it poses are huge: what was McNamara's role in the Vietnam conflict? Following his involvement in the devastation of Japan during World War Two, should McNamara be considered a war criminal? How did Kennedy and Kruschev avert nuclear war in October 1962? The manifest sobriety of the film's subject matter notwithstanding, Morris's highly wrought and flashy visual style has, in the estimation of some critics, served to undermine rather than enhance his serious intentions, as if having directed so many successful commercials (his client list includes Nike, Apple, Southern Comfort, Citibank, Miller, Adidas, Volkswagen) somehow tarnishes his documentary status. This discussion will offer a largely more positive view of *The Fog of War*. For the most part it will argue – through a close examination of the film's analysis of recent American history and McNamara's place within it – that the immense visual pleasure the film affords its spectators is a vital component of the complex dialectical debates that inform the arguments around which the film is structured. However, in discussing the end of the film, this analysis will also assess how Morris's visual style contributes to a sense of McNamara being treated far too uncritically.

Dialectics inform *The Fog of War*, they are part of its formal and intellectual fabric. The fundamental dialectical collision, which underpins other subsidiary dialectical collisions, is between hindsight and presentness, that is between history negotiated after the event and history as it is being lived. McNamara, in undertaking the journey he outlines in *The Fog of War*, is reconciling two personal perspectives: the 'presentness' of living the events he much later is recounting for the benefit of Morris's camera. For some, *The Fog of War* is an elegant apologia; as J. Hoberman asks, however, 'Is *The Fog of War* a *mea culpa*? And if so, whose? Is it McNamara's apology or is it Morris' apology for McNamara?' (Hoberman 2004: 20). For Errol Morris (who at the time protested against the Vietnam War and McNamara's role in it) what he found in McNamara's 1995 autobiography *In Retrospect: The Tragedy and Lessons of Vietnam* – which he characterises not as a confessional apology but 'an attempt to go back into history and try to understand it' (Thomson 2004: 10) – is arguably what he has sought to replicate in *The Fog of War*. Morris interprets his subject as grappling with, trying to understand the historical moments he lived through and shaped; he is not overtly critical of McNamara, letting him talk largely unprompted and not proffering (as many articles on the film have done since [cf. Hoberman 2004; Kaplan 2003]) a counterview to the ones he puts forward. When the subject is one of the most controversial (and in many quarters reviled) figures of twentieth century US history, this becomes a meaningful and controversial choice, although an explicable one, if indeed Morris's intention, as it appears to be, is to centre *The Fog of War* on McNamara's reassessment of his own actions.[4]

The most important dialectical strand within this overarching structure is the collision between divergent histories: the view of history promulgated by McNamara and incompatible and opposing views of those same events voiced outside the film. For all the breadth of its historical scope *The Fog of War* is very much one man's view, as Morris interviews only McNamara – and illustrates only McNamara's words (he could conceivably have created an internal dialectic within the film between McNamara's words and the counterarguments to them, much as Emile de Antonio does in *Millhouse* or *In the Year of the Pig*). Just as it is now impossible to watch *Être et avoir* without recalling the legal battles between Lopez, the children's families and the film's producers, it is virtually impossible to view *The Fog of War* without recourse to alternative historical viewpoints. A problem for some critics is that such counterpoints to McNamara are not included within the documentary itself. J. Hoberman is unremittingly critical of *The Fog of War*, calling it 'important – as well as self-important' and surmising 'McNamara's bad teeth and liver spots notwithstanding, the beauty of *The Fog of War* is entirely skin deep' (Hoberman 2004: 21 and 22). Within his critique Hoberman also objects to McNamara's versions of events, in particular his suggestion that Kennedy was waiting until after the 1964 election to pull out of South Vietnam and that Johnson was to blame 'for the debacle' (p. 21). Even more devastating is Gary Indiana's hilarious condemnation of *The Fog of War* for *Artforum*, in which, after likening Morris's treatment of 'human oddities' to the work of painter Francis Bacon, he goes on:

> While Morris's visual sense is rather quotidian and hardly as exalted as Bacon's iconic genius, he has a definite flair for turning humans into talking sea cucumbers obsessed with philosophical or historical matters clearly beyond their intelligence. That they also seem beyond the director's intelligence accounts for the quirky hilarity that rescues much of Morris's work from being taken seriously.

Indiana concludes his attack by observing that 'throughout *The Fog of War* it's abundantly clear that McNamara remains, on the cusp of senescence, incapable of feeling much culpability about anything' (Indiana 2004).

Other articles, like Hoberman's, go into more detail on the issue of McNamara's lack of introspection and self-criticism and Morris's concomitant lack of trenchant, critical historical investigation. In an article reproduced on Errol Morris's official website (www.errolmorris.com) Fred Kaplan takes exception to the manner in which *The Fog of War* characterises the ultimately peaceful conclusion to the Cuban Missile Crisis. McNamara recounts (as has been known for a while) that Nikita Kruschev sent Kennedy two telegrams, the first offering to remove his missiles from Cuba if the US agreed never to invade, the second saying he would remove the missiles if the US removed its missiles from Turkey. Kaplan accuses McNamara of still propagating the myth that Kennedy 'accepted the first telegram and simply ignored the second' despite having gone on record, some twenty years after the crisis, saying that he knew that 'in fact, Kennedy acceded to the missile trade' (Kaplan 2003). Kaplan identifies two further 'falsehoods' in McNamara's account: first, the content of the second telegram (in the film he remains vague about what it said) and second that former US ambassador to the Soviet Union Llewellyn 'Tommy' Thompson was the one to persuade Kennedy 'to resolve the crisis through diplomacy, not force'. Kaplan argues: 'This too is misleading. A full hearing of the tapes indicates that Kennedy didn't need anybody to steer him toward negotiation … McNamara tries to paint himself as no less dovish than Kennedy on dealing with the Russians. Yet, as he must know on some level, the opposite was true' (Kaplan 2003).

It is, however, possible and valid to argue that what is present in *The Fog of War* is McNamara's implied internal struggle between what he knows he did and what he would like to be remembered for having thought, though not done (his evasiveness at the end of the film when questioned directly about his culpability, for example). The tension created by McNamara's refusal to engage in any meaningful analysis of the image he has constructed of himself is permitted to surface, even if only incidentally. In McNamara's tears when insisting that his years as Secretary of Defense 'were some of the best years of our lives and *all* members of my family benefited from it'[5] – we sense that he or some member(s) of his family were close to breakdown, and indeed Hoberman attests that Lyndon Johnson in part relieved McNamara of his duties (whether McNamara was sacked or resigned is never entirely clear) because he thought he was 'close to a nervous breakdown' (Hoberman 2004: 22). This might not resonate with the guilt Indiana would like McNamara to have displayed, although it is a fleeting recognition of the personal suffering his actions caused. As with many documentary subjects (in this instance the life and culpability of Robert McNamara), alternative, conflicting interpretations of that subject exist, all possessing a degree of plausibility and credibility. The readings of McNamara's political career offered by Indiana, Hoberman or Kaplan are all convinced of their own validity and largely convincing to those who encounter them; however, what Morris indicates – and indeed constructs a metaphor for with the very style of *The Fog of War* – is that truth is fragmentary and too multifarious to be treated or presented linearly. Coupled with this, there is the additional problem that the idiosyncrasies of Morris's *mise-en-scène*, the flamboyance of his trademark audiovisual style seems automatically to persuade critics that his films, because they are far removed from the realist aesthetic of much documentary, have disengaged from reality itself and are thereby fabrications rather than verifiable renditions of the truth.

In Morris's film Hoberman finds not only 'tabloid sensationalism' and 'lofty detachment' but also 'moral equivocation' (Hoberman 2004: 21); it seems fair to guess that Hoberman, like Indiana, responds negatively to Morris's film-making style. Any documentary filmmaker who prioritises style as well as content (not necessarily style *over* content) is still readily damned, as if a distinctive and non-realist *mise-en-scène* by its very nature obscures, even represses reality. The tabloid portion of Hoberman's critique is probably referring to images such as the creative graphic sequence in which numbers superimposed onto aerial black and white archive footage of the firebombing of Japan during World War Two fall like bombs towards the ground. In interview Morris has professed to being particularly proud of this sequence:

> I love the falling numbers over Japan, the whole sequence of the firebomb-ing of Japan. And McNamara is telling you a very, very, *very* powerful story, a very important story. But I like to think that it's been communicated visu-ally. The voice-over, the visuals combine in a way that a story is told. History can easily become overburdened by details. And so, in telling history, you have to chart a course through a morass of material. You have to tell a story, and you have to communicate the story powerfully.
>
> (Cunningham 2005: 60)

This comment gives both the essence of Morris's style and the likely reason for people not liking *The Fog of War*. Morris does not want simply to convey a story verbally or through purely illustrative archive material; he uses reconstruction, computer graphics and traditionally cinematic techniques such as intricate light-ing and an intrusive, repetitive score to create an evocative synthesis of what he considers his overall story to be. Morris's documentaries offer his spectator immense visual pleasure. However, his critics would argue that such sumptuous-ness diverts attention from the films' superficiality (as Hoberman says: the beauty of *The Fog of War* is 'skin deep'), Morris serving their cause well by making remarks such as 'History can easily become overburdened by details', as if the aesthetically pleasing conjunction of visual and historical material takes automatic priority over detail. Another feature of *The Fog of War* that makes it especially vulnerable to such attacks is the use of the 'eleven lessons'. These are Morris's lessons (another attempt at helpful synthesis?) not McNamara's, as the latter has stated,[6] and they help to divide up – appearing as intertitles – the otherwise sprawling and unchronological subject matter. As Indiana rails, the eleven lessons 'range from clichés as old as von Clausewitz ... to specious dicta ... to secular mysticism ... to corporate-training-manual exhortations' (Indiana 2004). The 'lesson' that introduces the firebombing sequence ('Maximize Efficiency') Indiana places within the final category.

McNamara, under the command of General Curtis LeMay, was used as a number-cruncher: he was part of the team who calculated the impact of LeMay's daily airstrikes, creating tables to analyse each operation's success rate in order to make future missions more efficient. The graphic showing the numbers tumbling through the night skies is directly illustrative of McNamara's role (McNamara says that he does not want to think that his reports were the reason for the decimation of Tokyo, but the sequence apportions some blame to him); it also serves as a shorthand assimilation of McNamara's attitude to and portrayal of LeMay as obsessed by target destruction over and above anything else. When then such a sequence leads into archive showing fires raging and demonstrating the aftermath of the attacks (Tokyo looks like Hiroshima) it becomes clear that the tabloidish simplification of the numbers graphics are but one component of a more complex and 'serious' argument involving bombing and numbers. One conclusion could be that LeMay became convinced of the efficacy of firebombing after looking at the tables prepared by McNamara and colleagues, the numbers prompting him to order more attacks.

As he then details the extent of the firebombing raids (over numerous Japanese cities) and the extent of the damage on the ground to each city, McNamara goes on to draw parallels between these targets and comparably sized American cities as a means of evoking the scale of these raids and making the impact of them relevant to his home audience. Another graphic sequence begins in which, over similar aerial archive footage of a devastated Japanese landscape, percentage figures indicating the portion of the city destroyed in each raid, accompanied by the name of a city in the US, which then fades and is replaced by the name of the Japanese city that was actually hit. The series of names and figures speed up and the sequence culminates in McNamara making the observation that 'proportionality should be a guideline of war'. The lack of proportionality described by McNamara and the accompanying images underlines his contention that, although it was the dropping of the Atom bombs on Hiroshima and Nagasaki that effectively ended the war, Japan had already been devastated in 'one of the most brutal wars in history'. This World War Two portion of *The Fog of War* draws to a close with McNamara recounting how LeMay had said to him after the war's end that what they had done was immoral and that, had America lost the war, they would have been prosecuted as war criminals. McNamara's concluding interrogatory is one of a series of questions that (interestingly or irritatingly, depending on your point of view) are left hanging in the air. He asks: what makes it immoral if you lose but not if you win? He is looking directly into the camera, even more intently than usual via the Interrotron, but then the sequence ends, to be replaced by the beginning of the section about America's involvement in Indochina. McNamara almost succeeds in deflecting attention from himself with his belligerent stare, daring Morris and us to respond. This daring, however, is topped by a subtle camera move by cinematographer Bob Chappell as he continues a 'snail-paced zoom and slight Dutch (tilt)' (Davis 2004: 30) into McNamara's face, a move which effectively reverses the scrutinising look to probe McNamara instead. Is this final stand-off insufficiently penetrating in its targeting of McNamara? In that *The Fog of War* never gets a confession of guilt out of McNamara, perhaps, but in that this mutual stare more or less explicitly affirms that both we and McNamara cannot but think that he and LeMay were, but for the Japanese surrender, war criminals it is enough.

Clearly for many there is a fundamental discordance in *The Fog of War* between the weightiness of the subject matter and the inventiveness of its *mise-en-scène*. Is it too much to suggest that this collision between subject and visual style is maybe an intentional dialectic? Throughout the Vietnam sections, for example, Morris uses, on several occasions, lines of dominoes falling to denote the disastrous 'domino-effect' of Johnson's escalation of the Vietnam War. This visual metaphor is striking in its obviousness, but it functions on various levels, not least a narrative one as a means of linking the two sections on Vietnam, which are interrupted by a long chunk of McNamara discussing the immediate postwar period and his time at Ford. The dominoes' final appearance comes as McNamara comments that historians are not fond of talking about what might have been, at which point the undulating lines of flattened dominoes go into reverse and rise up. Shot in extreme close-up these sequences are memorable in their beauty, especially on the big screen, on which their tactile roundedness, the grain in their discoloured ivory and their weight are emphasised. What, though, do these dominoes signify? At the most basic level they represent the 'domino effect' (or chaos theory), namely that one action, if the wrong one, can lead to another and then to another until events get out of control. If this is all they mean, then the tumbling dominoes are a crass metaphor indeed. Their extraordinary lusciousness and old-fashionedness are richly suggestive of other things: the lives of the men lost in that futile war, the realisation that the US could never return to a pre-Vietnam state of consciousness, the inability of successive American elder statesmen, McNamara included, to think through the consequences of their actions and pronouncements until it is too late. They also make one wonder what might have become of McNamara had he not left his position as President of Ford Motor Company (a position he assumed 9 November 1960, the day after Kennedy was elected) to become Secretary of Defense.

Most plausibly the dominoes are intended to work on the spectator of *The Fog of War* on a primal, emotional level – to make us feel again (as McNamara and Morris are living again) the panic and dread of the Vietnam period. Such a basic gut response to documentary is rare, and it links Morris's work more readily to mainstream fiction films. Another point at which the physical response takes precedence over the intellectual response is during 'Lesson #6: Get the Data' as McNamara talks about his pioneering research at Ford Motors into safety features such as seat belts. Again the actual and the metaphoric are linked: McNamara talks about the experiments he and his scientist colleagues ran at Cornell University, dropping eggs in boxes and swaddled human skulls down flights of stairs to test the theory that, in order to save lives on the road, car drivers and passengers needed to be appropriately and sufficiently packaged. Illustrative of this, there is a generically inevitable series of lyrical, slow motion shots of old-fashioned egg boxes and skulls wrapped in creamy bandages falling through the well of a traditional, highly polished spiralling staircase. Eggs ooze and skulls splinter in a sequence that is both amusing and chilling in its literalness. The punchline is, of course, that even after the introduction of seat belts, people refused to use them until they became mandatory.

It is, as argued earlier, the very sumptuousness of Morris's visual style that lays *The Fog of War* open to charges of evasiveness and letting its subject off the hook. *The Fog of War*'s grandiose elegance renders what McNamara is talking about strange and distant as opposed to relevant and immediate (despite, as many critics at the time of its release noted, the obvious parallels with Donald Rumsfeld and the second Iraq War); it also creates around McNamara himself an aura of gravitas, an elegance and ease that he lacked whilst living the events under discussion. Beyond their relationship to the words of McNamara, *The Fog of War*'s reconstructions are also illustrative of the film's attitudes to its documentary roots, namely Morris's persistent distrust, as evidenced by all his films, in any notion of a fixed truth, exemplified in *The Fog of War* by his repeated use of dual exposure, the superimposition of one image on another to create an instantaneous dialectic through collage. The beauty of many of these reconstructions is a means (as the film's harshest critics characterise it) of eliding and masking the true brutality of McNamara and the history he is trying to rewrite, but it also functions as a visual counterpoint and thus a means of accentuating that brutality. Just as the filmic elegance of the skulls floating past the Cornell staircase cannot disguise the potential gruesomeness of a fatal car crash, so the falling dominoes emphasise both McNamara's evasiveness and the shameful violence of Vietnam. One is reminded of Claude Lanzmann's protestation that we have become immune to the impact of Holocaust archive; it is not only through the faithful re-use of familiar war images that Vietnam can be accurately evoked. At its best, Morris's amalgam of archive and reconstruction in *The Fog of War* compels the spectator to look at even familiar images differently.

At the film's heart, however, is Morris's ambivalent attitude towards McNamara, whose policies he protested against at the time but whom he clearly came to like and respect over the course of filming his eight hours of interview with him. McNamara's life was monumental and the film's style clearly reflects its importance, although it could be argued that to reflect McNamara's importance in this way is to abdicate responsibility for critiquing it. The film's very style lends a homogeneity to McNamara's life, drawing otherwise heterogeneous strands together to offer a not totally convincing portrait of an intelligent, ruthless but in old age humane man who is tortured if not by guilt then by not fully knowing the extent to which he could have done things differently in the past. If one contrasts *The Fog of War* with *Millhouse: A White Comedy* (discussed in Chapter Five), then the ultimately unsatisfying evasiveness of Morris's style becomes apparent. Each tells the story of a significant and vilified American political figure, but whereas the rawness of de Antonio's 'collage junk' style (the archive he uses is unaltered and often rather poor quality) fails to elide the fragmentariness and ugliness of Nixon's career, Morris's smooth rendition of McNamara's life makes the unsatisfactory ellipses in that rendition fall away, repressed by the consistency of *The Fog of War*'s tone and look. Although, as Morris attests, 'If you were trying to make a movie about the twentieth century in some oddball fashion … you could do no better than to create a profile of this man' (Cunningham 2005: 61), *The Fog of War* leaves us with little definitive sense of McNamara. There is a tangible sense that Morris does not want to push this octogenarian further than he wishes to go, and so it is left to McNamara to define the parameters of the film's representation of him. There is an equally strong sense, though, that in its foginess, in its decision not to push McNamara, *The Fog of War* is criticising McNamara's evasiveness.

Nowhere is this duality clearer than in the Epilogue, which films McNamara for the only time without the use of the Interrotron, although the interview we hear is from another time, this being again the only time this documentary convention of overlaying an interviewee's voice over them doing something else is used. McNamara, in the most conventional set up of the entire film, is at the wheel of his car. The atypical dislocation between image and sound is important here as it compels us to look at McNamara more closely and not merely listen to his words. He is being scrutinised via a series of reflective surfaces – his spectacles, the windscreens and the rear-view mirror – as Morris is heard to put to him the most important questions of all: Why did he not speak out against the war once he had left the Johnson administration? Does he feel responsible or guilty? As McNamara on the screen stares inscrutably at the road, we hear his refusal to answer either question directly,[7] although the use of the rear-view mirror particularly and some bizarre framing (at one point the lower part of McNamara's face slumps out of shot) underlines his evasiveness and our growing frustration with it. Rather than nailing him (this old man driving a car seems much more vulnerable than the magisterial presence in the specially lit studio) Morris feeds McNamara his lifeline. It is also intriguing that this most conventional of sequences reveals some of the limitations of Morris's meticulously orchestrated method – that had he done a more conventional interview with McNamara, he might have caught him off guard, less closed and self-preserving. After McNamara has reiterated that he does not want to say anything further about Vietnam, Morris asks his subject 'Is it a feeling that you're damned if you do (speak) and if you don't?' McNamara seizes on this, his face perks up and his voice is far more upbeat as he agrees, then adding the final smooth and witty reply 'I'd rather be damned if I don't'. This is a disastrous place to end, as this Epilogue undoes any previous subtle attempts to put McNamara's limited self-scrutiny into a broader, more critical perspective. Like Richard Nixon at the end of Oliver Stone's film, McNamara here suddenly becomes the fatally flawed but fundamentally endearing elder statesman, the closing titles (again reminiscent of *Nixon*) spelling out McNamara's achievements after Vietnam, such as his presidency of the World Bank from 1968–81. We are left with the sense that Morris colludes with McNamara's desire to absolve himself. What one person says about themselves is notoriously untrustworthy – as Morris indicated *par excellence* in *The Thin Blue Line* and elsewhere in *The Fog of War*.

Capturing the Friedmans

Personal testimony, however, is certainly not the only truth, nor, if some of the reviews of *Capturing the Friedmans* are anything to go by, are personal testimony and truth even consistently or reliably related. Andrew Jarecki's *Capturing the Friedmans* is almost entirely based on conflicting personal confessions. It tells the story of a middle-class Long Island family which, in the mid-1980s, was torn apart by the convictions of father Arnold and youngest son Jessie on several counts of child abuse. Most members of the family have always protested their innocence, and some of the evidence against Arnold and Jessie does seem flimsy: testimonies from some former pupils in their computer class who, under hypnosis, found themselves remembering repeated episodes of abuse they had hitherto repressed; testimonies extracted by police officers over-eager, the film implies, to find the two members of the Friedman family guilty. Arnie killed himself in prison in 1995 whilst Jessie served 13 of his 18-year sentence and was released on 7 December 2001. An interesting but significant aside to *Capturing the Friedmans* is that Jarecki (co-founder of the phone service and Internet site *Moviefone*, which was sold to AOL for \$388 million) had started out making a documentary about professional birthday party clowns in which eldest son David Friedman featured (as the top New York clown 'Silly Billy'). It was only after David had revealed to Jarecki some of his family's hidden history – and also told him of the existence of years of family home movie footage, shot by himself (latterly) and his father – that he embarked on *Capturing the Friedmans*, which took three years to make. Not unlike Errol Morris's films, *Capturing the Friedmans* poses several questions that it does not, in the end, answer, and one of these is David wondering whether or not the revelations about his family would ruin his career (in interviews given after the film's release he maintains that it did not prove damaging [see Farndale 2004: 25]).

Stylistically, the similarities with *The Fog of War* are few; however, several reviewers likened *Capturing the Friedmans* to Morris's documentaries. Xan Brooks in *Sight and Sound* classifies Jarecki's film as 'coloured by the influence of Errol Morris in its gallery of oddballs and its teasing lack of judgement' (Brooks 2004: 41) and Michael Atkinson in *The Village Voice* comments that Jarecki proves himself 'Morris-like' in his decision to let 'the asinine authorities talk until they've buried themselves in righteous dung' (2003).[8] Paul Arthur remarks about the film (in a similar though more measured vein to Gary Indiana when criticising *The Fog of War*) that it 'floats an unusual number of particularly meaty themes' which it never sets out to resolve, instead leaving it up to the viewer 'to think about particular issues far in excess of *Capturing the Friedmans'* ability to develop them' (Arthur 2003b: 6). Arthur goes beyond the comparisons with Morris as he posits:

> Jarecki, like [Michael] Moore and Steve James and a dozen other 'cutting edge' documentary practitioners, traffics in grossly manipulative dramatic structures and effects of a kind usually associated with classical Hollywood and not seen in the ranks of nonfiction since the days of Robert Flaherty's *Man of Aran* (1934) and *Louisiana Story* (1948) … the line from, say, *Roger and Me* (1989) through *Hoop Dreams* (1994) to *Spellbound,* is an accelerating arc of dramatic liberties and expressive 'distortions' of actuality.
> (Arthur 2003b: 5)

Although Arthur finds 'nothing inherently wrong with this approach' he argues that the style is little more than a 'confluence of certain formal prerogatives' that go some way towards explaining the recent surge in documentary's popularity (p. 5). A fundamental difference between *Capturing the Friedmans* or other recent documentaries and *Man of Aran*, however, is that Jarecki has used 'manipulative' dramatic techniques out of choice whilst Flaherty did, at least in part, out of necessity. Neither Morris in *The Fog of War* nor Jarecki in *Capturing the Friedmans* suggests that documentary's role is to be conclusive or to offer answers to questions posed, either via filmmakers' interventions (for example voice-over) or through the opinions of subjects interviewed for either film. Despite Arthur's identification of a homogeneity amongst recent successful theatrical release documentaries, a film such as *Capturing the Friedmans* is the opposite, in this respect, to Michael Moore's polemical films, which put forward a stridently defined (some might add simplistic) argument and viewpoint.

In his article, Arthur offers a précis of several critical responses to *Capturing the Friedmans*, and what is interesting here is the manner in which the documentary's moral elusiveness (that Jarecki never feels compelled to even obliquely state as Morris does via the tensions within his *mise-en-scène* in *The Fog of War*, what his opinions of his subjects are) is used as evidence of both the film's failure and of its success (see Arthur 2003b: 7). Roger Ebert opens his review by recounting how, when asked after the Sundance screenings of *Capturing the Friedmans* whether or not he thought Arnold Friedman was guilty of child molestation, Jarecki replied that he did not know. Ebert goes on: 'Neither does the viewer of this film', concluding his positive review with the thought that 'The film is an instructive lesson about the elusiveness of facts' (Ebert 2003). Another critic to view the film's ambivalence as constructive is James Berardinelli who ends his review by implicating us all in the Friedmans' plight:

> In the end, while Jarecki may not be able to answer our most basic questions about the guilt or innocence of the Friedmans, he makes a profound statement that, in situations like this, no one can be completely innocent and everyone is a victim.
>
> (2003)

This is more of a rhetorical flourish than a logical statement and, as Arthur counters after quoting likeminded reviews: 'Frankly, I'm not sure how or why my spectatorship implicates me in the cycle of mutually-enhancing exploitation engaged in by Jarecki and his eager (or reluctant, it hardly matters) cast of characters' (Arthur 2003b: 7). The elusiveness of *Capturing the Friedmans* apparently gives license to several reviewers to enjoy dabbling in unspecificity themselves. Michael Atkinson's review culminates, for example, in the nonsensical assertion:

> The glibbest way to read *Capturing the Friedmans* is as a *Blue Velvet*-y exposé of suburban turmoil. But paedophilia ends up being merely the

Macguffin; the authentic tragedy here, so honestly and sublimely manifested, is the damage inflicted upon love by natural and unnatural forces'.

(Atkinson 2003)

By sleight of hand Atkinson here dispenses with the really problematic subject of
Capturing the Friedmans, namely paedophilia, by relegating it to the status of a
Macguffin, a distracting, inconsequential red herring. This move is deeply
morally dubious. Atkinson then goes on to suggest that the film's 'authentic
tragedy' is something so woolly as to be irrelevant in itself.

Capturing the Friedmans is a fascinating but equivocal and evasive film and in
its treatment of its subject it is not surprising that it elicits such enthusiastic
though meaningless critiques as Atkinson's cited above. On certain issues the
film is categorical (Jarecki clearly sides with David, for instance, in its marginalisation and criticism of his mother Elaine) whilst on others it is wilfully nebulous
(Arnold's guilt or otherwise, what David knew, how the police conducted their
enquiries etc). Jarecki acknowledged the difficulty of working with this material
when he compares the making of *Capturing the Friedmans* to 'unraveling different aspects of [a] mystery' (Fairweather 2003: 8). He then develops this notion
of mystery solving when he says 'I found that there were many smart, articulate
people willing to talk to me, but the amazing thing was that none of these smart
people could agree on anything. So it fell to me to try to develop the truest story
I could' (p. 6). The 'truest story', in terms of how Jarecki packages and presents
it, turns out to be an inconclusive one; as the director subsequently comments,
the making of *Capturing the Friedmans* 'demonstrated for me, in the most direct
way, the elusive nature of truth' (p. 9). In a film about a subject as challenging
as this, however, for the director not to attempt a greater unravelling of the mys-
teries of truth is frustrating. Like Errol Morris with Robert S. McNamara, there
is a strong suspicion that Andrew Jarecki ultimately decides to let his interviewees off the hook – or at least not to probe their inconsistencies, prejudices and
maybe even lies. 'One thing I realised early on is that memory is totally dynamic'
Jarecki surmises; he then continues:

> I also felt that while not everyone in the film tells the truth, I don't find
> most of them to be consciously lying about anything. They are adjusting
> their memory at the same time they are adjusting their story. So when the
> police detective in this story tells me something, and we see a photograph a
> moment later disproving what she says, I don't think it means she was delib-
> erately trying to mislead me. Or at least that's not how she would see it.

(Fairweather 2003: 9)

This is an extraordinary statement from a documentary filmmaker who has made
a film that touches on subjects as momentous as paedophilia and possible miscar-
riages of justice; extraordinary precisely because Jarecki does not (as Morris does
in *The Thin Blue Line,* for instance) confront the complex fallibilities of human
memory within the film itself, but rather glosses over moments when this fallibil-

ity is uncomfortably in evidence. It is morally as well as practically easier not to take sides in such a case, but Jarecki's non-judgemental attitude sometimes seems naïve or fraudulent in itself. On the subject of the documentary's handling of the police, it seems fairly clear from the way in which sequences are edited that Jarecki believes they were, if not liars, then over-eager to find evidence to condemn Arnold and Jessie Friedman. At no time, however, does he push them on this; nor does he construct sequences as I argue Morris does in *The Fog of War* that formally raise questions about his subjects' possible culpability.

As a means of addressing some of these issues, this discussion will now focus on how archival material is used in *Capturing the Friedmans* and the way in which authorial attitudes are implied. One thing that is notable and odd about the Friedmans is that so much of the family's history has been recorded for posterity on film and video. First Arnold and then David were the obsessive family archivists, although it becomes apparent from the presence of footage of Arnold's dead sister dancing as a child that the capturing of family moments on film is a long-standing Friedman tradition. This need to capture events on film and video (and the 'Capturing' of the documentary's title is, most likely, intentionally ironic) is compulsive and perhaps an avoidance mechanism. Early on Elaine Friedman recounts how the cops, after having searched Arnold's study, showed her some of the pornography they had found: 'And you know, I didn't see it. My eyes were in the right direction, but my brain saw nothing'. Later the lawyers showed Elaine the same material and this time she did see it and was shocked, remembering: 'I couldn't believe what I saw'. The same superficiality and innocence, of looking but not seeing could be attributed to the home movie footage. This is particularly the case with the material David shot of Arnold after he was, following six months in jail, allowed home to prepare for his and Jessie's trial and before he begins serving his sentence. On the night before the latter, David videos Arnold dancing with his sons and giving a flamboyant rendition of 'I'm in Heaven' on the piano. The perversity, in this context, of Arnold's forced joviality is more than stoical gallows humour and Jarecki's editing of this sequence is an avoidance tactic of its own. The image of Arnold Friedman acting up to the camera amidst sequences showing his family falling apart, the sons turning on their mother and Elaine revealing that her husband has confessed to two acts of child molestation not just one is illustrative not merely of Arnold's public denial of the impact on him of the charges but of Jarecki's equally significant refusal to make known what he thinks happened. Jarecki, arguably like Arnie Friedman, is letting the home movie footage – because it is so overwhelming and elusive at the same time – mask his own prevarication.

The family archive material is so compelling because it is so far removed from the grim story *Capturing the Friedmans* tells, a duality emphasised by Jarecki as he juxtaposes Elaine's comment 'I had a good family, right? ... Where did this [Arnold's child pornography] come from?' with a happy family snapshot (reproduced for much of the pre-publicity material with Elaine looking over at Arnold and David as they smile for the camera) and some home movie of a Thanksgiving celebration. *Capturing the Friedmans* is performative in the least complicated, most accessible way in that it revels in, at every turn, the critical conundrum: we can never know the 'real' person or family history or truth. Jarecki is not interested in deciding whether he thinks Arnold and/or Jessie Friedman were guilty of the crimes they were charged with; he is not even ostensibly interested – despite the comparisons made between *Capturing the Friedmans* and the films of Errol Morris – in endlessly reworking and re-examining the alternative perspectives on a case. What *Capturing the Friedmans* does is present rather than analyse various levels of performance and suggest, via their endless juxtaposition, that truth is an elusive thing.

The Friedman family members offer two primary levels of performance: to each other in their home movies and to Jarecki in interview. Why the film makes its spectator feel uncomfortable much of the time is that the dynamic relationship created by the normative documentary between an individual talking about themselves and being filmed doing something which approximates being themselves is here almost entirely absent – except for the scene during the Epilogue when Elaine is waiting to be reunited with Jessie, who has just been released from prison, a scene that stands out as humane and straightforward in an otherwise manic and heightened world. The Friedmans experience their past lives not via memory but via film and video footage; this makes even the past feel like a perpetual present, as past actions are always there to see, always available to be endlessly replayed. Because the Friedmans have committed so much to film and tape, it is as if the act of memorising has been bypassed. When asked by Jarecki in interview about his memories of the last night before Jessie was due to enter his plea (of guilty), David comments that he does not remember that night beyond what is committed to tape – a filmed video diary in which he is seen crying and admitting 'I'm so scared', then footage of an argument between Elaine and the boys. These tapes are the Friedmans' memories, and only Elaine (when she tells David she does not want to be filmed) objects to the ever-present camera. Jarecki constructs a documentary around the reams of home movie footage that echo this dislocation between memory and past action; as Arthur notes 'In terms of structure, *Capturing the Friedmans* doles out its information in a manner intended to build suspense and provide "shocking" revelations' (2003b: 6). As instances of this tactic Arthur identifies the withholding of Arnold's suicide whilst in prison until relatively late (as he asks: does knowledge of this suicide 'influence our final assessment of his guilt or innocence?' [p. 6]) and the very late revelation that Arnold's brother Howard is gay. For Arthur the latter suggests that Howard's 'ardent defense of Arnold is somehow related to his sexual orientation' (p. 6). Just as home movies only give their audiences snatches of family life and are incapable of ultimately revealing either what happens in between or how the home movie relates to what happens in between, so *Capturing the Friedmans* is fragmentary – intrigued by the act of performance rather than its revelations.

The other level on which the Friedmans perform is in interview to Jarecki. Two members stand out in terms of how they use and are presented in these situations: David and Elaine. The former uses his interviews with Jarecki to continue his diatribe against Elaine, a mother whom he hates and blames for having deserted her husband in his hour of need. David's belief is that Elaine violated the rules of marriage when she divorced Arnold after his conviction; he also maintains that she was sexually ignorant, a view backed up by Howard who mentions that Elaine 'had her problems'. In the context of a film about paedophilia and alleged child abuse the defence on camera – that is, in the very public domain – of Arnold, the alleged abuser and self-confessed paedophile, for his relative sexual maturity is complicated; that these comments are made by his eldest son and his brother (whom Arnold told Elaine he had abused) is staggering. There is a lack of self-analysis in David, just as there is a lack of analytical questioning from Jarecki. Against David's allegations about Elaine Jarecki posits Elaine's version: that Arnold treated sex like work and bypassed foreplay, that 'there was really nothing between us except these children that he yelled at'. About Arnie's child pornography Elaine muses 'He just wanted to look at these pictures and ... meditate, or ...'. It seems that every member of the Friedman family is in denial of some sort, and that *Capturing the Friedmans* refuses to probe their lack of introspection. *Capturing the Friedmans* is kaleidoscopic in that it deals in fragments of home movie turns, interviews, newsreels, but like a kaleidoscope the individual pieces make interesting shapes but shapes that in the end do not create a distinct overall form and, most importantly, lack argument and meaning. This is the nature of memory and amateur film, perhaps. In another documentary to have come out recently – Jonathan Caouette's *Tarnation* (2004) – there is a more extreme use of home movie footage as Caouette pieces together his cruel and disturbed upbringing and charts his relationship with his schizophrenic mother. *Tarnation,* however, is autobiographical and is aesthetically cogent and cohesive in its evocation of mental illness, depression and individuation through frenzied juxtaposition of snippets of home movies Jonathan has been shooting obsessively throughout his life. The various family members in both *Tarnation* and *Capturing the Friedmans* (except for Elaine who, at one point, tells David she no longer wants to be filmed) are more relaxed with the camera than with each other; performing for each other or in the case of *Capturing the Friedmans* the director is easier than relating to each other. This dysfunctionalism, though, is inherent to the subject matter of *Tarnation,* and Caouette's autobiography is tangibly therapeutic.[9]

With every frenetically edited sequence *Tarnation* illustrates the vulnerability of memory and the vulnerability of the individual whose memories are made up of an endless stream of consciousness spew of undigested movie footage. As in *Capturing the Friedmans,* several inconsistencies and differences are left unresolved, for example that Caouette's grandparents (who effectively brought him up) first decided to start Renee, his mother, on a programme of ECT after an accident but are later declared, by Caouette, to be insane themselves. The elusiveness of *Tarnation* is excusable as the film is entirely and overtly from one autobiographical point of view; the elusiveness of *Capturing the Friedmans* is more problematic. When Paul Arthur identifies Jarecki's predilection for creating suspense he is pinpointing the reasons for *Capturing the Friedmans* being for the viewer frustrating: it makes us want to discover what the truth about Arnold and Jessie is, while at the same time telling us – through its non-analytical and judgemental tendency – that we shall never know and that not knowing and concomitantly the slipperiness of truth are conceptually interesting ends in themselves. Why Nick Broomfield's *Tracking Down Maggie* does not work is ultimately that Broomfield, who specialises in the imploding, near-failing documentary, never gets close to interviewing Margaret Thatcher; even the last vestige of the traditional documentary is missing. Conversely, why *The Thin Blue Line* was so notable and influential was that it offered both a discursive examination of the unreliability of memory or the mutability of truth as well as a clinching, revelatory finale as David Harris confesses on tape to the murder Randall Adams has hitherto been imprisoned for.

Although the rawness of *Tarnation* is more of an assault on the spectator's senses (the chaotic speed of some of the sequences, the mix of words on the screen and images, the loud musical accompaniment), *Capturing the Friedmans* is a more saccharine viewing experience. The problem lies in its moral elusiveness, in Jarecki's coupling of voyeurism and detachment – that we are invited to gawp at the Friedmans and intrude upon their lives whilst simultaneously being distanced from them by feeling compelled to agree with the film's overall stance of 'we will never know the truth' as Howard puts it towards the end. The whole film makes us feel uncomfortable with proffering an opinion on the evidence, and although Jarecki at heart arguably sides with the Friedmans, this is never made explicit. We respond ambivalently to both sides – the family on one hand and the cops and legal authorities on the other – and to side with either one or the other would be obliquely to acknowledge our own perversity on some level, because *Capturing the Friedmans* makes the act of wanting to discover the truth a perverse pursuit in itself.

Touching the Void

Kevin Macdonald's film about the first successful – but near-fatal – scaling of Siula Grande in the Peruvian Andes in 1985 by Joe Simpson and Simon Yates is thematically at least a simpler film than *Capturing the Friedmans*. Simpson and Yates got to the summit of Siula Grande but, during the descent, Simpson broke one leg. Yates then tried to lower Simpson down the mountain using a rope, but when during a blizzard Simpson plunged into a crevasse, he realised that either they would both die or he had to cut the rope between them and save himself. Yates decided upon the latter, a decision that later meant his ostracisation in certain mountaineering circles but one which Simpson has always maintained was sensible and logical (as Yates recounts at the end of *Touching the Void*, the first thing Simpson said to him when they were finally reunited was 'I'd have done the same'). Simpson survived the fall into the crevasse (and again Yates was criticised for not checking the crevasse before leaving his partner for dead) and the latter part of *Touching the Void* tells the story of his tenacious, brave descent of Siula Grande to safety. The film uses the title of Simpson's successful book about the climb, but unlike its predecessor it juxtaposes Simpson's account with the words of Yates and Richard Hawking who was left to look after base camp as well as with self-consciously beautiful, awesome shots of Siula Grande. On the DVD of *Touching the Void* is the short film *Return to Siula Grande* which shows the climbers returning to the mountain for the first time since their dramatic ascent of 1985. This could have formed the basis for a more straightforward rendition of Simpson and Yates' story as Macdonald includes in this accompanying documentary Simpson's explicit fear of returning to the site of the accident that 'defined my life', for instance, or Yates' own misgivings about going back. Instead *Touching the Void* is a detailed and poetically cinematic account of the climbers' ascent and descent; as one review stated: 'Macdonald shrewdly perceives that we need to know little about these two men beyond their reactions to the situation' (Falcon 2004: 35). What Falcon says earlier in his review about *Touching the Void* being similar to reality television and predecessors such as *Rescue 999* in its placement of dramatic reconstruction alongside specially shot to-camera interviews with the protagonists is also true, although Macdonald creates from these conventionally prosaic, pedestrian techniques 'unprecedented levels of cinematic spectacle' (p. 34).

Particularly Joe Simpson, as he describes at the beginning of *Touching the Void* how climbing is a blend of 'ballet and gymnastics' giving the climber a sense of 'power and space', conveys the euphoria associated with successful climbing; not just that it is 'great fun' as Simpson again says in the pre-credit sequence, but that it is an experience of magnitude, life-changing. An indispensable component of the drama that, at the outset, *Touching the Void* establishes is the contrast between men and mountains: the awesomeness of the latter temporarily controlled by the pluck, skill and good luck of the former. *Touching the Void* is a straightforward documentary if compared, for example, to *The Fog of War,* which takes more chances aesthetically and stylistically; it is also a far more emotive film than the films discussed so far in this chapter bar *Être et avoir,* although the emotion generated there is cute, even saccharine as opposed to heightened and nearly tragic. The drama inherent within *Touching the Void* finds an echo in its adherence to a simple three-act structure. The first 'act' is the euphoric early stage of the climb, culminating in Simpson and Yates's successful ascent of Siula Grande; the second comprises their descent and Simpson's accident; the third centres on his near death and ultimately his survival as he is discovered by Yates and Hawking, having managed to drag himself to base camp despite his shattered leg. The spectator's responses are guided and predictable and, at its conclusion, *Touching the Void* becomes a classically Aristotelean cathartic experience: in having identified with Simpson especially and thus felt drained as the life literally drains from him (he describes the slow 'reduction' that is his body closing down), we are then moved to tears and feel a swelling of happiness as we identify with his realisation – just after declaring 'I knew I was dead then' – that he is saved. *Touching the Void* elicits responses that are as primal as they are intellectual.

The first 'act' is characterised not only by ultimate success but also by explanation – of why and how climbers climb. This is classic exposition. Simpson and Yates explain, for instance, that they left their third man, Hawking, at base camp, that they used the 'purest' mode of climbing, namely 'Alpine style', which entails taking all necessary food and equipment and doing the climb swiftly, bypassing the need to prepare camps and lay ropes. Just as the effect of the film's finale is predicated upon the contrast between Simpson believing he is about to die and discovering that he will live, so early on a similar effect is generated by the sharp difference between the climbers' euphoria at both the dependency of this 'Alpine style' (as Simpson comments, you inevitably put 'immense trust' in the abilities of your partner) and success of ascending Siula Grande so quickly and the later accident as Simpson's dependency on Yates almost costs him his life. At this stage, Simpson and Yates are demonstrably able to surmount the physical problems presented to them: their commentary informs us that the climb was difficult, a truth verified by a camera shot down a sheer face of ice, and they find themselves hampered by a blizzard on Day Two, nevertheless, on Day Three the weather clears and they not only can see for the first time what they have been trying to climb but they get to the summit (17 minutes into a 1 hour 40 movie). This early climax, the reason Simpson and Yates's climb would have entered into history if their descent had not gone so badly wrong, is celebrated cinematically by choral music, aerial views of the peak and swooping, sideways helicopter shots of the slopes. Immediately after this, Simpson sets up the drama of 'Act Two' by mentioning that 80 per cent of accidents happen on descent not ascent, a statistic supported by his description of the ridge being far harder to pass than they had envisaged and images of the meringue-like folds of snow that disguise its shape and force.

'Act Two' differs visually from what preceded it in that it lacks the grand, awe-inspiring shots of the mountain's form and its lush, egg-white peaks, which return towards the end of the film. Instead, the drama of Simpson's two falls – the one that broke his leg so badly that his calf bone went through his knee and into his thigh and the slip that necessitated the cutting of the rope – is illustrated by more talking (Simpson and Yates in interview describing the effect of Simpson's accident – 'we're stuffed' as Yates puts it – and what they subsequently did in attempt to both get down the mountain) and intense close-ups, this time of Simpson slipping through the snow, for instance, as Yates lowered him down. Emphasised here is the physicality and cruelty of climbing, not the majestic beauty of mountains; there is also the motivation here not to detract from the controversy and potential tragedy of Yates' decision to cut the rope between himself and Joe Simpson. The dramatic impact of this pivotal section of *Touching the Void* is heightened by the repeated use of close-up. The interviews are consistently shot in extreme close-up, inviting the spectator's scrutiny of and empathy towards two figures who, for much of the documentary, remain relatively inscrutable and closed. Even when Simpson is recounting his belief that he was on the verge of death (when, just before Richard Hawking tells how he was woken by Joe calling out for help) and is in tears, he is sufficiently in control to continue telling the story of his rescue. The point about these interviews is that they deal in fact (the sequence of events), not in emotion or emotional responses; the revelation of emotion is done by the spectator.

The stylistic changes between these first two sections of *Touching the Void* function as signals for the changes that have occurred to the men's fortunes. On one level there are the practical problems that in the first 'act' Simpson and Yates had surmounted with relative ease but which now cause them real difficulty, such as the realisation that, needing water after Simpson's fall, they had used up too much gas earlier and so could not make a 'brew' (using melted snow) to rehydrate him after the loss of pints of blood. Reflecting this shift, the grind and danger of mountaineering has replaced the spectacle of it – tensely, rapidly edited sequences of close-up images of the climbers slipping down the mountain, of attaching and releasing the rope, of Simpson trying in vain the climb up the rope once he had fallen off the ledge. Even the sound is magnified. Complementing these shots is the exaggerated sound of Simpson and Yates's descent: the scrunching of boots breaking the fresh snow, the teeth-tingling slide of smooth outer clothing on its surface or the more decisive thud as they attempt to burrow their feet deeper in order to come to a stop in between moves.

The climax of 'Act Two' is Joe's 150 foot fall into a crevasse, his surprise at being alive and his realisation that he was alone and probably going to die. This, of course, is one time when Simpson (recounting how alone he felt) is left to describe the moment on his own. This slightly lengthier interview with Simpson allows him to divulge his equivocal responses to the accident. He tells firstly of being 'very scared' and then explains that, at only 25, he was 'super ambitious' and this accident 'hadn't been part of our game plan'; this then leads into a critical self-description of himself losing control – crying and behaving, in his estimation, childishly. Simpson is portrayed as cold, hard and macho and his concluding comment here is 'I thought I'd be tougher than that'. Because the interviews with Simpson and Yates in particular, but also Hawking, are utilised to recreate the events on Siula Grande in 1985, such retrospective comments as Simpson's here function more as evocations of what it was like living through those events than as commentaries on what those events might, with hindsight, be argued to mean. The dramatic impact of *Touching the Void* stems from the underpinning desire to create a sense of presentness, to give the events of 1985 a contemporary dynamism that takes the film beyond being a historical document, a marriage of style and content that dominates the third 'act'.

Documentary is commonly thought of as a cerebral, intellectual genre (Bill Nichols' notion of a 'discourse of sobriety'); quite often it is virtually the opposite: emotion-driven, sensual and – in that it sometimes asks its spectator to respond to it spontaneously on a gut, almost physical emotive level – primal in its appeal. This is the case with the final, longest section of *Touching the Void*, which is structured around a trio of emotions and emotive situations: the immense physical effort needed and the danger to Simpson of finding a way out of the crevasse then dragging himself down Siula Grande to base camp, his despair at believing he is going to die and the final elation as he is discovered by Hawking and Yates. At a couple of key moments (when Simpson describes being on the point of death and when he has been rescued and taken to base camp) the exhausting drama of Simpson's epic bid for survival is temporarily broken by humour. In that we find ourselves laughing out loud, these interruptions in themselves prompt non-cerebral responses, thereby facilitating the release of some of the tension and anxiety generated by our enforced and prolonged identification with Simpson during his painful descent of the mountain. What Macdonald does here is to mix catharsis with a complex and sudden reversal of not fortune exactly, but emotion.

The magnitude of Simpson's physical challenge is expressed visually, through the repeated use (once he has struggled out of the crevasse and into the daylight) of long shots of the mountainside. As before, these shots evoke as well as represent the thrill and sensual attraction of mountaineering; however, because of the intervening accident and the knowledge that Yates has left Simpson for dead, the aesthetic beauty of such images is complicated. Here the significant juxtaposition is a manifestly physical one. Whereas before similar big mountain shots were linked more to Simpson's imagination (metaphors for his ambition and the exhilaration of climbing), in this final 'act' they have become the tangible obstacle between death and survival. As a means of representing this, Macdonald more than once emphatically juxtaposes the hugeness of the mountain with the minuteness and insignificance of Joe, making it hard for the spectator in the first instance to pick him out. This contrast parallels directly what Simpson is saying in interview, that, despite his relief at having scrambled out of the crevasse, he was 'only just started, mate' and that the only way he could cope conceptually with the idea that, with one destroyed leg, he had to negotiate the mountain and its glaciers without food or water if he was to live, was to break up his trek into 20-minute chunks. An awful irony of this last 'act' of *Touching the Void* is that whilst Simpson cannot contemplate the 'big picture', the film shows us nothing but. As Joe Simpson himself repeatedly signals, he frequently doubted he could go on; his resignation that he might not be able to is indicated by the extreme long shots of him (or rather the actor playing him) crawling through the snow and his decision to try to get back is interpreted via two speeded up sequences that transfer onto the act of watching the documentary the stress Simpson was under. A similar merging of Simpson's thoughts and needs and spectatorship comes during the sequence showing Simpson's need for water: his frustration at being able to hear water but not find any is, by now predictably, signalled by idealised images of a glistening and rolling stream. When Joe eventually finds some water and drinks, his comment is: 'it was like putting fuel in'. Maybe the poetic grandeur of Macdonald's images comes from the need to compensate for Simpson's own persistent lack of poetry.

This lack of poetry – or, perhaps more accurately, his refusal to wallow in the potential tragedy of his plight – is reinforced by the use of humour at two crucial moments in the story. The tone of 'Act Three' of *Touching the Void* is dictated by Simpson's proximity to death, a proximity that, as he repeatedly reminds us, was a constant, not a fluctuating presence. During what turns out to be his last night alone on the mountain, Simpson describes himself falling apart, a mental and physical disintegration marked filmically by an illogical, fragmented series of fleeting and warped images. Symptomatic of his and the film's divorce from logicality, Simpson cannot recall thinking about loved ones as he feels himself sliding into death, drifting deliriously in and out of sleep. Instead a tune came into his head: Boney M's 'Brown Girl in the Ring'. Simpson remembers trying to get the tune out of his head and thinking 'Bloody hell, I'm going to die to Boney M'. The effect of this sequence, particularly in the cinema, is overwhelming. As a moment of release, of letting the spectator siphon off the emotional intensity that has been building up through this final section, this juxtaposition of a jolly, inane tune and what Simpson believes to be near-death delirium has the spontaneous effect of making any audience laugh – rather hysterically, it has to be said – as one. 'Brown Girl in the Ring' is played loud, and the volume is important because it creates a powerful synergy between Simpson, the film and the audience: Simpson describes his consciousness being invaded by 'Brown Girl in the Ring', the documentary is interrupted and engulfed by it and we, as the audience (which is why this moment is so much more powerful in the cinema), find our collective consciousness being equally invaded. As Simpson is just about to describe how he realised, by the smell, that he had reached the base camp latrines, the jollity of 'Brown Girl in the Ring' is not entirely inappropriate.

The final bit of humour comes right at the end of *Touching the Void*, after Joe Simpson has been found in an 'awful state' by Yates and Hawking and taken to the tent. This is an overwhelming moment, one not lessened by being recounted years later by the protagonists of the story. Until they agreed to participate in Macdonald's documentary, neither climber had returned to Siula Grande and although there had not been a silence around the events *Touching the Void* describes, there is a palpable sense that neither Simpson nor Yates has relived this scene in quite this way. Despite its inconducive subject matter (an expedition that goes wrong merely provides a narrative populated by solitary figures) the option on Joe Simpson's book has been taken out by various Hollywood producers (and Tom Cruise was at one point in the frame to act in it),[10] but as yet not made into a feature film. As a result of its narrative, there are few scenes in which Simpson and Yates function conventionally as buddies, sharing an experience, but this is one of them, as the story of their reunion is told equally by both of them and Joe recalls 'I remember that feeling of being held'. The melodramatic potential of this tearful reunion is punctured by Richard Hawking remembering Joe asking 'Where are my trousers?' – soaked in urine, they had been removed and burnt – and smiling as he says: 'It was the same old Joe back again'.

For a documentary about past events of which no archive material exists, there is remarkably little reconstruction in *Touching the Void*. It is interesting to speculate why Kevin Macdonald chose to use reconstruction here, except that it is, as a documentary style, very much in vogue. As one harsh critique of *Touching the Void* observes, 'The quality of the acting is not the problem, it's the contrast between the fake and the genuine that makes the former insupportable. To have performers feigning agony while real agony is being discussed on the soundtrack is distracting at the very least' (*Los Angeles Times* critic Kenneth Turan quoted in Powers [2004: 25]). The acting, though, is minimal – and minimalist – and there are two forms of reconstruction going on in *Touching the Void*: those involving actors and those involving climbers (Turan seems to think they are one and the same). The former are used minimally for close-ups and (mute) conversations; there are indeed instances when the gulf between the acting and what Simpson and Yates are recalling is vast, as when Simpson's description, whilst stuck in the crevasse, of the pain he is in is accompanied by an awkward-sounding scream on the soundtrack. These close-ups with actors were filmed in the Alps, when the filming on Siula Grande itself had finished. The bulk of the reconstructions are performed by professional climbers in the Andes; these and the words of Simpson *et al.* are much more significant factors in *Touching the Void* than the scenes with actors, because the documentary is not simply a good yarn, it is also a film about mountaineering. The relative inauthenticity, when contrasted with the climbing sequences or the interviews, of the actors is the real *Rescue 999* touch. It is harder to defend Macdonald's decision to include these sequences, as some of the exchanges between actors are superfluous, in that they illustrate but do not expand upon what is being said in voice-over. The effect, however, of these three layers of reconstruction or storytelling (interviews, re-enactments using actors and re-enactments using climbers) is to perpetuate and strengthen the film's sense of presentness, of re-evoking the events on Siula Grande as opposed to merely re-telling them. These are composite performances and so the protagonists of *Touching the Void* become composite characters: we are shown facets of their stories, sometimes in great detail, but we are not given a rounded picture of any of them. This has the twin effect of making us focus on the specific events of *Touching the Void* and not to be concerned with their implications and ramifications (there are scant references, for example, to what happened afterwards except the odd mention of Joe Simpson's success as a writer as well as a mountaineer and the criticism of Simon Yates). Although someone would come out of *Touching the Void* and probably say they had got to know quite a lot about Joe Simpson, the film does not give a sense of his character, merely of his responses to the events on Siula Grande. His 'character', if indeed we want to, we have to piece together ourselves out of the fragments offered; although the events on which the film is based are obviously tackled with hindsight, neither the action nor the characters are completed, finished. In this they are inherently performative, evolving out of a specific conjunction of elements (reconstruction, interview, return to Siula Grande) and not fixed or reflective of what might or might not be the 'true' character of Simpson or Yates. It matters very little to how one enjoys and watches *Touching the Void* how Joe Simpson is or comes across in 'real life' – when not reliving the most momentous, defining moment of that life.

Conclusion

The four documentaries discussed here by no means form a homogenous group except in that they were made and released at roughly the same time. What is interesting about them historically is that they represent an important moment in documentary history when, among cinema audiences, some non-fiction films rivalled their fiction counterparts for popularity. In terms of the theory and history of documentary proposed in this book, what is also a significant feature of these films is what they say about how non-fiction is evolving. That *Être et avoir* is atypical within this context by virtue of being a traditional observational documentary, marks an important transition. When the first edition of *New Documentary* appeared it was still the case that a substantial portion of documentary output on television or in the cinema had its roots in observation, the one clear and consistent exception being the historical archive-based documentary. The relative marginalisation of observation since 2000 logically has occurred at a time when the inherent drama of documentary has been increasingly sought and exploited, a shift illustrated by a number of things: the omnipresence of dramatic reconstruction in historical documentaries, the dominance on television of sellable and reusable generic formats and even the tailoring of ostensibly observational material to suit the predetermined script or drama (the last is an accusation levelled at *Spellbound* of which Paul Arthur remarks: 'no one seemed bothered by fakery in *Spellbound* by which director Jeff Blitz seems to track kids' preparations for a national spelling bee by interviewing them *after the fact*' (Arthur 2003b: 6). In the same article (about *Capturing the Friedmans*) Arthur discusses the possible explanations for 'a burst of recent documentary box-office successes', commenting that, a few exceptions notwithstanding, 'the line from, say, *Roger and Me* (1989) through *Hoop Dreams* (1994) to *Spellbound*, is an accelerating arc of dramatic liberties and expressive "distortions" of actuality' (p. 5). Arthur is not automatically critical of this development, although he does link it not only to 'a confluence of certain formal prerogatives' or 'ethical stances' but also to 'marketing calculations' (p. 5): documentary for both television and the cinema has become a more commercial enterprise and the move towards an overt use of drama alongside the covert presence of dramatic license, the preponderance of computerised special effects or the manipulation or re-editing of information to suit a film's argument or narrative (alongside the case of *Spellbound* one could place the liberties Michael Moore has always taken with editing) are moves that exemplify the commercialisation of non-fictional output and its concomitant shift away from the observational mode. The historical and the formal have thus, to a degree, become intertwined as the growing popularity of documentary in recent years has come about at a time when documentary has changed and relaxed its formal and aesthetic parameters. As John Corner (2002) has remarked in relation to post-millennial television documentary, we are now in a 'post-documentary' era. Rather than categorise recent developments in documentary as 'post' documentary, I would argue that it is more constructive to view these changes as symptomatic of documentary's renewed (for this is not an entirely unprecedented phenomenon) interest in the more overt forms of performativity: reconstruction, acknowledgement of and interplay with the camera, image manipulation, performance. Documentary now widely acknowledges and formally engages with its own constructedness, its own performative agenda; it is not that reality has changed, but rather the ways in which documentary – mainstream as well as independent – has chosen to represent it.

Notes

Introduction

1 This category is dropped by the time Nichols comes to offer a further expanded set of modes in *Introduction to Documentary*. See above, page 4.

PART I

Ground rules

1 The event: archive and newsreel

1 The Grassy Knoll is on Elm Street just to the right and front of the presidential limousine as Kennedy was shot.
2 'The Zapruder Footage', *The Late Show* (BBC2, 22.11.1993).
3 The Warren Commission (so called because its president was Justice Earl Warren) was set up on 29 November 1963 by President Johnson to investigate the assassination of John Kennedy. Its findings were that Lee Harvey Oswald alone killed Kennedy from the sixth floor of the Texas School Book Depository, a building behind and to the right of the President's car. In order to prove their findings (and thus to refute all claims of a conspiracy) the Warren Commission had to prove that the shots could have all been fired by one person which necessitated what became known as the 'magic bullet theory': the theory that one bullet could have entered Kennedy's neck from the back, exited, changed direction in the air, hit Governor Connally (also in the car) twice before emerging from his body unscathed. The Warren Commission's report omitted certain key frames from the Zapruder film (Nos 208–11), despite asserting that the first bullet struck Kennedy at frame 210, claiming this was an oversight. Very quickly the report's use of the Zapruder film to substantiate its claims became the focus of conspiracy theorists who believed the Commission deliberately obscured the truth of Kennedy's assassination. In May 1964 the Commission conducted a re-enactment of the assassination based on the Zapruder footage. As Simon comments, 'The re-enactment's production as representation thus came to substitute for the real event but was used in a process that rewrote the event' (Simon 1996: 39).
4 Certain frames from Nix's film disappeared, conspiracy theorists assume because they would have contradicted the Warren Commission Report's findings. Also, in *The Men Who Killed President Kennedy* (Central Television, 1988), Beverly, one of Jack Ruby's ex-employees, maintains that the home movie she shot from just behind Morland was handed over to the FBI but subsequently disappeared.
5 From the introductory commentary of *The Men Who Killed President Kennedy* (Central Television, 1988).
6 *The Men Who Killed President Kennedy*.

7   *The Late Show* (BBC2, 22.11.93).
8   *Don Delillo: the word, the image and the gun* (*Omnibus*, BBC1, 27.9.91).
9   Cf. *The Trial of Lee Harvey Oswald* (David Greene, 1976) and *The Trial of Lee Harvey Oswald* (London Weekend Television, 1986). The former dramatisation of Oswald's hypothetical trial presumes that Ruby did not kill Oswald so the latter was able to stand trial but ends just before the verdict is announced, thereby circumventing the problem of establishing his guilt or innocence. The latter was part of an occasional LWT series in which individuals were put on trial in a studio but using real lawyers, witnesses and jury members; the verdict in this instance was that Oswald acted alone in the murder of President Kennedy. (The other people put on trial in the series were Richard III, Roger Hollis and – using a slightly different format whereby her policies are tried as opposed to her – Margaret Thatcher.)
10   Just such an example of the 'strange incidents' impinges directly on *Rush to Judgement* as one of the eye-witnesses, railway worker Lee Bowers, is killed in a car accident three months after giving the interview. De Antonio does not explicitly make the connection between Bowers' interview (in which he talks of seeing three cars apparently casing the car park behind the Grassy Knoll in the run up to the assassination) and his death, but coupled with Jones' powerful words the implication is obvious.
11   Although often compared to Shub, de Antonio said, early in his career, he had not yet seen any of her work (see Crowdus and Georgakas 1988: 170).
12   Richard Roud, who originally turned down *Point of Order* for screening in New York, only three months later, 'made the discovery that *Point of Order* was a film, after all, and invited it to the London festival' (Weiner 1971: 10).
13   De Antonio refers specifically in this interview to Rauchenberg and Jasper Johns, also to the composer John Cage who appears in *Mr Hoover and I*. Cf. also de Antonio's film *Painters Painting*.
14   Cf. Chapter 5 for a discussion of Umberto Eco's analysis of one of Nixon's 1973 television addresses during the Watergate investigations for a further examination of how the public perception of Nixon's character contributed to his downfall.
15   This footage has appeared in several other films, notably *The Atomic Café*, presumably because of its fine comic potential. Not only is there Nixon, the carved out pumpkin and the piece of film, but also there is Nixon's mute accomplice with his amazingly restless eyebrows.
16   A conclusion pursued to a ludicrous extreme in Oliver Stone's *Nixon* with the president's confrontation with 'the Beast' for example under the Lincoln memorial.

2 Narration: the film and its voice

1   There is also the issue of where the archival material originates (more fully discussed in Chapter 1); for example, that the Nazi footage of Himmler has been appropriated for anti-Nazi purposes.
2   It has often been said that Kenneth Branagh sees himself as the new Laurence Olivier. His narration for *Cold War* further substantiates this.
3   As in Bill Couturie's *Dear America: Letters Home From Vietnam* (1987), in which it is the actors, and not the GIs whose letters they are reading, whom Couturie lists in the film's title sequence, the presence of Olivier perhaps blurs the issue of how an audience receives the statements he is making. One critic of *Dear America* comments that, in that film, 'Historical context dissolves into subjectivity' (Hoberman 1988: 44), suggesting that the images themselves, through the pre-eminence afforded the actors, uncomfortably become part of a narrativised, mythologised history – one which derives as much of its capacity to move from the mechanisms of drama as it does from the strength of the 'truth' being documented.

4   This is in keeping with the series' 'identity'. *The World at War* did not approach its subject entirely chronologically; instead each episode dealt with a particular campaign, set of events or issues which often spanned several years. 'Genocide' held an ambivalent position within this formulaic structure: it was at once both set apart, more important than the episodes around it (hence the appearance of Olivier at the beginning) and it needed to conform to the series identity.

5   For an explanation of this notion of one primary collision that in turn brings about a series of secondary collisions cf. Part Two of Lukács (1937).

6   Dan White was sentenced on 21 May 1979, having been found guilty of voluntary manslaughter rather than murder. He was paroled 6 January 1985 after serving five years, one month in Soledad Prison. Although the then Mayor Dianne Feinstein publicly urged White not to return to San Francisco as there had been unrest and several rallies upon his release, White did return and lived 'quietly without incident until he committed suicide by asphyxiation in the garage of his home on October 21 1985' (www.backdoor.com/castro/soledadpage.html).

7   Although this is not emphasised in the film, it is significant that one of the earlier pieces of archive shows Moscone in interview condemning the use of capital punishment.

8   On some prints of the film the title is given as *San Pietro*, although in most writing about the film and in catalogues it is generally known now as *The Battle of San Pietro*, as indeed it is in the US War Department copy of the 'Narration Script' of October 1944 and other army documents reprinted in Culbert (1990: 227–320).

9   I do not agree with Dai Vaughan that our interpretation is still dependent on how we interpret the soldier's look. Vaughan comments: 'If we assume that he [the soldier] can see the statue, we read pained inscrutability into his expression; if we assume that he cannot, we read irony into the juxtaposition' ('Arms and the Absent', *Sight and Sound*, 48:3, Summer 1979: 183).

10   For the army correspondence relating to *The Battle of San Pietro* see Culbert (1990).

11   There is some controversy about the authenticity of Huston's material and whether or not he restaged his battle scenes. As Edgerton indicates, the film itself makes clear at the end that 'All scenes in this picture were photographed within range of enemy small arms or artillery fire. For purposes of continuity a few of these scenes were shot before and after the actual battle of San Pietro'. In an interview Huston gave on his war trilogy – which forms the basis for Midge Mackenzie's documentary *John Huston: War Stories* (1998) – Huston comments how he and one of his crew were lucky to survive one particular round of enemy attacks, and were saved only by a low wall just in front of them, which took the force of the mortar blast. It is clear from the *verite* quality of some of Huston's footage that he was filming at times during actual battles.

12   Cf. Edgerton (1987): this sequence is generally acknowledged to have been shot after the battle of San Pietro had ended, perhaps as late as 22 January 1944 (p. 32).

13   I am indebted to Doug Pye for this observation.

14   Cf. Spender (1985).

15   Marker's accreditation of himself as 'editor' is quite common; at the end of *The Last Bolshevik*, for example, appears 'written and edited by Chris Marker'. Either one takes this as a perhaps pretentious self-effacing gesture on Marker's part, or possibly as an indication that he genuinely does not believe in single authorship and wants to emphasise this to his audience. The fact that so many of his films are compilations, using visual material from a variety of eclectic sources, suggests that Marker's concerns are more democratic that didactic. (Cf. also Chapter 2 on archive documentaries.)

16   Cf. William Shakespeare, *Othello:* 'She lov'd me for the dangers I had pass'd, and I loved her that she did pity them' (Act I, Scene iii, ll. 167–8).

17   Cf. Horak (1997: 29ff) for a discussion of Marker's two types of documentaries.

PART II

The legacy of direct cinema

1   For a lengthier discussion of *Crisis* and *Primary* see Chapter 5.

3 Documentary journeys

1   For example in Britain, Chris Terrill (cf. Chapter 4 of this book) and Nicholas Barker (cf. Chapter 6).

2   This is Moran's term for describing how the majority of the interviewees in *Seven Up* conform to the social expectations of the Jesuit maxim and the first programme, despite not wishing to or trying not to.

3   Arguably hooks is being unduly harsh on the first point, as *Hoop Dreams* has indicated, through its representation of both William and Arthur's less than perfect fathers, the importance of good fathering to the success of black families.

4   For a full discussion of this see Chapter 7.

5   The issue of ethics is interesting with respect to such a violation of documentary 'rules' as the hiring of a location with which the interviewee is not associated. In addition, there is the hiring of the locomotive Henrik Gawkowski drives into the station at Treblinka and the use of hidden cameras (and lies) to extract interviews from ex-SS such as Franz Suchomel. Of the last, Marcel Ophuls says, 'I can hardly find the words to express how much I approve of this procedure [Lanzmann's promise to Suchomel that his identity will not be revealed], how much I sympathise with it. This is not a matter of means and ends, this is a matter of moral priorities' (Ophuls 1985: 22).

6   It is interesting that in an interview I have seen with Karski since he appeared in *Shoah,* he was far more composed and polished.

4 New observational documentary: from 'docusoaps' to reality television

1   At the time of filming, 17 of the 250 crew were women.

2   *The Cruise* likewise followed *Eastenders* when it began transmission in December 1997.

3   There have been four UK series of *Celebrity Big Brother* to date: 2001, 2002, 2005, 2006.

PART III

Performance

5 The president and the image

1   See Chapter 1 for a discussion of Kennedy's assassination.

2   Kennedy received 303 Electoral College votes against Nixon's 219, whilst the popular vote in 1960 was much closer: 34,226,731 for Kennedy and 34,108,157 for Nixon – the smallest margin ever recorded (Matthews 1996: 156).

3   Roosevelt himself was aware of the potential effect of his physical frailty, appearing for press photographs at the Yalta conference in an ordinary chair.

4   Johnson's most significant domestic legislation came out of the two 'Great Society' congresses: the 88th (1963–4) and the 89th (1965–6). These achieved the Civil

Rights Act, major tax cuts, a widespread anti-poverty programme, the Urban Mass Transportation Act, the Medicare Bill for all over 65s and poor, aid to school districts with larger than average numbers of poor families, the Voting Rights Act which abolished literacy tests and other devices designed to keep blacks from voting, an expanded housing programme, a new Immigration Act that ended the 1924 quota system, a permanent food stamps programme, etc. (White T. 1982: 124–6).

5   There were four photographers on *Primary*. Richard Leacock, D.A. Pennebaker, Terrence McCartney-Filgate and Albert Maysles.

6   As the action in *Crisis* was filmed simultaneously much of the time, there was not time for one crew to do all the filming. The four directors involved were: Richard Leacock, James Lipscomb (who also narrated), D.A. Pennebaker and Hope Ryden.

7   Cf. Richard Leacock's comment (made in 1963): 'Obviously we [the filmmakers] have our own bias and selection, obviously we're not presenting the Whole Truth. I'm not being pretentious and ridiculous: we're presenting the filmmaker's perception of an aspect of what happened' (Shivas 1963: 257).

8   *RFK*, David Grubin, 2004.

9   In the event Beatty turned the part down and Kennedy was played by Cliff Robertson.

10 The first of Nixon's many memoirs was entitled *Six Crises,* a structure that is mimicked by de Antonio's film *Millhouse* (see Chapter 1).

11 *Watergate 5: Impeachment* (1994).

12 Throughout his life Nixon effected this distanciation. In his 1978 memoirs he talks of 'A president's power begins slipping away the moment it is known that he is going to leave; I had seen that in 1952, in 1960, in 1968. On the eve of my resignation I knew that my role was already a symbolic one, and that Gerald Ford's was now the constructive one' (Nixon 1978: 1077). No acknowledgement, therefore, of the difference between criminality and unpopularity or completion of a second term in office.

13 Watergate was a traumatic break with history and led to the 1974 Presidential Records and Materials Preservation Act which stipulated that papers and tapes should be kept with the National Archives; was the motivation behind the Privacy Act of the same year which extended the provisions of the Freedom of Information Act passed by the Johnson administration and permitted individuals to see personal information in their federal agency files and if need be correct them; led to the Ethics of Government Act, passed by the Senate in 1978 to establish a legal basis for the office of special prosecutor so that he or she could only be removed by impeachment or conviction for a crime (Ambrose 1991: 592).

14 Tanner challenges the 'super delegates' and makes the convention 'open', i.e. allowing each delegate to vote openly rather than have their votes counted as a block state vote, arguing that the 'super delegates' system is not representative of the earlier voting patterns in the primaries. This is a doomed gamble to try to thwart Dukakis who would inevitably win under the 'super delegates' system.

15 In 1994 Paula Jones brought – and later agreed to drop – sexual harassment charges against Clinton.

16 After Dan Quayle had had the temerity to compare himself to Jack Kennedy, Lloyd Bentsen had this to say: 'Senator, I served with Jack Kennedy. I knew Jack Kennedy. Jack Kennedy was a friend of mine. Senator, you're no Jack Kennedy'.

6 The performative documentary

1   The actor Ricky Tomlinson who plays the scab in *Dockers* is also an ex-dockers' union leader.

2   Cf. Chapter 2 in Nichols (1991: 32–75) for a discussion of the previous four modes.

3   Cf., though, the mention of Austin in Susan Scheibler, 'Constantly performing the documentary: the seductive promise of *Lightning Over Water*' in Renov (1993: 135–50), and Caryl Flinn, 'Containing fire: performance in *Paris is Burning*' in Grant and Sloniowski (1998: 429–45).

4   Cf. Bruzzi (1999: 32–4) for a further discussion of Barker's influence on *Modern Times*.

5   A quintessential example is *Lido* (6.12.95), a film made by Lucy Blakstad who was one of the Assistant Producers on *Signs of the Times*. *Lido* adopts many of the same techniques as Barker's series: posed interviews, a formalised and unspontaneous style, an open narrative structure.

6   '*The Thin Blue Line* was a project done by Errol Morris and though it helped me by taking my case to the public, I could not win my freedom in a theater. It had to be achieved in a courtroom. After my release, Mr Morris felt he had the exclusive rights to my life story. He did not. Therefore, it became necessary to file an injunction to sort out any legal questions on the issue. The matter was resolved before having to go before a judge. Mr Morris reluctantly conceded that I had the sole rights to my own life'. (Randall Adams in '72 Hours Away from Execution: Danny Yeager Interviews Randall Adams', *The Touchstone* 10:3, Summer 2000, www.rtix.com)

7   For a general discussion of *Handsworth Songs*, cf. Corner (1996); for a discussion specifically about its female voice-over, cf. Cook (1987).

8   Cf. Chapter 2 for a further discussion of women's voices in documentary.

9   Nichols in 'The voice of documentary' goes on to apply the term voice to 'interactive' documentaries, that is, those which (like the films of Emile de Antonio) formally as opposed to physically suggest their authorship.

10 Since serving in the army Black has been a UK government intelligence analyst and is (as of 2006) Director of Janusian Security Risk Management.

11 For a critical response to *Kurt and Courtney*'s depiction of Love, cf. Moran (1998).

12 Cf. *Signs and Meaning* (2nd edition), London: Secker & Warburg, 1972.

13 There have been rumours, strongly denied by Broomfield, that he and Fleiss had an affair, Nagy embellishing this by saying that they were engaged, a further rumour that Broomfield dismisses as 'ridiculous' (Brown M. 1996: 42).

PART IV

New directions

7 Contemporary documentaries: performance and success

1   See the discussion of reality television in Chapter 4.

2   To create the effect of Morris's interviewees looking to camera, whilst actually looking at an image of Morris, two cross-connected teleprompters are set at a 45-degree angle in front of the camera. Morris actually sits out of view of his interviewees, several feet away (Cf. Davis 2004: 28). Nunn suggests that 'the Interrotron enabled Morris to succeed in the illusion of closeness to his subject whilst appearing to be absent from the filmic process' (2004: 416). This complicated dissonance lends Morris's films a peculiarly intense coldness.

3   *The Thin Blue Line* was in many ways a classic piece of investigative filmmaking, successful in getting Randall Adams acquitted of murder; *A Short History of Time* attempted to convey through images the work and theories of cosmologist Stephen Hawking and *Mr Death* centred on Holocaust denier Fred Leuchter.

4   J. Hoberman recalls that Morris once told him: 'The idea is not to listen to what people say, but to keep them talking' (Hoberman 2004: 22).

5   Whether or not these tears are to be believed as sincere is debateable. See, for example, Rosenbaum in which he writes: 'At some point during the *New Yorker* conversa-

tion, someone – I can't recall whether or was Mr Morris or Mr (Mark) Singer – called crocodile tears, deliberately or inadvertently, "alligator tears". I like the notion of "alligator tears". In this film, McNamara reinvents crocodile tears, you might say; he transcends the more obvious crocodile tears and gives us – alligator tears. Alligator tears aren't insincere, not in the same way crocodile tears folklorically are. I'd define alligator tears as tears of equanimity, of self-righteousness posing as self-criticism: The fog of war ate my homework' (2003).

6   Cf. Desson Thomson 'With Enemies Like These ...', (*The Guardian,* 26 March 2004: 10) where McNamara states 'They're Errol Morris's lessons, not my lessons'.

7   McNamara replies, for example, to the first question 'I'm not going to say any more than I have ... a lot of people misunderstand the war, misunderstand me' and the second question he counters with 'I don't want to go any further ... I don't want to add anything on Vietnam'.

8   Atkinson is specifically referring to fellow *Village Voice* journalist Debbie Nathan.

9   See Paul Arthur 'Feel the Pain: First Person Docs are Soothing the Pain of their Makers. What Do They Do For Us?' (*Film Comment* 40:5, September–October 2004: 47–50).

10 Cf. Falcon (2004: 35).

Bibliography

Ambrose, Stephen (1991) *Nixon, Volume 3: Ruin and. Recovery, 1973–1990*, New York and London: Simon & Schuster.

Anonymous (1996) *Primary Colors: A Novel of Politics*, London: Vintage.

Apted, Michael (2006) Interview with the author, 4 January.

Arthos, John (1996) 'Narrative Manipulation and Documentary Truth: Putting the Move on Audiences in *Hoop Dreams*', *Film and Philosophy*, 3, 87–94.

Arthur, Paul (1993) 'Jargons of authenticity (three American moments)', in Michael Renov (ed.) *Theorizing Documentary*, London and New York: Routledge.

—— (1997) 'On the virtues and limitations of collage', *Documentary Box*, 11 (October): 1–7.

—— (2003a) 'Essay Questions: From Alain Resnais to Michael Moore', *Film Comment*, 39:1 (January): 58–63.

—— (2003b) 'True Confessions, Sort of: *Capturing the Friedmans* and the Dilemma of Theatrical Documentary', *Cineaste*, 28:4 (Fall) 4–7.

Atkinson, Michael (2003) 'All in the Family: The Hissing of Summer Lawns' [review of *Capturing the Friedmans*], *Village Voice*, 28 May–3 June, reproduced on www.villagevoice.com/film.

Austin, J. L. (1970) *Philosophical Papers* (2nd edition, edited by J. O. Urmson and G. J. Warnock), Oxford: Oxford University Press.

Bakker, Kees (2005) 'The Good, the bad and the documentary: on deontology of representation and ethics of interpretation', *Documentary Box*, 24: 24–33.

Barker, Nicholas (1999) Interview with the author, 10 September.

Barneveld, Anet van (2003) 'Nicolas Philibert lecture: the moment a subject transcends reality', *Dox*, 49 (November): 16–17.

Barthes, Roland (1957) *Mythologies*, London: Paladin [1973].

—— (1973) *S/Z*, Oxford: Blackwell [1996].

—— (1977) *Image/Music/Text* (selected and translated by Stephen Heath), London: Fontana.

Barnouw, Erik (1993) *Documentary: A History of the Non-fiction Film* (2nd revised edition), Oxford: Oxford University Press.

Barwell, Claire (1997a) '*Flâneur* of London', *Pix*, 2 (January): 158–59.

—— (1997b) 'Interview with Patrick Keiller', *Pix*, 2 (January): 160–65.

Bazin, André (1967) *What is Cinema?: Volume I* (selected and translated by Hugh Gray), Berkeley and Los Angeles: University of California Press.

BBC (1998) Unpublished minutes of editorial policy meeting, Tuesday 8 December.

Bell, Rachel (1998) Interview with the author, 17 December.

Benjamin, Walter (1955) *Illuminations* (translated by Harry Zohn), London: Fontana [1973].

Berardinelli, James (2003) '*Capturing the Friedmans*', reproduced on http://movie-reviews.colossus.net.

Bigio, Denise (1986) 'Michael Apted: Up, Up, and Away', *International Documentary*, 5:1 (April): 4–5, 20.

Billen, Andrew (1995) 'Where's Molly?', *Observer Review*, 10 December: 9.

Bishop, Louise (1996) 'Is there a producer in the house?', *Television*, 33:5 (July–August): 12–13.

—— (1998) 'Getting real', *Television*, 35:3 (April): 16–17.

Bonitzer, Pascal (1976) 'The silences of the voice'; reprinted in Philip Rosen (ed.) *Narrative, Apparatus, Ideology: A Film Reader*, New York: Columbia University Press [1986]: 319–34.

Branigan, Edward (1992) *Narrative Comprehension and Film*, London and New York: Routledge.

Brennan, Timothy (1990) 'The national longing for form', in Homi K. Bhabha (ed.) *Nation and Narration*, London and New York: Routledge.

Brenton, Sam and Cohen, Reuben (2003) *Shooting People: Adventures in Reality TV*, London: Verso.

Britton, Andrew (1992) 'Invisible eye', *Sight and Sound*, 1:10 (February): 27–9.

Broadcast (2004) 'Back to Reality', 20 February: 5.

—— (2004) Ofcom report on *Big Brother 4* fight, 22 October: 6.

Brooks, Xan (2004) 'Family Viewing' (Review of *Capturing the Friedmans*), *Sight and Sound*, 14:4 (April): 40–1.

Broomfield, Nick (1993) 'Heroes and villains: Pier Paolo Pasolini', *The Independent Magazine*, 6 February: 46.

Brown, Maggie (1996) 'Fetishes', *Daily Telegraph Weekend Magazine*, 10 August: 41–2.

—— (2003) 'Real to Reel', *Guardian*, 17 November.

Brown, Thomas (1988) *JFK: History of an Image*, London: I.B. Taurus & Co. Ltd.

Bruzzi, Stella (1998) 'The President and the Image', *Sight and Sound*, 8:7 (July): 16–19.

—— (1999) 'Butterfly on the wall', *Sight and Sound*, 9:1 (January): 32–4.

Burch, Noël (1969) *The Theory of Film Practice* (translated by Annette Michelson), London: Secker & Warburg [1973].

Burgoyne, Robert (1996) 'Modernism and the narrative of *JFK*', in Vivian Sobchack (ed.) *The Persistence of History: Cinema, Television and the Modern Event*, London and New York: Routledge.

Butler, Judith (1990) *Gender Trouble: Feminism and the Subversion of Identity*, London and New York: Routledge.

—— (1993) *Bodies that Matter: On the Discursive Limitations of 'Sex'*, London and New York: Routledge.

Carr, E.H. (1961) *What is History?* Harmondsworth: Penguin [1986].

Carroll, Noël (1996a) *Theorising the Moving Image*, Cambridge: Cambridge University Press.

—— (1996b) 'Nonfiction film and postmodern skepticism', in David Bordwell and Noël Carroll (eds) *Post-Theory: Reconstructing Film Studies*, Madison: University of Wisconsin Press.

Cavalcanti, Alberto (1939) 'Sound in films', *Films*, 1:1 (November): 25–39.

Ciment, Michel (1988) 'Joy to the World! An Interview with Marcel Ophuls', *American Film*, 13:10 (September): 38–43.

Cipriano, Katherine (2005) 'Hoops: Escape or Illusion? A Review Essay', *Film and History*, 35:2: 78–80.

Clark, Bernard (2002) 'The box of tricks', in ed. Institute of Ideas *Reality TV: How Real is Real?*, London: Hodder and Stoughton.

Cleave, Maureen (1991) 'Molly's hidden depths', *The Evening Standard*, 27 March: 26.

Colombat, André Pierre (1993) *The Holocaust in French Film* (Metuchen), New York and London: Scarecrow Press.

Comolli, Jean-Louis (1980) 'Machines of the visible', in Teresa de Lauretis and Stephen Heath (eds) *The Cinematic Apparatus*, London: Macmillan.

Comolli, Jean-Louis and Narboni, Jean (1969) 'Cinema/ideology/criticism', reprinted in Bill Nichols (ed.) *Movies and Methods*, Berkeley and Los Angeles: University of California Press [1976].

Cook, Pam (1987) *'Handsworth Songs'*, *Monthly Film Bulletin*, 638: 77–8.

Corner, John (1996) *The Art of Record: A Critical Introduction to Documentary*, Manchester: Manchester University Press.

—— (2002) 'Performing the real: documentary diversions', *Television and New Media*, 3:3 (August): 255–69.

Cousins, Mark (2004) 'What's up doc?', *Sight and Sound*, 14:2 (February): 5.

Crowdus, Gary (1990) 'Reflections on *Roger and Me*: Michael Moore and his Critics', *Cineaste*, 17:4: 27–30.

Crowdus, Gary and Georgakas, Dan (1988) 'History is the theme of all my films: an interview with Emile de Antonio', in Alan Rosenthal (ed.) *New Challenges for Documentary*, Berkeley and Los Angeles: University of California Press.

Culbert, David (ed.) (1990) *Film and Propaganda in America: A Documentary [Volume III: World War II – Part 2]*, New York and London: Greenwood Press.

Cummings, Dolan (2002) 'Introduction', ed. Institute of Ideas *Reality TV: How Real is Real?*, London: Hodder and Stoughton.

Cunningham, Megan (2005) *The Art of Documentary: Ten Conversations with Leading Directors, Cinematographers, Editors and Producers*, Berkeley: New Riders.

Dale, Peter (1998) 'Documentaries in danger', *Broadcast*, 23 October: 17.

Davis, Bob (2004) 'A Troubled Legacy', *American Cinematographer*, 85:3 (March): 28–32.

de Beauvoir, Simone (1985) 'Preface' to Claude Lanzmann *Shoah: An Oral History of the Holocaust*, New York: Pantheon Books: iii–vi.

Diamond, Edwin and Silverman, Robert A. (1997) *White House to Your House: Media and Politics in Virtual America*, Cambridge, Mass, and London: MIT Press.

Doane, Mary Ann (1980) 'The voice in the cinema: the articulation of the body and space', *Yale French Studies*, 60 (Fall): 33–50.

Doherty, Thomas (1987) 'Representing the holocaust: Claude Lanzmann's *Shoah*', *Film and History*, 17:1 (February): 2–8.

Dorey, John (2000) *Freakshow: First Person Media and Factual Television*, London: Pluto Press.

Drew, Robert (1983) 'Narration can be a killer'; reprinted in Kevin Macdonald and Mark Cousins (eds) *Imagining Reality: The Faber Book of Documentary*, London: Faber & Faber [1996]: 271–73.

Dunkley, Chris (2002) 'It's not new and it's not clever', in ed. Institute of Ideas *Reality TV: How Real is Real?*, London: Hodder and Stoughton.

Durgnat, Raymond (1967) *Franju*, London: Studio Vista.

Ebert, Roger (2003) '*Capturing the Friedmans*', *Chicago Sun-Times*, 6 June. Reproduced on http://rogerebert.suntimes.com.

Eco, Umberto (1985) 'Strategies of lying', in Marshall Blonsky, *On Signs: A Semiotics Reader*, Oxford: Blackwell: 3–11.

Edgerton, Gary (1987) 'Revisiting the recordings of wars past: remembering the documentary trilogy of John Huston', *Journal of Popular Film and Television*, 15:1 (Spring): 27–41.

Eisenstein, Sergei (1926) 'Béla forgets the scissors', reprinted in Richard Taylor and Ian Christie (eds) *The Film Factory: Russian and Soviet Cinema in Documents, 1896–1939*, London and New York: Routledge [1994]: 145–49.

Eisenstein, Sergei, Pudovkin, Vsevelod and Alexandrov, Grigori (1928) 'Statement on sound', reprinted in Richard Taylor and Ian Christie (eds) *The Film Factory: Russian and Soviet Cinema in Documents, 1896–1939*, London and New York: Routledge [1994]: 234–35.

Fairweather, Kathleen (2003) 'A Family Affair', *International Documentary*, 22: 6: 8–9.

Falcon, Richard (2004) 'White Ladder' (review of *Touching the Void*), *Sight and Sound* 14:1 (January): 34–5.

Farndale, Nigel (2004) 'The Camera Never Lies', *Sunday Telegraph Magazine*, 14 March: 21–7.

Fielder, Mark (1998) Interview with the author, 27 November.

Flinn, Caryl (1998) 'Containing fire: performance in *Paris is Burning*', in Barry Keith Grant and Jeanette Sloniowski (eds) *Documenting the Documentary: Close Readings of Documentary Film and Video*, Detroit: Wayne State University Publishing.

Freeman, Hadley (2005) 'Pick 'n' mix', *The Guardian G2*, 10 August: 2–3.

French, Sean (1989) 'Shooting from the heart', *The Observer*, 12 November: 4.

Gant, Charles (2005) 'Does truth pay?', *Sight and Sound*, 15:9 (September): 8.

Gentleman, Amelia (2004a) 'Defeat for teacher who sued over film profits', *Guardian*, 29 September: 15.

Gentleman, Amelia (2004b) 'Film's fallen hero fights for his class', *Observer*, 3 October (www.observer.guardian.co.uk)

Glitz, Michael (1993) 'The house that "Dave" built', *Premiere* [US], 6:10 (June): 34–5.

Graef, Roger (1998) 'The truth is in there', *Sunday Times*, 5 April.

Grant, Barry Kieth and Sloniowski, Jeanette (eds) (1998) *Documenting the Documentary: Close Readings of Documentary Film and Video*, Detroit: Wayne State University Press.

Groskop, Viv (2005) 'Do the maths', *Daily Telegraph Magazine*, 28 May: 38, 41–4.

Guynn, William (1990) *A Cinema of Nonfiction*, London and Toronto: Associated University Presses.

Hamann, Paul (1998) 'The Docusoap debate', *European Media: Business and Finance*, 8:20 (October): 5, 6.

Hammen, Scott (1996) 'John Huston at War', excerpt reprinted in Macdonald, Kevin and Cousins, Mark (eds) *Imagining Reality: The Faber Book of Documentary*, London: Faber and Faber.

Hill, Annette (2002) '*Big Brother*: the real audience', *Television and New Media*, 3:3 (August): 323–340.

Hoberman, J. (1988) 'America Dearest', *American Film*, XIII:7 (May): 39–45, 54–6.

—— (1996) '*Shoah*: Witness to annihilation', in Kevin Macdonald and Mark Cousins (eds) *Imagining Reality: The Faber Book of Documentary*, London: Faber & Faber: 316–22.

—— (2004) 'Warmonger Blues', *Sight and Sound*, 14:4 (April): 20–2.

Hodges, Mike (1997) 'The secret city', *Pix*, 2 (January): 166–7.

hooks, bell (1995) 'Dreams of Conquest', *Sight and Sound*, 5:4 (April): 22–3.

Horak, Jan-Christopher (1997) *Making Images Move: Photographers and Avant-garde Cinema*, Washington and London: Smithsonian Institute Press.

Hughes, P. (2003) 'Welcome to my world', *Broadcast*, 13 June: 15.

Hughes, Robert (1980) *The Shock of the New: Art and the Century of Change*, London: Thames & Hudson [1993].

Humphrys, John (2005) 'First do no harm: the James McTaggart Lecture 2004', in ed. Bob Franklin *Television Policy: The MacTaggart Lectures*, Edinburgh: Edinburgh University Press.

Indiana, Gary (2004) '*The Fog of War*' (Film Review), *Artforum*, January. Reproduced on www.findarticles.com.

Innes, Christopher (1979) *Modern German Drama: A Study in Form*, Cambridge: Cambridge University Press.

Insdorf, Annette (1989) *Indelible Shadows: Film and the Holocaust* (2nd edition), Cambridge: Cambridge University Press.

Izod, John and Kilborn, Richard (1997) *An Introduction to TV Documentary: Confronting Reality*, New York and Manchester: Manchester University Press.

Jacobsen, Kurt (1996) 'Memories of Insustice: Marcel Ophuls' Cinema of Conscience', *Film Comment*, 32:4 (July–August): 61–7.

Johnson, Thomas J. (1995) *The Rehabilitation of Richard Nixon: The Media's Effect on Collective Memory*, New York and London: Garland Publishing Inc.

Jones, Kent (2004) 'This Means War!', *Film Comment* 40:4 (July/August): 19–20.

Kaplan, Fred (2003) 'The Evasions of Robert McNamara: What's True and What's a Lie in *The Fog of War*?', reproduced on www.errolmorris.com.

Kellman, Steven G. (1988) 'Cinema of/as atrocity: *Shoah*'s guilty conscience', *The Gettys-burg Review*, 1: 22–30.

Kolker, Robert Phillip (1971) 'Circumstantial evidence: an interview with David and Albert Maysles', *Sight and Sound* 40:4 (Autumn): 183–86.

Kozloff, Sarah (1988) *Invisible Storytellers: Voice-over Narration in American Fiction Film*, Berkeley and Los Angeles: University of California Press.

Kuhn, Annette (1978) 'The camera I: observations on documentary', *Screen*, 19:2 (Summer): 71–83.

Lambert, Stephen (2005) Interview with the author, 22 July.

Lanzmann, Claude (1985a) 'The being of nothingness: an interview with Claude Lanzmann', reproduced in Kevin Macdonald and Mark Cousins (eds) *Imagining Reality: The Faber Book of Documentary*, London: Faber & Faber [1996]: 322–25.

—— (1985b) *Shoah: An Oral History of the Holocaust*, New York: Pantheon Books.

—— (1990) 'Seminar with Claude Lanzmann: 11 April, 1990'; *Yale French Studies, 79: Literature and the Ethical Question*: 82–100.

Lawson, Mark (1995) 'High flyer on the wall', *The Guardian*, 10 October: 10–11.

Leeman, Lisa (2003) 'How Close is Too Close? A Consideration of the Filmmaker-Subject Relationship', *International Documentary*, 22:5 (June): 14–18.

Levin, G. Roy (1971) *Documentary Explorations: 15 Interviews with Filmmakers*, New York: Doubleday.

Leyda, Jay (1983) *Kino: A History of Russian and Soviet Film* (3rd edition), Princeton: Princeton University Press.

—— (1996) 'Esther Shub and the art of compilation', in Kevin Macdonald and Mark Cousins (eds) *Imagining Reality: The Faber Book of Documentary*, London: Faber & Faber.

Lichfield, John (2004) 'When avoir becomes more important than être', *Independent,* 19 May: 5.

Lukács, Georg (1937) *The Historical Novel* (translated by Hannah and Stanley Mitchell), Harmondsworth: Penguin [1981].

McCann (1998) 'ITV gives new docu-soap prime billing', *The Independent*, 23 February.

Macdonald, Kevin and Cousins, Mark (1996) (eds) *Imagining Reality: The Faber Book of Documentary*, London: Faber & Faber.

McGregor, Alex (1995) 'This old house', *American Cinematographer*, 76:11 (November): 83–6.

Mamber, Stephen (1972a) 'Cinéma-vérité in America', *Screen*, 13:2 (Summer): 79–107.

—— (1972b) 'Part II – Direct cinema and the crisis structure', *Screen*, 13:3 (Autumn): 114–36.

—— (1974) *Cinéma Vérité in America: Studies in Uncontrolled Documentary*, Cambridge, Mass, and London: MIT Press.

Mapplebeck, Victoria (2002) 'Money Shot', in eds. Institute of Ideas *How Real is Real?* London: Hodder and Stoughton.

Marker, Chris (1984) 'Terminal Vertigo' [an interview by computer with Chris Marker], *Monthly Film Bulletin*, 51 (606, July): 196–97.

Matthews, Christopher (1996) *Kennedy and Nixon: The Rivalry that Shaped Postwar America*, New York: Simon & Schuster.

Michelson, Annette (ed.) (1984) *Kino-eye: The Writings of Dziga Vertov* (translated by Kevin O'Brien), Berkeley and Los Angeles: University of California Press.

Moi, Toril (1987) *French Feminist Thought*, Oxford: Blackwell.

Monsell, Thomas (1998) *Nixon on Stage and Screen: The Thirty-seventh President as Depicted in Films, Television, Plays and Opera*, Jefferson, North Carolina and London: McFarland & Company Inc.

Moran, Caitlin (1998) 'You give Love a bad name', *Time Out*, 1077 (June): 18–21.

Moran, Joe (2002) 'Childhood, class and memory in the *Seven Up* films', *Screen*, 43:4 (Winter): 387–402.

Murray, Susan and Ouellette, Laurie (eds.) (2004) *Reality TV: Remaking Television Culture*, New York: New York University Press.

Nahra, Carol (1999) 'Michael Apted and *42 Up*', *International Documentary*, 18:1–2 (January–February): 22–3.

Nichols, Bill (1981) *Ideology and the Image: Social Representation in the Cinema*, Bloomington and Indianapolis: Indiana University Press.

—— (1983) 'The voice of documentary', reprinted in Rosenthal [1988]: 48–63.

—— (1991) *Representing Reality: Issues and Concepts of Documentary*, Bloomington and Indianapolis: Indiana University Press.

—— (1994) *Blurred Boundaries: Questions of Meaning in Contemporary Culture*, Bloomington and Indianapolis: Indiana University Press.

—— (2001) *Introduction to Documentary*, Bloomington: Indiana University Press

Nixon, Richard (1978) *The Memoirs of Richard Nixon*, London: Arrow Books [1979].

Nunn, Heather (2004) 'Errol Morris: Documentary as Psychic Drama', *Screen* 45:4: 413–22.

O'Connor, John E. (2005) 'Introduction: Historians on Michael Moore and *Fahrenheit 9/11*', *Film and History*, 35:2: 7.

Ophuls, Marcel (1985) 'Closely watched trains', *American Film*, 11:2 (November): 18–22, 79.

—— (2004) 'Film and History: Questions to Filmmakers and Historians', *Cineaste* 29:2 (Spring), Ophuls' contribution: 57.

Ouellette, Laurie (1995) 'Camcorder dos and don'ts: popular discourses on amateur video and participatory television', *Velvet Light Trap*, 36 (Autumn): 33–44.

Paterson, Elaine (1989) 'Heller let loose', *Time Out*, 1007: 6–13, 52–3.

Pearson, Allison (1998) 'All the world's a soap set', *The Daily Telegraph*, 28 May.

Piper, Helen (2004) 'Reality TV, *Wife Swap* and the drama of banality', *Screen* 45:4 (Winter): 273–86.

Plantinga, Carl (1997) *Rhetoric and Representation in Nonfiction Film*, Cambridge: Cambridge University Press.

Powers, Tom (2004) 'Reenact Naturally: New Docs are Recasting the Old Practice of Dramatization', *International Documentary*, 23:5 (June): 25–7.

Rafferty, Terrence (1984) 'Marker changes trains', *Sight and Sound*, 53:4 (Autumn): 284–88.

Ranney, Austin (1983) *Channels of Power: The Impact of Television on American Politics*, New York: Basic Books.

Renov, Michael (1986) 'Re-thinking Documentary: towards a taxonomy of mediation', *Wide Angle*, 8: 3–4.

—— (ed.) (1993) *Theorizing Documentary*, London and New York: Routledge.

—— (2004) *The Subject of Documentary*, Minneapolis: University of Minnesota Press.

Robinson, Julie (2002) '*7 Up* and Up and Up', *Directors Guild of America Magazine*, 27:3 (Fall): 36–7.

Roscoe, Jane and Hight, Craig (2001) *Faking It: Mock-documentary and the Subversion of Factuality*, Manchester: Manchester University Press

Rosenbaum, Ron (2003) 'New Morris Film Traps McNamara in a *Fog of War*', review of *The Fog of War* for *New York Observer*, 29 September, reprinted on www.errolmorris.com.

Rosenthal, Alan (1978) 'Emile de Antonio: an interview', *Film Quarterly*, 31:1 (Fall): 4–17.

—— (1988) *New Challenges for Documentary*, Berkeley and Los Angeles: University of California Press.

Rotha, Paul (1930) *The Film Till Now: A Survey of World Cinema* (new edition), London: Vision Press Ltd [1963].

—— (1952) *The Documentary Film* (2nd edition), London: Faber (originally published 1935).

Sei Shonagon (1971) *The Pillow Book of Sei Shonagon* (translated by Ivan Morris), Harmondsworth: Penguin.

Shearman, Nick (1998) Interview with the author, 26 November.

—— (2005) Interview with the author, 18 July.

Shivas, Mark (1963) 'Interview with Richard Leacock', in Kevin Macdonald and Mark Cousins (eds) *Imagining Reality: The Faber Book of Documentary*, London: Faber & Faber [1996].

Sight and Sound (2004) 'Editorial: To be or to have', 14:11 (November): 3.

Silverman, Kaja (1988) *The Acoustic Mirror: The Female Voice in Psychoanalysis and Cinema*, Bloomington and Indianapolis: Indiana University Press.

Simon, Art (1996) *Dangerous Knowledge: The JFK Assassination in Art and Film*, Philadelphia: Temple University Press.

Sinclair, Iain (1997) *Lights Out for the Territory*, London: Granta.

Smith, Gavin (2004) 'The Ending is up to You: Michael Moore Interviewed', *Film Comment* 40:4 (August): 21–6.

Sobchack, Vivian (ed.) (1996) *The Persistence of History: Cinema, Television and the Modern Event*, London and New York: Routledge.

Spencer, Megan (1999) 'Sideshow alley: the documentaries of Nick Broomfield', *IF*, 15 (July).

Spender, Dale (1985) *Man Made Language* (2nd edition), London: Routledge & Kegan Paul.

Taubin, Amy (2003) '*To Be or To Have* (review)', *Film Comment*, 39:5 (September/October): 74.

Terrill, Chris (1998) Interview with the author, 8 December.

Thomson, Desson (2004) 'With Enemies Like These ...', *The Guardian*, 26 March, 10–11.

Titus, Constandina (1983) 'Back to ground zero: old footage through new lenses', *Journal of Popular Film and Television*, 11:1 (Spring): 3–11.

Toplin, Robert Brent (2005) 'The Long Battle Over *Fahrenheit 9/11:* A Matter of Politics, not Aesthetics', *Film and History* 35:2: 8–10.

Tretyakov, Sergey, Shklovsky, Victor, Shub, Esther and Brik, Osip (1927) 'Symposium on Soviet Documentary', in Lewis Jacobs (ed.) *The Documentary Tradition* (2nd edition), Toronto: J. McLeod [1979].

Tuchman, Mitch (1990) 'Freedom of information', *Film Comment*, 26:4 (July–August): 66–8.

Vaughan, Dai (1974) 'The space between shots', *Screen*, 15:1 (Spring): 73–85.

—— (1979) 'Arms and the absent', *Sight and Sound*, 48:3 (Summer): 182–87.

—— (1999) *For Documentary: Twelve Essays*, Berkeley and Los Angeles: University of California Press.

Wasson, Haidee (1995) 'Assassinating an image: the strange life of Kennedy's death', *CineAction!*, 38 (September): 5–11.

Watson, Paul (1998) *The Daily Mail*, 17 February.

Waugh, Thomas (1985) 'Beyond *Vérité:* Emile de Antonio and the New Documentary of the Seventies', in Bill Nichols (ed.) *Movies and Methods II*, Berkeley and Los Angeles: University of California Press: 233–58.

Weiner, Bernard (1971) 'Radical scavenging: an interview with Emile de Antonio', *Film Quarterly*, 25:1 (Fall): 3–15.

Weiss, Marc N. (1974) 'Emile de Antonio', *Film Library Quarterly*, 7(2): 29–35.

Weiss, Peter (1971) 'The material and the models: notes towards a definition of documentary theatre', *Theatre Quarterly*, 1: 41–5.

White, Hayden (1987) *The Content of the Form: Narrative, Discourse and Historical Representation*, Baltimore and London: Johns Hopkins University Press.

—— (1996) 'The modernist event', in Vivian Sobchack (ed.) *The Persistence of History: Cinema, Television and the Modernist Event*, London and New York: Routledge.

White, Theodore (1982) *America in Search of Itself: The Making of the President, 1956–1980*, New York: Harper & Row.

Williams, Linda (1993) 'Mirrors without memories: truth, history and the new documentary', *Film Quarterly*, 46:3 (Spring): 9–21.

Winston, Brian (1993) 'The documentary film as scientific inscription', in Michael Renov (ed.) *Theorizing Documentary*, London and New York: Routledge: 37–57.

—— (1995) *Claiming the Real: The Documentary Film Revisited*, London: British Film Institute.

—— (2000) *Lies, Damn Lies and Documentaries*, London: British Film Institute.

Wise, Damon (2002) 'Boom Raider', *Sight and Sound*, 12:5 (May): 16–18.

Wise, Mike (2004) 'Looking Back at Broken "Dreams"', *Washington Post*, 5 July: D1 (www.washingtonpost.com)

Wood, David (2004) 'Has TV got nasty?', *Broadcast*, 9 July: 21.

Wood, Jason (2005) ed. *Nick Broomfield: Documenting Icons*, London: Faber and Faber.

Youdelman, Jeffrey (1982) 'Narration, Invention, History'; reprinted in Alan Rosenthal (ed.) *New Challenges for Documentary*, Berkeley and Los Angeles: University of California Press [1988].

Zimmerman, Patricia (1995) *Reel Families: A Social History of Amateur Film*, Bloomington and Indianapolis: Indiana University Press.

Index

Related titles from Routledge

Screening the Past

Pam Cook

This lively and accessible collection explores film culture's obsession with the past, offering searching and provocative analyses of a wide range of titles from *Mildred Pierce* and *Brief Encounter* to *Raging Bull* and *In the Mood for Love*.

Screening the Past engages with current debates about the role of cinema in mediating history through memory and nostalgia, suggesting that many films use strategies of memory to produce diverse forms of knowledge which challenge established ideas of history, and the traditional role of historians. The work of contemporary directors such as Martin Scorsese, Kathryn Bigelow, Todd Haynes and Wong Kar-wai is used to examine the different ways they deploy creative processes of memory, arguing that these movies can tell us much about our complex relationship to the past, and about history and identity.

Pam Cook also investigates the recent history of film studies, reviewing the developments that have culminated in the exciting, if daunting, present moment. Classic essays sit side by side with new research, contextualised by introductions which bring them up to date, and provide suggestions for further reading. The result is a rich and stimulating volume that will appeal to anyone with an interest in cinema, memory and identity.

ISBN 10: 0-415-18374X (hbk)
ISBN 10: 0-415-183758 (pbk)

ISBN 13: 9-78-0-415-183741 (hbk)
ISBN 13: 9-78-0-415-183758 (pbk)

Available at all good bookshops
For ordering and further information please visit:

www.routledge.com

Related titles from Routledge

Cinema Studies: The Key Concepts
Second Edition
Susan Hayward

This is the essential guide for anyone interested in film. Now in its second edition, the text has been completely revised and expanded to meet the needs of today's students and film enthusiasts. Some 150 key genres, movements, theories and production terms are explained and analyzed with depth and clarity. Entries include:

- Auteur Theory
- Blaxploitation
- British New Wave
- Feminist Film Theory
- Intertextuality
- Method Acting
- Pornography
- Third World Cinema
- Vampire Movies

A bibliography of essential writings in cinema studies completes an authoritative yet accessible guide to what is at once a fascinating area of study and arguably the greatest art form of modern times.

ISBN 10: 0-415-227399 (hbk)
ISBN 10: 0-415-227402 (pbk)

ISBN 13: 9-78-0-415-227391 (hbk)
ISBN 13: 9-78-0-415-227407 (pbk)

Available at all good bookshops
For ordering and further information please visit:

www.routledge.com

Related titles from Routledge

The Film Cultures Reader
Edited by Graeme Turner

This companion reader to *Film as Social Practice* brings together key writings on contemporary cinema, exploring film as a social and cultural phenomenon.

Key features of the reader include:

- thematic sections, each with an introduction by the editor
- a general introduction by Graeme Turner
- sections: understanding film, film technology, film industries, meanings and pleasures, identities, audiences and consumption

Contributors include:

Tino Balio, Sabrina Barton, Tony Bennett, Jacqueline Bobo, Edward Buscombe, Stella Bruzzi, Jim Collins, Barbara Creed, Richard Dyer, Jane Feuer, Miriam Hansen, John Hill, Marc Jancovich, Susan Jeffords, Isaac Julien, Annette Kuhn, P. David Marshall, Judith Mayne, Kobena Mercer, Tania Modleski, Steve Neale, Tom O'Regan, Stephen Prince, Thomas Schatz, Gianluca Sergi, Ella Shohat, Jackie Stacey, Janet Staiger, Robert Stam, Chris Straayer, Yvonne Tasker, Stephen Teo, Janet Wollacott, Justin Wyatt.

ISBN 10: 0-415-25281-4 (hbk)
ISBN 10: 0-415-25282-2 (pbk)

ISBN 13: 9-78-0-415-25281-2 (hbk)
ISBN 13: 9-78-0-415-25282-9 (pbk)

Available at all good bookshops
For ordering and further information please visit:

www.routledge.com

Related titles from Routledge

Cinema and Nation
Edited by Mette Hjort and Scott Mackenzie

Ideas of national identity, nationalism and
transnationalism are now a central feature of
contemporary film studies, as well as primary concerns
for film-makers themselves.

Embracing a range of national cinemas including
Scotland, Poland, France, Turkey, Indonesia, India,
Germany and America, *Cinema and Nation* considers
the ways in which film production and reception are
shaped by ideas of national belonging and examines
the implications of globalisation for the concept of
national cinema.

In the first three Parts, contributors explore sociological
approaches to nationalism, challenge the established
definitions of 'national cinema', and consider the ways
in which states – from the old Soviet Union to
contemporary Scotland – aim to create a national
culture through cinema. The final two Parts address the
diverse strategies involved in the production of national
cinema and consider how images of the nation are used
and understood by audiences both at home and
abroad.

ISBN 10: 0-415-20862-9 (hbk)
ISBN 10: 0-415-20863-7 (pbk)

ISBN 13: 9-78-0-415-20862-8 (hbk)
ISBN 13: 9-78-0-415-20863-5 (pbk)

Available at all good bookshops
For ordering and further information please visit:

www.routledge.com

Related titles from Routledge

Genre and Hollywood
Steve Neale

Genre and Hollywood provides a comprehensive introduction to the study of genre. In this important new book, Steve Neale discusses all the major concepts, theories and accounts of Hollywood and genre, as well as the key genres which theorists have written about, from horror to the Western. He also puts forward new arguments about the importance of genre in understanding Hollywood cinema.

Neale takes issue with much genre criticism and genre theory, which has provided only a partial and misleading account of Hollywood's output. He calls for broader and more flexible conceptions of genre and genres, for more attention to be paid to the discourses and practices of Hollywood itself, for the nature and range of Hollywood's films to be looked at in more detail, and for any assessment of the social and cultural significance of Hollywood's genres to take account of industrial factors.

In detailed, revisionist accounts of two major genres – film noir and melodrama – Neale argues that genre remains an important and productive means of thinking about both New and old Hollywood, its history, its audiences and its films.

ISBN 10: 0-415-026059 (hbk)
ISBN 10: 0-415-026067 (pbk)

ISBN 13: 9-78-0-415-026055 (hbk)
ISBN 13: 9-78-0-415-026062 (pbk)

Available at all good bookshops
For ordering and further information please visit:

www.routledge.com